CHAMBERS

Dictionary of
Abbreviations

GW00643724

CHAMBERS

Dictionary of
Abbreviations

Edited by
David Edmonds

CHAMBERS

CHAMBERS
An imprint of Larousse plc
43–45 Annandale Street
Edinburgh EH7 4AZ

Copyright © Larousse plc 1995

A CIP catalogue record for this book
is available from the British Library

ISBN 0-550-18304-3 (Hardback)
ISBN 0-550-18305-1 (Paperback)

Typeset by Hewer Text Composition Services, Edinburgh

Printed in England by Clays Ltd, St Ives plc

Contents

Preface

This book lists and explains more than ten thousand abbreviations which have been selected to meet the needs of ordinary people in the home, school and office. Special attention has been paid to sporting and commercial terms, to medical abbreviations (including those infuriating scraps of Latin that still litter prescriptions and case-notes), to basic computing terms, and to the acronyms of major business, governmental, and international organizations. Foreign abbreviations likely to be met with in the UK or seen by travellers abroad are also included, and the terms used in newspaper classified advertisements have received a special study. A series of inset panels distributed throughout the book brings together key information on such topics as food additives, international airport and airline codes, academic qualifications, chemical elements, chess notation, and British and American postcodes, all of which also receive a full treatment in the main dictionary. A list of these panels and their page numbers appears on p.xi below.

Acknowledgement is due to Dr R E Allen, Publishing Director of Larousse plc, for unfailing support and encouragement, to Adonis Petrides for help with motoring terms, to Johnny Cowee and Tim and Pauline Parry for advice on medical matters, and to Dr Caroline Fraser for help with Russian transliterations.

How to use this dictionary

1. The headwords are listed in alphabetical order, as are the senses within each headword. Where several headwords are composed of identical letters, they are listed in the order AA, Aa, aa.

2. In cases where the reader may be uncertain how to say the headword it is followed by a pronunciation in conventional script.

3. Each headword is followed by one of five indicators, which show how the abbreviation was made. The indicator *contraction* is used in cases where letters were taken out of the centre of the word leaving (at least) the first and last letters intact (eg Dr = Doctor, abp = archbishop), *shortening* where the end of the word has been removed (eg abbr. = abbreviation, Tues. = Tuesday), and *acronym* where the headword is built from the initial letters of the words it replaces (eg Nato = North Atlantic Treaty Organization, nimby = not in my back yard, Cento = Central Treaty Organization). *Symbol* is reserved for the chemical elements (since here the headword is not always derived from the element's current name); and initialisms (eg BBC, MSc, asap), which are pronounced as individual letters, are all called *abbrev*.

4. Next come the meanings; if the headword has several meanings, they are separated by black lozenges ♦. If the expansion is a foreign word or phrase its language will be named, and a translation given; where necessary an explanatory note may follow, as in the following example:

   dim. *shortening* ... diminuendo (Italian, = diminishing) (music)

5. No firm rules can be given for the capitalization and punctuation of abbreviations. *PTO* is no more or less correct than *p.t.o.* or *pto*, and all will be found in what we read. To avoid cluttering the dictionary, we have selected the form which currently seems most common and corresponds to the publishers' house style. This reflects the current tendency of omitting points in acronyms, initialisms and contractions, and retaining them in shortenings. Again, an ordinary word such as *position* can be abbreviated in many different ways (eg *pos.*, *posit.*, *postn*, *posn*), and there is usually no real means of deciding which is better than the others; we have therefore adopted the most widely current form when this can be determined.

Panels

In order to help the user find abbreviations relating to specific subject areas we have included in the text some special panels which bring together information on key topics. These panels can be found on the pages listed below:

A

A *abbrev.* ◆ absolute (temperature)
◆ Academician ◆ Academy ◆ ace (cards)
◆ adult (former cinema film censorship
classification) ◆ advanced ◆ amateur
◆ America ◆ American ◆ ammeter
◆ ampere ◆ analog ◆ answer ◆ area
◆ Associate ◆ atomic ◆ atomic weight
◆ Australia ◆ Australian ◆ Austria
(international vehicle registration)
Å *abbrev.* ◆ Ångström
a *abbrev.* ◆ about ◆ absent ◆ acceleration
◆ accepted ◆ acre ◆ acreage ◆ acting
◆ active ◆ adjective ◆ advance
◆ afternoon ◆ alto ◆ anno (Latin, = in
the year) ◆ annus (Latin, = year)
◆ anonymous ◆ ante (Latin, = before)
◆ anterior ◆ are (metric unit of area)
◆ arrive ◆ atto-
A0 *abbrev.* ◆ 841 × 1189 mm (paper size)
A1 *abbrev.* ◆ 594 × 841 mm (paper size)
A2 *abbrev.* ◆ 420 × 594 mm (paper size)
A3 *abbrev.* ◆ 297 × 420 mm (paper size)
A4 *abbrev.* ◆ 210 × 297 mm (paper size)
A5 *abbrev.* ◆ 148 × 210 mm (paper size)
A6 *abbrev.* ◆ 105 × 148 mm (paper size)
A7 *abbrev.* ◆ 74 × 105 mm (paper size)
A8 *abbrev.* ◆ 52 × 74 mm (paper size)
A9 *abbrev.* ◆ 37 × 52 mm (paper size)
A10 *abbrev.* ◆ 26 × 37 mm (paper size)
AA *abbrev.* ◆ achievement age
◆ Advertising Association ◆ age
allowance (taxation) ◆ Alcoholics
Anonymous ◆ American Airlines
(airline baggage code) ◆ anti-aircraft
◆ Architectural Association ◆ Associate
in Arts ◆ Associate of Arts ◆ Australian
Army ◆ Automobile Association
◆ adult-accompanied (former cinema
film censorship classification)

◆ Bournemouth (British vehicle
registration mark)
AAA *abbrev.* ◆ Amateur Athletic
Association ◆ anti-aircraft artillery
AA & QMG *abbrev.* ◆ Assistant Adjutant
and Quartermaster General
AAAS *abbrev.* ◆ American Academy of
Arts and Sciences
AAC *abbrev.* ◆ Amateur Athletic Club
◆ anno ante Christum (Latin, = in the
year before Christ) ◆ Army Air Corps
(US)
AAEW *abbrev.* ◆ Atlantic Airborne Early
Warning
AAG *abbrev.* ◆ Assistant Adjutant-
General
AAM *abbrev.* ◆ air-to-air missile
A & A *abbrev.* ◆ additions and
amendments
A & C *abbrev.* ◆ addenda and corrigenda
A & E *abbrev.* ◆ accident and emergency
(hospital department)
a & h *abbrev.* ◆ accident and health
a & i *abbrev.* ◆ accident and indemnity
A & M *abbrev.* ◆ Agricultural and
Mechanical ◆ Ancient and Modern
(hymn-book)
A & N *abbrev.* ◆ Army and Navy (club)
◆ Army and Navy (stores)
A & R *abbrev.* ◆ artists and recording
◆ artists and repertoire
a & s *abbrev.* ◆ accident and sickness
A & W *abbrev.* ◆ alive and well
aaO *abbrev.* ◆ am angeführten Orte
(German, = at the place quoted)
AAP *abbrev.* ◆ Australian Associated
Press
AAQMG *abbrev.* ◆ Assistant Adjutant
and Quartermaster General

aar *abbrev.* ✦ against all risks ✦ average annual rainfall

AAS *abbrev.* ✦ Academiae Americanae Socius (Latin, = Fellow of the American Academy)

A'asia *contraction* ✦ Australasia

AB *abbrev.* ✦ Aberdeen (UK postcode) ✦ able-bodied (seaman) ✦ Advisory Board ✦ Artium Baccalaureus (Latin, = Bachelor of Arts) (US) ✦ Worcester (British vehicle registration mark)

A/B *abbrev.* ✦ Aktiebolaget (Swedish, = Limited)

Ab *abbrev.* ✦ antibody

ab. *shortening* ✦ about

a/b *abbrev.* ✦ airbags ✦ airborne

ABA *abbrev.* ✦ Amateur Boxing Association ✦ American Bar Association ✦ Antiquarian Booksellers' Association ✦ Association of British Archaeologists

Abb. *shortening* ✦ Abbess ✦ Abbey ✦ Abbot

ABBA *abbrev.* ✦ Amateur Basketball Association

abbr. *shortening* ✦ abbreviated ✦ abbreviation

abbrev. *shortening* ✦ abbreviated ✦ abbreviation

ABC *abbrev.* ✦ Aerated Bread Company ✦ American Broadcasting Company ✦ Arab Banking Corporation ✦ Associated British Cinemas ✦ Audit Bureau of Circulations ✦ Australian Broadcasting Corporation

ABCC *abbrev.* ✦ Association of British Chambers of Commerce ✦ Association of British Correspondence Colleges

---

SOME COMMON ABBREVIATIONS

This list contains some of the abbreviations we meet with every day. Fuller information on these items may be found at their alphabetical place in this dictionary.

AD	*in the year of Our Lord (with date in Christian era)*	**F**	*Fahrenheit*
AH	*in the year of the Hegira (with date in Muslim era)*	**f**	*following (page etc)*
		HGV	*heavy goods vehicle*
am	*before noon*	**ie**	*that is*
b	*born*	**l**	*line*
BC	*before Christ (with date before Christian era)*	**m**	*married*
		MS	*manuscript*
C	*Celsius; centigrade*	**NB**	*note carefully*
c	*circa (with approximate dates etc)*	**p**	*page*
cent.	*century*	**pm**	*after noon*
cf	*compare*	**PS**	*postscript*
ch.	*chapter*	**PTO**	*please turn over*
d	*daughter; died*	**QED**	*which was to be proved*
do	*ditto*	**RSVP**	*please reply*
Dr	*Doctor*	**s**	*son*
EC	*European Community*	**sae**	*stamped addressed envelope*
eg	*for example*	**SOS**	*international distress signal*
et al.	*and elsewhere; and other (people or things)*	**UK**	*United Kingdom*
		USA	*United States of America*
etc.	*and the rest*	**v, vs**	*versus*
		viz.	*namely*

ABCD *abbrev.* ◆ atomic, biological and chemical protection and damage control

abd *contraction* ◆ abdicated ◆ abridged

abd. *shortening* ◆ abdomen ◆ abdominal

Aber. *shortening* ◆ Aberdonensis (Latin, = of Aberdeen)

ABF *abbrev.* ◆ Actors' Benevolent Fund ◆ Army Benevolent Fund

Abf. *shortening* ◆ Abfahrt (German, = departure)

abf *abbrev.* ◆ absolute bloody final

ABFM *abbrev.* ◆ American Board of Foreign Missions

abgk. *shortening* ◆ abgekürzt (German, = abbreviated)

ABH *abbrev.* ◆ actual bodily harm

Abh. *shortening* ◆ Abhandlungen (German, = Transactions)

ABI *abbrev.* ◆ Association of British Insurers

ABIA *abbrev.* ◆ Association of British Introduction Agencies

ab init. *shortening* ◆ ab initio (Latin, = from the beginning)

abl. *shortening* ◆ ablative

ABM *abbrev.* ◆ anti-ballistic missile

ABO *symbol* ◆ antigen-based bloodgroup-classification

A-bomb *contraction* ◆ atomic bomb

ABP *abbrev.* ◆ arterial blood pressure ◆ Associated Book Publishers

abp *contraction* ◆ archbishop

ABPA *abbrev.* ◆ Australian Book Publishers' Association

abr. *shortening* ◆ abridged ◆ abridgement

ABRC *abbrev.* ◆ Advisory Board for Research Councils

ABRO *abbrev.* ◆ Animal Breeding Research Organization

ABRSM *abbrev.* ◆ Associated Board of the Royal Schools of Music

ABS *abbrev.* ◆ Antiblockiersystem (German, = anti-lock system) (car brakes) ◆ Associate of the Building Societies Institute ◆ Association of Broadcasting Staff

abs. *shortening* ◆ absence ◆ absent ◆ absolute ◆ absolutely ◆ absorbent ◆ abstract

ABSA *abbrev.* ◆ Association for Business Sponsorship of the Arts

abse. re. *shortening* ◆ absente reo (Latin, = the accused being absent)

abs. feb. *shortening* ◆ absente febre (Latin, = when the fever has gone)

absol. *shortening* ◆ absolute ◆ absolutely

abs. re. *shortening* ◆ absente reo (Latin, = the accused being absent)

abstr. *shortening* ◆ abstract

Abt. *shortening* ◆ Abteilung (German, = part)

abt *contraction* ◆ about

ABTA *abbrev.* ◆ Association of British Travel Agents

abv. *shortening* ◆ above

ABZ *abbrev.* ◆ Aberdeen (airport baggage label)

AC *abbrev.* ◆ adult contemporary (music) ◆ Aero Club ◆ Air Canada (airline baggage code) ◆ air-conditioned ◆ air-conditioning ◆ Air Corps ◆ aircraftman ◆ Alpine Club ◆ alternating current ◆ ante Christum (Latin, = before Christ) ◆ appellation contrôlée (French, = regulated naming) (of origin of wines) ◆ Assistant Commissioner ◆ athletic club ◆ Coventry (British vehicle registration mark) ◆ Companion of the Order of Australia

Ac *symbol* ◆ actinium (chemical element)

ac *abbrev.* ◆ ante cibum (Latin, = before food)

a/c *abbrev.* ◆ account ◆ account current

ACA *abbrev.* ◆ Associate of the Institute of Chartered Accountants

acad. *shortening* ◆ academic ◆ academy

ACARD *abbrev.* ◆ Advisory Council for Applied Research and Development

Acas *pronounced* ay-cass *acronym* ◆ Advisory, Conciliation, and Arbitration Service

ACC *abbrev.* ◆ Accra (airport baggage label) ◆ Association of County Councils

acc. *shortening* ◆ acceptance ◆ accompanied ◆ according ◆ account ◆ accountant ◆ accusative

ACCA *abbrev.* ◆ Associate of the Chartered Association of Certified Accountants

acce *contraction* ◆ acceptance

accel. *shortening* ◆ accelerando (Italian, = getting faster) (music)

access. *shortening* ◆ accessory

ACCM *abbrev.* ◆ Advisory Council for the Church's Ministry

ACCME *abbrev.* ◆ Accreditation Council for Continuing Medical Education

accom. *shortening* ◆ accommodation

accomp. *shortening* ◆ accompanied ◆ accompaniment

accred. *shortening* ◆ accredited

ACCT *abbrev.* ◆ Association of Cinematograph, Television and Allied Technicians

acct *contraction* ◆ account ◆ accountant

accum. *shortening* ◆ accumulated ◆ accumulative

accus. *shortening* ◆ accusative

AC/DC *abbrev.* ◆ alternating current/ direct current ◆ bisexual

ACdre *abbrev.* ◆ Air Commodore

ACE *abbrev.* ◆ Advisory Centre for Education ◆ Allied Command Europe ◆ Association for the Conservation of Energy

ACER *abbrev.* ◆ Australian Council for Educational Research

ACF *abbrev.* ◆ Army Cadet Force

ACGB *abbrev.* ◆ Arts Council of Great Britain

ACGI *abbrev.* ◆ Associate of the City and Guilds of London Institute

ACGME *abbrev.* ◆ Accreditation Council for Graduate Medical Education

ACGS *abbrev.* ◆ Assistant Chief of General Staff

ACH *abbrev.* ◆ automated clearing house

ACI *abbrev.* ◆ Alderney (airport baggage label) ◆ Army Council Instruction

ACIA *abbrev.* ◆ Associate of the Corporation of Insurance Brokers

ACIB *abbrev.* ◆ Associate of the Chartered Institute of Bankers

ACIGS *abbrev.* ◆ Assistant Chief of the Imperial General Staff

ACII *abbrev.* ◆ Associate of the Chartered Insurance Institute

ACIS *abbrev.* ◆ Associate of the Chartered Institute of Secretaries

ack. *shortening* ◆ acknowledge ◆ acknowledged ◆ acknowledgement

ack-ack *abbrev.* ◆ anti-aircraft (military telephonists' former phoneticization of AA)

ACLU *abbrev.* ◆ American Civil Liberties Union

ACM *abbrev.* ◆ Air Chief Marshal

ACMA *abbrev.* ◆ Associate of the Institute of Cost and Management Accountants

acn *abbrev.* ◆ all concerned notified

a/con. *shortening* ◆ air conditioning

Acord *acronym* ◆ Advisory Council on Research and Development

Acorn *acronym* ◆ A Classification of Residential Neighbourhoods (socio-economic classification used in market research etc) ◆ associative content retrieval network ◆ automatic checkout and recording network

Acost *acronym* ◆ Advisory Committee on Science and Technology

ACP *abbrev.* ◆ African, Caribbean and Pacific ◆ Associate of the College of Preceptors

ACPO *abbrev.* ◆ Association of Chief Police Officers

acpt. *shortening* ◆ acceptance

ACPU *abbrev.* ◆ auxiliary computer power unit

acq. *shortening* ◆ acquire ◆ acquisition ◆ acquittal

acrd *contraction* ◆ accrued

Acre *acronym* ◆ Action with Communities in Rural England

ACS *abbrev.* ◆ active control system ◆ Association of Commonwealth Students

ACSA *abbrev.* ◆ Associate of the Institute of Chartered Secretaries and Administrators

a/cs pay. *shortening* ◆ accounts payable

a/cs rec. *shortening* ◆ accounts receivable

ACT *abbrev.* ◆ advance corporation tax ◆ Australian Capital Territory

act. *shortening* ◆ acting ◆ active ◆ actual ◆ actuary

actg *contraction* ◆ acting

ACTH *abbrev.* ◆ adrenocorticotrophic hormone

ACTS *abbrev.* ◆ Action of Churches Together in Scotland

ACTT *abbrev.* ◆ Association of Cinematograph Television and Allied Technicians

ACTU *abbrev.* ◆ Australian Council of Trade Unions

ACU *abbrev.* ◆ Association of Commonwealth Universities

acv *abbrev.* ◆ actual cash value ◆ air-cushion vehicle

ACW *abbrev.* ◆ aircraftswoman ◆ automatic car wash

ACY *abbrev.* ◆ average crop yield

AD *abbrev.* ◆ active duty ◆ air defence ◆ Alzheimer's Disease ◆ anno domini (Latin, = in the year of Our Lord) ◆ Gloucester (British vehicle registration mark) ◆ Dame of the Order of Australia

ad *abbrev.* ◆ accidental damage ◆ accumulated dose (radiation) ◆ after date ◆ ante diem (Latin, = before the day)

SOME POPULAR ACRONYMS

Some of these will be in the panel on p.145 in a few years' time; some people may think they should be there already.

Acas *Advisory and Conciliation Service*	**Opec** *Organization of Oil-Producing Countries*
Aids *acquired immune deficiency syndrome*	**Oxfam** *Oxford Committee for Famine Relief*
Amstrad *Alan Michael Sugar Trading*	**Pep** *personal equity plan*
Asda *Associated Dairies*	**quango** *quasi-autonomous non-governmental organization*
Bupa *British United Provident Association*	**quasar** *quasi-stellar object*
Camra *Campaign for Real Ale*	**Salt** *Strategic Arms Limitation Talks* or *Treaty*
Ernie *Electronic Random Number Indicator Equipment*	**Serps** *State Earnings-Related Pension Scheme*
Esso *Standard Oil (from the initials)*	**Start** *Strategic Arms Reduction Talks* or *Treaty*
Interpol *International Criminal Police Organization*	**Tesco** *T E Stockwell and J Cohen*
Naafi *Navy, Army, and Air Force Institutes*	**Tessa** *Tax-Exempt Special Savings Account*
Nato *North Atlantic Treaty Organization*	**Tina** *there is no alternative*
nimby *not in my back yard*	**Unesco** *United Nations Educational, Scientific and Cultural Organization*
Offer *Office of Electricity Regulation*	
Ofgas *Office of Gas Supply*	**VAT** *Value Added Tax*
Oftel *Office of Telecommunications*	**Wasp** *white Anglo-Saxon Protestant*
Ofwat *Office of Water Services*	**yuppy** *young urban professional*

ad. *shortening* ◆ adapted ◆ advertisement

adap. *shortening* ◆ adapted

Adas *pronounced* ay-das *acronym*
◆ Agricultural Development and
Advisory Service ◆ automatic data
acquisition system

ADC *abbrev.* ◆ advice of duration and
charge ◆ aide-de-camp ◆ analogue-to-
digital converter

ADD *abbrev.* ◆ Addis Ababa (airport
baggage label)

add. *shortening* ◆ addendum ◆ addition
◆ additional ◆ address

addn *contraction* ◆ addition

ADE *abbrev.* ◆ Aden (airport baggage
label)

adf *abbrev.* ◆ after deducting freight
◆ automatic direction finder

ad fin. *shortening* ◆ ad finem (Latin, =
near the end)

ad gr. gust. *shortening* ◆ ad gratum
gustum (Latin, = to an agreeable taste)

ADHD *abbrev.* ◆ attention deficit
hyperactivity disorder

ADI *abbrev.* ◆ acceptable daily intake
◆ Approved Driving Instructor

ad init. *shortening* ◆ ad initium (Latin, =
near the beginning)

ad int. *shortening* ◆ ad interim (Latin, =
for the moment)

adj. *shortening* ◆ adjacent ◆ adjective
◆ adjourned ◆ adjustment ◆ adjutant

Adj.-Gen. *shortening* ◆ Adjutant-General

Adjt *contraction* ◆ Adjutant

Adjt-Gen. *shortening* ◆ Adjutant-General

ADL *abbrev.* ◆ activities of daily life
◆ Ada design language

ad lib. *shortening* ◆ ad libitum (Latin, = as
you like)

ad loc. *shortening* ◆ ad locum (Latin, = at
the place cited)

Adm. *shortening* ◆ Admiral ◆ Admiralty

adm. *shortening* ◆ admission

admin. *shortening* ◆ administration
◆ administrative ◆ administrator

admos *acronym* ◆ automatic device for
mechanical order selection

ADP *abbrev.* ◆ adenosine diphosphate
◆ automatic data processing

ADT *abbrev.* ◆ Atlantic Daylight Time

adt *abbrev.* ◆ any damn thing (in placebo
prescription)

ADTS *abbrev.* ◆ automatic data and
telecommunications service

adv. *shortening* ◆ advance ◆ advent
◆ adverb ◆ adversus (Latin, = against)
◆ advisory ◆ advocate

advt *contraction* ◆ advertisement

ADX *abbrev.* ◆ automatic data exchange
◆ automatic digital exchange

AE *abbrev.* ◆ account executive ◆ age
exemption ◆ Air Efficiency Award
◆ American English ◆ Bristol (British
vehicle registration mark)

ae. *shortening* ◆ aetatis (Latin, = of his or
her age)

AEA *abbrev.* ◆ Atomic Energy Authority

AEB *abbrev.* ◆ Associated Examining
Board

AEC *abbrev.* ◆ Atomic Energy
Commission (US)

aec *abbrev.* ◆ additional extended cover
◆ at earliest convenience

AED *abbrev.* ◆ automated engineering
design

AEEU *abbrev.* ◆ Amalgamated
Engineering and Electrical Union

AEF *abbrev.* ◆ Allied Expeditionary Force

AEI *abbrev.* ◆ Associated Electrical
Industries

AELTC *abbrev.* ◆ All England Lawn
Tennis Club

AENA *abbrev.* ◆ All England Netball
Association

AERE *abbrev.* ◆ Atomic Energy Research
Establishment

Aeroflot *acronym* ◆ Aero Flotilla (Soviet
state airline)

aeron. *shortening* ◆ aeronautic

aesth. *shortening* ◆ aesthetic ◆ aesthetics

aet *abbrev.* ◆ after extra time

aet. *shortening* ◆ aetatis (Latin, = of his or
her age)

AEU *abbrev.* ◆ Amalgamated
Engineering Union

AEU(TASS) *abbrev.* ✦ Amalgamated Engineering Union (Technical, Administrative and Supervisory Section)

AEW *abbrev.* ✦ airborne early warning

AF *abbrev.* ✦ Admiral of the Fleet ✦ Air France (airline baggage code) ✦ Anglo-French ✦ Associate Fellow ✦ audio frequency ✦ Truro (British vehicle registration mark)

Af *abbrev.* ✦ Afgháni (Afghan monetary unit)

a/f *abbrev.* ✦ as found

AFA *abbrev.* ✦ Amateur Fencing Association ✦ Amateur Football Association ✦ Associate of the Faculty of Actuaries

AFAM *abbrev.* ✦ Ancient Free and Accepted Masons

Afasic *acronym* ✦ Association for All Speech-Impaired Children

AFC *abbrev.* ✦ Air Force Cross ✦ Association Football Club

afc *abbrev.* ✦ automatic flight control ✦ automatic frequency control

afce *abbrev.* ✦ automatic flight control equipment

afco *abbrev.* ✦ automatic fuel cut-off

afcs *abbrev.* ✦ automatic flight control system

afd *abbrev.* ✦ accelerated freeze-drying

aff. *shortening* ✦ affairs ✦ affectionate ✦ affectionately ✦ affiliated ✦ affirmative

affil. *shortening* ✦ affiliated

afft *contraction* ✦ affidavit

AFG *abbrev.* ✦ Afghanistan (international vehicle registration)

Afg. *shortening* ✦ Afghan ✦ Afghanistan

AFHQ *abbrev.* ✦ Allied Forces Headquarters

AFL-CIO *abbrev.* ✦ American Federation of Labor and Congress of Industrial Organizations

AFM *abbrev.* ✦ Air Force Medal ✦ audio-frequency modulation

AFP *abbrev.* ✦ Agence France Presse

AFPRB *abbrev.* ✦ Armed Forces Pay Review Board

AFr *abbrev.* ✦ Algerian franc (monetary unit) ✦ Anglo-French

Afr. *shortening* ✦ Africa ✦ African

AFRAeS *abbrev.* ✦ Associate Fellow of the Royal Aeronautical Society

AFRC *abbrev.* ✦ Agricultural and Food Research Council

Afrik. *shortening* ✦ Afrikaans

afsd *contraction* ✦ aforesaid

aft. *shortening* ✦ after ✦ afternoon

ag. *shortening* ✦ against ✦ agricultural

AFV *abbrev.* ✦ armoured fighting vehicle

AG *abbrev.* ✦ Adjutant-General ✦ Aktiengesellschaft (German, = joint stock company) ✦ Attorney-General ✦ Hull (British vehicle registration mark)

A-G *abbrev.* ✦ Attorney-General

Ag *symbol* ✦ argentum (Latin, = silver) (chemical element)

AGA *abbrev.* ✦ air-ground-air ✦ appropriate to gestational age

Aga *acronym* ✦ Aktiebolaget Gasackumulator (Swedish, = Gasometer Company) (makers of kitchen ranges)

agb *abbrev.* ✦ any good brand

AGCA *abbrev.* ✦ automatic ground-controlled approach

AGCL *abbrev.* ✦ automatic ground-controlled landing

agcy *contraction* ✦ agency

agd *contraction* ✦ agreed

AGE *abbrev.* ✦ automatic guidance electronics

Agfa *acronym* ✦ Aktiengesellschaft für Anilinfabrikation (German, = Dye-Manufacture Company)

aggr. *shortening* ✦ aggregate

Agip *acronym* ✦ Agenzia Generale Italia Petroli (Italian, = Italian General Petrol Agency)

Agitprop *acronym* ✦ Agitpropbyuro (Russian, = Bureau for Agitation and Propaganda)

AGL *abbrev.* ✦ above ground level

AGM *abbrev.* ✦ air-to-ground missile ✦ annual general meeting

AGR *abbrev.* ◆ advanced gas-cooled reactor

agr. *abbrev.* ◆ agreed ◆ agreement ◆ agriculture

agric. *shortening* ◆ agriculture ◆ agricultural

AGSM *abbrev.* ◆ Associate of the Guildhall School of Music and Drama

agst *contraction* ◆ against

AGT *abbrev.* ◆ advanced gas turbine

agt *contraction* ◆ agent ◆ agreement

agw *abbrev.* ◆ actual gross weight

agy *contraction* ◆ agency

AH *abbrev.* ◆ anno Hegirae (Latin, = in the year of the Hegira) ◆ Norwich (British vehicle registration mark)

ah *abbrev.* ◆ ampere hour

AHA *abbrev.* ◆ Area Health Authority

ahd *contraction* ◆ ahead

ahl *abbrev.* ◆ ad hunc locum (Latin, = at this place)

AHQ *abbrev.* ◆ Allied Headquarters ◆ Army Headquarters

ahr *abbrev.* ◆ acceptable hazard rate

AHS *abbrev.* ◆ anno humanae salutis (Latin, = in the year of human salvation)

ahv *abbrev.* ◆ ad hanc vocem (Latin, = at this word)

AI *abbrev.* ◆ Air India (airline baggage code) ◆ air interception ◆ Amnesty International ◆ artificial insemination ◆ artificial intelligence

AIA *abbrev.* ◆ Associate of the Institute of Actuaries

AIB *abbrev.* ◆ Associate of the Institute of Bankers

AICC *abbrev.* ◆ All-India Congress Committee

AID *abbrev.* ◆ acute infectious disease ◆ Agency for International Development (US) ◆ artificial insemination by donor

Aids *acronym* ◆ acquired immune deficiency syndrome

AIH *abbrev.* ◆ artificial insemination by husband

Ailas *acronym* ◆ automatic instrument landing approach system

AIMechE *abbrev.* ◆ Associate of the Institution of Mechanical Engineers

AIMinE *abbrev.* ◆ Associate of the Institute of Mining Engineers

AInstP *abbrev.* ◆ Associate of the Institute of Physics

AIQS *abbrev.* ◆ Associate of the Institute of Quantity Surveyors

air con. *shortening* ◆ air conditioning

AISA *abbrev.* ◆ Associate of the Incorporated Secretaries Association

AIStructE *abbrev.* ◆ Associate of the Institution of Structural Engineers

AJ *abbrev.* ◆ ankle jerk ◆ Manchester (British vehicle registration mark)

aj *abbrev.* ◆ antijamming

AJAG *abbrev.* ◆ Assistant Judge Advocate General

AK *abbrev.* ◆ above knee ◆ Alaska (US postcode) ◆ Knight of the Order of Australia ◆ Sheffield (British vehicle registration mark)

aka *abbrev.* ◆ also known as

AKC *abbrev.* ◆ Associate of King's College

AL *abbrev.* ◆ Alabama (US postcode) ◆ Albania (international vehicle registration) ◆ Anglo-Latin ◆ Nottingham (British vehicle registration mark) ◆ St Albans (UK postcode)

Al *symbol* ◆ aluminium (chemical element)

al. *shortening* ◆ alcohol ◆ alcoholic ◆ alii (Latin, = others)

ALA *abbrev.* ◆ all letters answered ◆ Associate of the Library Association

Ala. *shortening* ◆ Alabama

ALAC *abbrev.* ◆ Artificial Limb and Appliance Centre

Alas. *shortening* ◆ Alaska

ALAWP *abbrev.* ◆ all letters answered with photograph

Alb. *shortening* ◆ Albania ◆ Albanian ◆ Alberta

Alban. *shortening* ◆ Albanensis (Latin, = of St Albans)

ALBM *abbrev.* ◆ air-launched ballistic missile

ALC *abbrev.* ◆ Alicante (airport baggage label)

alc. *shortening* ◆ alcohol

Alcan *acronym* ◆ Aluminium Company of Canada

ALCM *abbrev.* ◆ air-launched cruise missile

ALD *abbrev.* ◆ adrenoleukodystrophy

Ald. *shortening* ◆ Alderman

A-level *contraction* ◆ Advanced Level

ALF *abbrev.* ◆ Animal Liberation Front

Alf *acronym* ◆ automatic letter facer (mail sorting machine)

Alg. *shortening* ◆ Algeria ◆ Algerian ◆ Algiers

alg. *shortening* ◆ algebra ◆ algebraic

Algol *acronym* ◆ Algebraically Oriented Language (computer language)

align. *shortening* ◆ alignment

alk. *shortening* ◆ alkali ◆ alkaline

ALL *abbrev.* ◆ acute lymphoblastic leukaemia

alleg. *shortening* ◆ allegation ◆ allegorical ◆ allegory

allo *contraction* ◆ allegro (Italian, = lively) (music)

all'ott. *shortening* ◆ all'ottava (Italian, = at the octave) (music)

ALP *abbrev.* ◆ automated language processing

alp. *shortening* ◆ alpine

ALPA *abbrev.* ◆ Airline Pilots' Association

alph. *shortening* ◆ alphabetic

alphanum. *shortening* ◆ alphanumeric

Alpurcoms *acronym* ◆ all-purpose communications system

ALR *abbrev.* ◆ American Law Reports

ALS *abbrev.* ◆ approach lighting system ◆ Associate of the Linnean Society

Alsat. *shortening* ◆ Alsatian

al seg. *shortening* ◆ al segno (Italian, = to the sign) (music) ◆ al segno (Italian, = at the sign) (music)

alt. *shortening* ◆ alteration ◆ altered ◆ alternate ◆ alternative ◆ altitude ◆ alto

alt. dieb. *shortening* ◆ alternis diebus (Latin, = every other day)

alt. hor. *shortening* ◆ alternis horis (Latin, = every other hour)

alt. noct. *shortening* ◆ alternis noctibus (Latin , = every other night)

ALU *abbrev.* ◆ arithmetic logic unit

alum. *shortening* ◆ aluminium ◆ alumnus (Latin, = former pupil)

AM *abbrev.* ◆ Air Marshal ◆ Albert Medal ◆ amplitude modulation ◆ anno mundi (Latin, = in the year of the world) ◆ Artium Magister (Latin, = Master of Arts) (US) ◆ Associate Member ◆ Ave Maria (Latin, = Hail Mary) ◆ Swindon (British vehicle registration mark)

Am *symbol* ◆ americium (chemical element)

Am. *shortening* ◆ America ◆ American

aM *abbrev.* ◆ am Main (German, = on the Main) (with names of places near this German river)

am *abbrev.* ◆ ante meridiem (Latin, = before noon)

am. *shortening* ◆ amateur ◆ ammeter

AMA *abbrev.* ◆ against medical advice ◆ American Medical Association ◆ Association of Metropolitan Authorities ◆ Australian Medical Association

amalg. *shortening* ◆ amalgamated

amat. *shortening* ◆ amateur

amb. *shortening* ◆ ambassador

ambig. *shortening* ◆ ambiguity ◆ ambigous

AMC *abbrev.* ◆ American Motors Corporation

AMCS *abbrev.* ◆ Airborne Missile Control System

am. cur. *shortening* ◆ amicus curiae (Latin, = friend of the court)

AMDG *abbrev.* ◆ ad majorem Dei gloriam (Latin, = to the greater glory of God)

amdmt *contraction* ◆ amendment

Amer. *shortening* ◆ America ◆ American

Amex *acronym* ◆ American Express ◆ American Stock Exchange

AMF *abbrev.* ◆ Allied Mobile Force (Nato)

amg *contraction* ◆ among

AMI *abbrev.* ◆ acute myocardial infarction

AMIGasE *abbrev.* ◆ Associate Member of the Institution of Gas Engineers

AMIMarE *abbrev.* ◆ Associate Member of the Institute of Marine Engineers

AMIMinE *abbrev.* ◆ Associate Member of the Institute of Mining Engineers

AMIPA *abbrev.* ◆ Associate Member of the Institute of Practitioners in Advertising

AMIPM *abbrev.* ◆ Associate Member of the Institute of Personnel Management

AMIStructE *abbrev.* ◆ Associate Member of the Institution of Structural Engineers

AML *abbrev.* ◆ acute myelogenous leukaemia

AMM *abbrev.* ◆ Amman (airport baggage label) ◆ anti-missile missile

AMMA *abbrev.* ◆ Assistant Masters' and Mistresses' Association

AMORC *abbrev.* ◆ Ancient Mystical Order Rosae Crucis (official title of the Rosicrucians)

amort. *shortening* ◆ amortization

AMP *abbrev.* ◆ adenosine monophosphate

amp. *shortening* ◆ amplification ◆ amplitude

amph. *shortening* ◆ amphibian ◆ amphibious

AMPS *abbrev.* ◆ automated message-processing system

AMR *abbrev.* ◆ automatic message routeing

AMRAAM *abbrev.* ◆ advanced medium-range air-to-air missile

AMS *abbrev.* ◆ Amsterdam (airport baggage label)

AMSA *abbrev.* ◆ advanced manned strategic aircraft

AMSL *abbrev.* ◆ above mean sea level

Amstrad *acronym* ◆ Alan Michael Sugar Trading

amt *contraction* ◆ amount

amu *abbrev.* ◆ atomic mass unit

AN *abbrev.* ◆ Anglo-Norman ◆ Nicaragua (international civil aircraft marking) ◆ Reading (British vehicle registration mark)

an *abbrev.* ◆ above named

a/n *abbrev.* ◆ advice note

an. *shortening* ◆ anno (Latin, = in the year) ◆ anonymous

anal. *shortening* ◆ analogous ◆ analogy ◆ analysis ◆ analytic

anat. *shortening* ◆ anatomic ◆ anatomy

ANC *abbrev.* ◆ African National Congress

anc. *shortening* ◆ ancient ◆ anciently

AND *abbrev.* ◆ Andorra (international vehicle registration)

and. *shortening* ◆ andante (Italian, = flowing) (speed-indicator in music)

Anfo *acronym* ◆ ammonium nitrate and fuel oil

Ang. *shortening* ◆ Anglice (Latin, = in English)

Anh. *shortening* ◆ Anhang (German, = appendix)

ANK *abbrev.* ◆ Ankara (airport baggage label)

Ank. *shortening* ◆ Ankunft (German, = arrival)

ANL *abbrev.* ◆ Anti-Nazi League

Anm. *shortening* ◆ Anmerkung (German, = note) (in book etc)

anme *contraction* ◆ anonyme (French, = limited liability)

ann. *shortening* ◆ annals ◆ anno (Latin, = in the year) ◆ annual ◆ annuity

annul. *shortening* ◆ annulled ◆ annulment

anon. *shortening* ◆ anonymous

ANS *abbrev.* ◆ Army Nursing Service ◆ autonomic nervous system

ans. *shortening* ◆ answer

ANSI *abbrev.* ◆ American National Standards Institute

ant. *shortening* ◆ anticipated ◆ antonym

anthol. *shortening* ◆ anthology

anthropol. *shortening* ◆ anthropological ◆ anthropologist ◆ anthropology

antilog *shortening* ◆ antilogarithm

antiq. *shortening* ◆ antiquarian ◆ antiquities

ANU *abbrev.* ◆ Australian National University

a/nw *contraction* ◆ as new

ANZAAS *abbrev.* ◆ Australian and New Zealand Association for the Advancement of Science

Anzac *acronym* ◆ Australian and New Zealand Army Corps

Anzus *acronym* ◆ Australia, New Zealand and the United States (former defensive alliance)

AO *abbrev.* ◆ Army Order ◆ Carlisle (British vehicle registration mark)

aO *abbrev.* ◆ an der Oder (German, = on the Oder) (with names of places near this German river)

a/o *abbrev.* ◆ account of

AOB *abbrev.* ◆ any other business

AOC *abbrev.* ◆ Air Officer Commanding ◆ appellation d'origine contrôlée (French, = regulated naming of origin) (of wines)

AOCB *abbrev.* ◆ any other competent business

AOD *abbrev.* ◆ Ancient Order of Druids ◆ Army Ordnance Department

AOF *abbrev.* ◆ Ancient Order of Foresters

AOH *abbrev.* ◆ Ancient Order of Hibernians

AOK *abbrev.* ◆ all items satisfactory

AONB *abbrev.* ◆ Area of Outstanding Natural Beauty

AOR *abbrev.* ◆ adult-oriented rock ◆ album-oriented rock ◆ album-oriented radio

aor. *shortening* ◆ aorist

a/or *contraction* ◆ and/or

AP *abbrev.* ◆ Air Police ◆ American plan ◆ anti-personnel ◆ armour-piercing ◆ Associated Press ◆ Brighton (British vehicle registration mark) ◆ Pakistan (international civil aircraft marking)

ap *abbrev.* ◆ additional premium ◆ ante prandium (Latin, = before meals) ◆ author's proof

ap. *shortening* ◆ apostle ◆ apothecary ◆ apparent ◆ apparently ◆ apud (Latin, = in the works of)

APACS *abbrev.* ◆ Association for Payment Clearing Services

APC *abbrev.* ◆ armoured personnel carrier ◆ aspirin, phenacetin and caffeine ◆ automatic public convenience

APCT *abbrev.* ◆ Association of Polytechnic and College Teachers

Apex *acronym* ◆ Apex Trust for the Advancement of the Employment Prospects of Ex-Offenders ◆ advance purchase excursion ◆ Association of Professional, Executive, Clerical and Computer Staff

APH *abbrev.* ◆ antepartum haemorrhage

APL *abbrev.* ◆ A Programming Language

apo. *shortening* ◆ apogee

Apoc. *shortening* ◆ Apocalypse ◆ Apocrypha ◆ Apocryphal

Apocr. *shortening* ◆ Apocrypha ◆ Apocryphal

apos. *shortening* ◆ apostrophe

app. *shortening* ◆ apparatus ◆ apparent ◆ apparently ◆ appeal ◆ appendix ◆ applied ◆ appointment ◆ appreciated ◆ apprentice ◆ approval ◆ approved ◆ approximate

app. crit. *shortening* ◆ apparatus criticus (Latin, = critical apparatus) (listing variant readings to an edited text)

appr. *shortening* ◆ apprentice ◆ approved

appro. *shortening* ◆ approval

approx. *shortening* ◆ approximate ◆ approximately ◆ approximation

appurts *contraction* ◆ appurtenances

APR *abbrev.* ◆ annual percentage rate

Apr. *shortening* ◆ April

APRC *abbrev.* ◆ anno post Romam conditam (Latin, = in the year from the founding of Rome)

APS *abbrev.* ✦ Associate of the Pharmaceutical Society

APT *abbrev.* ✦ advanced passenger train ✦ automatic picture transmission

apt *contraction* ✦ appartment

APWR *abbrev.* ✦ advanced pressurised water reactor

apx. *shortening* ✦ approximately

AQ *abbrev.* ✦ achievement quotient

aq. *shortening* ✦ aqua (Latin, = water) ✦ aqueous

AQPS *abbrev.* ✦ autre que pur sang (French, = other than pure blood) (horse-breeding)

AR *abbrev.* ✦ Aerolineas Argentinas (airline baggage code) ✦ Anna Regina (Latin, = Queen Anne) ✦ anno regni (Latin, = in the year of the reign of) ✦ annual return ✦ Arkansas (US postcode) ✦ army regulation ✦ artificial respiration ✦ autonomous region ✦ autonomous republic ✦ Chelmsford (British vehicle registration mark)

Ar *symbol* ✦ argon (chemical element)

Ar. *shortening* ✦ Arab ✦ Arabia ✦ Arabian ✦ Arabic ✦ Aramaic

aR *abbrev.* ✦ am Rhein (German, = on the Rhine) (with names of places near this river)

a/r *abbrev.* ✦ all risks

ARA *abbrev.* ✦ Aircraft Research Association ✦ Amateur Rowing Association ✦ Associate of the Royal Academy ✦ Association of the River Authorities

Arab. *shortening* ✦ Arabia ✦ Arabian ✦ Arabic

ARAD *abbrev.* ✦ Associate of the Royal Academy of Dancing

ARAM *abbrev.* ✦ Associate of the Royal Academy of Music

Aram. *shortening* ✦ Aramaic

ARAS *abbrev.* ✦ Associate of the Royal Astronomical Society

arb. *shortening* ✦ arbitration ✦ arbitrator

arbor. *shortening* ✦ arboriculture

ARC *abbrev.* ✦ Aeronautical Research Council ✦ Aids-related complex ✦ Arthritis and Rheumatism Council

ARCA *abbrev.* ✦ Associate of the Royal College of Art

arccos *shortening* ✦ arc cosine

arccosec *shortening* ✦ arc cosecant

arccot *shortening* ✦ arc cotangent

arch. *shortening* ✦ archaic ✦ archaism ✦ archery ✦ archipelago ✦ architect ✦ architectural ✦ architecture

archaeol. *shortening* ✦ archaeology

archbp *contraction* ✦ archbishop

archd. *shortening* ✦ archdeacon ✦ archduke

archit. *shortening* ✦ architect ✦ architectural ✦ architecture

ARCIC *abbrev.* ✦ Anglican–Roman Catholic International Commission

ARCM *abbrev.* ✦ Associate of the Royal College of Music

ARCO *abbrev.* ✦ Associate of the Royal College of Organists

arcsec *shortening* ✦ arc secant

arcsin *shortening* ✦ arc sine

arctan *shortening* ✦ arc tangent

ARCUK *abbrev.* ✦ Architects' Registration Council of the United Kingdom

ARCVS *abbrev.* ✦ Associate of the Royal College of Veterinary Surgeons

ARD *abbrev.* ✦ acute respiratory disease

ARDS *abbrev.* ✦ adult respiratory distress syndrome

ARE *abbrev.* ✦ Admiralty Research Establishment ✦ Arab Republic of Egypt

Arels-Felco *acronym* ✦ Association of Recognized English Language Schools/Federation of English Language Course Organizations

ARF *abbrev.* ✦ acute renal failure ✦ acute respiratory failure

Arg. *shortening* ✦ Argentina ✦ Argentine

ARI *abbrev.* ✦ acute respiratory infection

ARIA *abbrev.* ✦ automated radioimmunoassay

ARIBA *abbrev.* ◆ Associate of the Royal Society of British Architects

ARICS *abbrev.* ◆ Professional Associate of the Royal Institution of Chartered Surveyors

arith. *shortening* ◆ arithmetic ◆ arithmetical

Ariz. *shortening* ◆ Arizona

Ark. *shortening* ◆ Arkansas

ARM *abbrev.* ◆ artificial rupture of the membranes

Arm. *shortening* ◆ Armenia ◆ Armenian ◆ Armoric

Arms *acronym* ◆ Action for Research into Multiple Sclerosis

ARN *abbrev.* ◆ Stockholm, Arlanda airport (airport baggage label)

ARP *abbrev.* ◆ air raid precautions

arp. *shortening* ◆ arpeggiato (Italian, = harped) (played as a broken chord)

Arpanet *acronym* ◆ Advanced Research Projects Agency Network

ARPS *abbrev.* ◆ Associate of the Royal Photographic Society

ARR *abbrev.* ◆ anno regni reginae (Latin, = in the year of the queen's reign) ◆ anno regni regis (Latin, = in the year of the king's reign)

arr. *shortening* ◆ arranged ◆ arranger ◆ arrival ◆ arrived

ARSA *abbrev.* ◆ Associate of the Royal Society of Arts

ARSR *abbrev.* ◆ air route surveillance radar

art. *shortening* ◆ article ◆ artificial ◆ artillery

ARTC *abbrev.* ◆ air route traffic control

artic. *shortening* ◆ articulated

arty *contraction* ◆ artillery

ARV *abbrev.* ◆ Aids-associated retrovirus

AS *abbrev.* ◆ Advanced Supplementary (examination) ◆ al segno (Italian, = to the sign) (music) ◆ air speed ◆ air staff ◆ all sections ◆ Anglo-Saxon ◆ anno salutis (Latin, = in the year of salvation) ◆ antisubmarine ◆ Assistant Secretary ◆ Inverness (British vehicle registration mark)

A/S *abbrev.* ◆ Aksjeselskap (Norwegian, = limited company) ◆ Aktieselskab (Danish, = joint-stock company)

As *symbol* ◆ arsenic (chemical element)

ASA *abbrev.* ◆ Advertising Standards Authority ◆ Amateur Swimming Association ◆ American Standards Association

asap *abbrev.* ◆ as soon as possible

ASB *abbrev.* ◆ Alternative Service Book ◆ anencephaly and spina bifida

asb. *shortening* ◆ asbestos

ASBM *abbrev.* ◆ air-to-surface ballistic missile

Ascii *pronounced* as-kee *acronym* ◆ American Standard Code for Information Interchange (computer code)

ASD *abbrev.* ◆ atrial septal defect

Asda *acronym* ◆ Associated Dairies

Asdic *acronym* ◆ Anti-Submarine Detection Investigation Committee (name for sonar equipment)

ASE *abbrev.* ◆ Association for Science Education

Asean *acronym* ◆ Association of South East Asian Nations

Ash *acronym* ◆ Action on Smoking and Health

ASI *abbrev.* ◆ airspeed indicator

ASIAD *abbrev.* ◆ Associate of the Society of Industrial Artists and Designers

ASIF *abbrev.* ◆ Amateur Swimming International Federation

ASIO *abbrev.* ◆ Australian Security Intelligence Organization

ASL *abbrev.* ◆ above sea level ◆ American Sign Language

Aslef *acronym* ◆ Associated Society of Locomotive Engineers and Firemen

Aslib *acronym* ◆ Association for Information Management (orig. Association of Special Libraries and Information Bureaux)

ASM *abbrev.* ◆ air-to-surface missile ◆ assistant stage manager

ASR *abbrev.* ✦ airport surveillance radar ✦ air-sea rescue ✦ answer, send and receive ✦ automatic send and receive

A/SRS *abbrev.* ✦ air-sea rescue service

Ass. *abbrev.* ✦ Associate ✦ Associated ✦ Association

ass. *shortening* ✦ assistance ✦ assistant ✦ assurance

Asset *acronym* ✦ Association of Supervisory Staffs, Executives, and Technicians

assim. *shortening* ✦ assimilated

assmt *contraction* ✦ assessment

assn *contraction* ✦ association

assoc. *shortening* ✦ associate ✦ associated ✦ association

ASSR *abbrev.* ✦ Autonomous Soviet Socialist Republic

asst *contraction* ✦ assistant

asstd *contraction* ✦ assorted

AST *abbrev.* ✦ advanced supersonic transport ✦ Atlantic Standard Time ✦ automatic station tuning

ASTM *abbrev.* ✦ American Society for Testing and Materials

ASTMS *abbrev.* ✦ Association of Scientific, Technical and Managerial Staffs

astr. *shortening* ✦ astronomical ✦ astronomy

astrol. *shortening* ✦ astrological ✦ astrology

astron. *shortening* ✦ astronomical ✦ astronomy

ASV *abbrev.* ✦ American Standard Version (translation of Bible)

ASVA *abbrev.* ✦ Associate of the Incorporated Society of Valuers and Auctioneers

ASW *abbrev.* ✦ antisubmarine warfare

AT *abbrev.* ✦ achievement test ✦ administrative trainee ✦ alternative technology ✦ antitank ✦ appropriate technology ✦ attainment target ✦ automatic transmission ✦ Hull (British vehicle registration mark)

At *symbol* ✦ astatine (chemical element)

ATA *abbrev.* ✦ Air Transport Association (US) ✦ Air Transport Auxiliary

AT & T *abbrev.* ✦ American Telephone and Telegraph Company

ATB *abbrev.* ✦ advanced technology bomber

ATC *abbrev.* ✦ air-traffic control ✦ Air Training Corps ✦ automatic train control

ATCC *abbrev.* ✦ air traffic control centre

ATCL *abbrev.* ✦ Associate of Trinity College, London

ATCRBS *abbrev.* ✦ air traffic control radar beacon system

ATD *abbrev.* ✦ actual time of departure

ATE *abbrev.* ✦ automatic test equipment

ATH *abbrev.* ✦ Athens (airport baggage label)

athl. *shortening* ✦ athlete ✦ athletic

ATL *abbrev.* ✦ Association of Teachers and Lecturers

Atl. *shortening* ✦ Atlantic

Atlas *acronym* ✦ automated telephone line address system ✦ automatic tabulating, listing and sorting package

ATLB *abbrev.* ✦ Air Transport Licensing Board

ATM *abbrev.* ✦ anti-tank missile ✦ automated teller machine ✦ automatic teller machine

atm. *shortening* ✦ atmosphere ✦ atmospheric

at. no. *shortening* ✦ atomic number

at. numb. *shortening* ✦ atomic number

ATP *abbrev.* ✦ adenosine triphosphate ✦ advanced turboprop ✦ Automatic Train Protection

ATR *abbrev.* ✦ advanced test reactor

ATS *abbrev.* ✦ anti-tetanus serum ✦ Auxiliary Territorial Service

ats *abbrev.* ✦ at the suit of

att. *shortening* ✦ attached ✦ attorney

Att.-Gen. *shortening* ✦ Attorney-General

attn *contraction* ✦ for the attention of

attrac. *shortening* ✦ attractive

attrib. *shortening* ✦ attributed ✦ attributive ✦ attributively

atty *contraction* ✦ attorney

Atty-Gen. *shortening* ✦ Attorney-General

ATV *abbrev.* ◆ all-terrain vehicle
◆ Associated Television
at. wt *contraction* ◆ atomic weight
AU *abbrev.* ◆ astronomical unit
◆ Nottingham (British vehicle
registration mark)
ÅU *abbrev.* ◆ Ångström unit
Au *symbol* ◆ aurum (Latin, = gold)
(chemical element)
AUC *abbrev.* ◆ anno urbis conditae
(Latin, = in the year from the building
of the city) ◆ ab urbe condita (Latin, =
from the building of the city)
aud. *shortening* ◆ audit ◆ audited
◆ auditor
AUEW *abbrev.* ◆ Amalgamated Union of
Engineering Workers
AUEW-TASS *abbrev.* ◆ Amalgamated
Union of Engineering Workers,
Technical, Administrative and
Supervisory Section
Aufl. *shortening* ◆ Auflage (German, =
edition)
Aug. *shortening* ◆ August
aug. *shortening* ◆ augment
◆ augmentative
augm. *shortening* ◆ augment
◆ augmentative ◆ augmenté (French, =
enlarged)
AUH *abbrev.* ◆ Abu Dhabi (airport
baggage label)
AUS *abbrev.* ◆ Australia (international
vehicle registration)
Aus. *shortening* ◆ Austria ◆ Austrian
Ausg. *shortening* ◆ Ausgabe (German, =
edition)
Austr. *shortening* ◆ Australia
◆ Australian
Austral. *shortening* ◆ Australia
◆ Australian
AUT *abbrev.* ◆ Association of University
Teachers
auth. *shortening* ◆ authentic ◆ author
◆ authority ◆ authorized
auto. *shortening* ◆ automatic
autobiog. *shortening* ◆ autobiographical
◆ autobiography
aux. *shortening* ◆ auxiliary

AV *abbrev.* ◆ audio-visual ◆ Authorized
Version (of the Bible) ◆ Peterborough
(British vehicle registration mark)
Av. *shortening* ◆ Avenue ◆ Avocat
(French, = lawyer)
av *abbrev.* ◆ annos vixit (Latin, = lived (so
many) years)
av. *shortening* ◆ average
a/v *abbrev.* ◆ ad valorem (Latin, =
according to value) (tax system)
avail. *shortening* ◆ available
AVB *abbrev.* ◆ atrioventricular block
AVC *abbrev.* ◆ additional voluntary
contribution ◆ automatic volume control
avdp. *shortening* ◆ avoirdupois
Ave *contraction* ◆ Avenue
avge *contraction* ◆ average (cricket)
AVI *abbrev.* ◆ Automatic Vehicle
Identification
AVM *abbrev.* ◆ Air Vice-Marshal
◆ automatic vending machine
avoir. *shortening* ◆ avoirdupois
AVR *abbrev.* ◆ Army Volunteer Reserve
Avro *acronym* ◆ A. V. Roe Ltd (aircraft
manufacturer)
AVS *abbrev.* ◆ Anti-Vivisection Society
AW *abbrev.* ◆ alloy wheels ◆ Shrewsbury
(British vehicle registration mark)
a/w *abbrev.* ◆ actual weight ◆ artwork
Awacs *pronounced* ay-wax *acronym*
◆ airborne warning and control system
Awol *acronym* ◆ absent without official
leave
AWRE *abbrev.* ◆ Atomic Weapons
Research Establishment
awu *abbrev.* ◆ atomic weight unit
AX *abbrev.* ◆ Cardiff (British vehicle
registration mark)
ax. *shortening* ◆ axiom
AY *abbrev.* ◆ Finnair (airline baggage
code) ◆ Leicester (British vehicle
registration mark)
AZ *abbrev.* ◆ Alitalia (airline baggage
code) ◆ Arizona (US postcode) ◆ Belfast
(British vehicle registration mark)
Azapo *acronym* ◆ Azanian People's
Organization
AZT *abbrev.* ◆ azidothymidine

B

B *abbrev.* ◆ Bachelor ◆ baht (Thai monetary unit) ◆ balboa (Panamanian monetary unit) ◆ Baron ◆ bass (music) ◆ bathroom ◆ Belgium (international vehicle registration) ◆ Birmingham (UK postcode) ◆ bishop (chess) ◆ black (pencil) ◆ bolívar (Venezuelan monetary unit) ◆ breathalyzer ◆ Britain ◆ British ◆ Taiwan (international civil aircraft marking)

B *symbol* ◆ boron (chemical element)

b *abbrev.* ◆ bag ◆ bale ◆ ball ◆ barrel ◆ billion ◆ bloody ◆ book ◆ born ◆ bowled ◆ breadth ◆ bye (cricket)

B0 *abbrev.* ◆ 1000 × 1414 mm (paper size)

B1 *abbrev.* ◆ 707 × 1000 mm (paper size)

B2 *abbrev.* ◆ 500 × 707 mm (paper size)

B3 *abbrev.* ◆ 353 × 500 mm (paper size)

B4 *abbrev.* ◆ 250 × 353 mm (paper size)

B5 *abbrev.* ◆ 176 × 250 mm (paper size)

B6 *abbrev.* ◆ 125 × 176 mm (paper size)

B7 *abbrev.* ◆ 88 × 125 mm (paper size)

B8 *abbrev.* ◆ 62 × 88 mm (paper size)

B9 *abbrev.* ◆ 44 × 62 mm (paper size)

B10 *abbrev.* ◆ 31 × 44 mm (paper size)

BA *abbrev.* ◆ Bachelor of Arts ◆ Bath (UK postcode) ◆ Booksellers' Association ◆ British Academy ◆ British Airways ◆ British Airways (airline baggage code) ◆ British Association ◆ Manchester (British vehicle registration mark)

Ba *symbol* ◆ barium (chemical element)

BAA *abbrev.* ◆ British Airports Authority ◆ British Archaeological Association ◆ British Astronomical Association

BAAB *abbrev.* ◆ British Amateur Athletic Board

BAAF *abbrev.* ◆ British Agencies for Adoption and Fostering

BAAS *abbrev.* ◆ British Academy for the Advancement of Science

Babs *acronym* ◆ blind approach beacon system

BABT *abbrev.* ◆ British Approval Board for Telecommunications

BAC *abbrev.* ◆ blood alcohol concentration ◆ British Aircraft Corporation

bac. *shortening* ◆ baccalauréat (French, = baccalaureate) (school-leaving examination)

BACAN *abbrev.* ◆ British Association for the Control of Aircraft Noise

bach. *shortening* ◆ bachelor

BACM *abbrev.* ◆ British Association of Colliery Management

BACO *abbrev.* ◆ British Aluminium Company

BACS *abbrev.* ◆ Bankers' Automated Clearing Service

bact. *shortening* ◆ bacterium ◆ bacteriological ◆ bacteriology

bacteriol. *shortening* ◆ bacteriological ◆ bacteriology

BADA *abbrev.* ◆ British Antique Dealers' Association

BAdmin *abbrev.* ◆ Bachelor of Administration

BAE *abbrev.* ◆ Badminton Association of England

BAe *abbrev.* ◆ British Aerospace

BAEA *abbrev.* ◆ British Actors' Equity Association

BAF *abbrev.* ◆ British Athletics Federation

BAFM *abbrev.* ◆ British Association of the Friends of Museums

Bafta *acronym* ◆ British Academy of Film and Television Arts

BAG *abbrev.* ◆ Bank Action Group

Baga *acronym* ◆ British Amateur Gymnastics Association

BAGB *abbrev.* ◆ Bicycle Association of Great Britain

BAgr *abbrev.* ◆ Bachelor of Agriculture

BAgric *abbrev.* ◆ Bachelor of Agriculture

BAgrSc *abbrev.* ◆ Bachelor of Agricultural Science

BAH *abbrev.* ◆ Bahrain (airport baggage label)

BAIR *abbrev.* ◆ British Airports Information Retrieval

BAJ *abbrev.* ◆ Bachelor of Arts, Journalism

BAK *abbrev.* ◆ Baku (airport baggage label)

BAL *abbrev.* ◆ Baltimore (airport baggage label) ◆ blood alcohol level

bal. *shortening* ◆ balance

balc. *shortening* ◆ balcony

BALH *abbrev.* ◆ British Association for Local History

ball. *shortening* ◆ ballast ◆ ballistics

BALPA *abbrev.* ◆ British Air Line Pilots' Association

BaM *abbrev.* ◆ barium meal

BAMA *abbrev.* ◆ British Aerosol Manufacturers Association

BANC *abbrev.* ◆ British Association of National Coaches ◆ British Association of Nature Conservationists

B & B *abbrev.* ◆ bed and breakfast

b & c *abbrev.* ◆ building and contents

B & D *abbrev.* ◆ bondage and discipline ◆ bondage and domination

b & e *abbrev.* ◆ beginning and ending

B & FBS *abbrev.* ◆ British and Foreign Bible Society

B and S *abbrev.* ◆ brandy and soda

b & w *abbrev.* ◆ black and white

BAO *abbrev.* ◆ Bachelor of Arts, Obstetrics ◆ Bankruptcy Annulment Order

BAOR *abbrev.* ◆ British Army of the Rhine

Bap. *shortening* ◆ Baptist

bap. *shortening* ◆ baptized

BAppArts *abbrev.* ◆ Bachelor in Applied Arts

BAppSc *abbrev.* ◆ Bachelor in Applied Science

Bapt. *shortening* ◆ Baptist

bapt. *shortening* ◆ baptism ◆ baptized

BAR *abbrev.* ◆ base address register ◆ buffer address register

bar. *shortening* ◆ baritone ◆ barometer ◆ barometric ◆ barrel ◆ barrister

Barb *acronym* ◆ Broadcasters' Audience Research Board

Barb. *shortening* ◆ Barbados

BArch *abbrev.* ◆ Bachelor of Architecture

BArchE *abbrev.* ◆ Bachelor of Architectural Engineering

barg. *shortening* ◆ bargain

barit. *shortening* ◆ baritone

BARLA *abbrev.* ◆ British Amateur Rugby League Association

Bart *contraction* ◆ Baronet

Bart's *contraction* ◆ St Bartholomew's Hospital, London

BAS *abbrev.* ◆ Bachelor of Agricultural Science ◆ Bachelor of Applied Science ◆ British Antarctic Survey

BASc *abbrev.* ◆ Bachelor of Agricultural Science ◆ Bachelor of Applied Science

BASF *abbrev.* ◆ Badische Anilin und Soda-Fabrik (German, = Baden Aniline and Soda Manufactory)

Basic *acronym* ◆ Beginners' All-Purpose Symbolic Instruction Code (computer programming language) ◆ British-American Scientific International Commercial (a limited form of English)

BASW *abbrev.* ◆ British Association of Social Workers

BAT *abbrev.* ◆ British-American Tobacco Company

bat *abbrev.* ◆ best available technology

bat. *shortening* ◆ battalion ◆ battery

bath. *shortening* ◆ bathroom

bathrm *contraction* ◆ bathroom

batt. *shortening* ✦ battalion
battn *contraction* ✦ battalion
BAU *abbrev.* ✦ British Association Unit
✦ business as usual
BAWA *abbrev.* ✦ British Amateur
Wrestling Association
BAWLA *abbrev.* ✦ British Amateur
Weightlifters' Association
BB *abbrev.* ✦ Blackburn (UK postcode)
✦ Boys' Brigade ✦ Brigitte Bardot ✦ soft
black (pencil) ✦ Newcastle upon Tyne
(British vehicle registration mark)
bb *abbrev.* ✦ bail bond ✦ bank book
BBA *abbrev.* ✦ Bachelor of Business
Administration ✦ born before arrival
✦ British Backgammon Association
✦ British Board of Agrément
b/bar *contraction* ✦ bull-bar
BBB *abbrev.* ✦ softest black (pencil)
BBBC *abbrev.* ✦ British Boxing Board of
Control
BBC *abbrev.* ✦ British Broadcasting
Corporation
BBCC *abbrev.* ✦ British Bottle Collectors'
Club
BBCCS *abbrev.* ✦ British Beer Can
Collectors Society
BBCS *abbrev.* ✦ British Beer Mat
Collectors Society ✦ British Butterfly
Conservation Society
BBEM *abbrev.* ✦ bed, breakfast and
evening meal
BBF *abbrev.* ✦ British Baseball Federation
BBFC *abbrev.* ✦ British Board of Film
Classification
BBIP *abbrev.* ✦ British Books in Print
BBKA *abbrev.* ✦ British Beekeepers
Association
BBL *abbrev.* ✦ British Bridge League
bbl *symbol* ✦ barrel
BBMC *abbrev.* ✦ British Board of Marbles
Control
BBQ *abbrev.* ✦ barbecue
BBQC *abbrev.* ✦ British Board of Quality
Control
BBS *abbrev.* ✦ Bachelor of Business
Science ✦ Bachelor of Business Studies
✦ bulletin board system

BC *abbrev.* ✦ Baccalaureus Chirurgiae
(Latin, = Bachelor of Surgery)
✦ Bachelor of Chemistry ✦ Bachelor of
Commerce ✦ Badminton Club
✦ Basketball Club ✦ Battery
Commander ✦ before Christ ✦ Billiards
Club ✦ birth control ✦ Board of Control
✦ Boat Club ✦ Bomber Command
✦ Borough Council ✦ Bowls Club
✦ Boxing Club ✦ British Coal ✦ British
Columbia ✦ British Council ✦ bronchial
carcinoma ✦ Leicester (British vehicle
registration mark)
bc *abbrev.* ✦ basso continuo (music)
✦ bayonet cap (light bulbs) ✦ budgeted
cost ✦ bulk carrier
BCA *abbrev.* ✦ British Chicken Association
BCAB *abbrev.* ✦ British Computer
Association for the Blind
BCAC *abbrev.* ✦ British Conference on
Automation and Computation
BCAL *abbrev.* ✦ British Caledonian
(airline baggage label)
BCAP *abbrev.* ✦ British Code of
Advertising Practice
BCAR *abbrev.* ✦ British Civil
Airworthiness Requirements ✦ British
Council for Aid to Refugees
BCBC *abbrev.* ✦ British Citizens Band
Council
BCC *abbrev.* ✦ basal-cell carcinoma
✦ British Caravanners Club ✦ British
Council of Churches ✦ Bus and Coach
Council
bcc *abbrev.* ✦ blind carbon copy
BCCA *abbrev.* ✦ British Cyclo-Cross
Association
BCCI *abbrev.* ✦ Bank of Credit and
Commerce International
BCD *abbrev.* ✦ binary coded decimal
BCDP *abbrev.* ✦ balloon catheter
dilatation of the prostate
BCE *abbrev.* ✦ Bachelor of Chemical
Engineering ✦ Bachelor of Civil
Engineering ✦ before Christian era
✦ before common era
BCF *abbrev.* ✦ British Chess Federation
✦ British Cycling Federation

BCG *abbrev.* ◆ bacillus of Calmette and Guérin (TB inoculation)
BCh *abbrev.* ◆ Baccalaureus Chirurgiae (Latin, = Bachelor of Surgery)
bch *contraction* ◆ bunch
BChD *abbrev.* ◆ Baccalaureus Chirurgiae Dentalis (Latin, = Bachelor of Dental Surgery)
BChE *abbrev.* ◆ Bachelor of Chemical Engineering
BChemEng *abbrev.* ◆ Bachelor of Chemical Engineering
BChir *abbrev.* ◆ Baccalaureus Chirurgiae (Latin, = Bachelor of Surgery)
BCIS *abbrev.* ◆ Building Cost Information Service
BCL *abbrev.* ◆ Bachelor of Civil Law ◆ Bachelor of Canon Law
BCMA *abbrev.* ◆ British Complementary Medicine Association ◆ British Country Music Association
BCN *abbrev.* ◆ Barcelona (airport baggage label)
bcn *contraction* ◆ beacon
BCO *abbrev.* ◆ British College of Optometrists
BCOG *abbrev.* ◆ British College of Obstetricians and Gynaecologists
BCom *abbrev.* ◆ Bachelor of Commerce
BComm *abbrev.* ◆ Bachelor of Commerce
BComSc *abbrev.* ◆ Bachelor of Commercial Science
BCP *abbrev.* ◆ Book of Common Prayer
BCPL *abbrev.* ◆ Basic Computer Programming Language
BCRC *abbrev.* ◆ British Cave Rescue Council
BCRU *abbrev.* ◆ British Committee on Radiological Units
BCRUM *abbrev.* ◆ British Committee on Radiation Units and Measurements
BCS *abbrev.* ◆ Bachelor of Chemical Science ◆ Bachelor of Commercial Science ◆ British Cardiac Society ◆ British Computer Society ◆ British Crossbow Society
BCSI *abbrev.* ◆ British Campaign to Stop Immigration

bcst *contraction* ◆ broadcast
BCT *abbrev.* ◆ Building Conservation Trust
BCU *abbrev.* ◆ British Canoe Union
BD *abbrev.* ◆ Bachelor of Divinity ◆ Bahrain Dinar (monetary unit) ◆ Bangladesh (international vehicle registration) ◆ bank draft ◆ battle dress ◆ bile duct ◆ bomb disposal ◆ Bradford (UK postcode) ◆ British Midland (airline baggage code) ◆ Northampton (British vehicle registration mark)
Bd *contraction* ◆ Band (German, = volume)
bd *abbrev.* ◆ bis die (Latin, = twice a day) ◆ bill discounted
bd *contraction* ◆ board ◆ bond ◆ bound
b/d *abbrev.* ◆ banker's draft ◆ barrels per day ◆ brought down
BDA *abbrev.* ◆ bomb damage assessment ◆ British Darts Organization ◆ British Deaf Association ◆ British Dental Association ◆ British Diabetic Association ◆ British Dyslexia Association
BDBJ *abbrev.* ◆ Board of Deputies of British Jews
BDDA *abbrev.* ◆ British Deaf and Dumb Association
bde *contraction* ◆ brigade
BDentSc *abbrev.* ◆ Bachelor of Dental Science
BDF *abbrev.* ◆ Ballroom Dancers Federation
BDFA *abbrev.* ◆ British Dairy Farmers' Association
bdg *contraction* ◆ binding
BDL *abbrev.* ◆ below detectable limits
BDH *abbrev.* ◆ British Drug Houses Ltd
BDI *abbrev.* ◆ Barbados (British vehicle registration mark) ◆ British Dyslexia Institute ◆ Bundesverband der Deutschen Industrie (German, = Federation of German Industry)
bdi *abbrev.* ◆ both dates included
bdle *contraction* ◆ bundle
BDM *abbrev.* ◆ branch delegates' meeting

BDO *abbrev.* ◆ British Darts Organization

Bdr *contraction* ◆ Bombardier

BDRA *abbrev.* ◆ British Drag Racing Association

bdrm *contraction* ◆ bedroom

BDS *abbrev.* ◆ Bachelor of Dental Surgery ◆ Barbados (international vehicle registration) ◆ Brindisi (airport baggage label) ◆ British Deer Society ◆ British Dragonfly Society ◆ British Driving Society

bds *abbrev.* ◆ bis in die sumendus (Latin, = to be taken twice daily)

bds *contraction* ◆ boards

BDSc *abbrev.* ◆ Bachelor of Dental Science

BDST *abbrev.* ◆ British Double Summer Time

BDU *abbrev.* ◆ bomb disposal unit

BE *abbrev.* ◆ Bachelor of Economics ◆ Bachelor of Engineering ◆ Board of Education ◆ Leicester (British vehicle registration mark)

Be *symbol* ◆ beryllium (chemical element)

be *abbrev.* ◆ best estimate ◆ bill of entry ◆ bill of exchange

BEA *abbrev.* ◆ British Epilepsy Association ◆ British Esperanto Association ◆ British European Airways

BEAB *abbrev.* ◆ British Electrical Approvals Board

BEAMA *abbrev.* ◆ British Electrical and Allied Manufacturers' Association

bearb. *shortening* ◆ bearbeitet (German, = compiled) ◆ bearbeitet (German, = edited)

BEC *abbrev.* ◆ Building Employers' Confederation

BEc *abbrev.* ◆ Bachelor of Economics

bec. *shortening* ◆ because

BEcon *abbrev.* ◆ Bachelor of Economics

Bectu *acronym* ◆ Broadcasting, Entertainment, Cinematograph and Theatre Union

BEd *abbrev.* ◆ Bachelor of Education

bedrm *contraction* ◆ bedroom

Beds. *shortening* ◆ Bedfordshire

BEE *abbrev.* ◆ Bachelor of Electrical Engineering

BEF *abbrev.* ◆ British Equestrian Federation ◆ British Expeditionary Force

bef *abbrev.* ◆ blunt end first

bef. *shortening* ◆ before

BEFA *abbrev.* ◆ British Emigrant Families Association

BEG *abbrev.* ◆ Belgrade (airport baggage label)

beg. *shortening* ◆ beginning

Beibl. *shortening* ◆ Beiblatt (German, = supplement)

BEIC *abbrev.* ◆ British Egg Industry Council

Bel. *shortening* ◆ Belgian ◆ Belgium

Bel & Dr. *shortening* ◆ Bel and the Dragon (book of Bible)

Belf. *shortening* ◆ Belfast

Belg. *shortening* ◆ Belgian ◆ Belgium

BEM *abbrev.* ◆ British Empire Medal

ben. *shortening* ◆ benediction

benef. *shortening* ◆ benefice

Benelux *acronym* ◆ Belgium, Netherlands, Luxembourg

BEng *abbrev.* ◆ Bachelor of Engineering

beq. *shortening* ◆ bequeath

beqt *contraction* ◆ bequest

BER *abbrev.* ◆ Berlin (airport baggage label)

Ber. *shortening* ◆ Berlin

Berks. *shortening* ◆ Berkshire

Berl. *shortening* ◆ Berlin

Berm. *shortening* ◆ Bermuda

Bersa *acronym* ◆ British Elastic Rope Sports Association

BES *abbrev.* ◆ Bachelor of Engineering Science ◆ Business Expansion Scheme

BESI *abbrev.* ◆ bus electronic scanning indicator

B ès L *abbrev.* ◆ Bachelier ès Lettres (French, = Bachelor of Letters)

BESS *abbrev.* ◆ Bank of England Statistical Summary

bet. *shortening* ◆ between

betw. *shortening* ◆ between

BeV *abbrev.* ◆ billion electron-volts

bev. *shortening* ◆ bevel ◆ beverage
BEY *abbrev.* ◆ Beirut (airport baggage label)
BF *abbrev.* ◆ Stoke-on-Trent (British vehicle registration mark)
bf *abbrev.* ◆ bring forward ◆ brought forward ◆ bloody fool
BFA *abbrev.* ◆ Bachelor of Fine Arts
b'fast *contraction* ◆ breakfast room
BFBB *abbrev.* ◆ British Federation of Brass Bands
BFFC *abbrev.* ◆ British Federation of Folk Clubs
BFFS *abbrev.* ◆ British Federation of Film Societies
BFI *abbrev.* ◆ British Film Institute
BFMP *abbrev.* ◆ British Federation of Master Printers
BFN *abbrev.* ◆ British Forces' Network (radio)
BFO *abbrev.* ◆ beat frequency oscillator
BFor *abbrev.* ◆ Bachelor of Forestry
BForSc *abbrev.* ◆ Bachelor of Forestry Science
BFPO *abbrev.* ◆ British Forces Post Office
BFr *abbrev.* ◆ Belgian franc (monetary unit)
BFS *abbrev.* ◆ Belfast (airport baggage label)
BFSS *abbrev.* ◆ British Field Sports Society
BG *abbrev.* ◆ blood group ◆ Brigadier General ◆ Bulgaria (international vehicle registration) ◆ Liverpool (British vehicle registration mark)
bg *contraction* ◆ bag
b/g *abbrev.* ◆ bonded goods
BGA *abbrev.* ◆ British Gliding Association
BGC *abbrev.* ◆ bank giro credit
BGH *abbrev.* ◆ bovine growth hormone
bgl *abbrev.* ◆ below ground level
BGM *abbrev.* ◆ Bethnal Green Museum
BGRB *abbrev.* ◆ British Greyhound Racing Board
BGS *abbrev.* ◆ Brigadier, General Staff ◆ British Geological Survey ◆ British Geriatrics Society
bgt *contraction* ◆ bought

BGW *abbrev.* ◆ Baghdad (airport baggage label)
BH *abbrev.* ◆ Bournemouth (UK postcode) ◆ Luton (British vehicle registration mark)
bh *abbrev.* ◆ bloody hell
b/h *abbrev.* ◆ bill of health
BHA *abbrev.* ◆ British Handball Association ◆ British Homeopathic Association ◆ British Humanist Association
B'ham *shortening* ◆ Birmingham
BHB *abbrev.* ◆ British Hockey Board
BHC *abbrev.* ◆ British High Commissioner
BHE *abbrev.* ◆ Bachelor of Home Economics
BHF *abbrev.* ◆ British Heart Foundation
BHGA *abbrev.* ◆ British Hang Gliding Association
BHL *abbrev.* ◆ biological half-life
Bhm *contraction* ◆ Birmingham
BHO *abbrev.* ◆ Bhopal (airport baggage label)
BHort *abbrev.* ◆ Bachelor of Horticulture
BHortSc *abbrev.* ◆ Bachelor of Horticultural Science
bhp *abbrev.* ◆ brake horse-power
BHQ *abbrev.* ◆ Brigade Headquarters
BHS *abbrev.* ◆ British Home Stores ◆ British Horse Society
BHX *abbrev.* ◆ Birmingham (airport baggage label)
BI *abbrev.* ◆ Befrienders International
Bi *symbol* ◆ bismuth (chemical element)
Bib. *shortening* ◆ Bible
bib. *shortening* ◆ biblical
bibl. *shortening* ◆ biblical ◆ bibliographical ◆ bibliography
biblio. *shortening* ◆ bibliography
bibliog. *shortening* ◆ bibliography
BICC *abbrev.* ◆ Berne International Copyright Convention ◆ British Insulated Callender's Cables Ltd
BID *abbrev.* ◆ Bachelor of Industrial design ◆ brought in dead
bid *abbrev.* ◆ bis in die (Latin, = twice daily)

BIE *abbrev.* ♦ Bachelor of Industrial Engineering

bienn. *shortening* ♦ biennial

BIET *abbrev.* ♦ British Institute of Engineering Technology

BIFU *abbrev.* ♦ Banking, Insurance and Finance Union

BIHA *abbrev.* ♦ British Ice Hockey Association

BIIBA *abbrev.* ♦ British Insurance and Investment Brokers' Association

BIM *abbrev.* ♦ British Institute of Management

bin. *shortening* ♦ binary

bind. *shortening* ♦ binding

BIO *abbrev.* ♦ Bilbao (airport baggage label)

biochem. *shortening* ♦ biochemical ♦ biochemistry

biodeg. *shortening* ♦ biodegradable

biog. *shortening* ♦ biographer ♦ biographical ♦ biography

biol. *shortening* ♦ biological ♦ biology

Bios *pronounced* buy-os *acronym* ♦ basic input-output system

BIQ *abbrev.* ♦ Biarritz (airport baggage label)

BIR *abbrev.* ♦ British Institute of Radiology

BIRE *abbrev.* ♦ British Institution of Radio Engineers

Birm. *shortening* ♦ Birmingham

BIRS *abbrev.* ♦ British Institute of Recorded Sound

BIS *abbrev.* ♦ Bank for International Settlements ♦ British Interplanetary Society ♦ business information system

BISF *abbrev.* ♦ British Iron and Steel Federation

bish. *shortening* ♦ bishop

Bispa *acronym* ♦ British Independent Steel Producers' Association

Bisync *acronym* ♦ binary synchronous communications

bit *contraction* ♦ binary digit

bit. *shortening* ♦ bitumen ♦ bituminous

bitum. *shortening* ♦ bituminous

biv. *shortening* ♦ bivouac

BIWS *abbrev.* ♦ Bureau of International Whaling Statistics

BJ *abbrev.* ♦ Bachelor of Journalism ♦ Ipswich (British vehicle registration mark)

BJA *abbrev.* ♦ British Judo Association

BJJA *abbrev.* ♦ British Ju Jitsu Association

BJuris *abbrev.* ♦ Bachelor of Jurisprudence

BK *abbrev.* ♦ Portsmouth (British vehicle registration mark)

Bk *symbol* ♦ berkelium (chemical element)

bk *contraction* ♦ bank ♦ book

BKA *abbrev.* ♦ British Karate Association

bkble *contraction* ♦ bookable

bkd *contraction* ♦ booked

bkfst *contraction* ♦ breakfast

bkg *contraction* ♦ banking

bkgd *contraction* ♦ background

B/kit *contraction* ♦ body kit

BKK *abbrev.* ♦ Bangkok (airport baggage label)

bklt *contraction* ♦ booklet

BKM *abbrev.* ♦ Moscow (airport baggage label)

bkpg *contraction* ♦ bookkeeping

bkrpt *contraction* ♦ bankrupt

bks *contraction* ♦ barracks

BL *abbrev.* ♦ Bachelor of Law ♦ Bachelor of Letters ♦ Bolton (UK postcode) ♦ British Legion ♦ British Leyland ♦ British Library ♦ Reading (British vehicle registration mark)

bl *abbrev.* ♦ bill of lading

bl *contraction* ♦ barrel

bl. *shortening* ♦ bale

Blaise *acronym* ♦ British Library Automated Information Service

BLAVA *abbrev.* ♦ British Laboratory Animals Veterinary Association

BLBSD *abbrev.* ♦ British Library, Bibliographic Services Division

bldg *contraction* ♦ building

BLDSC *abbrev.* ♦ British Library, Document Supply Centre

Blesma *acronym* ♦ British Limbless Ex-Servicemen's Association

BLHSS *abbrev.* ♦ British Library, Humanities and Social Sciences

BLibSc *abbrev.* ♦ Bachelor of Library Science

BLitt *abbrev.* ♦ Baccalaureus Litterarum (Latin, = Bachelor of Letters)

blk *contraction* ♦ black ♦ block

BLL *abbrev.* ♦ Bachelor of Laws

BLLD *abbrev.* ♦ British Library, Lending Division

BLNL *abbrev.* ♦ British Library Newspaper Library

BLQ *abbrev.* ♦ Bologna (airport baggage label)

BLRD *abbrev.* ♦ British Library, Reference Division

BLS *abbrev.* ♦ Bachelor of Library Science

BLT *abbrev.* ♦ bacon, lettuce and tomato (sandwich filling)

blt *contraction* ♦ built

blvd *contraction* ♦ boulevard

BM *abbrev.* ♦ Bachelor of Medicine ♦ Bachelor of Music ♦ British Museum ♦ Luton (British vehicle registration mark)

BMA *abbrev.* ♦ British Medical Association ♦ British Midland Airways ♦ Stockholm (airport baggage label)

BMath *abbrev.* ♦ Bachelor of Mathematics

BMATT *abbrev.* ♦ British Military Advisory and Training Team

BMBF *abbrev.* ♦ British Mountain Bike Federation

BMC *abbrev.* ♦ British Motor Corporation

BMD *abbrev.* ♦ births, marriages and deaths

BMDO *abbrev.* ♦ Ballistic Missile Defence Organization (US)

BME *abbrev.* ♦ Bachelor of Mechanical Engineering ♦ Bachelor of Mining Engineering

BMed *abbrev.* ♦ Bachelor of Medicine

BMEP *abbrev.* ♦ brake mean effective pressure

BMet *abbrev.* ♦ Bachelor of Metallurgy

BMetE *abbrev.* ♦ Bachelor of Metallurgical Engineering

BMEWS *abbrev.* ♦ ballistic missile early warning system

BMI *abbrev.* ♦ ballistic missile interceptor ♦ body mass index

BMJ *abbrev.* ♦ British Medical Journal

BML *abbrev.* ♦ British Museum Library

bmp *abbrev.* ♦ brake mean power

BMR *abbrev.* ♦ basal metabolic rate

BMRB *abbrev.* ♦ British Market Research Bureau

BMS *abbrev.* ♦ Baptist Missionary Society

bms *abbrev.* ♦ business modelling system

BMTA *abbrev.* ♦ British Motor Trade Association

BMus *abbrev.* ♦ Bachelor of Music

BMW *abbrev.* ♦ Bayerische Motoren Werke (German, = Bavarian Motor Works)

BMWS *abbrev.* ♦ ballistic missile weapon system

BMX *abbrev.* ♦ bicycle motocross

BN *abbrev.* ♦ Bachelor of Nursing ♦ bank note ♦ Brighton (UK postcode) ♦ Manchester (British vehicle registration mark)

Bn *contraction* ♦ Baron

bn *contraction* ♦ bassoon ♦ battalion ♦ billion

BNA *abbrev.* ♦ British Nursing Association

BNB *abbrev.* ♦ British National Bibliography

BNC *abbrev.* ♦ British National Corpus

BNCAR *abbrev.* ♦ British National Committee for Antarctic Research

BNCC *abbrev.* ♦ British National Committee for Chemistry

BNCSR *abbrev.* ♦ British National Committee on Space Research

BNE *abbrev.* ♦ Brisbane (airport baggage label)

BNEC *abbrev.* ♦ British National Export Council ♦ British Nuclear Energy Council

BNF *abbrev.* ◆ Backus-Naur Form (computer programming notation) ◆ British Nutrition Foundation

BNFL *abbrev.* ◆ British Nuclear Fuels plc (orig. British Nuclear Fuels Limited)

BNHQ *abbrev.* ◆ battalion headquarters

BNI *abbrev.* ◆ Benin (airport baggage label)

bnkg *contraction* ◆ banking

BNJ *abbrev.* ◆ Bonn (airport baggage label)

BNO *abbrev.* ◆ bowels not opened

BNOC *abbrev.* ◆ British National Oil Corporation ◆ British National Opera Company

BNP *abbrev.* ◆ British National Party

BNS *abbrev.* ◆ British Numismatic Society

BNSc *abbrev.* ◆ Bachelor of Nursing Science

BNurs *abbrev.* ◆ Bachelor of Nursing

BO *abbrev.* ◆ body odour ◆ Bolivia (international vehicle registration) ◆ bowels opened ◆ box office ◆ branch office ◆ broker's order ◆ brought over ◆ buyer's option ◆ Cardiff (British vehicle registration mark)

BOA *abbrev.* ◆ British Olympic Association ◆ British Optical Association ◆ British Orthopaedic Association

BOAC *abbrev.* ◆ British Overseas Airways Corporation (airline baggage code) ◆ British Overseas Airways Corporation

BOBS *abbrev.* ◆ Board of Banking Supervision

BOC *abbrev.* ◆ British Oxygen Corporation

BOCM *abbrev.* ◆ British Oil and Cake Mills Limited

BOD *abbrev.* ◆ biological oxygen demand ◆ Bordeaux (airport baggage label)

Bod. *shortening* ◆ Bodleian Library

Bodl. *shortening* ◆ Bodleian Library

Bod. Lib. *shortening* ◆ Bodleian Library

Body *acronym* ◆ British Organ Donor Society

BoE *abbrev.* ◆ Bank of England

BOF *abbrev.* ◆ beginning of file ◆ British Orienteering Federation

BOG *abbrev.* ◆ Bogotá (airport baggage label)

BOH *abbrev.* ◆ Bournemouth (airport baggage label)

Bol. *shortening* ◆ Bolivia ◆ Bolivian

bol. *shortening* ◆ bolus (Latin, = pill)

Boltop *acronym* ◆ better on lips than on paper

BOM *abbrev.* ◆ Bombay (airport baggage label)

Bomb. *shortening* ◆ Bombardier

BON *abbrev.* ◆ British Organization of Non-Parents

BOP *abbrev.* ◆ Boys' Own Paper

BOptom *abbrev.* ◆ Bachelor of Optometry

bor. *shortening* ◆ borough

Boss *acronym* ◆ Bureau of State Security (South Africa)

BOT *abbrev.* ◆ beginning of tape

BoT *abbrev.* ◆ Board of Trade

bot. *shortening* ◆ botanical ◆ botanist ◆ botany ◆ bottle ◆ bottom ◆ bought

BOTB *abbrev.* ◆ British Overseas Trade Board

Boul. *shortening* ◆ Boulevard (French) (precedes name)

BP *abbrev.* ◆ Bachelor of Pharmacy ◆ Bachelor of Philosophy ◆ before present (with radiocarbon dates) ◆ British Petroleum ◆ British Pharmacopoeia ◆ Portsmouth (British vehicle registration mark)

bp *abbrev.* ◆ bills payable ◆ birthplace ◆ blood pressure ◆ boiling point

bp *contraction* ◆ bishop

BPAS *abbrev.* ◆ British Pregnancy Advisory Service

BPC *abbrev.* ◆ Book Prices Current ◆ British Pharmaceutical Codex ◆ British Pharmacopoeia Commission

BPCC *abbrev.* ◆ British Printing and Communication Corporation

BPCRA *abbrev.* ◆ British Professional Cycle Racing Association

bpd *abbrev.* ◆ barrels per day
BPE *abbrev.* ◆ Bachelor of Physical Education
BPH *abbrev.* ◆ benign prostatic hypertrophy
BPh *abbrev.* ◆ Bachelor of Philosophy
bph *abbrev.* ◆ barrels per hour
BPharm *abbrev.* ◆ Bachelor of Pharmacy
BPhil *abbrev.* ◆ Bachelor of Philosophy
bpi *abbrev.* ◆ bits per inch ◆ bytes per inch
BPIF *abbrev.* ◆ British Printing Industries Federation
bpl. *shortening* ◆ birthplace
bpm *abbrev.* ◆ barrels per minute
BPO *abbrev.* ◆ Berlin Philharmonic Orchestra
bps *abbrev.* ◆ bits per second ◆ bytes per second
BPsych *abbrev.* ◆ Bachelor of Psychology
Bq *shortening* ◆ becquerel
BR *abbrev.* ◆ block release ◆ Brazil (international vehicle registration) ◆ British Caledonian (airline baggage code) ◆ British Rail ◆ Bromley (UK postcode) ◆ Newcastle upon Tyne (British vehicle registration mark)
Br *contraction* ◆ birr (Ethiopian monetary unit) ◆ Brother
Br *symbol* ◆ bromine (chemical element)
Br. *shortening* ◆ Britain ◆ British
br *abbrev.* ◆ bank rate ◆ bedroom ◆ bills receivable
br. *shortening* ◆ branch ◆ bridge ◆ brother ◆ brown
BRA *abbrev.* ◆ British Rheumatism and Arthritis Association
Braz. *shortening* ◆ Brazil ◆ Brazilian
BRC *abbrev.* ◆ British Rabbit Council ◆ business reply card
BRCS *abbrev.* ◆ British Red Cross Society
brd *contraction* ◆ board (food)
BRDC *abbrev.* ◆ British Racing Drivers' Club
brdcst *contraction* ◆ broadcast
BRE *abbrev.* ◆ Bachelor of Religious Education ◆ Bremen (airport baggage label) ◆ Building Research Establishment

breathtkg *contraction* ◆ breathtaking
b/rec. *shortening* ◆ bills receivable
BREL *abbrev.* ◆ British Rail Engineering Limited
Bret. *shortening* ◆ Breton
brev. *shortening* ◆ brevet
BRF *abbrev.* ◆ Bible Reading Fellowship ◆ British Road Federation
brf. *shortening* ◆ brief
BRI *abbrev.* ◆ Bari (airport baggage label)
Brig. *shortening* ◆ Brigade ◆ Brigadier
Brig. Gen. *shortening* ◆ Brigadier General
brill. *shortening* ◆ brillante (Italian, = brilliant) (music)
Brit. *shortening* ◆ Britain ◆ Britannia ◆ British ◆ Briton
Brit. Mus. *shortening* ◆ British Museum
Brit. Pat. *shortening* ◆ British Patent
brk *contraction* ◆ brick
brkf. *shortening* ◆ breakfast
brklyr *contraction* ◆ bricklayer
brkt *contraction* ◆ bracket
brkwtr *contraction* ◆ breakwater
BRM *abbrev.* ◆ British Racing Motors
BRN *abbrev.* ◆ Bahrain (international vehicle registration) ◆ Bern (airport baggage label)
BRNC *abbrev.* ◆ Britannia Royal Naval College
bro. *shortening* ◆ brother
Bros *contraction* ◆ Brothers
BRPB *abbrev.* ◆ British Rail Properties Board
BRS *abbrev.* ◆ British Road Services
BRU *abbrev.* ◆ Brunei (international vehicle registration) ◆ Brussels (airport baggage label)
Brum. *shortening* ◆ Brummagem (Birmingham)
bryol. *shortening* ◆ bryology
BS *abbrev.* ◆ Bachelor of Science ◆ Bachelor of Surgery ◆ Bahamas (international vehicle registration) ◆ breath sounds ◆ blood sugar ◆ British Standard ◆ Bristol (UK postcode) ◆ Building Society ◆ Inverness (British vehicle registration mark)

bs *abbrev.* ◆ balance sheet ◆ bill of sale ◆ bullshit

b/s *abbrev.* ◆ building society

BSA *abbrev.* ◆ Bachelor of Agricultural Science ◆ Birmingham Small Arms Company ◆ British School at Athens ◆ body surface area

BSAC *abbrev.* ◆ British Sub-Aqua Club

BSAgr *abbrev.* ◆ Bachelor of Science in Agriculture

BSArch *abbrev.* ◆ Bachelor of Science in Architecture

BSB *abbrev.* ◆ Brasilia (airport baggage label) ◆ British Satellite Broadcasting

BSBA *abbrev.* ◆ Bachelor of Science in Business Administration

BSBus *abbrev.* ◆ Bachelor of Science in Business

BSC *abbrev.* ◆ Bachelor of Science in Commerce ◆ British Safety Council ◆ British Steel Corporation ◆ British Sugar Corporation ◆ Broadcasting Standards Council ◆ Building Societies Commission

BSc *abbrev.* ◆ Bachelor of Science

bsc *abbrev.* ◆ binary synchronous communications

bsc *contraction* ◆ basic

BScAg *abbrev.* ◆ Bachelor of Science in Agriculture

BScChemE *abbrev.* ◆ Bachelor of Science in Chemical Engineering

BScD *abbrev.* ◆ Bachelor of Dental Science

BSCE *abbrev.* ◆ Bachelor of Science in Civil Engineering

BScEng *abbrev.* ◆ Bachelor of Science in Engineering

BScMed *abbrev.* ◆ Bachelor of Medical Science

BSCP *abbrev.* ◆ British Standard Code of Practice

BScSoc *abbrev.* ◆ Bachelor of Social Sciences

BScTech *abbrev.* ◆ Bachelor of Technical Science

BSE *abbrev.* ◆ Bachelor of Science in Education ◆ bovine spongiform encephalopathy

BSF *abbrev.* ◆ Bachelor of Science in Forestry

BSG *abbrev.* ◆ British Standard Gauge

bsh. *shortening* ◆ bushel

BSHA *abbrev.* ◆ Bachelor of Science in Hospital Administration

BSI *abbrev.* ◆ British Standards Institution

BSIE *abbrev.* ◆ Bachelor of Science in Industrial Engineering

BSJA *abbrev.* ◆ British Show Jumping Association

bskt *contraction* ◆ basket

BSkyB *abbrev.* ◆ British Sky Broadcasting

BSL *abbrev.* ◆ Basle (airport baggage label) ◆ British Sign Language

BSM *abbrev.* ◆ British School of Motoring

bsmt *contraction* ◆ basement

BSN *abbrev.* ◆ Bachelor of Science in Nursing

BSR *abbrev.* ◆ Basra (airport baggage label) ◆ Board for Social Responsibility (Church of England) ◆ British School at Rome

BSS *abbrev.* ◆ Bachelor of Social Science ◆ British Standards Specification

BST *abbrev.* ◆ bovine somatotrophin ◆ British Standard Time ◆ British Summer Time

BT *abbrev.* ◆ Belfast (UK postcode) ◆ British Telecom ◆ Leeds (British vehicle registration mark)

Bt *contraction* ◆ Baronet

bt *contraction* ◆ beat ◆ bought

BTA *abbrev.* ◆ British Tourist Authority

BTCV *abbrev.* ◆ British Trust for Conservation Volunteers

BTEC *abbrev.* ◆ Business and Technician Education Council

btf *abbrev.* ◆ balance to follow

BTG *abbrev.* ◆ British Technology Group

BTh *abbrev.* ◆ Bachelor of Theology

bth *contraction* ◆ bath ◆ berth

bth. *shortening* ◆ bathroom

BThU *abbrev.* ◆ British Thermal Unit

btm *contraction* ◆ bottom

BTN *abbrev.* ◆ Brunei (airport baggage label)

BTO *abbrev.* ◆ big-time operator ◆ British Trust for Ornithology

BTS *abbrev.* ◆ Bood Transfusion Service

BTU *abbrev.* ◆ Board of Trade unit ◆ British Thermal Unit

btw. *shortening* ◆ between

BU *abbrev.* ◆ Bakers, Food and Allied Workers Union ◆ Baptist Union of Great Britain and Ireland ◆ Manchester (British vehicle registration mark)

bu *abbrev.* ◆ base unit

bu. *shortening* ◆ bushel

BUAV *abbrev.* ◆ British Union for the Abolition of Vivisection

BUC *abbrev.* ◆ Bangor University College

Bucks. *shortening* ◆ Buckinghamshire

BUCOP *abbrev.* ◆ British Union Catalogue of Periodicals

BUD *abbrev.* ◆ Budapest (airport baggage label)

bud. *abbrev.* ◆ budget

BUE *abbrev.* ◆ Buenos Aires (airport baggage label)

BUF *abbrev.* ◆ British Union of Fascists

Buglr *contraction* ◆ Bugler

BUJ *abbrev.* ◆ Baccalaureus Utriusque Juris (Latin, = Bachelor of Both Laws) (canon and civil)

Bulg. *shortening* ◆ Bulgaria ◆ Bulgarian

bull. *shortening* ◆ bulletin

Bupa *acronym* ◆ British United Provident Association

BUR *abbrev.* ◆ Burma (international vehicle registration)

burg. *shortening* ◆ burgess ◆ burgomaster

burl. *shortening* ◆ burlesque

bus. *shortening* ◆ business

BUSF *abbrev.* ◆ British Universities Sports Federation

BV *abbrev.* ◆ Beata Virgo (Latin, = Blessed Virgin) ◆ bene vale (Latin, = farewell) ◆ Besloten Vennootschap (Dutch, = Company Limited) ◆ blood

vessel ◆ blood volume ◆ Preston (British vehicle registration mark)

BVA *abbrev.* ◆ British Veterinary Association

BVetMed *abbrev.* ◆ Bachelor of Veterinary Medicine

BVetSc *abbrev.* ◆ Bachelor of Veterinary Science

BVI *abbrev.* ◆ British Virgin Islands (international vehicle registration)

BVM *abbrev.* ◆ Bachelor of Veterinary Medicine ◆ Beata Virgo Maria (Latin, = Blessed Virgin Mary)

BVM & S *abbrev.* ◆ Bachelor of Veterinary Medicine and Surgery

BVP *abbrev.* ◆ British Visitors' Passport

BVS *abbrev.* ◆ Bachelor of Veterinary Surgery

BVSc *abbrev.* ◆ Bachelor of Veterinary Science

BW *abbrev.* ◆ biological warfare ◆ body water ◆ body weight ◆ British Waterways ◆ Oxford (British vehicle registration mark)

b/w *abbrev.* ◆ black and white

BWB *abbrev.* ◆ British Waterways Board

bwd *contraction* ◆ backward

BWR *abbrev.* ◆ boiling-water reactor

BWSF *abbrev.* ◆ British Water Ski Federation

BWV *abbrev.* ◆ Bach Werke Verzeichnis (German, = Catalogue of Bach's Works)

BX *abbrev.* ◆ Haverfordwest (British vehicle registration mark)

BY *abbrev.* ◆ north-west London (British vehicle registration mark)

BYO *abbrev.* ◆ bring your own

BYOB *abbrev.* ◆ bring your own booze

BYOG *abbrev.* ◆ bring your own girl

BYT *abbrev.* ◆ bright young things

Byz. *shortening* ◆ Byzantine

BZ *abbrev.* ◆ Down (British vehicle registration mark)

BZE *abbrev.* ◆ Belize (airport baggage label)

BZV *abbrev.* ◆ Brazzaville (airport baggage label)

C

C *abbrev.* ♦ Cape ♦ cancer ♦ castle (chess) ♦ Catholic ♦ Celsius ♦ centigrade ♦ clubs (cards) ♦ cocaine (slang) ♦ Coloured (South Africa) ♦ Command paper (series 1870–99) ♦ Conservative ♦ Corps ♦ coulomb ♦ Council ♦ County ♦ Cuba (international vehicle registration) ♦ kilocalorie

C *symbol* ♦ carbon (chemical element)

c *abbrev.* ♦ canine (dentistry) ♦ capacity ♦ caput (Latin, = chapter) ♦ carat ♦ cathode ♦ caught by (cricket) ♦ cent (monetary unit) ♦ centavo (monetary unit) ♦ centi- ♦ centime (monetary unit) ♦ century ♦ circa (Latin, = about) ♦ cold ♦ college ♦ colt ♦ constant (mathematics) ♦ contralto ♦ cubic

C4 *abbrev.* ♦ Channel Four (commercial television channel)

CA *abbrev.* ♦ California (US postcode) ♦ cardiac arrest ♦ Carlisle (UK postcode) ♦ Central America ♦ certificate of airworthiness ♦ Chargé d'Affaires ♦ Chartered Accountant ♦ chief accountant ♦ chronological age ♦ Church Army ♦ Civil Aviation Administration of China (airline baggage code) ♦ Classical Association ♦ College of Arms ♦ consular agent ♦ Consumers' Association ♦ County Alderman ♦ Court of Appeal ♦ current assets

Ca *contraction* ♦ Compagnia (Italian, = Company) ♦ Companhia (Portuguese, = Company) ♦ Compañia (Spanish, = Company)

Ca *symbol* ♦ calcium (chemical element)

ca *abbrev.* ♦ coll'arco (Italian, = with the bow) (music)

ca *contraction* ♦ carcinoma ♦ circa (Latin, = about)

ca. *shortening* ♦ case

c/a *abbrev.* ♦ capital account ♦ credit account ♦ current account

CAA *abbrev.* ♦ Campaign for the Abolition of Angling ♦ Civil Aviation Authority

CAADRP *abbrev.* ♦ civil aircraft airworthiness data recording program

CAAIS *abbrev.* ♦ computer-assisted action information system

CAAT *abbrev.* ♦ Campaign Against Arms Trade

CAB *abbrev.* ♦ Citizens' Advice Bureau

cab. *shortening* ♦ cabin

CABG *abbrev.* ♦ coronary artery bypass graft

CABS *abbrev.* ♦ coronary artery bypass surgery

CAC *abbrev.* ♦ Campaign Against Censorship ♦ Central Advisory Committee ♦ Central Arbitration Committee

CACC *abbrev.* ♦ Civil Aviation Communications Centre ♦ Council for the Accreditation of Correspondence Colleges

CACE *abbrev.* ♦ Central Advisory Council for Education

CACLB *abbrev.* ♦ Churches' Advisory Committee on Local Broadcasting

CACM *abbrev.* ♦ Central American Common Market

CACTM *abbrev.* ♦ Central Advisory Council for the Ministry

Cad *acronym* ♦ computer-aided design ♦ computer-aided draughting ♦ compact audio disc

cadav. *shortening* ✦ cadaver
Cadcam *acronym* ✦ computer-aided design and manufacture
CADD *abbrev.* ✦ computer-aided drafting and design
CADE *abbrev.* ✦ computer-aided design evaluation
Cadmat *acronym* ✦ computer-aided design, manufacture and testing
Cadpos *acronym* ✦ Communications and Data Processing Operations System
CAE *abbrev.* ✦ computer-aided engineering
CAEC *abbrev.* ✦ Central American Economic Community
Caerns. *shortening* ✦ Caernarvonshire
CAES *abbrev.* ✦ compressed air energy storage
CAEU *abbrev.* ✦ Council of Arab Economic Unity
caf *abbrev.* ✦ cost and freight
cafm *abbrev.* ✦ commercial air freight movement
Cafod *acronym* ✦ Catholic Fund for Overseas Development
CAFU *abbrev.* ✦ Civil Aviation Flying Unit
CAI *abbrev.* ✦ Cairo (airport baggage label) ✦ computer-aided instruction
CAIB *abbrev.* ✦ Certified Associate of the Institute of Bankers
Caith. *shortening* ✦ Caithness (former Scottish county)
CAL *abbrev.* ✦ Conversational Algebraic Language (computer language)
Cal *acronym* ✦ computer-aided learning
Cal. *shortening* ✦ kilocalorie ✦ California
cal. *shortening* ✦ calando (Italian, = decreasing) ✦ calendar ✦ calibre ✦ calorie
calc. *shortening* ✦ calculated ✦ calculation ✦ calculus
Calif. *shortening* ✦ California
caln *contraction* ✦ calculation
calo. *shortening* ✦ calando (Italian, = decreasing) (music)
Caltech *acronym* ✦ California Institute of Technology

Calv. *shortening* ✦ Calvinistic
CAM *abbrev.* ✦ Cameroon (international vehicle registration) ✦ Commonwealth Association of Museums ✦ computer-aided manufacture
Cam. *shortening* ✦ Cambodia ✦ Cambodian
cam. *shortening* ✦ camouflage
Camb. *shortening* ✦ Cambrian ✦ Cambridge ✦ Cambridgeshire
Cambs. *shortening* ✦ Cambridgeshire
Camra *acronym* ✦ Campaign for Real Ale
CAN *abbrev.* ✦ Committee on Aircraft Noise (ICAO)
Can. *shortening* ✦ Canada ✦ Canadian ✦ Canal ✦ Cantoris (section of church choir)
can. *shortening* ✦ canon ✦ canto ✦ canton
Cana *acronym* ✦ Clergy Against Nuclear Arms
Canad. *shortening* ✦ Canadian
Canc. *shortening* ✦ Cancellarius (Latin, = Chancellor)
canc. *shortening* ✦ cancellation ✦ cancelled
Cancirco *pronounced* kan-ser-ko *acronym* ✦ Cancer International Research Co-operative
Cand *acronym* ✦ Campaign Against Nuclear Dumping
cand. *shortening* ✦ candidate
C & A *abbrev.* ✦ Clemens and Auguste (Christian names of the Breeninkmeyer brothers, Dutch founders of the store chain)
c and b *abbrev.* ✦ caught and bowled by (cricket)
c & c *abbrev.* ✦ carpets and curtains
c & d *abbrev.* ✦ collection and delivery
C & E *abbrev.* ✦ Customs and Excise
c & f *abbrev.* ✦ cost and freight
C & G *abbrev.* ✦ City and Guilds of London Institute ✦ Cheltenham and Gloucester Building Society
c & i *abbrev.* ✦ cost and insurance
c & lc *abbrev.* ✦ capital and lower case (printing instruction)
c & p *abbrev.* ✦ carriage and packing

c & r *abbrev.* ✦ convalescence and rehabilitation

c & sc *abbrev.* ✦ capital and small capitals (printing instruction)

C & W *abbrev.* ✦ country and western (music)

Can. Fr. *shortening* ✦ Canadian French

Can. Pac. *shortening* ✦ Canadian Pacific

Cant. *shortening* ✦ Canterbury ✦ Canticles (book of Bible) ✦ Cantonese

Cantab. *shortening* ✦ Cantabrigiensis (Latin, = of Cambridge)

Cantran *acronym* ✦ cancelled in transmission

Cantuar. *shortening* ✦ Cantuariensis (Latin, = of Canterbury)

canv. *shortening* ✦ canvas

CAO *abbrev.* ✦ Chief Administrative Officer

CAP *abbrev.* ✦ Church Action on Poverty ✦ Code of Advertising Practice ✦ Common Agricultural Policy ✦ computer-aided production

Cap. *shortening* ✦ Captain

cap *abbrev.* ✦ codice di avviamento postale (Italian, = postcode)

cap. *shortening* ✦ capacity ✦ capiat (Latin, = let him take) ✦ capital ✦ capitalize ✦ capital letter ✦ caput (Latin, = chapter)

CAPD *abbrev.* ✦ continuous ambulatory peritoneal dialysis

Capn *contraction* ✦ Captain

Capric. *shortening* ✦ Capricorn

CAPS *abbrev.* ✦ Captive Animals' Protection Society

CAPT *abbrev.* ✦ Citizens Against the Poll Tax

Capt. *shortening* ✦ Captain

capt. *shortening* ✦ caption

CAR *abbrev.* ✦ Central African Republic ✦ compounded annual rate

Car. *shortening* ✦ County Carlow ✦ Carolus (Latin, = Charles)

car. *shortening* ✦ carat

CARA *abbrev.* ✦ combat air rescue aircraft

Caraf *acronym* ✦ Christians Against Racism and Fascism

carb. *shortening* ✦ carbonate ✦ carburettor

CARD *abbrev.* ✦ compact automatic retrieval device

Card *acronym* ✦ Campaign Against Racial Discrimination

Card. *shortening* ✦ Cardinal

Cards. *shortening* ✦ Cardigan (former Welsh county)

Care *acronym* ✦ Christian Action for Research and Education ✦ Co-operative for American Relief Everywhere

Carib. *shortening* ✦ Caribbean

Caricom *acronym* ✦ Caribbean Community and Common Market

Carliol. *shortening* ✦ Carliolensis (Latin, = of Carlisle)

Carms. *shortening* ✦ Carmarthen (former Welsh county)

Carns. *shortening* ✦ Caernarvon (former Welsh county)

carp. *shortening* ✦ carpenter ✦ carpentry

carr. fwd *contraction* ✦ carriage forward

Cart *acronym* ✦ collision avoidance radar trainer

cart. *shortening* ✦ cartage ✦ carton

cartog. *shortening* ✦ cartographic ✦ cartography

CAS *abbrev.* ✦ Casablanca (airport baggage label) ✦ Catgut Acoustical Society ✦ Chief of Air Staff ✦ Collision Avoidance System

cas. *shortening* ✦ castle ✦ casual ✦ casualty

Case *acronym* ✦ Campaign for State Education ✦ computer-aided software engineering ✦ computer-aided systems engineering

cash. *shortening* ✦ cashier

cass. *shortening* ✦ cassette

CAT *abbrev.* ✦ Centre for Alternative Technology ✦ College of Advanced Technology ✦ computerized axial tomography ✦ computer-aided translation ✦ computer-aided typesetting

Cat. *shortening* ✦ Catalan

cat. *shortening* ◆ catalogue ◆ catamaran ◆ catapult ◆ catechism ◆ category

catachr. *shortening* ◆ catachresis ◆ catachrestic

Catal. *shortening* ◆ Catalan ◆ Catalonian

CATE *abbrev.* ◆ Committee for the Accreditation of Teacher Education

Cath. *shortening* ◆ Catholic

cath. *shortening* ◆ cathedral ◆ cathode

catk *contraction* ◆ counterattack

CATU *abbrev.* ◆ Ceramic and Allied Trades Union

CATV *abbrev.* ◆ cable television ◆ community antenna television

caus. *shortening* ◆ causation ◆ causative

Cav. *shortening* ◆ County Cavan

Caviar *acronym* ◆ Cinema and Video Industry Audience Research

CAYA *abbrev.* ◆ Catholic Association of Young Adults

CAX *abbrev.* ◆ Carlisle (airport baggage label)

CB *abbrev.* ◆ Bolivia (international civil aircraft marking) ◆ Cambridge (UK postcode) ◆ cash book ◆ Citizens' Band ◆ Companion of the Order of the Bath ◆ confined to barracks ◆ contrabasso (Italian, = double bass) ◆ County Borough ◆ Manchester (British vehicle registration mark)

cb *abbrev.* ◆ centre of buoyancy ◆ circuit breaker

c/b *abbrev.* ◆ caught and bowled (cricket) ◆ cost–benefit

CBA *abbrev.* ◆ cost–benefit analysis ◆ Council for British Archaeology

CBC *abbrev.* ◆ Canadian Broadcasting Corporation ◆ complete blood count

cbd *abbrev.* ◆ cash before delivery

CBE *abbrev.* ◆ Commander of the Order of the British Empire

ADVERTSPEAK 1: Cars

There are many jokes about second-hand car salesmen, but even before you reach the showroom the language of their advertisements, which often consist of nothing but abbreviations, may leave you baffled. As motor gadgetry grows new abbreviations are invented, and little standardization has yet taken place. A selection of the usual abbreviations for some common items is given below: these all, together with many other motor items and a number of variant forms, appear in the dictionary.

a/b	*airbag*	**fsh**	*full service history*
a/con.	*air conditioning*	**GTS**	*gran turismo sports; gran turismo special*
at	*automatic transmission*		
aw	*alloy wheels*	**hfs**	*heated front seats*
b/bar	*bull-bar*	**hlww**	*headlamp wash and wipe*
b/kit	*body kit*	**irl**	*infra-red locking*
cc	*cruise control*	**lhd**	*left-hand drive*
ch.	*chassis*	**lwb**	*long wheelbase*
cl	*central locking*	**mod.**	*model*
demo	*demonstration model*	**obc**	*on-board computer*
eds	*electrically adjusted driver's seat*	**otg**	*outside temperature gauge*
esc	*electric seat control; etched security code*	**pas**	*power-assisted steering*
		rhd	*right-hand drive*
esr	*electric sun roof*	**r/r**	*roof rails*
ew	*electric widows*	**s/susp**	*sports suspension*
far	*front arm rests*	**T**	*thousand (mileage)*

CBEL *abbrev.* ◆ Cambridge Bibliography of English Literature

CBF *abbrev.* ◆ cerebral blood flow

CBI *abbrev.* ◆ Confederation of British Industry

cbi *abbrev.* ◆ complete background investigation ◆ computer-based information

CBIS *abbrev.* ◆ computer-based information system

cbk *contraction* ◆ chequebook

CBL *abbrev.* ◆ commercial bill of lading

CBMIS *abbrev.* ◆ computer-based management information system

C-bomb *contraction* ◆ cobalt bomb

CBR *abbrev.* ◆ complete bed rest ◆ crude birth rate

CBRW *abbrev.* ◆ chemical, biological and radiological warfare ◆ chemical, biological and radiological weapons

CBS *abbrev.* ◆ Columbia Broadcasting System

CBSI *abbrev.* ◆ Chartered Building Societies' Institute

CBSO *abbrev.* ◆ City of Birmingham Symphony Orchestra

CBT *abbrev.* ◆ computer-based training

CBU *abbrev.* ◆ Clearing Banks Union ◆ cluster bomb unit

CBW *abbrev.* ◆ chemical and biological warfare

CBX *abbrev.* ◆ company branch exchange

CC *abbrev.* ◆ Bangor (British vehicle registration mark) ◆ Cape Colony ◆ Cape Coloured ◆ Central Committee ◆ Chamber of Commerce ◆ Charity Commission ◆ Chess Club ◆ Chile (international civil aircraft marking) ◆ City Council ◆ closed circuit ◆ confined to camp ◆ Countryside Commission ◆ County Council ◆ County Councillor ◆ Cricket Club ◆ Croquet Club ◆ cruise control ◆ Cycling Club

cc *abbrev.* ◆ carbon copy ◆ colour code ◆ cubic centimetre

CCA *abbrev.* ◆ County Councils Association ◆ current cost accounting

CCAT *abbrev.* ◆ Central Council for the Amateur Theatre

CCBN *abbrev.* ◆ Central Council for British Naturism

CCBW *abbrev.* ◆ Committee on Chemical and Biological Warfare

CCC *abbrev.* ◆ Camping and Caravanning Club of Great Britain and Ireland ◆ Central Criminal Court ◆ Council for the Care of Churches

ccc *abbrev.* ◆ cwmni cyfyngedig cyhoeddus (Welsh, = public limited company)

CCCBR *abbrev.* ◆ Central Council of Church Bell Ringers

CCCC *abbrev.* ◆ Charity Christmas Card Council

CCCM *abbrev.* ◆ Central Committee for Community Medicine (BMA)

CCCO *abbrev.* ◆ Committee on Climatic Changes and the Ocean

CCCP *abbrev.* ◆ Soyuz Sovietskikh Sotsialichestkikh Respublik (Russian, = Union of Soviet Socialist Republics) (CCCP is a transliteration of the Cyrillic characters for SSSR)

CCCR *abbrev.* ◆ closed-chest cardiac resuscitation ◆ Co-ordinating Committee for Cancer Research

CCD *abbrev.* ◆ charge coupled device

ccei *abbrev.* ◆ composite cost–effectiveness index

CCF *abbrev.* ◆ Central Control Function ◆ Combined Cadet Force ◆ Common Cold Foundation ◆ congestive cardiac failure

CCFA *abbrev.* ◆ Combined Cadet Force Association

CCGB *abbrev.* ◆ Cycling Council of Great Britain

CCHE *abbrev.* ◆ Central Council for Health Education

CChem *abbrev.* ◆ Chartered Chemist

CCHMS *abbrev.* ◆ Central Committee for Hospital Medical Services (BMA)

CCIA *abbrev.* ◆ Commission of the Churches on International Affairs (WCC)

CCIS *abbrev.* ♦ command control information system

CCITU *abbrev.* ♦ Co-ordinating Committee of Independent Trade Unions

CCIVS *abbrev.* ♦ Co-ordinating Committee for International Voluntary Service

CCJ *abbrev.* ♦ Council for Christians and Jews

CCLGF *abbrev.* ♦ Consultative Committee on Local Government Finance

CCM *abbrev.* ♦ Cornish Chamber of Mines

CCNR *abbrev.* ♦ Consultative Committee on Nuclear Research

CCOA *abbrev.* ♦ County Court Officers' Association

CCP *abbrev.* ♦ Chinese Communist Party ♦ Code of Civil Procedure

ccp *abbrev.* ♦ credit-card purchase

CCPR *abbrev.* ♦ Central Council for Physical Recreation

CCR *abbrev.* ♦ critical compression ratio

CCS *abbrev.* ♦ Caracas (airport baggage label) ♦ casualty clearing station

CCSC *abbrev.* ♦ Central Consultants and Specialists Committee (BMA)

CCSEM *abbrev.* ♦ computer-controlled scanning electron microscope

CCSU *abbrev.* ♦ Council of Civil Service Unions

CCT *abbrev.* ♦ common customs tariff ♦ compulsory competitive tendering

CCTA *abbrev.* ♦ Central Computer and Telecommunications Agency

CCTV *abbrev.* ♦ closed circuit television

CCU *abbrev.* ♦ Calcutta (airport baggage label) ♦ coronary care unit

CCW *abbrev.* ♦ International Committee on Chemical Warfare

ccw *abbrev.* ♦ counterclockwise

CCWC *abbrev.* ♦ Campaign for Cold Weather Credits

CCWM *abbrev.* ♦ Congregational Council for World Mission

CD *abbrev.* ♦ Brighton (British vehicle registration mark) ♦ Chancery Division ♦ Civil Defence ♦ compact disc ♦ compact disc player ♦ contagious disease ♦ Corps Diplomatique (French, = Diplomatic Corps)

Cd *abbrev.* ♦ coefficient of drag

Cd *contraction* ♦ Command paper (series 1900–18)

Cd *symbol* ♦ cadmium (chemical element)

cd *abbrev.* ♦ candela ♦ cash discount ♦ cum dividend (with dividend)

cd *contraction* ♦ could

c/d *abbrev.* ♦ carried down

CDAA *abbrev.* ♦ Churches Drought Action in Africa

cdbd *contraction* ♦ cardboard

CDC *abbrev.* ♦ command and data-handling console ♦ Commonwealth Development Corporation ♦ Control Data Corporation

CDEE *abbrev.* ♦ Chemical Defence Experimental Establishment

C de G *abbrev.* ♦ Croix de Guerre (French, = War Cross)

CDEU *abbrev.* ♦ Christian Democratic European Union

cd fwd *contraction* ♦ carried forward

CDH *abbrev.* ♦ congenital disease of the heart

CDI *abbrev.* ♦ compact-disk interactive

CDL *abbrev.* ♦ central door locking

CDN *abbrev.* ♦ Canada (international vehicle registration)

Cdn *abbrev.* ♦ Canadian

cDNA *abbrev.* ♦ complementary DNA

CDR *abbrev.* ♦ crude death rate

Cdr *contraction* ♦ Commander

Cdre *contraction* ♦ Commodore

CD-ROM *abbrev.* ♦ compact disk read-only memory

CDSC *abbrev.* ♦ Communicable Disease Surveillance Centre

CDSE *abbrev.* ♦ computer-driven simulation environment

CDSO *abbrev.* ♦ Companion of the Distinguished Service Order

CDT *abbrev.* ◆ Central Daylight Time ◆ craft, design, technology

cdt *contraction* ◆ cadet ◆ commandant

CDTV *abbrev.* ◆ compact disk television

CDV *abbrev.* ◆ canine distemper virus ◆ Civil Defence Volunteers ◆ compact disk video

CDW *abbrev.* ◆ collision damage waiver

CE *abbrev.* ◆ Chancellor of the Exchequer ◆ chemical engineer ◆ chief engineer ◆ Church of England ◆ civil engineer ◆ Common Entrance ◆ Common Era ◆ Communauté Européenne (French, = European Community) (EC toy safety approval mark) ◆ Council of Europe ◆ Peterborough (British vehicle registration mark)

Ce *symbol* ◆ cerium (chemical element)

ce *abbrev.* ◆ caveat emptor (Latin, = let the buyer beware) ◆ circular error

CEA *abbrev.* ◆ Cinematograph Exhibitors Association of Great Britain

Cebar *pronounced* see-bar *acronym* ◆ chemical, biological and radiological warfare

Cebis *pronounced* see-bis *acronym* ◆ Centre for Environment and Business in Scotland

CEC *abbrev.* ◆ Catholic Education Council ◆ Central Ethical Committee (BMA) ◆ Centre for Economic Co-operation (UN)

CECS *abbrev.* ◆ Church of England Children's Society

ced *abbrev.* ◆ computer entry device

CEDC *abbrev.* ◆ Committee on Economic Co-operation among Developing Countries (UN)

CEDO *abbrev.* ◆ Centre for Education Development Overseas

CEE *abbrev.* ◆ Common Entrance Examination

CEEC *abbrev.* ◆ Council for European Economic Co-operation

CEG *abbrev.* ◆ Computer Education Group

CEGB *abbrev.* ◆ Central Electricity Generating Board

CEI *abbrev.* ◆ Committee for Environmental Information ◆ Council of Engineering Institutions

cel. *shortening* ◆ celebrated

celeb. *shortening* ◆ celebrity

celest. *shortening* ◆ celestial

Cels *contraction* ◆ Celsius

Celt. *shortening* ◆ Celtic

cem. *shortening* ◆ cement ◆ cemetery

CEMS *abbrev.* ◆ Church of England Men's Society

Cen *pronounced* sen *acronym* ◆ Comité Européen de Normalisation (French, = European Standardization Committee)

Cenelec *acronym* ◆ Commission Européene de Normalisation Electrotechnique (French, = European Electrotechnical Standardization Committee)

CEng *abbrev.* ◆ Chartered Engineer

cens. *shortening* ◆ censor ◆ censorship

cent. *shortening* ◆ central ◆ century

Centa *pronounced* sen-ta *acronym* ◆ Combined Edible Nut Trade Association

centenn. *shortening* ◆ centennial

Cento *acronym* ◆ Central Treaty Organization

CEO *abbrev.* ◆ Chief Executive Officer

CEP *abbrev.* ◆ circular error probability

CEPR *abbrev.* ◆ Centre for Economic Policy Research

CEPS *abbrev.* ◆ Central Europe Pipeline System (Nato) ◆ Centre for European Policy Studies

CEPT *abbrev.* ◆ Conférence Européenne des Administrations des Postes et des Télécommunications (French , = European Conference of Postal and Telecommunications Administrations)

CEQ *abbrev.* ◆ Cannes (airport baggage label)

CER *abbrev.* ◆ Cherbourg (airport baggage label) ◆ Community of European Railways

cer. *shortening* ◆ ceramic

ceram. *shortening* ◆ ceramic

CERC *abbrev.* ◆ Civil Engineering Research Council

Ceres *acronym* ◆ Consumers for Ethics in Research Group

Cern *pronounced* sern *acronym* ◆ Conseil Européen pour la Recherche Nucléaire (French, = European Council for Nuclear Physics)

Cert *acronym* ◆ Charities Effectiveness Review Trust (NCVO)

cert. *shortening* ◆ certificate ◆ certificated ◆ certify ◆ certified

CertEd *abbrev.* ◆ Certificate in Education

certif. *shortening* ◆ certificate ◆ certificated ◆ certify ◆ certified

cerv. *shortening* ◆ cervical

CES *abbrev.* ◆ Centre for Environmental Studies

CESC *abbrev.* ◆ Conference on European Security and Co-operation

CESP *abbrev.* ◆ Confederation of European Socialist Parties

Cespa *acronym* ◆ Campaign for Equal State Pension Ages

Cessac *acronym* ◆ Church of England Soldiers', Sailors' and Airmen's Clubs

Cestr. *shortening* ◆ Cestrensis (Latin, = of Chester)

CET *abbrev.* ◆ Central European Time ◆ Common External Tariff (EC)

cet. par. *shortening* ◆ ceteris paribus (Latin, = other things being equal)

CEWC *abbrev.* ◆ Council for Education in World Citizenship

CF *abbrev.* ◆ Canada (international civil aircraft marking) ◆ Cardiff (UK postcode) ◆ Chaplain to the Forces ◆ cost and freight ◆ cystic fibrosis ◆ Reading (British vehicle registration mark)

Cf *symbol* ◆ californium (chemical element)

cf *abbrev.* ◆ carried forward ◆ centre-forward ◆ confer (Latin, = compare) ◆ cost and freight

cf *contraction* ◆ calf

c/f *abbrev.* ◆ carried forward

CFAL *abbrev.* ◆ current food additives legislation

CFB *abbrev.* ◆ Commonwealth Forestry Bureau

CFBAC *abbrev.* ◆ Central Fire Brigades Advisory Council of England and Wales

CFC *abbrev.* ◆ chlorofluorocarbon

CFD *abbrev.* ◆ computational fluid dynamics

cfd *abbrev.* ◆ cubic feet per day

CFE *abbrev.* ◆ College of Further Education ◆ Conventional Forces in Europe

CFDT *abbrev.* ◆ Confédération Française Démocratique du Travail (French, = French Democratic Confederation of Labour)

CFE *abbrev.* ◆ College of Further Education ◆ Conventional Forces in Europe

CFF *abbrev.* ◆ Chemins de Fer Fédéraux Suisses (French, = Swiss Federal Railways)

cfg *abbrev.* ◆ cubic feet of gas

cfh *abbrev.* ◆ cubic feet per hour

CFI *abbrev.* ◆ Campaign for Freedom of Information ◆ Court of First Instance (EEC)

cfi *abbrev.* ◆ cost, freight and insurance

CFLP *abbrev.* ◆ Central Fire Liaison Panel

cfm *abbrev.* ◆ cubic feet per minute

CfN *abbrev.* ◆ Council for Nature

CFO *abbrev.* ◆ Chief Fire Officer

CFOA *abbrev.* ◆ Chief Fire Officers' Association

CFP *abbrev.* ◆ Common Fisheries Policy (EC)

CFR *abbrev.* ◆ commercial fast reactor

cfs *abbrev.* ◆ cubic feet per second

CFSL *abbrev.* ◆ Central Forensic Science Laboratory

CFT *abbrev.* ◆ Cystic Fibrosis Trust

cft *abbrev.* ◆ cubic feet

CFU *abbrev.* ◆ Corfu (airport baggage label)

CFWI *abbrev.* ◆ County Federation of Women's Institutes

CG *abbrev.* ◆ Bournemouth (British vehicle registration mark) ◆ captain-general ◆ Captain of the Guard ◆ coastguard ◆ Coldstream Guards ◆ commanding general ◆ consul general ◆ Covent Garden (opera house) ◆ Croix de Guerre (French, = War Cross)

CG18 *abbrev.* ◆ Gatt Consultative Group of Eighteen (nations)

cg *abbrev.* ◆ centigram ◆ centre of gravity

CGA *abbrev.* ◆ colour graphics adapter ◆ Country Gentlemen's Association

cga *abbrev.* ◆ cargo proportion of general average

CGAT *abbrev.* ◆ City Gallery Arts Trust

CGB *abbrev.* ◆ Commonwealth Geographical Bureau

CGBR *abbrev.* ◆ central government borrowing requirement

CGC *abbrev.* ◆ Commonwealth Games Council

CGE *abbrev.* ◆ Conservative Group for Europe

cge *contraction* ◆ carriage

cge fwd *contraction* ◆ carriage forward

cge pd *contraction* ◆ carriage paid

CGF *abbrev.* ◆ Commonwealth Games Federation

CGH *abbrev.* ◆ Cape of Good Hope ◆ São Paulo (airport baggage label)

cgh *abbrev.* ◆ computer-generated hologram

CGI *abbrev.* ◆ Catholic Guides of Ireland ◆ City and Guilds of London Institute

cgi *abbrev.* ◆ corrugated galvanized iron

CGIL *abbrev.* ◆ Confederazione Generale Italiana del Lavoro (Italian, = General Italian Confederation of Labour)

CGLI *abbrev.* ◆ City and Guilds of London Institute

CGM *abbrev.* ◆ Conspicuous Gallantry Medal

cgm *contraction* ◆ centigram

CGN *abbrev.* ◆ Cologne (airport baggage label)

cgo *contraction* ◆ cargo

CGP *abbrev.* ◆ College of General Practitioners

CGPM *abbrev.* ◆ Conférence Générale des Poids et Mesures (French, = General Conference on Weights and Measures)

CGS *abbrev.* ◆ Chief of the General Staff ◆ Cottage Gardens Society

cgs *abbrev.* ◆ centimetre-gram-second

CGT *abbrev.* ◆ capital gains tax ◆ Confédération Général du Travail (French, = General Confederation of Labour)

CGT-FO *abbrev.* ◆ Confédération Générale du Travail—Force Ouvrière (French, = General Confederation of Labour—Workers' Force)

CH *abbrev.* ◆ Chester (UK postcode) ◆ Companion of Honour ◆ clearing house ◆ Confederatio Helvetica (Latin, = Switzerland) (international vehicle registration) ◆ customs house ◆ Nottingham (British vehicle registration mark)

Ch. *shortening* ◆ China ◆ Chinese ◆ Christ ◆ Chronicles (book of Bible)

ch *abbrev.* ◆ central heating ◆ centre half ◆ clearing house ◆ club house ◆ court house ◆ customs house

ch. *abbrev.* ◆ chain ◆ champion ◆ chaplain ◆ chapter ◆ chart ◆ chassis ◆ check (chess) ◆ chestnut ◆ chief ◆ child ◆ choir ◆ church

chamb. *shortening* ◆ chamberlain

chan. *shortening* ◆ channel

Chanc. *shortening* ◆ Chancery

chanc. *abbrev.* ◆ chancellor

chap. *shortening* ◆ chapel ◆ chaplain ◆ chapter

Chaps *acronym* ◆ Clearing House Automated Payment System

chapt. *shortening* ◆ chapter

Char *acronym* ◆ Campaign for Homeless People (orig. Campaign for Homeless and Rootless)

char. *shortening* ◆ character ◆ charity

CHAS *abbrev.* ◆ Catholic Housing Aid Society

CHB *abbrev.* ◆ complete heart block

ChB *abbrev.* ◆ Chirurgiae Baccalaureus (Latin, = Bachelor of Surgery)

CHCF *abbrev.* ◆ Catholic Handicapped Children's Fellowship

CHD *abbrev.* ◆ coronary heart disease

ChD *abbrev.* ◆ Chirurgiae Doctor (Latin, = Doctor of Surgery)

Ch. Div. *shortening* ◆ Chancery Division

CHDL *abbrev.* ◆ computer hardware description language

CHE *abbrev.* ◆ Campaign for Homosexual Equality

ChE *abbrev.* ◆ Chemical Engineer ◆ chief engineer

Cheka *acronym* ◆ Chrezvychainaya Comissiya po Bor'bye s Kontrrevolyutsiye, Sabotagem i Spekulyatsiye (Russian, = Special Commission for Combating Counter-Revolution, Sabotage, and Speculation) (Soviet secret police, 1917–22)

CHEL *abbrev.* ◆ Cambridge History of English Literature

chem. *shortening* ◆ chemical ◆ chemistry

ChemE *abbrev.* ◆ Chemical Engineer

Ches. *shortening* ◆ Cheshire

CHF *abbrev.* ◆ congestive heart failure

chf *contraction* ◆ chief

ch. fwd *contraction* ◆ charges forward

chg. *shortening* ◆ charge

chgd *contraction* ◆ charged

CHI *abbrev.* ◆ Chicago (airport baggage label)

childn *contraction* ◆ children

Chin. *shortening* ◆ China ◆ Chinese

CHIPS *abbrev.* ◆ Clearing House Inter-Bank Payments System

ChJ *abbrev.* ◆ Chief Justice

chkpt *contraction* ◆ checkpoint

CHLW *abbrev.* ◆ commercial high-level waste

ChM *abbrev.* ◆ Chirurgiae Magister (Latin, = Master of Surgery)

chm. *shortening* ◆ chairman ◆ checkmate (chess) ◆ choirmaster

chmn *contraction* ◆ chairman

CHO *abbrev.* ◆ Confederation of Healing Organizations

choc. *shortening* ◆ chocolate

CHOGM *abbrev.* ◆ Commonwealth Heads of Government Meeting

CHESS NOTATION

The following are commonly found in the descriptions of games in books and newspaper reports:

B	*bishop*	**Kt**	*knight*
C	*castle*	**N**	*knight*
ch.	*check*	**P**	*pawn*
chm.	*checkmate*	**Q**	*queen*
ep	*en passant*	**QB**	*queen's bishop*
K	*king; knight*	**QBP**	*queen's bishop's pawn*
KB	*king's bishop*	**QKt**	*queen's knight*
KBP	*king's bishop's pawn*	**QKtP**	*queen's knight's pawn*
KKt	*king's knight*	**QN**	*queen's knight*
KKtP	*king's knight's pawn*	**QNP**	*queen's knight's pawn*
KN	*king's knight*	**QP**	*queen's pawn*
KNP	*king's knight's pawn*	**QR**	*queen's rook*
KP	*king's pawn*	**QRP**	*queen's rook's pawn*
KR	*king's rook*	**R**	*rook*
KRP	*king's rook's pawn*		

choirm. *shortening* ◆ choirmaster
chor. *shortening* ◆ choral ◆ chorus
CHP *abbrev.* ◆ combined heat and power
ch. pd *contraction* ◆ charges paid
CHQ *abbrev.* ◆ Corps Headquarters
chq. *shortening* ◆ cheque
Chr. *shortening* ◆ Christ ◆ Christian
CHRI *abbrev.* ◆ Commonwealth Human Rights Initiative
Chron. *shortening* ◆ Chronicles (book of Bible)
chron. *shortening* ◆ chronicle ◆ chronological ◆ chronology
CHSA *abbrev.* ◆ Chest, Heart and Stroke Association
chw *abbrev.* ◆ constant hot water
CI *abbrev.* ◆ cardiac index ◆ cerebral infarction ◆ Channel Islands ◆ Chief Inspector ◆ China Airlines (airline baggage code) ◆ Commonwealth Institute ◆ Communist International ◆ Côte d'Ivoire (French, = Ivory Coast) (international vehicle registration) ◆ counter-intelligence
Ci *shortening* ◆ curie
ci *abbrev.* ◆ cast iron
CIA *abbrev.* ◆ Cancer Information Association ◆ Central Intelligence Agency (US) ◆ Chemical Industries Association
cia *abbrev.* ◆ cash in advance
Cia. *shortening* ◆ Compagnia (Italian, = Company) ◆ Compañía (Spanish, = Company)
CIAC *abbrev.* ◆ Construction Industry Advisory Council
CIArb *abbrev.* ◆ Chartered Institute of Arbitrators
CIAS *abbrev.* ◆ Conference of Independent African States
CIB *abbrev.* ◆ Campaign for an Independent Britain ◆ Chartered Institute of Bankers ◆ Corporation of Insurance Brokers
CIBS *abbrev.* ◆ Chartered Institute of Building Societies
CIC *abbrev.* ◆ Cinema International Corporation ◆ Commander-in-Chief

CICB *abbrev.* ◆ Criminal Injuries Compensation Board
Cicestr. *shortening* ◆ Cicestrensis (Latin, = of Chichester)
CID *abbrev.* ◆ Council of Industrial Design ◆ Criminal Investigation Department
CIDST *abbrev.* ◆ Committee for Scientific and Technical Information and Documentation (EC)
CIE *abbrev.* ◆ Companion of the Order of the Indian Empire ◆ Córas Iompair Éireann (Gaelic, = Transport Organization of Ireland)
Cie *contraction* ◆ Compagnie (French, = Company)
CIEE *abbrev.* ◆ Companion of the Institution of Electrical Engineers
cif *abbrev.* ◆ cost, insurance, freight
CIFA *abbrev.* ◆ Corporation of Insurance and Financial Advisers
cifc *abbrev.* ◆ cost, insurance, freight and commission
cifci *abbrev.* ◆ cost, insurance, freight, commission and interest
CIFE *abbrev.* ◆ Colleges and Institutes of Further Education
cife *abbrev.* ◆ cost, insurance, freight and exchange
cifi *abbrev.* ◆ cost, insurance, freight and interest
CIGA *abbrev.* ◆ Compagnia Italiana dei Grandi Alberghi (Italian, = Italian Grand Hotels Company)
CIGAS *abbrev.* ◆ Cambridge Intercollegiate Graduate Application Scheme
CIGS *abbrev.* ◆ Chief of the Imperial General Staff
CIHE *abbrev.* ◆ Council for Industry and Higher Education
CII *abbrev.* ◆ Chartered Insurance Institute
CIJ *abbrev.* ◆ Chartered Institute of Journalists
CIM *abbrev.* ◆ Commission for Industry and Manpower ◆ computer input on

microfilm ◆ computer-integrated manufacture

CIMA *abbrev.* ◆ Chartered Institute of Management Accountants

CIMB *abbrev.* ◆ Construction Industry Manpower Board

C-in-C *abbrev.* ◆ Commander-in-Chief

CIO *abbrev.* ◆ Church Information Office

CIOB *abbrev.* ◆ Chartered Institute of Building

CIP *abbrev.* ◆ cataloguing in publication ◆ Common Industrial Policy

CIPA *abbrev.* ◆ Chartered Institute of Patent Agents

CIPFA *abbrev.* ◆ Chartered Institute of Public Finance and Accountancy

CIPM *abbrev.* ◆ Comité International des Poids et Mesures (French, = International Committee on Weights and Measures)

CIR *abbrev.* ◆ Commission on Industrial Relations

cir. *shortening* ◆ circle ◆ circuit ◆ circular

circ. *shortening* ◆ circa (Latin, = about) ◆ circulate ◆ circulation ◆ circumference

circs *contraction* ◆ circumstances

circum. *shortening* ◆ circumference

CIS *abbrev.* ◆ cataloguing in source ◆ Commonwealth of Independent States

CISC *abbrev.* ◆ complex instruction-set computer

CISCO *abbrev.* ◆ Civil Service Catering Organization

CISL *abbrev.* ◆ Confederazione Italiana Sindacati Lavoratori (Italian, = Italian Confederation of Trade Unions)

CISS *abbrev.* ◆ Centre for International Sports Studies

Cist. *shortening* ◆ Cistercian

CIT *abbrev.* ◆ Compagnia Italiana Turismo (Italian, = Italian Tourism Company) ◆ Chartered Institute of Transport

cit *abbrev.* ◆ compression in transit

cit. *shortening* ◆ citation ◆ cited ◆ citizen

CITB *abbrev.* ◆ Construction Industry Training Board

CITES *abbrev.* ◆ Convention on International Trade in Endangered Species

cito disp. *shortening* ◆ cito dispensetur (Latin, = let there quickly be dispensed)

CIU *abbrev.* ◆ Club and Institute Union

civ. *shortening* ◆ civil ◆ civilian

CIWF *abbrev.* ◆ Compassion in World Farming

CJ *abbrev.* ◆ Chief Justice ◆ Gloucester (British vehicle registration mark)

cj. *shortening* ◆ conjectural

CJD *abbrev.* ◆ Creutzfeldt-Jakob disease

CJEC *abbrev.* ◆ Court of Justice of the European Communities

CK *abbrev.* ◆ certified kosher ◆ Preston (British vehicle registration mark)

ck *contraction* ◆ check

ckd *abbrev.* ◆ completely knocked down (disassembled)

ckout *contraction* ◆ checkout

ckpt *contraction* ◆ cockpit

CL *abbrev.* ◆ Sri Lanka (international vehicle registration) (orig. Ceylon) ◆ Norwich (British vehicle registration mark)

Cl *symbol* ◆ chlorine (chemical element)

cl *abbrev.* ◆ centilitre ◆ central locking

cl. *shortening* ◆ clarinet ◆ class ◆ classification ◆ clause ◆ cloth

CLA *abbrev.* ◆ Country Landowners' Association

Clap *acronym* ◆ Citizens Lobbying Against Prostitution (US)

Clar. *shortening* ◆ Clarenceux (King of Arms)

clar. *shortening* ◆ clarinet

Clarnico *acronym* ◆ Clark, Nichols and Coombes Ltd (confectioners)

class. *shortening* ◆ classical ◆ classification

CLAW *abbrev.* ◆ Consortium of Local Authorities in Wales

CLB *abbrev.* ◆ Church Lads' Brigade

CLCB *abbrev.* ◆ Committee of the London Clearing Banks

CLD *abbrev.* ◆ chronic liver disease

cld *contraction* ◆ called ◆ cancelled ◆ cleared ◆ coloured ◆ cooled

Clear *acronym* ◆ Campaign for Lead-Free Air

cler. *shortening* ◆ clerical

cl. gt *contraction* ◆ cloth gilt

CLIC *abbrev.* ◆ Cancer and Leukaemia in Childhood Trust

clim. *shortening* ◆ climatic

clin. *shortening* ◆ clinic ◆ clinical

CLit *abbrev.* ◆ Companion of Literature

clk *contraction* ◆ clerk

clkrm *contraction* ◆ cloakroom

clks *contraction* ◆ cloaks (cloakroom)

clkws. *shortening* ◆ clockwise

CLL *abbrev.* ◆ chronic limphocytic leukaemia

CLLR *abbrev.* ◆ International Symposium on Computing in Literary and Linguistic Research

Cllr *contraction* ◆ Councillor

CLO *abbrev.* ◆ cod liver oil

Clo. *shortening* ◆ Close

cloakrm *contraction* ◆ cloakroom

c/lock. *shortening* ◆ central locking

CLP *abbrev.* ◆ Constituency Labour Party

CLPA *abbrev.* ◆ Common Law Procedure Acts

CLR *abbrev.* ◆ computer language recorder

CLS *abbrev.* ◆ Certificate in Library Science

cls. *shortening* ◆ close

CLSB *abbrev.* ◆ Committee of London and Scottish Bankers

CLT *abbrev.* ◆ computer language translator

CLU *abbrev.* ◆ Chartered Life Underwriter

CM *abbrev.* ◆ Chelmsford (UK postcode) ◆ Chirurgiae Magister (Latin, = Master of Surgery) ◆ command module ◆ Corresponding Member ◆ Liverpool (British vehicle registration mark)

Cm *symbol* ◆ curium (chemical element)

cm *abbrev.* ◆ centimetre

CMA *abbrev.* ◆ Church Music Association ◆ Country Music Association

CMAC *abbrev.* ◆ Catholic Marriage Advisory Council

CMB *abbrev.* ◆ Chase Manhattan Bank ◆ Christian Mission to Buddhists

CMC *abbrev.* ◆ Catholic Media Council ◆ Collective Measures Committee (UN)

Cmd *contraction* ◆ Command paper (series 1919–56)

Cmdr *contraction* ◆ Commander

Cmdre *contraction* ◆ Commodore

cmdt *contraction* ◆ commandant

cmdg *contraction* ◆ commanding

CMF *abbrev.* ◆ Coal Merchants' Federation

CMG *abbrev.* ◆ Companion of the Order of St Michael and St George

CMHR *abbrev.* ◆ combustion modified highly resilient

CMI *abbrev.* ◆ computer-managed instruction

CML *abbrev.* ◆ Central Music Library ◆ chronic myeloid lukaemia ◆ computer-managed learning ◆ Council of Mortgage Lenders ◆ current mode logic

cml *shortening* ◆ commercial

cmn *contraction* ◆ commission

Cmnd *shortening* ◆ Command paper (series 1956–)

cmnr *contraction* ◆ commissioner

CMO *abbrev.* ◆ Chief Medical Officer

Cmos *pronounced* see-mos *acronym* ◆ complementary metal oxide semiconductor

CMP *abbrev.* ◆ Christian Movement for Peace ◆ Commissioner of the Metropolitan Police

cmpd *contraction* ◆ compound

cm. pf. *shortening* ◆ cumulative preference (shares)

CMR *abbrev.* ◆ cerebral metabolic rate

CMS *abbrev.* ◆ Catholic Missionary Society ◆ Church Missionary Society ◆ cras mane sumendus (Latin, = to be taken tomorrow morning)

CMV *abbrev.* ✦ cytomegalovirus

CN *abbrev.* ✦ Newcastle upon Tyne (British vehicle registration mark) ✦ Code Napoléon (French, = Napoleonic Code) (French legal system)

C/N *abbrev.* ✦ carbon/nitrogen (atmospheric ratio)

cn *abbrev.* ✦ credit note

CNAA *abbrev.* ✦ Council for National Academic Awards

CNAR *abbrev.* ✦ compound net annual rate

CNC *abbrev.* ✦ computer numeric control

CNCIEC *abbrev.* ✦ China National Coal Import and Export Corporation

CND *abbrev.* ✦ Campaign for Nuclear Disarmament

CNDA *abbrev.* ✦ Cherished Numbers Dealers Association

CNF *abbrev.* ✦ Commonwealth Nurses' Federation

CNG *abbrev.* ✦ compressed natural gas

CNIP *abbrev.* ✦ Ciskei National Independence Party

cnl *contraction* ✦ cancel

CNN *abbrev.* ✦ Cable News Network ✦ Certified Nursery Nurse

CNMB *abbrev.* ✦ Central Nuclear Measurements Bureau (EC)

CNR *abbrev.* ✦ Canadian National Railways

CNIEC *abbrev.* ✦ China National Import and Export Corporation

CNP *abbrev.* ✦ Council for National Parks

CNR *abbrev.* ✦ Canadian National Railways

cnr *contraction* ✦ corner

CNRS *abbrev.* ✦ Centre National de la Recherche Scientifique (French, = National Centre for Scientific Research)

CNS *abbrev.* ✦ central nervous system ✦ Chief of Naval staff ✦ cras nocte sumendus (Latin, = to be taken tomorrow night)

CNSLD *abbrev.* ✦ chronic non-specific lung disease

CNT *abbrev.* ✦ Commission for the New Towns

cntr. *shortening* ✦ contribute

CO *abbrev.* ✦ Colchester (UK postcode) ✦ Colombia (international vehicle registration) ✦ Colorado (US postcode) ✦ combined operations ✦ Commanding Officer ✦ Commissioner for Oaths ✦ Commonwealth Office ✦ conscientious objector ✦ Crown Office ✦ Exeter (British vehicle registration mark)

Co *symbol* ✦ cobalt (chemical element)

c/o *abbrev.* ✦ care of ✦ carried over ✦ complains of

Co. *shortening* ✦ Company ✦ County

COA *abbrev.* ✦ change of address ✦ condition on admission

coad. *shortening* ✦ coadjutor

COAS *abbrev.* ✦ Council of the Organization of American States

cob *abbrev.* ✦ close of business

Cobol *pronounced* koe-bol *acronym* ✦ Common Business-Oriented Language

COC *abbrev.* ✦ combined oral contraceptive

coc. *shortening* ✦ cocaine

coch. *shortening* ✦ cochleare (Latin, = spoonful)

Cocom *acronym* ✦ Co-ordinating Committee for Export Controls (Nato)

COD *abbrev.* ✦ cause of death

cod *abbrev.* ✦ cash on delivery

cod. *shortening* ✦ codex ✦ codicil

Codasyl *pronounced* koe-di-sil *acronym* ✦ Conference on Data Systems Languages

codec *acronym* ✦ coder/decoder

CODOT *abbrev.* ✦ Classification of Occupations and Directory of Occupational Titles

COE *abbrev.* ✦ Chamber Orchestra of Europe

COED *abbrev.* ✦ computer-operated electronic display

co-ed. *shortening* ✦ coeducational

coeff. *shortening* ✦ coefficient

C of A *abbrev.* ✦ Certificate of Airworthiness

C of C *abbrev.* ✦ Chamber of Commerce

C of E *abbrev.* ✦ Church of England ✦ Council of Europe

Coffer *acronym* ✦ Coalition for Fair Electricity Regulation

C of I *abbrev.* ✦ Church of Ireland

C of S *abbrev.* ✦ Chief of Staff ✦ Church of Scotland

cog *abbrev.* ✦ centre of gravity

cog. *shortening* ✦ cognate

COGB *abbrev.* ✦ Certified Official Government Business

Cogene *acronym* ✦ Committee on Genetic Experimentation

COGMA *abbrev.* ✦ Concrete Garage Manufacturers' Association

coh *abbrev.* ✦ cash on hand

Cohse *pronounced* koh-zee *acronym* ✦ Confederation of Health Service Employees

COI *abbrev.* ✦ Central Office of Information

COID *abbrev.* ✦ Council on International Development

COIE *abbrev.* ✦ Committee on Invisible Exports

COIF *abbrev.* ✦ Control of Intensive Farming

COL *abbrev.* ✦ centrally operated locking ✦ computer-orientated language ✦ cost of living

Col. *shortening* ✦ Colonel ✦ Colorado ✦ Colossians (book of Bible)

col. *shortening* ✦ colonial ✦ colony ✦ colour ✦ column

Cola *acronym* ✦ Camping and Outdoor Leisure Association

COLD *abbrev.* ✦ chronic obstructive lung disease

Coling *acronym* ✦ International Conference on Computational Linguistics

coll. *shortening* ✦ colleague ✦ collected ✦ collective ✦ collection ✦ collector ✦ college ✦ colloquial

collab. *shortening* ✦ collaboration

collat. *shortening* ✦ collateral ✦ collaterally

collect. *shortening* ✦ collectively

colloq. *shortening* ✦ colloquial ✦ colloquially

coll'ott. *shortening* ✦ coll'ottava (Italian, = in octaves) (music)

collr *contraction* ✦ collector

Colo. *shortening* ✦ Colorado

colog *shortening* ✦ cologarithm

Coloss. *shortening* ✦ Colossians (book of Bible)

COLS *abbrev.* ✦ communications for online systems

Col.-Sergt *contraction* ✦ Colour-Sergeant

Col.-Sgt *contraction* ✦ Colour-Sergeant

Com *acronym* ✦ computer output on microfilm ✦ computer output on microfiche

Com. ✦ Commander ✦ Commissioner ✦ Commodore ✦ Commonwealth ✦ Communist

com. *shortening* ✦ comedy ✦ commerce ✦ commercial ✦ commission ✦ committee ✦ common ✦ commune ✦ communication

Coma *acronym* ✦ Committee on Medical Aspects of Food Policy

Comal *acronym* ✦ Common Algorithmic Language

COMARE *abbrev.* ✦ Committee on Medical Aspects of Radiation in the Environment

comb. *shortening* ✦ combination ✦ combined ✦ combustion

comdg *contraction* ✦ commanding

Comdr *contraction* ✦ Commander

comdt *contraction* ✦ commandant

Comecon *pronounced* kom-i-kon *acronym* ✦ Council for Mutual Economic Assistance (of Communist bloc, 1949–91)

Comex *acronym* ✦ New York Commodity Exchange

Cominform *acronym* ✦ Communist Information Bureau

Comint *acronym* ✦ Communications Intelligence

Comintern *acronym* ◆ Communist International (1919–43)

coml *contraction* ◆ commercial

Comm. *shortening* ◆ Commodore

comm. *shortening* ◆ commander
◆ commentary ◆ commerce
◆ committee ◆ communal
◆ communication

commem. *shortening* ◆ commemoration
◆ commemorative

commiss. *shortening* ◆ commissary

commissr *contraction* ◆ commissioner

commn *contraction* ◆ commission

comms *contraction* ◆ communications

commun. *shortening* ◆ communication

comp. *shortening* ◆ companion
◆ comparative ◆ compare
◆ compensation ◆ competitor
◆ compiled ◆ compiler ◆ composer
◆ composite ◆ compositor ◆ compound
◆ compounded ◆ comprehensive
◆ comprising

Compa. *shortening* ◆ Company (now only on Bank of England notes)

Compac *acronym* ◆ Commonwealth Trans-Pacific Telephone Cable

compar. *shortening* ◆ comparative
◆ comparison

compd *contraction* ◆ compound

compl. *shortening* ◆ complement
◆ complete ◆ complimentary

complx. *shortening* ◆ complexion
◆ complexioned

Compsac *acronym* ◆ International Computer Software and Applications Conference

comr *contraction* ◆ commissioner

Comsat *acronym* ◆ communications satellite

Com. Ver. *shortening* ◆ Common Version (of the Bible)

Con. *shortening* ◆ Conservative ◆ Consul

con. *shortening* ◆ confidence
◆ conditioning ◆ contra (Latin, = against) ◆ conservation

Conba *acronym* ◆ Council of National Beekeeping Associations of the United Kingdom

conc. *shortening* ◆ concentrated
◆ concentration ◆ concise

conch. *shortening* ◆ conchology

concr. *shortening* ◆ concrete

cond. *shortening* ◆ condensed
◆ condition ◆ conditional ◆ conduct
◆ conductor

con esp. *shortening* ◆ con espressione (Italian, = with expression)

con espr. *shortening* ◆ con espressione (Italian, = with expression)

conf. *shortening* ◆ confectionery
◆ conference ◆ confidential ◆ confession

confed. *shortening* ◆ confederate
◆ confederated ◆ confederation

Cong. *shortening* ◆ Congregation
◆ Congregational ◆ Congress
◆ Congressional

cong. *shortening* ◆ congregation
◆ congregational

CONGU *abbrev.* ◆ Council of National Golf Unions

conj. *shortening* ◆ conjecture
◆ conjugation ◆ conjunction

Conn. *shortening* ◆ Connecticut

conn. *shortening* ◆ connected
◆ connection

cons. *shortening* ◆ consecrated
◆ consecutive ◆ conservatoire
◆ conservatory ◆ consignment
◆ consider ◆ consonant

con. sec. *shortening* ◆ conic section

conserv. *shortening* ◆ conservatoire
◆ conservatory

consgt *contraction* ◆ consignment

consid. *shortening* ◆ consideration

consol. *shortening* ◆ consolidated

Const. *shortening* ◆ constable

const. *shortening* ◆ constant
◆ constitution ◆ constitutional
◆ construction

constit. *shortening* ◆ constituent

constr. *shortening* ◆ construction
◆ construe

cont. *shortening* ◆ container ◆ containing
◆ contents ◆ continent ◆ continental
◆ continue ◆ continued ◆ continuo

contag. *shortening* ◆ contagious

cont. bon. mor. *shortening* ◆ contra bonos mores (Latin, = contrary to good manners)

contd *contraction* ◆ contained ◆ continued

contemp. *shortening* ◆ contemporary

contr. *shortening* ◆ contract ◆ contracted ◆ contraction

cont. rem. *shortening* ◆ continuantur remedia (Latin, = let the remedies be continued)

contrib. *shortening* ◆ contribution ◆ contributor

Conv. *shortening* ◆ Convocation

conv. *shortening* ◆ convenience (store etc) ◆ convenient ◆ convention ◆ conventional ◆ conversion ◆ convertible

convce *contraction* ◆ conveyance

co-op. *shortening* ◆ co-operative

Cop. *shortening* ◆ Copernican

COPD *abbrev.* ◆ chronic obstructive pulmonary disease

SOME COMPUTER TERMS

In this list you will find a selection of the most common computing abbreviations. The dictionary lists several hundred more.

ADP	*automatic data processing*
AI	*artificial intelligence*
Algol	*Algebraically Oriented Language*
Ascii	*American Standard Code for Information Exchange*
Basic	*Beginners' All-Purpose Symbolic Instruction Code*
BCD	*binary coded decimal*
bit	*binary digit*
CD-ROM	*compact disk read-only memory*
CGA	*colour graphics adapter*
Cobol	*Common Business-Oriented Language*
CPU	*central processing unit*
Datanet	*data network*
DB	*database*
DD	*double density*
Diane	*Direct Information Access Network for Europe*
Dos	*Disk Operating System*
DP	*data processing*
DTP	*desktop publishing*
EAN	*European Academic Network; European Article Number*
E-mail	*electronic mail*
Fortran	*Formula Translation*
Gemcos	*Generalized Message Control System*
Gigo	*garbage in, garbage out*
HD	*high density*
Holmes	*Home Office large major enquiry system*
IT	*information technology*
Janet	*Joint Academic Network*
KB	*kilobyte*
kbyte	*kilobyte*
LSI	*large-scale integration*
MB	*megabyte*
Mbyte	*megabyte*
modem	*modulator-demodulator*
MS-Dos	*MicroSoft Disk-Operating System*
MSI	*medium-scale integration*
MT	*machine translation*
OCR	*optical character recognition*
OL	*on-line*
PC	*personal computer*
RAM	*random access memory*
ROM	*read-only memory*
SGML	*Standardized Generalized Mark-up Language*
UPC	*Universal Product Code*
VDT	*visual display terminal*
VDU	*visual display unit*
VGA	*visual graphics array*
wimp	*windows, icons, menus, pointer*
WYSIWYG	*what you see is what you get*

Coppso *acronym* ◆ Conference of Professional and Public Service Organizations

Copt. *shortening* ◆ Coptic

COPUOS *abbrev.* ◆ Committee on the Peaceful Uses of Outer Space (UN)

COR *abbrev.* ◆ Club of Rome

Cor. *shortening* ◆ Corinthians (books of Bible) ◆ Coroner

cor. *shortening* ◆ corner ◆ cornet ◆ corno (Italian, = horn) (instrument)

Coral *acronym* ◆ Common Real-Time Application Language

Corda *acronym* ◆ Coronary Artery Disease Research Association

Corgi *acronym* ◆ Confederation for Registration of Gas Installers

Corn. *shortening* ◆ Cornish ◆ Cornwall

corol. *shortening* ◆ corollary

Corp. *shortening* ◆ Corporal ◆ Corporation

corp. *shortening* ◆ corporal

corr. *shortening* ◆ corrected ◆ correction ◆ correlative ◆ correspond ◆ correspondence ◆ corrigenda ◆ corrupted ◆ corruption

correl. *shortening* ◆ correlative

corres. *shortening* ◆ corresponding

corresp. *shortening* ◆ correspondence

corrupt. *shortening* ◆ corruption

Cors. *shortening* ◆ Corsica ◆ Corsican

Cort *acronym* ◆ Council of Regional Theatres ◆ Council of Repertory Theatres

cort. *shortening* ◆ cortex

COS *abbrev.* ◆ Cinema Organ Society

CoS *abbrev.* ◆ Chief of Staff

cos *abbrev.* ◆ cash on shipment

cos *shortening* ◆ cosine

co. sa. *shortening* ◆ come sopra (Italian, = as above) (music)

Cosatu *acronym* ◆ Congress of South African Trade Unions

cosec *shortening* ◆ cosecant

COSFPS *abbrev.* ◆ Commons, Open Spaces and Footpaths Preservation Society

COSHH *abbrev.* ◆ Control of Substances Hazardous to Health

Cosla *acronym* ◆ Convention of Scottish Local Authorities

Cossec *acronym* ◆ Cambridge, Oxford and Southern School Examinations Council

cot *shortening* ◆ cotangent

cotan *shortening* ◆ cotangent

Cots *acronym* ◆ Childlessness Overcome through Surrogacy

coun. *shortening* ◆ councillor

cov. *shortening* ◆ covariance ◆ crossover value

Covers *pronounced* koh-vers *acronym* ◆ coversed sine

cov. pt *contraction* ◆ cover point (cricket)

Cow *acronym* ◆ Committee of the Whole (UN General Assembly)

Coy *contraction* ◆ Company

CP *abbrev.* ◆ cerebral palsy ◆ Clarendon Press ◆ Command Post ◆ Common Prayer ◆ Communist Party ◆ Congregatio Passionis (Latin, = Congregation of the Passion) (RC monastic order) ◆ Congress Party (India) ◆ Court of Probate ◆ Huddersfield (British vehicle registration mark)

cp *abbrev.* ◆ candlepower ◆ carriage paid ◆ chemically pure

cp. *shortening* ◆ compara (Latin, = compare)

CPA *abbrev.* ◆ critical path analysis

CPAC *abbrev.* ◆ Consumer Protection Advisory Committee

CPAG *abbrev.* ◆ Child Poverty Action Group

CP Air *abbrev.* ◆ Canadian Pacific Airlines (airline baggage code)

CPB *abbrev.* ◆ cardiopulmonary bypass

CPBF *abbrev.* ◆ Campaign for Press and Broadcasting Freedom

CPC *abbrev.* ◆ Clerk of the Privy Council

cpd *contraction* ◆ compound

cpff *abbrev.* ◆ cost plus fixed fee

CPG *abbrev.* ◆ Coronary Prevention Group

CPGB *abbrev.* ◆ Communist Party of Great Britain

CPH *abbrev.* ◆ Copenhagen (airport baggage label)

cph *abbrev.* ◆ cycles per hour

CPI *abbrev.* ◆ consumer price index

cpi *abbrev.* ◆ characters per inch

CPIC *abbrev.* ◆ Comprehensive Pig Information Centre

CPL *abbrev.* ◆ Cats' Protection League ◆ commercial pilot's licence

Cpl *contraction* ◆ Corporal

cpl *abbrev.* ◆ characters per line

CP/M *abbrev.* ◆ Control Program for Microcomputers ◆ Control Program/ Monitor

cpm *abbrev.* ◆ characters per minute ◆ critical path method ◆ cycles per minute

cpn *contraction* ◆ coupon

CPO *abbrev.* ◆ Chief Petty Officer ◆ Compulsory Purchase Order ◆ Crime Prevention Officer

cpp *abbrev.* ◆ critical path plan ◆ current purchasing power

cpps *abbrev.* ◆ critical path planning and scheduling

CPR *abbrev.* ◆ Canadian Pacific Railway ◆ cardiopulmonary resuscitation

CPRE *abbrev.* ◆ Council for the Protection of Rural England

CPRS *abbrev.* ◆ Central Policy Review Staff

CPS *abbrev.* ◆ Carnivorous Plant Society ◆ Crown Prosecution Service ◆ Custos Privati Sigilli (Latin, = Keeper of the Privy Seal)

cps *abbrev.* ◆ characters per second ◆ cycles per second

CPSA *abbrev.* ◆ Civil and Public Services Association ◆ Clay Pigeon Shooting Association

CPSU *abbrev.* ◆ Communist Party of the Soviet Union

CPT *abbrev.* ◆ Cape Town (airport baggage label)

cpt *abbrev.* ◆ critical path technique

CPU *abbrev.* ◆ central processing unit

CQF *abbrev.* ◆ Calais (airport baggage label)

CQM *abbrev.* ◆ Chief Quartermaster ◆ Company Quartermaster

CQMS *abbrev.* ◆ Company Quartermaster-Sergeant

CR *abbrev.* ◆ Carolina Regina (Latin, = Queen Caroline) ◆ Carolus Rex (Latin, = King Charles) ◆ carriage return ◆ Community of the Resurrection (Anglican monastic order) ◆ compression ratio ◆ conditioned reflex ◆ Costa Rica (international vehicle registration) ◆ credit rating ◆ current rate ◆ Custos Rotulorum (Latin, = Keeper of the Rolls) ◆ Portsmouth (British vehicle registration mark) ◆ Portugal (international civil aircraft marking)

Cr *contraction* ◆ Councillor

Cr *symbol* ◆ chromium (chemical element)

cr *contraction* ◆ creditor

cr. *shortening* ◆ created ◆ credit ◆ crescendo (Italian, = growing) (music) ◆ crown

CRA *abbrev.* ◆ Commercial Rabbit Association

CRAC *abbrev.* ◆ Careers Research and Advisory Centre

CRAD *abbrev.* ◆ Committee for Research into Apparatus for the Disabled

CRAE *abbrev.* ◆ Committee for the Reform of Animal Experimentation

Cramra *acronym* ◆ Convention on the Regulation of Antarctic Mineral Resource Activities

CRC *abbrev.* ◆ camera-ready copy ◆ Cancer Research Campaign ◆ cyclic redundancy check

CRCP *abbrev.* ◆ Certificant of the Royal College of Physicians

CRCS *abbrev.* ◆ Certificant of the Royal College of Surgeons

CRD *abbrev.* ◆ chronic respiratory disease

CRE *abbrev.* ◆ Commission for Racial Equality ◆ cumulative radiation effect

Cres. *shortening* ◆ Crescent

cres. *shortening* ◆ crescendo (Italian, = growing) (music)

cresc. *shortening* ◆ crescendo (Italian, = growing) (music)

crg. *shortening* ◆ carriage

CRI *abbrev.* ◆ Children's Relief International

CRIC *abbrev.* ◆ Commercial Radio International Committee

crim. con. *shortening* ◆ criminal conversation (adultery)

criminol. *shortening* ◆ criminology

CRIS *abbrev.* ◆ command retrieval information system

crit. *shortening* ◆ critical ◆ criticism

CRL *abbrev.* ◆ Certified Record Librarian ◆ Certified Reference Librarian

CRM *abbrev.* ◆ counter-radar missile

CRMF *abbrev.* ◆ Cancer Relief Macmillan Fund

CRMP *abbrev.* ◆ Corps of Royal Military Police

CRNA *abbrev.* ◆ Campaign for the Restoration of the National Anthem and Flag

CRO *abbrev.* ◆ Cave Rescue Organization of Great Britain ◆ Companies Registration Office ◆ Criminal Records Office ◆ Croatia (international vehicle registration)

CRS *abbrev.* ◆ Cereals Research Station

CRT *abbrev.* ◆ cathode ray tube ◆ composite rate tax

Crt *contraction* ◆ Court (street name)

crt *contraction* ◆ court (games)

cryst. *shortening* ◆ crystal ◆ crystalline ◆ crystallography

crystallog. *shortening* ◆ crystallography

CS *abbrev.* ◆ Caesarian Section ◆ Chemical Society ◆ Christian Science ◆ Civil Service ◆ Clerk to the Signet ◆ Corson and Stoughton (discoverers of the irritant chemical used in CS gas) ◆ Court of Session ◆ Czechoslovakia (international vehicle registration) ◆ Glasgow (British vehicle registration mark) ◆ Portugal (international civil aircraft marking)

Cs *symbol* ◆ caesium (chemical element)

cs *abbrev.* ◆ come sopra (Italian, = as above) (music)

c/s *abbrev.* ◆ cycles per second

CSA *abbrev.* ◆ Campaign for a Scottish Assembly ◆ Channel Swimming Association ◆ Child Support Agency

CSAB *abbrev.* ◆ Civil Service Appeal Board

CSB *abbrev.* ◆ Central Statistical Board

CSBF *abbrev.* ◆ Civil Service Benevolent Fund

CSBM *abbrev.* ◆ confidence- and security-building measures

CSC *abbrev.* ◆ Civil Service Commission ◆ Conspicuous Service Cross

csc *abbrev.* ◆ cosecant

CSCB *abbrev.* ◆ Committee of Scottish Clearing Bankers

CSCE *abbrev.* ◆ Conference on Security and Co-operation in Europe (Nato)

CSCFE *abbrev.* ◆ Civil Service Council for Further Education

CSD *abbrev.* ◆ Chartered Society of Designers ◆ Civil Service Department

CSE *abbrev.* ◆ Campaign for State Education ◆ Certificate of Secondary Education

cse *contraction* ◆ course

C-section *contraction* ◆ Caesarean section (colloquial)

CSEU *abbrev.* ◆ Confederation of Shipbuilding and Engineering Unions

CSF *abbrev.* ◆ cerebrospinal fluid

CSI *abbrev.* ◆ Chartered Surveyors Institution

CSIP *abbrev.* ◆ Committee for the Scientific Investigation of the Paranormal

CSIR *abbrev.* ◆ Council for Industrial and Scientific Research

CSIRO *abbrev.* ◆ Commonwealth Scientific and Industrial Research Organization

CSL *abbrev.* ◆ computer simulation language

CSM *abbrev.* ◆ cerebrospinal meningitis ◆ Committee on the Safety of Medicines ◆ Company Sergeant-Major

CSMA *abbrev.* ◆ carrier-sensed multiple access

CSO *abbrev.* ◆ Central Statistical Office ◆ community service order ◆ Montevideo (airport baggage label)

CSP *abbrev.* ◆ Chartered Society of Physiotherapists ◆ Council for Scientific Policy

CSPEC *abbrev.* ◆ Confederation of the Socialist Parties of the European Community

CSS *abbrev.* ◆ computer systems simulator

CSSR *abbrev.* ◆ Congregatio Sanctissimi Redemptoris (Latin, = Congregation of the Most Holy Redeemer) (Redemptorist Order)

CST *abbrev.* ◆ Central Standard Time ◆ College of Science and Technology ◆ College of Speech Therapists ◆ convulsive shock therapy

CSU *abbrev.* ◆ catheter specimen of urine ◆ Civil Service Union

CSV *abbrev.* ◆ community service volunteer

CSYS *abbrev.* ◆ Certificate of Sixth Year Studies

CT *abbrev.* ◆ Canterbury (UK postcode) ◆ cerebral thrombosis ◆ cerebral tumour ◆ Civic Trust ◆ College of Technology ◆ Connecticut (US postcode) ◆ computed tomography ◆ computer-aided axial tomography ◆ coronary thrombosis ◆ Lincoln (British vehicle registration mark)

Ct *contraction* ◆ Court

ct *contraction* ◆ carat ◆ cent (monetary unit) ◆ court

CTA *abbrev.* ◆ Cable Television Association

CTB *abbrev.* ◆ comprehensive test ban

CTBT *abbrev.* ◆ comprehensive test ban treaty

CTC *abbrev.* ◆ carbon tetrachloride ◆ city technology college ◆ Cyclists' Touring Club

CTCC *abbrev.* ◆ Central Transport Consultative Committee

CTD *abbrev.* ◆ classified telephone directory

ctd *contraction* ◆ coated ◆ continued ◆ crated

CTEB *abbrev.* ◆ Council of Technical Examining Bodies

CTF *abbrev.* ◆ Catholic Teachers' Federation

ctl *contraction* ◆ central

CTGWE *abbrev.* ◆ Christmas Tree Growers of Western Europe

CTMB *abbrev.* ◆ Canal Transport Marketing Board

CTMO *abbrev.* ◆ Community Trade Marks Office (EC)

CTN *abbrev.* ◆ confectioner, tobacconist and newsagent (shop)

ctn *shortening* ◆ cotangent

ctn *contraction* ◆ carton

CTNC *abbrev.* ◆ Committee on Transnational Corporations (UN)

CTO *abbrev.* ◆ cancelled to order (stamps)

CTOL *abbrev.* ◆ conventional take-off and landing

Ctrl *contraction* ◆ Control (computer key)

CTS *abbrev.* ◆ Catholic Truth Society

CTT *abbrev.* ◆ capital transfer tax

cttee *contraction* ◆ committee

CTTH *abbrev.* ◆ Cathedrals through Touch and Hearing

CTU *abbrev.* ◆ Conservative Trade Unionists

CTUC *abbrev.* ◆ Commonwealth Trade Union Council

CTV *abbrev.* ◆ colour television ◆ continuous variable transmission

CTVM *abbrev.* ◆ Centre for Tropical Veterinary Medicine

CU *abbrev.* ◆ Cambridge University ◆ Church Union ◆ Cuba (international civil aircraft marking) ◆ Cubana Airlines (airline baggage code)

◆ Customs Union ◆ Newcastle upon Tyne (British vehicle registration mark)

Cu *symbol* ◆ cuprum (Latin , = copper) (chemical element)

cu. *shortening* ◆ cubic

CUA *abbrev.* ◆ Common User Access ◆ Conference of University Administrators

cub. *shortening* ◆ cubic

CUC *abbrev.* ◆ Coal Utilization Council

CUEP *abbrev.* ◆ Central Unit on Environmental Pollution

CUEW *abbrev.* ◆ Congregational Union of England and Wales

CUG *abbrev.* ◆ closed user group

CUK *abbrev.* ◆ São Paulo (airport baggage label)

CUKT *abbrev.* ◆ Carnegie United Kingdom Trust

CUL *abbrev.* ◆ Cambridge University Library

cul. *shortening* ◆ culinary

CUM *abbrev.* ◆ Cambridge University Mission

cum. *shortening* ◆ cumulative

Cumb. *shortening* ◆ Cumberland ◆ Cumbria

cum div. *shortening* ◆ cum dividend (with dividend)

cum. pref. *shortening* ◆ cumulative preference

CUNA *abbrev.* ◆ Credit Union National Association

CUNY *abbrev.* ◆ City University of New York

CUP *abbrev.* ◆ Cambridge University Press

cur. *shortening* ◆ currency ◆ current

cust. *shortening* ◆ custard ◆ custodian ◆ custody

CV *abbrev.* ◆ calorific value ◆ cardiovascular ◆ cerebrovascular ◆ cheval-vapeur (French, = horsepower) ◆ Common Version (of the Bible) ◆ Coventry (UK postcode) ◆ curriculum vitae ◆ Truro (British vehicle registration mark)

cv *abbrev.* ◆ cras vespere (Latin, = tomorrow evening)

cv. *abbrev.* ◆ cultivar

CVA *abbrev.* ◆ cerebrovascular accident (stroke)

CVCP *abbrev.* ◆ Committee of Vice Chancellors and Principals (of UK universities)

CVE *abbrev.* ◆ Certificate of Vocational Education

CVD *abbrev.* ◆ cerebrovascular disease

CVI *abbrev.* ◆ common variable immunodeficiency

CVL *abbrev.* ◆ Central Veterinary Laboratory

CVO *abbrev.* ◆ Commander of the Royal Victorian Order

CVS *abbrev.* ◆ cardiovascular system ◆ chorionic villus sampling

cvt. *shortening* ◆ convertible

CVWS *abbrev.* ◆ combat vehicle weapons system

CVWW *abbrev.* ◆ Council of Voluntary Welfare Work

CW *abbrev.* ◆ chemical warfare ◆ chemical weapons ◆ child welfare ◆ continuous wave ◆ Crewe (UK postcode) ◆ Preston (British vehicle registration mark)

CWA *abbrev.* ◆ Crime Writers' Association

CWBW *abbrev.* ◆ chemical and biological warfare

CWD *abbrev.* ◆ civilian war dead

CWG *abbrev.* ◆ Co-operative Women's Guild

CWGC *abbrev.* ◆ Commonwealth War Graves Commission

CWL *abbrev.* ◆ Cardiff (airport baggage label)

cwlth *contraction* ◆ commonwealth

CWM *abbrev.* ◆ Council for World Mission

CWME *abbrev.* ◆ Commission on World Mission and Evangelism (WCC)

CWO *abbrev.* ◆ chief warrant officer

cwo *abbrev.* ◆ cash with order

CWR *abbrev.* ◆ continuous welded rail

CWS *abbrev.* ◆ Co-operative Wholesale Society

cwt *contraction* ◆ hundredweight (Latin *centum* = 100)

CX *abbrev.* ◆ Cathay Pacific Airways (airline baggage code) ◆ Huddersfield (British vehicle registration mark) ◆ Uruguay (international civil aircraft marking)

CXR *abbrev.* ◆ chest X-ray

CXT *abbrev.* ◆ Common External Tariff (EC)

CY *abbrev.* ◆ Cyprus (international vehicle registration) ◆ Cyprus Airways (airline baggage code) ◆ Swansea (British vehicle registration mark)

cy *abbrev.* ◆ calendar year

cy *contraction* ◆ capacity ◆ currency

cyber. *shortening* ◆ cybernetics

cyc. *shortening* ◆ cycle ◆ cyclopedia

CYL *abbrev.* ◆ Communist Youth League

cyl. *shortening* ◆ cylinder ◆ cylindrical

Cym. *shortening* ◆ Cymric

CYMS *abbrev.* ◆ Catholic Young Men's Society

Cyp. *shortening* ◆ Cypriot ◆ Cyprus

CYS *abbrev.* ◆ Catholic Youth Services

CYSA *abbrev.* ◆ Community Youth Services Association

CYWU *abbrev.* ◆ Community Youth Workers' Union

CZ *abbrev.* ◆ Belfast (British vehicle registration mark) ◆ Canal Zone

D

D *abbrev.* ◆ Democrat ◆ Democratic ◆ Department ◆ Deus (Latin, = God) ◆ Deutsch (catalogue of Schubert's works) ◆ Deutschland (German, = Germany) (international civil aircraft marking) ◆ Deutschland (German, = Germany) (international vehicle registration) ◆ diamonds (cards) ◆ digital ◆ dimension ◆ dinar (Tunisian monetary unit) ◆ Director ◆ Dominus (Latin, = Lord) ◆ dong (Vietnamese monetary unit) ◆ Duchess ◆ Duke ◆ Dutch

3-D *abbrev.* ◆ three-dimensional

d *abbrev.* ◆ date ◆ daughter ◆ day ◆ dead ◆ deci- ◆ degree ◆ dele (Latin, = delete) ◆ denarius (Latin, = penny) (British monetary unit until 1971) ◆ departs ◆ depth ◆ deserted ◆ diameter ◆ died ◆ dividend ◆ dollar (monetary unit) ◆ dose ◆ duke

DA *abbrev.* ◆ Birmingham (British vehicle registration mark) ◆ Dan-Air (airline baggage code) ◆ Dartford (UK postcode) ◆ Depressives Anonymous ◆ developmental age ◆ dinar (Algerian monetary unit) ◆ Diploma in Anaesthetics ◆ Diploma of Art ◆ District Attorney (US) ◆ dopamine ◆ duck's arse (hairstyle)

D/A *abbrev.* ◆ digital-to-analogue

Da. *shortening* ◆ Danish

da *contraction* ◆ deca-

d/a *abbrev.* ◆ deposit account

DAAG *abbrev.* ◆ Deputy Assistant Adjutant-General

DAB *abbrev.* ◆ Dictionary of American Biography

DAC *abbrev.* ◆ digital-to-analogue converter

dachs. *shortening* ◆ dachshund

Dacor *acronym* ◆ data correction

dact. *shortening* ◆ dactyl

Daf *acronym* ◆ Doorn Automobielfabriek (Dutch, = Doorn Car Factory)

daf *abbrev.* ◆ described as follows

DAFS *abbrev.* ◆ Department of Agriculture and Fisheries for Scotland

DAG *abbrev.* ◆ Debendox Action Group ◆ Deputy Adjutant-General ◆ Divorce Action Group (Ireland)

Dagmar *acronym* ◆ defined advertising goals for measured advertising results

DAgr *abbrev.* ◆ Doctor of Agriculture

DAgrSc *abbrev.* ◆ Doctor of Agricultural Science

DAH *abbrev.* ◆ disordered action of the heart

DAI *abbrev.* ◆ death from accidental injuries

dal s. *shortening* ◆ dal segno (Italian, = from the sign) (music)

DAM *abbrev.* ◆ Damascus (airport baggage label)

dam. *shortening* ◆ damage

Dan. *shortening* ◆ Daniel (book of Bible) ◆ Danish

D & B *abbrev.* ◆ discipline and bondage ◆ Dun and Bradstreet (financial reports)

D & C *abbrev.* ◆ dilatation and curettage

d & d *abbrev.* ◆ deaf and dumb ◆ drunk and disorderly

D & HAA *abbrev.* ◆ Dock and Harbour Authorities Association

d & p *abbrev.* ◆ developing and printing

d & s *abbrev.* ◆ demand and supply

D & V *abbrev.* ◆ diarrhoea and vomiting

DAP *abbrev.* ✦ distributed array processor

dap *abbrev.* ✦ do anything possible ✦ documents against payment

DAppSc *abbrev.* ✦ Doctor of Applied Science

DAR *abbrev.* ✦ Dar-es Salaam (airport baggage label) ✦ Daughters of the American Revolution (US)

DArch *abbrev.* ✦ Doctor of Architecture

DAS *abbrev.* ✦ data acquisition system

das *abbrev.* ✦ delivered alongside ship

DASD *abbrev.* ✦ direct-access storage device

dash. *shortening* ✦ dashboard

Dass *acronym* ✦ Depressives Associated

DAT *abbrev.* ✦ dementia of the Altzheimer type ✦ digital audio tape

dat. *shortening* ✦ dative

Datacom *acronym* ✦ data communications

Datanet *acronym* ✦ data network

Datastor *acronym* ✦ data storage

Datec *acronym* ✦ Art and Design Committee of the Technician Education Council

Datel *acronym* ✦ Data and Telecommunications

Datran *acronym* ✦ data transmission

Datrec *acronym* ✦ data recording

dau. *shortening* ✦ daughter

DAW *abbrev.* ✦ Drama Association of Wales

DAWE *abbrev.* ✦ daughters already well-endowed

DB *abbrev.* ✦ database ✦ delayed broadcast ✦ Deutsche Bundesbahn (German, = German State Railways) ✦ Deutsche Bundesbank (German, = German State Bank) ✦ Manchester (British vehicle registration mark)

dB *abbrev.* ✦ decibel

db *abbrev.* ✦ daybook ✦ double bass ✦ double bed ✦ double-breasted ✦ draw bar

DBA *abbrev.* ✦ database administration ✦ dihydro-dimethyl-benzopyranbutyric acid (treatment for sickle-cell anaemia)

dba *abbrev.* ✦ doing business as ✦ doing business at

DBB *abbrev.* ✦ dinner, bed and breakfast

DBE *abbrev.* ✦ Dame Commander of the Order of the British Empire

DBib *abbrev.* ✦ Douay Bible

dbk *contraction* ✦ drawback

dbkn *contraction* ✦ debarkation

dbl. *shortening* ✦ double

dble *contraction* ✦ double

DBM *abbrev.* ✦ Diploma in Business Management

DBMC *abbrev.* ✦ Danish Bacon and Meat Council

DBMS *abbrev.* ✦ database management system

DBP *abbrev.* ✦ Deutsche Bundespost (German, = German State Post)

DBS *abbrev.* ✦ direct broadcast by satellite ✦ direct-broadcast satellite

dbs *abbrev.* ✦ damn bloody soon

DBST *abbrev.* ✦ Double British Summer Time

dbt *contraction* ✦ debit

DBV *abbrev.* ✦ Dubrovnik (airport baggage label)

DBW *abbrev.* ✦ desirable body weight

DC *abbrev.* ✦ da capo (Italian, = from the top) (music) ✦ death certificate ✦ Detective Constable ✦ direct current ✦ District Commissioner ✦ District Council ✦ District Commissioner ✦ District of Columbia ✦ Doctor of Chiropractic ✦ Douglas Commercial (aircraft manufacturers) ✦ Middlesborough (British vehicle registration mark)

DCA *abbrev.* ✦ Washington (airport baggage label)

DCAe *abbrev.* ✦ Diploma of the College of Aeronautics

DCAS *abbrev.* ✦ Divorce Conciliation and Advisory Service

DCB *abbrev.* ✦ Dame Commander of the Order of the Bath

DCC *abbrev.* ✦ digital compact cassette

DCCC *abbrev.* ✦ Domestic Coal Consumers Council

dcdr *contraction* ◆ decoder

DCE *abbrev.* ◆ data communications equipment ◆ Doctor of Civil Engineering

DCF *abbrev.* ◆ discounted cash flow

DCH *abbrev.* ◆ Diploma in Child Health

DCh *abbrev.* ◆ Doctor Chirurgiae (Latin, = Doctor of Surgery)

DChE *abbrev.* ◆ Doctor of Chemical Engineering

DCI *abbrev.* ◆ Detective Chief Inspector

dcisn *contraction* ◆ decision

DCL *abbrev.* ◆ Distillers Company Ltd ◆ Doctor of Civil Law

dcl. *shortening* ◆ declaration (cricket) ◆ declared (cricket)

DCM *abbrev.* ◆ Distinguished Conduct Medal

DCMG *abbrev.* ◆ Dame Commander of the Order of St Michael and St George

DCnL *abbrev.* ◆ Doctor of Canon Law

DComL *abbrev.* ◆ Doctor of Commercial Law

DCompL *abbrev.* ◆ Doctor of Comparative Law

DCP *abbrev.* ◆ Diploma in Clinical Pathology

DCS *abbrev.* ◆ Deputy Clerk of Session

DCVO *abbrev.* ◆ Dame Commander of the Royal Victorian Order

DD *abbrev.* ◆ dangerous drug ◆ Deo dedit (Latin, = gave to God) ◆ dishonourable discharge ◆ Divinitatis Doctor (Latin, = Doctor of Divinity) ◆ dono dedit (Latin, = gave as a gift) ◆ double density (of computer disk capacity) ◆ Dundee (UK postcode) ◆ Gloucester (British vehicle registration mark)

dd *abbrev.* ◆ days after date ◆ day's date ◆ delayed delivery ◆ delivered to docks ◆ direct debit ◆ due date

dd *contraction* ◆ dated ◆ delivered

d—d *contraction* ◆ damned

DDA *abbrev.* ◆ Dangerous Drugs Act ◆ Disabled Drivers' Association

DDC *abbrev.* ◆ Dewey Decimal Classification

ddc *abbrev.* ◆ direct digital control

DDD *abbrev.* ◆ dat, dicat, dedicat (Latin, = gives, devotes and dedicates) ◆ dono dedit dedicavit (Latin, = gave and dedicated as a gift)

DDE *abbrev.* ◆ direct data entry

DDH *abbrev.* ◆ Diploma in Dental Health

ddl *abbrev.* ◆ data definition language ◆ digital data link

ddp *abbrev.* ◆ distributed data processing

DDR *abbrev.* ◆ Deutsche Demokratische Republik (German, = German Democratic Republic) (the former East Germany)

DDRB *abbrev.* ◆ Doctors' and Dentists' Review Body

DDS *abbrev.* ◆ Dewey Decimal System ◆ digital data storage ◆ Doctor of Dental Surgery

DDSc *abbrev.* ◆ Doctor of Dental Science

DDT *abbrev.* ◆ dichloro-diphenyl-trichloro-ethane (insecticide)

DDTL *abbrev.* ◆ dreary desk-top lunch

DE *abbrev.* ◆ Dáil Éireann (Gaelic, = Assembly of Representatives) (lower house of Irish parliament) ◆ Delaware (US postcode) ◆ Department of Employment ◆ Derby (UK postcode) ◆ Haverfordwest (British vehicle registration mark)

de *abbrev.* ◆ deckle edge ◆ double entry

DEA *abbrev.* ◆ Drug Enforcement Administration (US)

deb. *shortening* ◆ debenture ◆ debit

debil. *shortening* ◆ debilitating ◆ debilitation

debk. *shortening* ◆ debarkation

DEC *abbrev.* ◆ Disasters Emergency Committee

Dec. *shortening* ◆ Decani (section of church choir) ◆ December ◆ Decorated (style of architecture)

dec. *shortening* ◆ deceased ◆ decimal ◆ declaration ◆ declared ◆ declension ◆ declination ◆ decorated ◆ decorative ◆ decrescendo (Italian, = decreasing) (music)

decaf. *shortening* ◆ decaffeinated

decasyll. *shortening* ◆ decasyllabic
◆ decasyllable
decd *contraction* ◆ deceased
decel. *shortening* ◆ deceleration
decid. *shortening* ◆ deciduous
decis. *shortening* ◆ decision
decl. *shortening* ◆ declension
decom. *shortening* ◆ decommission
DEcon *abbrev.* ◆ Doctor of Economics
DEconSc *abbrev.* ◆ Doctor of Economic
Science
decr. *shortening* ◆ decrease
decresc. *shortening* ◆ decrescendo
(Italian, = decreasing)
decrim. *shortening* ◆ decriminalization
DED *abbrev.* ◆ Department of Economic
Development (Northern Ireland)
DEd *abbrev.* ◆ Doctor of Education
ded. *shortening* ◆ dedicated ◆ dedication
◆ deduction
deduct. *shortening* ◆ deduction
◆ deductive
DEEP *abbrev.* ◆ Directly-Elected
European Parliament
def. *shortening* ◆ defective ◆ defendant
◆ deferred ◆ deficit ◆ definite
◆ definition
def. art. *shortening* ◆ definite article
Defcon *acronym* ◆ defence readiness
condition
defect. *shortening* ◆ defective
defl. *shortening* ◆ deflate ◆ deflation
deg. *shortening* ◆ degree
degen. *shortening* ◆ degeneration
degr. *shortening* ◆ degradation ◆ degree
dehyd. *shortening* ◆ dehydration
Del. *shortening* ◆ Delaware
del. *shortening* ◆ delegate ◆ delete
◆ delineavit (Latin, = drew it) ◆ deliver
delib. *shortening* ◆ deliberate
◆ deliberation
deliq. *shortening* ◆ deliquescent
dely *contraction* ◆ delivery
dem. *shortening* ◆ democratic ◆ demolish
◆ demolition ◆ demonstrative
demo. *shortening* ◆ demonstration
model
demon. *shortening* ◆ demonstrative

demons. *shortening* ◆ demonstrative
demonstr. *shortening* ◆ demonstrative
DemU *abbrev.* ◆ Democratic Unionist
demur. *shortening* ◆ demurrage
DEN *abbrev.* ◆ Denver (airport baggage
label) ◆ District Enrolled Nurse
Den. *shortening* ◆ Denmark
den. *shortening* ◆ denier
dendrochron. *shortening*
◆ dendrochronology
dendrol. *shortening* ◆ dendrological
◆ dendrology
DEng. *abbrev.* ◆ Doctor of Engineering
denom. *shortening* ◆ denomination
dens. *shortening* ◆ density
dent. *shortening* ◆ dental ◆ dentist
◆ dentistry
dep. *shortening* ◆ depart ◆ department
◆ departure ◆ dependant ◆ deponent
◆ deposed ◆ deposit ◆ deputy
Depca *acronym* ◆ International Study
Group for the Detection and Prevention
of Cancer
dept *contraction* ◆ department
der. *shortening* ◆ derivation ◆ derivative
◆ derived
Derby. *shortening* ◆ Derbyshire
DERE *abbrev.* ◆ Dounreay Experimental
Reactor Establishment
dereg. *shortening* ◆ deregulation
deriv. *shortening* ◆ derivation
◆ derivative ◆ derived
dermatol. *shortening* ◆ dermatology
DES *abbrev.* ◆ data encryption standard
◆ Department of Education and Science
des. *shortening* ◆ design ◆ desirable
desc. *shortening* ◆ descendant ◆ descent
descr. *shortening* ◆ description
desig. *shortening* ◆ designate
desp. *shortening* ◆ despatch
dest. *shortening* ◆ destination
◆ destroyer
destn *contraction* ◆ destination
DET *abbrev.* ◆ Detroit (airport baggage
label) ◆ diethyltriptamine (drug)
Det. *shortening* ◆ Detective
det. *shortening* ◆ detached ◆ determiner
detox. *shortening* ◆ detoxification

Deut. *shortening* ◆ Deuteronomy (book of Bible)

dev. *shortening* ◆ development

DEW *abbrev.* ◆ distant early warning

DF *abbrev.* ◆ Defender of the Faith ◆ direction-finding ◆ Djibouti franc (monetary unit) ◆ Gloucester (British vehicle registration mark)

d-f *abbrev.* ◆ double-fronted

DFC *abbrev.* ◆ Distinguished Flying Cross

DFD *abbrev.* ◆ data function diagram

DFDS *abbrev.* ◆ Det Forende Dampskibs-Selskab (Danish, = The United Steamship Company)

DFE *abbrev.* ◆ Department for Education

D/Fil *abbrev.* ◆ diesel filter

DFLP *abbrev.* ◆ Democratic Front for the Liberation of Palestine

DFM *abbrev.* ◆ Distinguished Flying Medal

DFS *abbrev.* ◆ disk filing system

dft *contraction* ◆ defendant ◆ draft

DG *abbrev.* ◆ Dei gratia (Latin, = by God's grace) ◆ Deutsche Grammophon (German, = German Gramophone Company) ◆ Director-General ◆ Directorate-General (of the EC) ◆ double glazed ◆ double glazing ◆ Dumfries (UK postcode) ◆ Gloucester (British vehicle registration mark)

dg *abbrev.* ◆ decigram

DGAA *abbrev.* ◆ Distressed Gentlefolk's Aid Association

DGAS *abbrev.* ◆ Double Glazing Advisory Service

DGCStJ *abbrev.* ◆ Dame Grand Cross of the Order of St John of Jerusalem

DGM *abbrev.* ◆ Diploma in General Medicine

Dgn *contraction* ◆ Dragoon

DGO *abbrev.* ◆ Diploma in Gynaecology and Obstetrics

DGS *abbrev.* ◆ Diploma in General Surgery ◆ Diploma in Graduate Studies

DH *abbrev.* ◆ dead heat ◆ Department of Health ◆ dirham (Moroccan monetary unit) ◆ Dudley (British vehicle registration mark) ◆ Durham (UK postcode)

Dh. *shortening* ◆ dirham (monetary unit of United Arab Emirates)

DHA *abbrev.* ◆ District Health Authority

DHC *abbrev.* ◆ Domestic Heating Council

DHDS *abbrev.* ◆ Dolmetsch Historical Dance Society

DHQ *abbrev.* ◆ District Headquarters ◆ Divisional Headquarters

DHSA *abbrev.* ◆ Diploma of Health Service Administration

DHSS *abbrev.* ◆ Department of Health and Social Security

dhw *abbrev.* ◆ domestic hot water

DI *abbrev.* ◆ Defence Intelligence ◆ Detective Inspector ◆ diabetes insipidus ◆ donor insemination

DIA *abbrev.* ◆ Driving Instructors' Association ◆ Washington (airport baggage label)

dia. *shortening* ◆ diameter

diag. *shortening* ◆ diagnosis ◆ diagonal ◆ diagram

dial. *shortening* ◆ dialect

diam. *shortening* ◆ diameter

Diamat *acronym* ◆ dialectical materialism

Diane *acronym* ◆ Direct Information Access Network for Europe

diaph. *shortening* ◆ diaphragm

dibas. *shortening* ◆ dibasic

DIC *abbrev.* ◆ Diamond Information Centre ◆ Diploma of Imperial College

DIChem *abbrev.* ◆ Diploma in Industrial Chemistry

dicot. *shortening* ◆ dicotyledon

dict. *shortening* ◆ dictation ◆ dictator ◆ dictionary

dictsort *acronym* ◆ dictionary sorter

DIE *abbrev.* ◆ Diploma in Industrial Engineering

dieb. alt. *abbrev.* ◆ diebus alternis (Latin, = every other day)

diff. *shortening* ◆ difference ◆ differential ◆ different

diff. calc. *shortening* ◆ differential calculus

diffr. *shortening* ◆ diffraction
diffu. *shortening* ◆ diffusion
Dig *acronym* ◆ Disablement Income Group
dig. *shortening* ◆ digest ◆ digestion ◆ digestive
DIH *abbrev.* ◆ Diploma in Industrial Health
dil. *shortening* ◆ dilute
DIM *abbrev.* ◆ Diploma in Industrial Management
dim. *shortening* ◆ dimension ◆ diminuendo (Italian, = diminishing) (music) ◆ diminutive
dimin. *shortening* ◆ diminuendo (Italian, = diminishing) (music) ◆ diminutive
DIMS *abbrev.* ◆ data and information management system
DIN *abbrev.* ◆ Deutsche Industrie-Norm (German, = German Industry Standard) (international standard paper sizes) ◆ Deutsches Institut für Normung (German, = German Standards Institute) ◆ Do It Now
din. *shortening* ◆ dinar (monetary unit) ◆ dining ◆ dinner
DIng *abbrev.* ◆ Doctor Ingeniariae (Latin, = Doctor of Engineering)
Dinky *acronym* ◆ dual income, no kids yet (used of couple)
dioc. *shortening* ◆ diocesan ◆ diocese
Dip. *shortening* ◆ Diploma
DipAD *abbrev.* ◆ Diploma in Art and Design
DipAgr *abbrev.* ◆ Diploma in Agriculture
DipALing *abbrev.* ◆ Diploma in Applied Linguistics
DipAppSc *abbrev.* ◆ Diploma in Applied Science
DipArch *abbrev.* ◆ Diploma in Architecture
DipBA *abbrev.* ◆ Diploma in Business Administration
DipCE *abbrev.* ◆ Diploma in Civil Engineering
DipChemEng *abbrev.* ◆ Diploma in Chemical Engineering
DipCom *abbrev.* ◆ Diploma in Commerce

DipDS *abbrev.* ◆ Diploma in Dental Surgery
DipEd *abbrev.* ◆ Diploma in Education
DipEng *abbrev.* ◆ Diploma in Engineering
DipESL *abbrev.* ◆ Diploma in English as a Second Language
DipGSM *abbrev.* ◆ Diploma in Music, Guildhall School of Music and Drama
DipHE *abbrev.* ◆ Diploma in Higher Education
diphth. *shortening* ◆ diphthong
dipl. *shortening* ◆ diploma ◆ diplomacy ◆ diplomatic
DipLSc *abbrev.* ◆ Diploma in Library Science
DipMechE *abbrev.* ◆ Diploma in Mechanical Engineering
DipN *abbrev.* ◆ Diploma in Nursing
DipRADA *abbrev.* ◆ Diploma of the Royal Academy of Dramatic Art
DipSoc *abbrev.* ◆ Diploma in Sociology
DipSS *abbrev.* ◆ Diploma in Social Studies
DipSW *abbrev.* ◆ Diploma in Social Work
DipTEFL *abbrev.* ◆ Diploma in Teaching English as a Foreign Language
DipTh *abbrev.* ◆ Diploma in Theology
dir. *shortening* ◆ direction ◆ director ◆ dirham (monetary unit of Morocco and the United Arab Emirates)
DIS *abbrev.* ◆ Development Information System (UN)
dis. *shortening* ◆ disabled ◆ discharge ◆ discontinued ◆ discount
disabil. *shortening* ◆ disability
disag. *shortening* ◆ disagreeable
disb. *shortening* ◆ disbursement
disc. *shortening* ◆ discount ◆ discover ◆ discoverer
discont. *shortening* ◆ discontinued
discr. *shortening* ◆ discretion
disemb. *shortening* ◆ disembark ◆ disembarkation
dishon. *shortening* ◆ dishonest ◆ dishonourable
disloc. *shortening* ◆ dislocation

Dismac *acronym* ◆ digital scene-matching area correlation sensors
disp. *shortening* ◆ dispensary
displ. *shortening* ◆ displacement
diss. *shortening* ◆ dissent ◆ dissertation
dissyl. *shortening* ◆ dissyllable
dist. *shortening* ◆ distance ◆ distilled ◆ distinguish ◆ distribute ◆ distributor ◆ district
distr. *shortening* ◆ distribution ◆ distributor
distrib. *shortening* ◆ distributive
DITB *abbrev.* ◆ Distributive Industry Training Board
div. *shortening* ◆ divide ◆ dividend ◆ divine ◆ divisi (Italian, = divided) (of musical parts) ◆ division ◆ divorce ◆ divorced
DIY *acronym* ◆ do-it-yourself
DJ *abbrev.* ◆ dinner jacket ◆ disc jockey ◆ dust jacket ◆ Liverpool (British vehicle registration mark)
DJF *abbrev.* ◆ Disk Jockeys Federation
DJI *abbrev.* ◆ Dow Jones Index (US Stock Exchange)
DJAG *abbrev.* ◆ Deputy Judge Advocate General
DJIA *abbrev.* ◆ Dow Jones Industrial Average (US Stock Exchange)
DK *abbrev.* ◆ Denmark and Greenland (international vehicle registration) ◆ Manchester (British vehicle registration mark)
dk *contraction* ◆ dark ◆ deck ◆ dock
dkhse *contraction* ◆ deckhouse
DKR *abbrev.* ◆ Dakar (airport baggage label)
Dkr *abbrev.* ◆ Danish krone (monetary unit)
dkt *contraction* ◆ docket
dkyd *contraction* ◆ dockyard
DL *abbrev.* ◆ Darlington (UK postcode) ◆ Deputy Lieutenant ◆ Portsmouth (British vehicle registration mark)
D/L *abbrev.* ◆ demand loan
dl *shortening* ◆ decilitre
DLCO-EA *abbrev.* ◆ Desert Locust Control Organization for Eastern Africa

dld *abbrev.* ◆ deadline date
dld *contraction* ◆ delivered
DLF *abbrev.* ◆ Disabled Living Foundation
DLIS *abbrev.* ◆ Desert Locust Information Service
DLitt *abbrev.* ◆ Doctor Litterarum (Latin, = Doctor of Letters)
DLO *abbrev.* ◆ dead letter office
DLP *abbrev.* ◆ Democratic Labour Party
DLR *abbrev.* ◆ Docklands Light Railway
dlr *contraction* ◆ dealer
dls *abbrev.* ◆ debt liquidation schedule
DLSc *abbrev.* ◆ Doctor of Library Science
dlvd *contraction* ◆ delivered
dlvr *contraction* ◆ deliver
dlvy *contraction* ◆ delivery
dly *contraction* ◆ daily
DM *abbrev.* ◆ Chester (British vehicle registration mark) ◆ Deutschmark (German monetary unit) ◆ diabetes mellitus ◆ diastolic murmur ◆ Doctor of Medicine ◆ Doctor of Music
dm *shortening* ◆ decimetre
DMA *abbrev.* ◆ Defence Manufacturers' Association ◆ direct memory access
D-Mark *contraction* ◆ Deutschmark (German currency unit)
dmc *abbrev.* ◆ direct manufacturing costs
DMD *abbrev.* ◆ Duchenne muscular dystrophy
dmd *contraction* ◆ demand
DMF *abbrev.* ◆ decayed, missing and filled (teeth) ◆ Disabled Motorists Federation
dmg. *shortening* ◆ damage
DML *abbrev.* ◆ data manipulation language
DMO *abbrev.* ◆ District Medical Officer
DMS *abbrev.* ◆ database management system
DMs *abbrev.* ◆ Doc Martens
DMT *abbrev.* ◆ dimethyltriptamine (drug)
DMU *abbrev.* ◆ directly managed unit (hospital in National Health Service)
DMus *abbrev.* ◆ Doctor of Music
DMZ *abbrev.* ◆ demilitarized zone

DN *abbrev.* ◆ debit note ◆ Diploma in Nursing ◆ Dominus Noster (Latin, = Our Lord) ◆ Doncaster (UK postcode) ◆ Leeds (British vehicle registration mark)

DNA *abbrev.* ◆ deoxyribonucleic acid ◆ District Nursing Association

dna *abbrev.* ◆ did not attend

DNB *abbrev.* ◆ Dictionary of National Biography

DNC *abbrev.* ◆ distributed numerical control

dnf *abbrev.* ◆ did not finish (race etc)

DNH *abbrev.* ◆ Department of National Heritage

DNJC *abbrev.* ◆ Dominus Noster Jesus Christus (Latin, = Our Lord Jesus Christ)

D-notice *contraction* ◆ Defence Notice (Government ban on publication of certain news items)

DNPP *abbrev.* ◆ Dominus Noster Papa Pontifex (Latin, = our lord the Pope)

DNR *abbrev.* ◆ do not resuscitate

Dnr *contraction* ◆ dinar (Yugoslavian monetary unit)

DNS *abbrev.* ◆ Department of National Savings

DO *abbrev.* ◆ deferred ordinary (shares) ◆ District Office ◆ Lincoln (British vehicle registration mark)

do *contraction* ◆ ditto

d/o *abbrev.* ◆ delivery order

DOA *abbrev.* ◆ date of availability ◆ dead on arrival

DOAE *abbrev.* ◆ Defence Operational Analysis Establishment

dob *abbrev.* ◆ date of birth

DObstRCOG *abbrev.* ◆ Diploma in Obstetrics of the Royal College of Gynaecologists and Obstetricians

DOC *abbrev.* ◆ Denominazione di Origine Controllata (Italian, = regulated naming of origin) (of wines) ◆ District Officer Commanding

doc. *shortening* ◆ document

DOCG *abbrev.* ◆ Denominazione di Origine Controllata Garantita (Italian, = guaranteed regulated naming of origin) (of wines)

Docomomo *acronym* ◆ International Working Party for the Documentation and Conservation of Buildings, Sites and Neighbourhoods of the Modern Movement

docu. *shortening* ◆ document ◆ documentary

dod *abbrev.* ◆ date of death

DOE *abbrev.* ◆ Department of Employment ◆ depends upon experience

DoE *abbrev.* ◆ Department of the Environment

D of L *abbrev.* ◆ Duchy of Lancaster

DOG *abbrev.* ◆ Directory of Opportunities for Graduates

DoH *abbrev.* ◆ Department of Health

DOHC *abbrev.* ◆ double overhead camshaft

DOI *abbrev.* ◆ died of injuries

DoI *abbrev.* ◆ Department of Industry

dol. *shortening* ◆ dolce (Italian, = sweet) (music) ◆ dollar (monetary unit)

dolciss. *shortening* ◆ dolcissimo (Italian, = very sweetly) (music)

DOM *abbrev.* ◆ Deo optimo maximo (Latin, = to God, the greatest and best) ◆ Dominican Republic (international vehicle registration) ◆ Dominus omnium magister (Latin, = God the master of all) ◆ dirty old man

Dom. *shortening* ◆ Dominical ◆ Dominican ◆ Dominus (Latin, = Lord)

dom *abbrev.* ◆ date of marriage

dom. *shortening* ◆ domestic ◆ domicile ◆ dominion

DOMS *abbrev.* ◆ Diploma in Ophthalmic Medicine and Surgery

Domsat *acronym* ◆ domestic communications satellite

Don. *shortening* ◆ County Donegal

don. *shortening* ◆ donec (Latin, = until)

Dor. *shortening* ◆ Dorian ◆ Doric

Dora *acronym* ◆ Defence of the Realm Act

Dors. *shortening* ◆ Dorset

Dos *acronym* ◆ Disk Operating System
dos *abbrev.* ◆ date of sale
dos. *shortening* ◆ dosage
DoT *abbrev.* ◆ Department of Transport
DOW *abbrev.* ◆ died of wounds
dow. *shortening* ◆ dowager
doz. *shortening* ◆ dozen
DP *abbrev.* ◆ data processing
◆ Democratic Party ◆ departure point
◆ displaced person ◆ Reading (British
vehicle registration mark)
dp *abbrev.* ◆ damp-proof ◆ dual purpose
d/p *abbrev.* ◆ delivery papers ◆ delivery
on payment
DPA *abbrev.* ◆ Data Protection Authority
dpa *abbrev.* ◆ deferred payment account
DPAA *abbrev.* ◆ Draught Proofing
Advisory Association
DPAS *abbrev.* ◆ Discharged Prisoners'
Aid Society
DPath *abbrev.* ◆ Diploma in Pathology
DPB *abbrev.* ◆ deposit pass book
DPC *abbrev.* ◆ Defence Planning
Committee (Nato)
dpc *abbrev.* ◆ damp-proof course
DPCM *abbrev.* ◆ differential pulse-code
modulation
DPE *abbrev.* ◆ Diploma in Physical
Education
DPH *abbrev.* ◆ Diploma in Public Health
DPh *abbrev.* ◆ Doctor of Philosophy
DPhil *abbrev.* ◆ Doctor of Philosophy
DPI *abbrev.* ◆ Department of Public
Information (UN)
dpi *abbrev.* ◆ dots per inch
DPM *abbrev.* ◆ Deputy Prime Minister
◆ Diploma in Psychological Medicine
DPMI *abbrev.* ◆ Dos/Protected Mode
Interface
dpob *abbrev.* ◆ date and place of birth
DPP *abbrev.* ◆ Director of Public
Prosecutions
dpp *abbrev.* ◆ deferred payment plan
DPR *abbrev.* ◆ Data Protection Register
DPRK *abbrev.* ◆ Democratic People's
Republic of Korea
DPS *abbrev.* ◆ Dales Pony Society

DPT *abbrev.* ◆ diphtheria, pertussis,
tetanus (vaccine)
dpt *contraction* ◆ department
dpty *contraction* ◆ deputy
dpu *abbrev.* ◆ data processing unit
DQ *abbrev.* ◆ direct question
◆ disqualified
DQMG *abbrev.* ◆ Deputy Quartermaster
General
DQMS *abbrev.* ◆ Deputy Quartermaster
Sergeant
DR *abbrev.* ◆ dead reckoning ◆ dining
room ◆ discount rate ◆ dry riser
◆ Exeter (British vehicle registration
mark)
D/R *abbrev.* ◆ deposit receipt
Dr *contraction* ◆ Doctor ◆ Driver
◆ Drummer
dr *contraction* ◆ debtor ◆ drawer
Dr. *shortening* ◆ Drive
dr. *shortening* ◆ drachm ◆ drachma
(Greek monetary unit)
Dram *acronym* ◆ dynamic random access
memory
dram. *shortening* ◆ dramatic ◆ dramatist
dram. pers. *shortening* ◆ dramatis
personae (Latin, = characters in the
play)
Drav. *shortening* ◆ Dravidian
Draw *acronym* ◆ direct read after write
draw. *shortening* ◆ drawing room
DRCOG *abbrev.* ◆ Diploma of the Royal
College of Obstetricians and
Gynaecologists
DRCPath *abbrev.* ◆ Diploma of the Royal
College of Pathologists
DRDW *abbrev.* ◆ direct read during write
DRV *abbrev.* ◆ dietary reference values
DRS *abbrev.* ◆ Dresden (airport baggage
label)
DS *abbrev.* ◆ Air Senegal (airline baggage
code) ◆ dal segno (Italian, = from the
sign) (music) ◆ debenture stock
◆ Detective Sergeant ◆ disseminated
sclerosis ◆ Doctor of Surgery ◆ Down's
syndrome ◆ Glasgow (British vehicle
registration mark)
D/S *abbrev.* ◆ dextrose saline

DSA *abbrev.* ◆ Down's Syndrome Association ◆ Driving Standards Agency

DSAC *abbrev.* ◆ Defence Scientific Advisory Council

DSB *abbrev.* ◆ Danske Statsbaner (Danish, = Danish State Railways)

DSC *abbrev.* ◆ Distinguished Service Cross

DSc *abbrev.* ◆ Doctor Scientiae (Latin, = Doctor of Science)

dsDNA *abbrev.* ◆ double-stranded deoxyribonucleic acid

DSM *abbrev.* ◆ deputy stage manager ◆ Distinguished Service Medal

dsmd *contraction* ◆ dismissed

DSO *abbrev.* ◆ Distinguished Service Order

DSP *abbrev.* ◆ Democratic Socialist Party

dsp *abbrev.* ◆ decessit sine prole (Latin, = died without issue) ◆ digital signal processing

dspl *contraction* ◆ disposal

dspn *contraction* ◆ disposition

dsRNA *abbrev.* ◆ double-stranded ribonucleic acid

DSS *abbrev.* ◆ decision support system ◆ Department of Social Security

DST *abbrev.* ◆ Daylight Saving Time ◆ Double Summer Time

DT *abbrev.* ◆ Daily Telegraph ◆ data transmission ◆ delerium tremens ◆ Dorchester (UK postcode) ◆ Sheffield (British vehicle registration mark)

dtba *abbrev.* ◆ date to be advised

DTC *abbrev.* ◆ Department of Technical Co-operation

DTD *abbrev.* ◆ document type definition

dtd *contraction* ◆ dated

DTE *abbrev.* ◆ data terminal equipment

DTech *abbrev.* ◆ Doctor of Technology

DTF *abbrev.* ◆ Dairy Trade Federation ◆ Domestic Textiles Federation

DTh *abbrev.* ◆ Doctor Theologiae (Latin, = Doctor of Theology)

DTheol *abbrev.* ◆ Doctor Theologiae (Latin, = Doctor of Theology)

DTI *abbrev.* ◆ Department of Trade and Industry

DTM *abbrev.* ◆ Dortmund (airport baggage label)

DTP *abbrev.* ◆ desktop publishing

DTR *abbrev.* ◆ double taxation relief

DTRP *abbrev.* ◆ Diploma in Town and Regional Planning

DTs *abbrev.* ◆ delirium tremens

DTT *abbrev.* ◆ Detroit (airport baggage label)

DU *abbrev.* ◆ Coventry (British vehicle registration mark) ◆ died unmarried ◆ duodenal ulcer

Du. *shortening* ◆ Dutch

DUB *abbrev.* ◆ Dublin (airport baggage label)

Dub. *shortening* ◆ County Dublin ◆ dubious

Dunelm. *shortening* ◆ Dunelmensis (Latin, = of Durham)

DUniv *abbrev.* ◆ Doctor of the University

duo. *shortening* ◆ duodecimo

DUP *abbrev.* ◆ Democratic Unionist Party

dup. *shortening* ◆ duplicate

DUR *abbrev.* ◆ Durban (airport baggage label)

Dur. *shortening* ◆ Durham

DUS *abbrev.* ◆ Düsseldorf (airport baggage label)

DV *abbrev.* ◆ Deo volente (Latin, = God willing) ◆ Douay Version (of Bible) ◆ double vision ◆ Exeter (British vehicle registration mark)

DVA *abbrev.* ◆ Dunkirk Veterans' Association

DVE *abbrev.* ◆ Diploma in Vocational Education

DVI *abbrev.* ◆ digital video imaging

DVLA *abbrev.* ◆ Driver and Vehicle Licensing Agency

DVM *abbrev.* ◆ Doctor of Veterinary Medicine

DVMS *abbrev.* ◆ Doctor of Veterinary Medicine and Surgery

dvr *contraction* ◆ driver

DVS *abbrev.* ◆ Doctor of Veterinary Surgery

DVSc *abbrev.* ◆ Doctor of Veterinary Science

DW *abbrev.* ◆ Cardiff (British vehicle registration mark)

dw *abbrev.* ◆ dead weight ◆ delivered weight ◆ dust wrapper

DWA *abbrev.* ◆ driving without awareness

DWAS *abbrev.* ◆ Doctor Who Appreciation Society

dwc *abbrev.* ◆ deadweight capacity

dwt *abbrev.* ◆ deadweight tonnage

dwt *contraction* ◆ pennyweight

DX *abbrev.* ◆ Ipswich (British vehicle registration mark) ◆ long distance

Dx *abbrev.* ◆ diagnosis

DXB *abbrev.* ◆ Dubai (airport baggage label)

DXR *abbrev.* ◆ deep X-ray

DXRT *abbrev.* ◆ deep X-ray therapy

DY *abbrev.* ◆ Benin (international vehicle registration) ◆ Brighton (British vehicle registration mark) ◆ Dudley (UK postcode)

DY *symbol* ◆ dysprosium (chemical element)

dy *contraction* ◆ delivery

DYB *abbrev.* ◆ do your best

dyn. *shortening* ◆ dynamics ◆ dynamo ◆ dynamometer ◆ dynasty ◆ dyne

DZ *abbrev.* ◆ Algeria (international vehicle registration) ◆ Antrim (British vehicle registration mark) ◆ drop zone

dz. *shortening* ◆ dozen

D-Zug *contraction* ◆ Durchgangzug (German, = through train)

E

E *abbrev.* ◆ earth (on electrical circuits) ◆ East ◆ Eastern ◆ east London (UK postcode) ◆ Ecstasy (slang term for the drug) ◆ Egyptian ◆ electromotive force ◆ emalangeni (Swaziland monetary unit) ◆ energy (physics) ◆ English ◆ España (Spanish, = Spain) (international vehicle registration) ◆ European (with EC codes for food additives etc) ◆ exa-

e *abbrev.* ◆ European (with weights that comply with EC directives)

EA *abbrev.* ◆ Dudley (British vehicle registration mark) ◆ East Anglia ◆ Eastern Airlines (airline baggage code) ◆ effective agent ◆ enemy aircraft

ea. *shortening* ◆ each

EAHF *abbrev.* ◆ eczema, asthma, hay fever

EAK *abbrev.* ◆ Kenya (international vehicle registration; orig. East Africa Kenya)

EAN *abbrev.* ◆ effective atomic number ◆ European Academic Network ◆ European Article Number (standard computer coding for retail items)

e & e *abbrev.* ◆ each and every

E & OE *abbrev.* ◆ errors and omissions excepted

eaon *abbrev.* ◆ except as otherwise noted

EAP *abbrev.* ◆ English for academic purposes

Earn *acronym* ◆ European Academic and Research Network

EAROM *acronym* ◆ electrically alterable read-only memory

EAS *abbrev.* ◆ electronic article surveillance ◆ equivalent air speed

easemt *contraction* ◆ easement

EA sh *abbrev.* ◆ East Africa shilling (monetary unit)

EAT *abbrev.* ◆ earliest arrival time ◆ estimated arrival time ◆ Tanzania (international vehicle registration; orig. East Africa Tanzania)

EAU *abbrev.* ◆ Uganda (international vehicle registration; orig. East Africa Uganda)

EAX *abbrev.* ◆ electronic automatic exchange

EB *abbrev.* ◆ Encyclopaedia Britannica ◆ epidermolysis bullosa (skin disease) ◆ Epstein-Barr (virus) ◆ Peterborough (British vehicle registration mark)

e-b *abbrev.* ◆ estate-bottled

EBB *abbrev.* ◆ Entebbe-Kampala, Uganda (airport baggage label)

Ebcdic *pronounced* eb-si-dik *acronym* ◆ extended binary coded decimal interchange code (computer code)

E-beam *contraction* ◆ electron beam

E-boat *contraction* ◆ Eilboot (German, = speedboat) (a fast German motor torpedo-boat) ◆ enemy boat

Ebor. *shortening* ◆ Eboracensis (Latin, = of York) ◆ Eboracum (Latin, = York)

EBRD *abbrev.* ◆ European Bank for Reconstruction and Development

EBS *abbrev.* ◆ emergency bed service ◆ emergency broadcast system

EBU *abbrev.* ◆ English Bridge Union ◆ European Badminton Union ◆ European Boxing Union ◆ European Broadcasting Union

EBV *abbrev.* ◆ Epstein-Barr Virus

EC *abbrev.* ◆ East Caribbean ◆ east central London (UK postcode) ◆ Ecuador (international vehicle

registration) ◆ Episcopal Church
◆ Established Church ◆ European
Community ◆ Executive Committee
◆ Preston (British vehicle registration
mark) ◆ Spain (international civil
aircraft marking)

Ec. *shortening* ◆ Ecuador

ECA *abbrev.* ◆ Economic Commission for
Africa

Ecat *acronym* ◆ emission computerized
axial tomography

ecc. *shortening* ◆ eccetera (Italian, = et
cetera)

Eccl. *shortening* ◆ Ecclesiastes (book of
Bible)

eccl. *shortening* ◆ ecclesiastical

Eccles. *shortening* ◆ Ecclesiastes (book of
Bible)

eccles. *shortening* ◆ ecclesiastical

Ecclus. *shortening* ◆ Ecclesiasticus (book
of Bible)

ECCM *abbrev.* ◆ electronic counter-
countermeasures

ECCP *abbrev.* ◆ European Committee on
Crime Problems

ECCU *abbrev.* ◆ English Cross-Country
Union

ECD *abbrev.* ◆ early closing day
◆ estimated completion date

ECd *abbrev.* ◆ East Caribbean dollar
(monetary unit)

ECDU *abbrev.* ◆ European Christian
Democratic Union

ECE *abbrev.* ◆ Economic Commission for
Europe

ECG *abbrev.* ◆ electrocardiogram
◆ electrocardiograph ◆ Export Credit
Guarantee

ECGD *abbrev.* ◆ Export Credits
Guarantee Department

ech. *shortening* ◆ echelon

ECHR *abbrev.* ◆ European Commission
on Human Rights ◆ European Court of
Human Rights

ECJ *abbrev.* ◆ European Court of Justice

ECLAC *abbrev.* ◆ Economic Commission
for Latin America and the Caribbean

ecli. *shortening* ◆ eclipse ◆ ecliptic

ECM *abbrev.* ◆ electronic
countermeasures ◆ environmental
corrosion monitor ◆ extended core
memory

ECMA *abbrev.* ◆ European Computer
Manufacturers Association

ECME *abbrev.* ◆ Economic Commission
for the Middle East

ECMWF *abbrev.* ◆ European Centre for
Medium-Range Weather Forecasting

ECO *abbrev.* ◆ English Chamber
Orchestra

eco. *shortening* ◆ ecological ◆ ecology

ECoG *abbrev.* ◆ electrocorticogram

ecol. *shortening* ◆ ecological ◆ ecology

E coli *contraction* ◆ Escherichia coli
(Latin) (sort of bacteria)

Ecom *acronym* ◆ electronic computer-
originated mail

econ. *shortening* ◆ economic ◆ economics
◆ economy

Ecosoc *acronym* ◆ United Nations
Economic and Social Council

Ecovast *acronym* ◆ European Council
for the Village and Small Town

Ecowas *acronym* ◆ Economic
Community of West African States

ECPS *abbrev.* ◆ European Centre for
Population Studies

ECR *abbrev.* ◆ electronic cash register

ECS *abbrev.* ◆ European
Communications Satellite

ECSC *abbrev.* ◆ European Coal and Steel
Community

ECST *abbrev.* ◆ European Convention on
the Suppression of Terrorism

ECT *abbrev.* ◆ electroconvulsive therapy

ECU *abbrev.* ◆ European Customs Union

Ecu *acronym* ◆ European Currency Unit

Ecua. *shortening* ◆ Ecuador
◆ Ecuadorean

Ecusa *acronym* ◆ Episcopal Church of
the United States of America

ECWA *abbrev.* ◆ Economic Commission
for Western Africa

ECY *abbrev.* ◆ European Conservation
Year

ECYO *abbrev.* ◆ European Community Youth Orchestra

ED *abbrev.* ◆ evening dinner ◆ Liverpool (British vehicle registration mark)

ed. *shortening* ◆ edited ◆ edition ◆ editor ◆ educated ◆ education

EdB *abbrev.* ◆ Bachelor of Education

EDBS *abbrev.* ◆ expert database system

EDC *abbrev.* ◆ ethylene dichloride ◆ European Defence Community ◆ expected date of confinement (childbirth)

EDD *abbrev.* ◆ English Dialect Dictionary

EdD *abbrev.* ◆ Doctor of Education

Edenburgen. *shortening* ◆ Edenburgensis (Latin, = of Edinburgh)

EDF *abbrev.* ◆ European Development Fund

EDI *abbrev.* ◆ Edinburgh (airport baggage label)

Edin. *shortening* ◆ Edinburgh

edit. *shortening* ◆ edited ◆ edition

EdM *abbrev.* ◆ Master of Education

Edm. & Ips. *shortening* ◆ Saint Edmundsbury and Ipswich (episcopal see)

edn *contraction* ◆ edition

edoc *abbrev.* ◆ effective date of change

E$ *abbrev.* ◆ Eurodollar

EDP *abbrev.* ◆ electronic data processing

EDS *abbrev.* ◆ electrically-adjusted driver's seat ◆ English Dialect Society

Edsat *acronym* ◆ educational television satellite

ED/st *abbrev.* ◆ electrically-adjusted driver's seat

EDT *abbrev.* ◆ Eastern Daylight Time (North America)

educ. *shortening* ◆ educated ◆ educational

EE *abbrev.* ◆ Early English ◆ errors excepted ◆ Lincoln (British vehicle registration mark)

EE & MP *abbrev.* ◆ Envoy Extraordinary and Minister Plenipotentiary

EEC *abbrev.* ◆ European Economic Community

EED *abbrev.* ◆ electro-explosive device

EEF *abbrev.* ◆ Engineering Employers' Federation

EEG *abbrev.* ◆ electroencephalogram ◆ electroencephalograph

EENT *abbrev.* ◆ eye, ear, nose and throat

EEO *abbrev.* ◆ Energy Efficiency Office

Eeprom *acronym* ◆ electrically erasable programmable memory (computing)

Eerom *acronym* ◆ electrically erasable read-only memory

EES *abbrev.* ◆ European Exchange System

EET *abbrev.* ◆ Eastern European Time

EETPU *abbrev.* ◆ Electrical, Electronic, Telecommunications and Plumbing Union

EETS *abbrev.* ◆ Early English Text Society

EEZ *abbrev.* ◆ exclusive economic zone

EF *abbrev.* ◆ Middlesborough (British vehicle registration mark)

EFA *abbrev.* ◆ essential fatty acids ◆ European Fighter Aircraft

EFDSS *abbrev.* ◆ English Folk Dance and Song Society

EFI *abbrev.* ◆ electronic fuel injection

EFL *abbrev.* ◆ English as a foreign language

EF/sts *contraction* ◆ electrically adjusted front seats

EFT *abbrev.* ◆ electronic funds transfer

Efta *acronym* ◆ European Free Trade Association

Eftpos *acronym* ◆ electronic funds transfer at point of sale

EFTS *abbrev.* ◆ electronic funds transfer system

EFU *abbrev.* ◆ European Football Union

efw *abbrev.* ◆ electric front windows

EG *abbrev.* ◆ equivalent grade ◆ Japan Asia Airways (airline baggage code) ◆ Peterborough (British vehicle registration mark)

Eg. *shortening* ◆ Egypt ◆ Egyptian

eg *abbrev.* ◆ exempli gratia (Latin, = for example)

EGA *abbrev.* ◆ enhanced graphics adapter

EGM *abbrev.* ◆ extraordinary general meeting

EGmbH *abbrev.* ◆ Eingetragene Gesellschaft mit beschränkter Haftung (German, = registered limited company)

EGU *abbrev.* ◆ English Golf Union

Egypt. *shortening* ◆ Egyptian

EH *abbrev.* ◆ Edinburgh (UK postcode) ◆ English horn ◆ Stoke-on-Trent (British vehicle registration mark)

EHF *abbrev.* ◆ European Hockey Federation ◆ extremely high frequency

EHO *abbrev.* ◆ Environmental Health Officer

EHP *abbrev.* ◆ effective horsepower ◆ electric horsepower

EHT *abbrev.* ◆ extra high tension

EI *abbrev.* ◆ Aer Lingus (airline baggage code) ◆ East Indian ◆ East Indies ◆ Ireland (international civil aircraft marking)

EIA *abbrev.* ◆ environmental impact assessment

EIB *abbrev.* ◆ European Investment Bank

EIC *abbrev.* ◆ East India Company

E-in-C *abbrev.* ◆ Engineer-in-Chief

E Ind. *shortening* ◆ East Indies

EJ *abbrev.* ◆ Haverfordwest (British vehicle registration mark) ◆ Ireland (international civil aircraft marking)

EIIR *abbrev.* ◆ Elizabetha Secunda Regina (Latin, = Queen Elizabeth the Second)

EIN *abbrev.* ◆ Eindhoven, Netherlands (airport baggage label)

EIS *abbrev.* ◆ Epidemic Intelligence Service

EIT *abbrev.* ◆ Eilat, Israel (airport baggage label)

EJ *abbrev.* ◆ elbow jerk

ejusd. *shortening* ◆ ejusdem (Latin, = of the same)

EK *abbrev.* ◆ East Kilbride ◆ Liverpool (British vehicle registration mark)

Ekco *acronym* ◆ E K Cole (manufacturer of electrical goods)

EL *abbrev.* ◆ Bournemouth (British vehicle registration mark) ◆ easy listening (type of music) ◆ Liberia (international civil aircraft marking)

el. *shortening* ◆ elect ◆ elected ◆ electric ◆ electricity ◆ elevation

ELA *abbrev.* ◆ Eritrean Liberation Army

elas. *shortening* ◆ elasticity

E-layer *contraction* ◆ Kennelly-Heaviside layer

eld. *shortening* ◆ elder ◆ eldest

ELDO *abbrev.* ◆ European Launcher Development Organization

elec. *shortening* ◆ electric ◆ electricity

elect. *shortening* ◆ election ◆ electric ◆ electrician ◆ electricity ◆ electronic

electron. *shortening* ◆ electronic ◆ electronics

elem. *shortening* ◆ element ◆ elementary

ELF *abbrev.* ◆ extra low frequency ◆ extremely low frequency

Elien. *shortening* ◆ Eliensis (Latin, = of Ely) (bishop's see)

Elint *pronounced* el-int *acronym* ◆ Electronic Intelligence

Eliz. *shortening* ◆ Elizabethan

ELT *abbrev.* ◆ English language teaching (to non-English speakers)

ELV *abbrev.* ◆ expendable launch vehicle

ELSS *abbrev.* ◆ emergency life support system

EM *abbrev.* ◆ electron microscope ◆ evening meal ◆ Liverpool (British vehicle registration mark)

EMA *abbrev.* ◆ European Monetary Agreement

E-mail *contraction* ◆ electronic mail

embryol. *shortening* ◆ embryological ◆ embryology

Emer. *shortening* ◆ Emeritus

emer. *shortening* ◆ emergency

EMF *abbrev.* ◆ electromotive force ◆ European Monetary Fund

EMI *abbrev.* ◆ Electrical and Musical Industries Limited (recording company)

emi *abbrev.* ◆ electromagnetic interference

EMP *abbrev.* ◆ electromagnetic pulse ◆ European Member of Parliament

Emp. *shortening* ◆ Emperor ◆ Empire ◆ Empress

emp. *shortening* ◆ employer ◆ employment ◆ employed

EMS *abbrev.* ◆ Emergency Medical Service ◆ European Monetary System ◆ expanded memory specification

EMU *abbrev.* ◆ economic and monetary union ◆ electromagnetic unit ◆ European Monetary Union

EN *abbrev.* ◆ Enfield (UK postcode) ◆ English Nature (formerly Nature Conservancy Council) ◆ Enrolled Nurse ◆ Manchester (British vehicle registration mark)

enc. *shortening* ◆ enclosed ◆ enclosure

encl. *shortening* ◆ enclosed ◆ enclosure

ency. *shortening* ◆ encyclopedia ◆ encyclopedic

encyc. *shortening* ◆ encyclopedia ◆ encyclopedic

encycl. *shortening* ◆ encyclopedia ◆ encyclopedic

ENE *abbrev.* ◆ east-north-east

ENG *abbrev.* ◆ electronic news gathering

EN(G) *abbrev.* ◆ Enrolled Nurse (General)

Eng. *shortening* ◆ England ◆ English

eng. *shortening* ◆ engineer ◆ engineering ◆ engraved ◆ engraver ◆ engraving

Eng. Tech. *shortening* ◆ Engineering Technician ◆ Engineering Technology

ENK *abbrev.* ◆ Enniskillen, Northern Ireland (airport baggage label)

enl. *shortening* ◆ enlarged ◆ enlargement

EN(M) *abbrev.* ◆ Enrolled Nurse (Mental)

ENO *abbrev.* ◆ English National Opera

ENP *abbrev.* ◆ electronic number plate

ENS *abbrev.* ◆ European Nuclear Society

Ens. *shortening* ◆ Ensign

ens. *shortening* ◆ en suite

Ensa *acronym* ◆ Entertainments National Services Association

ENT *abbrev.* ◆ ear, nose and throat

SOME CHEMICAL ELEMENTS

All the elements are listed in the dictionary. This list shows a selection of those best known to non-specialists.

Ag	silver	**Cu**	copper	**O**	oxygen
Al	aluminium	**F**	fluorine	**P**	phosphorus
Ar	argon	**Fe**	iron	**Pb**	lead
As	arsenic	**H**	hydrogen	**Po**	polonium
Au	gold	**Hg**	mercury	**Pt**	platinum
B	boron	**He**	helium	**Pu**	plutonium
Ba	barium	**I**	iodine	**Ra**	radium
Be	beryllium	**K**	potassium	**Rn**	radon
Bi	bismuth	**Kr**	krypton	**S**	sulphur
Br	bromine	**Li**	lithium	**Si**	silicon
C	carbon	**Mg**	magnesium	**Sb**	antimony
Ca	calcium	**Mn**	manganese	**Sn**	tin
Cd	cadmium	**Mo**	molybdenum	**Sr**	strontium
Cl	chlorine	**N**	nitrogen	**Ti**	titanium
Co	cobalt	**Na**	sodium	**W**	tungsten
Cr	chromium	**Ne**	neon	**U**	uranium
Cs	caesium	**Ni**	nickel	**Zn**	zinc

ent. *shortening* ◆ enter (stage direction)
◆ entertainment ◆ entomological
◆ entomology ◆ entrance

entom. *shortening* ◆ entomological
◆ entomology

Ent. Sta. Hall *shortening* ◆ Entered at
Stationers' Hall (former copyright
statement)

env. *shortening* ◆ envelope

Env. Ext. *shortening* ◆ Envoy
Extraordinary

eps *abbrev.* ◆ earnings per share

EO *abbrev.* ◆ Education Officer ◆ Equal
Opportunities ◆ Executive Officer
◆ Preston (British vehicle registration
mark)

eo *abbrev.* ◆ ex officio (Latin, = by right
of office)

EOA *abbrev.* ◆ examination, opinion and
advice

EOC *abbrev.* ◆ Equal Opportunities
Commission

Eoc. *shortening* ◆ Eocene

eod *abbrev.* ◆ every other day

EOF *abbrev.* ◆ end of file

eohp *abbrev.* ◆ except otherwise herein
provided

Eoka *pronounced* ay-oh-ka *acronym*
◆ Ethnike Organosis Kypriakou
Agonos (Greek, = National
Organization of the Cypriot Struggle)
(Greek Cypriot guerrilla force, 1955–9)

EOL *abbrev.* ◆ end of life

EORTC *abbrev.* ◆ European Organization
for Research into the Treatment of
Cancer

EP *abbrev.* ◆ electroplated ◆ European
Parliament ◆ extended play (record)
◆ Iran (international civil aircraft
marking) ◆ Swansea (British vehicle
registration mark)

ep *abbrev.* ◆ en passant (French, = while
passing) (chess)

ep. *shortening* ◆ epistle

EPA *abbrev.* ◆ Emergency Powers Act
◆ Employment Protection Act
◆ Environmental Protection Agency
(USA) ◆ European Productivity Agency

EPDA *abbrev.* ◆ Emergency Powers
Defence Act

EPG *abbrev.* ◆ Eminent Persons' Group

Eph. *shortening* ◆ Ephesians (book of
Bible)

epil. *shortening* ◆ epilogue

Epiph. *shortening* ◆ Epiphany

epis. *shortening* ◆ episcopal ◆ epistle

episc. *shortening* ◆ episcopal

epit. *shortening* ◆ epitaph ◆ epitome

EPNS *abbrev.* ◆ electroplated nickel
silver ◆ English Place-Name Society

Epoch *acronym* ◆ End Physical
Punishment of Children

Epos *acronym* ◆ electronic point of sale

EPP *abbrev.* ◆ European People's Party

Eprom *pronounced* ee-prom *acronym*
◆ erasable programmable memory ◆ a
chip with Eprom

eps *abbrev.* ◆ earnings per share
◆ electrically-positioned seats

EPT *abbrev.* ◆ Environmental Protection
Technology

EPU *abbrev.* ◆ European Payments
Union

eq. *shortening* ◆ equal ◆ equation
◆ equator ◆ equerry ◆ equity
◆ equivalent

eqn *contraction* ◆ equation

eqn. *shortening* ◆ equine

equil. *shortening* ◆ equilibrium

ER *abbrev.* ◆ Eastern Region ◆ East
Riding (former division of Yorkshire)
◆ Edwardus Rex (Latin, = King
Edward) ◆ Elizabetha Regina (Latin, =
Queen Elizabeth) ◆ Peterborough
(British vehicle registration mark)

Er *symbol* ◆ erbium (chemical element)

ERA *abbrev.* ◆ Education Reform Act
◆ Equal Rights Amendment (US)

Erasmus *acronym* ◆ European
Community Action Scheme for the
Mobility of University Students

ERB *abbrev.* ◆ electric roller blind

E-region *contraction* ◆ Kennelly-
Heaviside layer

ERBM *abbrev.* ◆ extended-range ballistic missile

ERF *abbrev.* ◆ Erfurt, Germany (airport baggage label)

ergon. *shortening* ◆ ergonomic ◆ ergonomics

ERI *abbrev.* ◆ Edwardus Rex Imperator (Latin, = Edward, King and Emperor)

Erit. *shortening* ◆ Eritrea

ERM *abbrev.* ◆ exchange rate mechanism

Ernie *acronym* ◆ electronic random number indicator equipment (to draw winning premium bonds)

Erom *pronounced* ee-rom *acronym* ◆ erasable read only memory

erron. *shortening* ◆ erroneous ◆ erroneously

ERU *abbrev.* ◆ English Rugby Union

ERZ *abbrev.* ◆ Erzurum, Turkey (airport baggage label)

ES *abbrev.* ◆ Dudley (British vehicle registration mark) ◆ El Salvador (international vehicle registration)

ES *abbrev.* ◆ en suite

Es *symbol* ◆ einsteinium (chemical element)

e/s *abbrev.* ◆ en suite

ESA *abbrev.* ◆ Environmentally Sensitive Area ◆ European Space Agency

ESB *abbrev.* ◆ Ankara (airport baggage label) ◆ electrical stimulation of the brain

ESC *abbrev.* ◆ electric seat control

Esc. *shortening* ◆ escudo (monetary unit)

esc. *shortening* ◆ escape (computer key)

ESCA *abbrev.* ◆ electronic spectroscopy for chemical analysis

ESCB *abbrev.* ◆ European System of Central Banks

Esd. *shortening* ◆ Esdras (books of Bible)

ESE *abbrev.* ◆ east-south-east

ESI *abbrev.* ◆ electricity supply industry

ESL *abbrev.* ◆ English as a second language

ESN *abbrev.* ◆ educationally subnormal

Esol *pronounced* ee-sol *acronym* ◆ English for speakers of other languages

ESOP *abbrev.* ◆ employee share ownership plan

ESP *abbrev.* ◆ English for special purposes ◆ English for specific purposes ◆ extrasensory perception

esp. *shortening* ◆ especially ◆ espressivo (Italian, = expressive) (music)

espec. *shortening* ◆ especially

Esprit *acronym* ◆ European Strategic Programme of Research into Information Technology

Esq. *shortening* ◆ Esquire

Esqr. *shortening* ◆ Esquire

ESR *abbrev.* ◆ electric sun roof

ESRC *abbrev.* ◆ Economic and Social Research Council

Esro *acronym* ◆ European Space Research Organization

ESS *abbrev.* ◆ evolutionarily stable strategy

Ess. *shortening* ◆ Essex

ess. *shortening* ◆ essence ◆ essential

Esso *acronym* ◆ Standard Oil (from the initals SO)

EST *abbrev.* ◆ earliest start time ◆ Eastern Standard Time (USA and Canada) ◆ electric shock treatment

est. *shortening* ◆ established ◆ estate ◆ estimated ◆ estuary

estab. *shortening* ◆ established

Estec *acronym* ◆ European Space Technology Centre

Esth. *shortening* ◆ Esther (book of Bible)

ESU *abbrev.* ◆ English-Speaking Union

esu *abbrev.* ◆ electrostatic unit

ESV *abbrev.* ◆ earth satellite vehicle ◆ emergency shut-down valve

ET *abbrev.* ◆ Arab Republic of Egypt (international vehicle registration; orig. Egypt) ◆ Eastern Time ◆ educational therapy ◆ embryo transfer ◆ Employment Trainee ◆ Employment Training ◆ English text ◆ English translation ◆ ephemeris time ◆ Ethiopia (international civil aircraft marking) ◆ Ethiopian Airlines (airline baggage code) ◆ extraterrestrial ◆ Sheffield (British vehicle registration mark)

ETA *abbrev.* ◆ Entertainment Trades' Alliance ◆ estimated time of arrival

Eta *pronounced* et-uh *acronym* ◆ Euzkadi ta Askatasuna (Basque, = Nation and Liberty) (a militant Basque separatist organization)

et al. *shortening* ◆ et alibi (Latin, = and elsewhere) ◆ et alii (Latin, = and others)

ETB *abbrev.* ◆ English Tourist Board

etc. *shortening* ◆ et cetera (Latin, = and the rest)

ETD *abbrev.* ◆ estimated time of departure

ETF *abbrev.* ◆ electronic transfer of funds

ETH *abbrev.* ◆ Eilat, Israel (airport baggage label) ◆ Ethiopia (international vehicle registration)

Eth. *shortening* ◆ Ethiopia ◆ Ethiopian ◆ Ethiopic

eth. *shortening* ◆ ether ◆ ethical ◆ ethics

ethnog. *shortening* ◆ ethnographical ◆ ethnography

ethnol. *shortening* ◆ ethnological ◆ ethnology

Etr. *shortening* ◆ Etruscan

et seq. *shortening* ◆ et sequens (Latin, = and the following)

ETTA *abbrev.* ◆ English Table Tennis Association

ETTU *abbrev.* ◆ European Table Tennis Union

ETU *abbrev.* ◆ Electrical Trades Union

ETUC *abbrev.* ◆ European Trade Union Confederation

etym. *shortening* ◆ etymological ◆ etmology

etymol. *shortening* ◆ etymological ◆ etmology

EU *abbrev.* ◆ Bristol (British vehicle registration mark) ◆ Evangelical Union ◆ European Union

Eu *symbol* ◆ Euler unit ◆ europium (chemical element)

euph. *shortening* ◆ euphemism ◆ euphemistic ◆ euphemistically

Eur. *shortening* ◆ Europe ◆ European

Euratom *acronym* ◆ European Atomic Energy Community

EuroJazz *contraction* ◆ European Community Youth Jazz Orchestra

EUW *abbrev.* ◆ European Union of Women

EV *abbrev.* ◆ Chelmsford (British vehicle registration mark) ◆ English Version (of the Bible)

eV *abbrev.* ◆ electron-volt

EVA *abbrev.* ◆ extravehicular activity (astronautics)

evac. *shortening* ◆ evacuate ◆ evacuation

eval. *shortening* ◆ evaluate ◆ evaluation

evan. *shortening* ◆ evangelical

evang. *shortening* ◆ evangelical

evap. *shortening* ◆ evaporate ◆ evaporation

evg *contraction* ◆ evening

EVR *abbrev.* ◆ electronic video recording and reproduction

EW *abbrev.* ◆ early warning ◆ electronic warfare ◆ Estonia (international vehicle registration) ◆ Peterborough (British vehicle registration mark)

ew *abbrev.* ◆ each way (betting) ◆ electric windows

EWO *abbrev.* ◆ European Women's Orchestra

EWR *abbrev.* ◆ Newark, New Jersey (airport baggage label)

EX *abbrev.* ◆ Emirates Airlines (airline baggage code) ◆ Exeter (UK postcode) ◆ Norwich (British vehicle registration mark)

Ex. *shortening* ◆ Exodus (book of Bible)

ex. *shortening* ◆ examination ◆ examined ◆ example ◆ excellent ◆ except ◆ excepted ◆ exception ◆ excess ◆ exchange ◆ excluding ◆ exclusive (of tax etc) ◆ excursion ◆ excursus ◆ executed ◆ executive ◆ export ◆ express ◆ extended ◆ extra

exag. *shortening* ◆ exaggerated

ex aq. *shortening* ◆ ex aqua (Latin, = from water)

ex b *abbrev.* ◆ ex bonus (without bonus)

Exc. *shortening* ◆ Excellency

exc. *shortening* ◆ excellent ◆ except ◆ exception ◆ excudit (Latin, = engraved it) ◆ excursion

ex cap. *shortening* ◆ ex capitalization (without capitalization)

exch. *shortening* ◆ exchange ◆ exchequer

excel. *shortening* ◆ excellent

excl. *shortening* ◆ exclamation ◆ excluding ◆ exclusive

ex cp *shortening* ◆ ex coupon (without interest on the coupon)

excptly *contraction* ◆ exceptionally

ex div. *shortening* ◆ ex dividend (without dividend)

exec. *shortening* ◆ execute ◆ executive ◆ executor

exes *contraction* ◆ expenses

ex. gr. *shortening* ◆ exempli gratia (Latin, = for example)

ex int. *shortening* ◆ ex interest (without interest)

ex lib. *shortening* ◆ ex libris (Latin, = from the books (of))

ex n *abbrev.* ◆ ex new (excluding new shares)

Exod. *shortening* ◆ Exodus (book of Bible)

ex off. *shortening* ◆ ex officio (Latin, = by right of office)

Exon. *shortening* ◆ Exonia (Latin, = Exeter) ◆ Exoniensis (Latin, = of Exeter)

exor *contraction* ◆ executor

ex p *abbrev.* ◆ ex parte (Latin, = in the interests of one party) (to a lawsuit)

exp. *shortening* ◆ expense ◆ experience ◆ experiment ◆ expired ◆ exponential ◆ export ◆ exporter ◆ exposed ◆ express ◆ expurgated

expl. *shortening* ◆ explanation ◆ explosion

exr *contraction* ◆ executor

exrx *contraction* ◆ executrix

exs *contraction* ◆ expenses

EXT *abbrev.* ◆ Exeter (airport baggage label)

ext. *shortening* ◆ extension ◆ extent ◆ exterior ◆ external ◆ externally ◆ extinct ◆ extra ◆ extract ◆ extraction ◆ extreme

exten. *shortening* ◆ extension

extr. *shortening* ◆ extraordinary

EXW *abbrev.* ◆ ex works

exx *contraction* ◆ executrix

EY *abbrev.* ◆ Bangor (British vehicle registration mark)

EYW *abbrev.* ◆ Key West, Florida (airport baggage label)

EZ *abbrev.* ◆ Belfast (British vehicle registration mark)

Ez. *shortening* ◆ Ezra (book of Bible)

Ezek. *shortening* ◆ Ezekiel (book of Bible)

Ezr. *shortening* ◆ Ezra (book of Bible)

F

F *abbrev.* ✦ Fahrenheit ✦ fail ✦ false ✦ farad ✦ fast ✦ Fellow ✦ fighter plane (US; as in *F-111* etc) ✦ fine (pencil) ✦ forte (Italian, = loud) (music) ✦ franc (monetary unit) ✦ France (international vehicle registration) ✦ France (international civil aircraft marking) ✦ Friday

F *symbol* ✦ fluorine (chemical element)

f *abbrev.* ✦ facing ✦ fair ✦ farthing (former UK monetary unit) ✦ fathom ✦ female ✦ feminine ✦ femto- ✦ firm (horse-racing) ✦ focal length ✦ fog ✦ folio ✦ following ✦ foot ✦ formula ✦ forte (Italian, = loud) (music) ✦ foul ✦ front ✦ function ✦ furlong ✦ furnished ✦ guilder (Netherlands monetary unit)

FA *abbrev.* ✦ Faculty of Actuaries ✦ Family Allowance ✦ field artillery ✦ Finnaviation (airline baggage code) ✦ Football Association ✦ fuck all ✦ Stoke-on-Trent (British vehicle registration mark)

FAA *abbrev.* ✦ Federal Aviation Administration ✦ Fleet Air Arm

fac. *shortening* ✦ façade ✦ facility ✦ facsimile ✦ faculty

Face *acronym* ✦ Fight Against Cuts in Education

facet. *shortening* ✦ facetious

facil. *shortening* ✦ facility

facs. *shortening* ✦ facsimile

FADO *abbrev.* ✦ Fellow of the Association of Dispensing Opticians

Fahr. *shortening* ✦ Fahrenheit

FAI *abbrev.* ✦ Fairbanks, Alaska (airport baggage label)

Falk. Is. *shortening* ✦ Falkland Islands

FAM *abbrev.* ✦ Free and Accepted Masons

fam. *shortening* ✦ familiar ✦ family

f & a *abbrev.* ✦ fore and aft

f & f *abbrev.* ✦ fixtures and fittings

F & M *abbrev.* ✦ foot and mouth

F & T *abbrev.* ✦ fire and theft

Fany *acronym* ✦ First Aid Nursing Yeomanry

FAO *abbrev.* ✦ Food and Agriculture Organization (UN)

fao *abbrev.* ✦ for attention of

FAR *abbrev.* ✦ front arm rests

far. *shortening* ✦ farriery ✦ farthing (former UK monetary unit)

FAS *abbrev.* ✦ Fellow of the Anthropological Society ✦ Fellow of the Antiquarian Society ✦ Fellow of the Society of Arts ✦ fetal alcohol syndrome ✦ free alongside ship

fasc. *shortening* ✦ fascicule

fav. *shortening* ✦ favourite

FB *abbrev.* ✦ Bristol (British vehicle registration mark) ✦ Fenian Brotherhood ✦ fire brigade ✦ Free Baptist

fb *abbrev.* ✦ freight bill ✦ full back

FBA *abbrev.* ✦ Fellow of the British Academy

FBAA *abbrev.* ✦ Fellow of the British Association of Accountants and Auditors

f'ball *contraction* ✦ football

FBCM *abbrev.* ✦ Federation of British Carpet Manufacturers

FBCS *abbrev.* ✦ Fellow of the British Computer Society

FBCO *abbrev.* ✦ Fellow of the British College of Ophthalmic Opticians

FBCS *abbrev.* ◆ Fellow of the British Computer Society

fbd *contraction* ◆ freeboard

FBI *abbrev.* ◆ Federal Bureau of Investigation ◆ Federation of British Industries

FBIBA *abbrev.* ◆ Fellow of the British Insurance Brokers' Association

FBIM *abbrev.* ◆ Fellow of the British Institute of Management

FBM *abbrev.* ◆ fleet ballistic missile ◆ Lubumbashi (airport baggage label)

FBOA *abbrev.* ◆ Fellow of the British Optical Association

FBR *abbrev.* ◆ fast-breeder reactor

FBU *abbrev.* ◆ Oslo (airport baggage label)

FBW *abbrev.* ◆ fly by wire

FC *abbrev.* ◆ Fighter Command ◆ football club ◆ Forestry Commission ◆ Free Church ◆ Oxford (British vehicle registration mark)

fc *abbrev.* ◆ follow copy ◆ fixed charge ◆ for cash

FCA *abbrev.* ◆ Fellow of the Institute of Chartered Accountants

fcap *contraction* ◆ foolscap

FCCA *abbrev.* ◆ Fellow of the Chartered Association of Certified Accountants

FCFC *abbrev.* ◆ Free Church Federal Council

fcg *contraction* ◆ facing

FCGI *abbrev.* ◆ Fellow of the City and Guilds of London Institute

fch *abbrev.* ◆ full central heating

FCIA *abbrev.* ◆ Fellow of the Corporation of Insurance Agents

FCIArb *abbrev.* ◆ Fellow of the Chartered Institute of Arbitrators

FCIB *abbrev.* ◆ Fellow of the Chartered Institute of Bankers

FCII *abbrev.* ◆ Fellow of the Chartered Insurance Institute

FCIMA *abbrev.* ◆ Fellow of the Chartered Institute of Management Accountants

FCMA *abbrev.* ◆ Fellow of the Institute of Cost and Management Accountants

fcng *contraction* ◆ facing

FCO *abbrev.* ◆ Foreign and Commonwealth Office

FCP *abbrev.* ◆ Fellow of the College of Preceptors

fcp *contraction* ◆ foolscap

FCS *abbrev.* ◆ Federation of Conservative Students

FCSA *abbrev.* ◆ Fellow of the Institute of Chartered Secretaries and Administrators

FCSD *abbrev.* ◆ Fellow of the Chartered Society of Designers

FCSP *abbrev.* ◆ Fellow of the Chartered Society of Physiotherapy

FCST *abbrev.* ◆ Fellow of the College of Speech Therapists

FCT *abbrev.* ◆ Fellow of the Association of Corporate Treasurers

FD *abbrev.* ◆ Dudley (British vehicle registration mark) ◆ Fidei Defensor (Latin, = Defender of the Faith) ◆ Financial Director

fd *abbrev.* ◆ flight deck ◆ focal distance ◆ free delivery ◆ free discharge ◆ free dispatch

fd *contraction* ◆ field ◆ fiord ◆ ford ◆ forward ◆ found ◆ founded ◆ fund

FDA *abbrev.* ◆ Food and Drugs Administration (US) ◆ First Division Association (union for senior civil servants)

FDC *abbrev.* ◆ first-day cover ◆ fleur de coin (French, = excellent impression) (numismatics; of coin in mint condition)

FDF *abbrev.* ◆ Fort de France, Martinique (airport baggage label) ◆ Food and Drink Federation

fdg *contraction* ◆ funding

FDR *abbrev.* ◆ Freie Demokratische Republik (German, = Free Democratic Republic) (the former West Germany)

fdr *contraction* ◆ founder

fdry *contraction* ◆ foundry

FDS *abbrev.* ◆ Fellow in Dental Surgery

FDSRCPS *abbrev.* ◆ Fellow in Dental Surgery of the Royal College of Physicians and Surgeons

FDSRCS *abbrev.* ◆ Fellow in Dental Surgery of the Royal College of Surgeons

FE *abbrev.* ◆ further education ◆ Lincoln (British vehicle registration mark)

Fe *symbol* ◆ ferrum (Latin, = iron) (chemical element)

fe *abbrev.* ◆ first edition

Feb. *shortening* ◆ February

fec. *shortening* ◆ fecit (Latin, = made it)

Fed. *shortening* ◆ Federal Reserve Board (US)

fed. *shortening* ◆ federal ◆ federated ◆ federation

FEDC *abbrev.* ◆ Federation of Engineering Design Consultants

FEI *abbrev.* ◆ Fédération Équestre Internationale (French, = International Equestrian Federation)

fem. *shortening* ◆ female ◆ feminine

Ferm. *shortening* ◆ Fermanagh

FES *abbrev.* ◆ Federation of Engineering Societies ◆ Fellow of the Entomological Society ◆ Fellow of the Ethnological Society ◆ foil, épée and sabre (fencing)

fest. *shortening* ◆ festival

FET *abbrev.* ◆ field-effect transistor

feud. *shortening* ◆ feudal

FEZ *abbrev.* ◆ Fez (airport baggage label)

FF *abbrev.* ◆ Bangor (British vehicle registration mark) ◆ Fianna Fáil (Gaelic, = Warriors of Ireland) (Irish political party) ◆ French franc (monetary unit)

ff *abbrev.* ◆ factory fitted ◆ fecerunt (Latin, = made it) ◆ fixed focus ◆ fortissimo (Italian, = very loud) (music) ◆ fully fashioned ◆ fully furnished ◆ fully fitted

FFA *abbrev.* ◆ Fellow of the Faculty of Actuaries

FFB *abbrev.* ◆ Fellow of the Faculty of Building

fff *abbrev.* ◆ fortississimo (Italian, = as loud as possible) (music)

FFHC *abbrev.* ◆ Freedom from Hunger Campaign

FFHom *abbrev.* ◆ Fellow of the Faculty of Homoeopathy

FFPS *abbrev.* ◆ Fellow of the Faculty of Physicians and Surgeons

FFR *abbrev.* ◆ Fellow of the Faculty of Radiologists

f/furn. *shortening* ◆ fully furnished

FG *abbrev.* ◆ Brighton (British vehicle registration mark) ◆ Federal Government ◆ Fine Gael (Gaelic, = Tribe of the Gaels) (Irish political party) ◆ fine grain ◆ full gilt

fg *abbrev.* ◆ fully good

FGCM *abbrev.* ◆ Field General Court Martial

FGO *abbrev.* ◆ Fleet Gunnery Officer

FGS *abbrev.* ◆ Fellow of the Geological Society

FGSM *abbrev.* ◆ Fellow of the Guildhall School of Music and Drama

FH *abbrev.* ◆ fire hydrant ◆ Gloucester (British vehicle registration mark)

f/h *abbrev.* ◆ fly half ◆ foghorn ◆ freehold

FHH *abbrev.* ◆ fetal heart heard

fhld *contraction* ◆ freehold

FHNH *abbrev.* ◆ fetal heart not heard

f/hold *contraction* ◆ freehold

fhp *abbrev.* ◆ friction horsepower

FHR *abbrev.* ◆ Federal House of Representatives ◆ fetal heart rate

FHS *abbrev.* ◆ Fellow of the Heraldry Society

FI *abbrev.* ◆ Faeroe Islands ◆ Falkland Islands ◆ Fiji Islands ◆ Finland (international vehicle registration) ◆ fire insurance ◆ Flugfelag-Icelandair (airline baggage code)

FIA *abbrev.* ◆ Fellow of the Institute of Actuaries

Fiat *acronym* ◆ Fabbrica Italiana Automobili Torino (Italian, = Italian Motor Works, Turin)

FIB *abbrev.* ◆ Fellow of the Institute of Bankers

fib. *shortening* ◆ fibula

FIBP *abbrev.* ◆ Fellow of the Institute of British Photographers

FICE *abbrev.* ◆ Fellow of the Institute of Civil Engineers

FICSA *abbrev.* ◆ Federation of International Civil Servants' Associations

fict. *shortening* ◆ fiction ◆ fictitious

FID *abbrev.* ◆ Falkland Island Dependencies ◆ Fellow of the Institute of Directors ◆ Field Intelligence Department

fid. *shortening* ◆ fiduciary

Fid. Def. *shortening* ◆ Fidei Defensor (Latin, = Defender of the Faith)

FIEE *abbrev.* ◆ Fellow of the Institute of Electrical Engineers

fi. fa. *shortening* ◆ fieri facias (Latin, = see that it is done) (sort of writ)

Fifa *acronym* ◆ Fédération Internationale de Football Association (French, = International Association Football Federation)

Fifo *acronym* ◆ first in, first out

FIFST *abbrev.* ◆ Fellow of the Institute of Food Science and Technology

fig. *shortening* ◆ figurative ◆ figure

FIGasE *abbrev.* ◆ Fellow of the Institution of Gas Engineers

FIH *abbrev.* ◆ Kinshasa (airport baggage label)

fil. *shortening* ◆ filament ◆ fillet ◆ filter ◆ filtrate

FIL *abbrev.* ◆ Fellow of the Institute of Linguists

Filo *acronym* ◆ first in, last out

FIMarE *abbrev.* ◆ Fellow of the Institute of Marine Engineers

Fimbra *acronym* ◆ Financial Intermediaries, Managers and Brokers Regulatory Association

FIMC *abbrev.* ◆ Fellow of the Institute of Management Consultants

FIMechE *abbrev.* ◆ Fellow of the Institution of Mechanical Engineers

FIMinE *abbrev.* ◆ Fellow of the Institute of Mining Engineers

FIMIT *abbrev.* ◆ Fellow of the Institute of Musical Instrument Technology

Fin. *shortening* ◆ Finistère ◆ Finland ◆ Finnish

fin. *shortening* ◆ ad finem (Latin, = towards the end) ◆ final ◆ finance

Fina *acronym* ◆ Fédération Internationale de Natation Amateur (French, = International Amateur Swimming Association)

Findus *acronym* ◆ Fruit Industries Ltd

Finn. *shortening* ◆ Finnish

Finnair *acronym* ◆ Finnish Airlines

fin. sec. *shortening* ◆ Financial Secretary

FInstP *abbrev.* ◆ Fellow of the Institute of Physics

fio *abbrev.* ◆ for information only

FIPA *abbrev.* ◆ Fellow of the Institute of Practitioners in Advertising

FIPM *abbrev.* ◆ Fellow of the Institute of Personnel Management

FIQS *abbrev.* ◆ Fellow of the Institute of Quantity Surveyors

FIR *abbrev.* ◆ fuel indicator reading

fir. *shortening* ◆ firkin

FIS *abbrev.* ◆ Family Income Supplement ◆ Fédération Internationale de Ski (French, = International Ski Federation) ◆ Fellow of the Institute of Statisticians

fis *abbrev.* ◆ flight information service

FISA *abbrev.* ◆ Fellow of the Incorporated Secretaries Association

Fisa *acronym* ◆ Fédération Internationale de Sport Automobile (French, = International Automobile Sports Federation) ◆ Finance Industry Standards Association

FIST *abbrev.* ◆ Fellow of the Institute of Science Technology

FIStructE *abbrev.* ◆ Fellow of the Institution of Structural Engineers

FISVA *abbrev.* ◆ Fellow of the Incorporated Society of Valuers and Auctioneers

FIUO *abbrev.* ◆ for internal use only

fixt. *shortening* ◆ fixtures

FJ *abbrev.* ◆ Air Pacific (airline baggage code) ◆ Exeter (British vehicle registration mark)

FJI *abbrev.* ◆ Fellow of the Institute of Journalists ◆ Fiji (international vehicle registration)

FK *abbrev.* ◆ Dudley (British vehicle registration mark) ◆ Falkirk (UK postcode)

fk *contraction* ◆ fork

FKC *abbrev.* ◆ Fellow of King's College, London

Fkr *abbrev.* ◆ Faroese krone (monetary unit)

FL *abbrev.* ◆ Flag Lieutenant ◆ Flight Lieutenant ◆ Florida (US postcode) ◆ Liechtenstein (international vehicle registration) ◆ Peterborough (British vehicle registration mark)

Fl. *shortening* ◆ Flanders ◆ Flemish

fl *abbrev.* ◆ falsa lectio (Latin, = erroneous reading) (textual criticism)

fl. *shortening* ◆ floor ◆ florin (monetary unit) ◆ floruit (Latin, = flourished) ◆ fluid

FLA *abbrev.* ◆ Fellow of the Library Association ◆ Future Large Aircraft (EC large military transport plane design project)

Fla *contraction* ◆ Florida

flag. *shortening* ◆ flageolet

fld *contraction* ◆ failed ◆ field ◆ fluid

fldg *contraction* ◆ folding

Flem. *shortening* ◆ Flemish

flex. *shortening* ◆ flexible

flg *contraction* ◆ flooring ◆ flying ◆ following

Flli *contraction* ◆ Fratelli (Italian, = Brothers)

FLN *abbrev.* ◆ Front de Libération Nationale (French, = National Liberation Front) (Algerian nationalist guerillas)

flor. *shortening* ◆ florin (monetary unit) ◆ floruit (Latin, = flourished)

FLQ *abbrev.* ◆ Front de Libération du Québec (French, = Quebec Liberation Front) (Francophone separatist group)

FLR *abbrev.* ◆ Florence (airport baggage label)

flr *contraction* ◆ failure ◆ floor

FLS *abbrev.* ◆ Fellow of the Linnean Society

flt *contraction* ◆ flat ◆ flight

Flt Cmdr *contraction* ◆ Flight Commander

fltg *contraction* ◆ floating

Flt Lt *contraction* ◆ Flight Lieutenant

Flt Off. *shortening* ◆ Flight Officer

Flt Sgt *contraction* ◆ Flight Sergeant

fluc. *shortening* ◆ fluctuation

fluor. *shortening* ◆ fluorescent ◆ fluoridation ◆ fluoride ◆ fluorspar

FM *abbrev.* ◆ Chester (British vehicle registration mark) ◆ Field Marshal ◆ frequency modulation

Fm *symbol* ◆ fermium (chemical element)

fm *abbrev.* ◆ fiat mistura (Latin, = let a mixture be made)

fm *contraction* ◆ farm ◆ fathom

FMCGs *abbrev.* ◆ fast-moving consumer goods

FMD *abbrev.* ◆ foot and mouth disease

fmd *contraction* ◆ formed

FMDV *abbrev.* ◆ foot and mouth disease virus

FMF *abbrev.* ◆ fetal movements felt

FMG *abbrev.* ◆ Malagasy franc (monetary unit)

Fmk *contraction* ◆ Finnish markka (monetary unit)

fml *contraction* ◆ formal

FMLN *abbrev.* ◆ Farabundo Martí Liberación Nacional (Spanish, = Farabundo Marti National Liberation Front) (El Salvador guerilla movement)

FMO *abbrev.* ◆ Fleet Medical Officer ◆ Flight Medical Officer

fmr *contraction* ◆ former

fmrly *contraction* ◆ formerly

FMS *abbrev.* ◆ Fellow of the Medical Society ◆ flexible manufacturing system ◆ flight management system

FN *abbrev.* ◆ Maidstone (British vehicle registration mark)

fn. *shortening* ◆ footnote

FNA *abbrev.* ◆ Freetown, Sierra Leone (airport baggage label)

fna *abbrev.* ◆ for necessary action

FNC *abbrev.* ◆ Funchal, Madeira Islands (airport baggage label)

fnd *contraction* ◆ found ◆ foundation ◆ foundered

fndry *contraction* ◆ foundry

FNJ *abbrev.* ◆ Feng Yang-Pyongyang, North Korea (airport baggage label)

FNLA *abbrev.* ◆ Frente Nacional de Libertação de Angola (Portuguese, = National Front for the Liberation of Angola)

FNO *abbrev.* ◆ Fleet Navigation Officer

FO *abbrev.* ◆ Field Officer ◆ Flag Officer ◆ Flying Officer ◆ Foreign Office ◆ formal offer ◆ Full Organ ◆ Gloucester (British vehicle registration mark)

fo *contraction* ◆ folio

FOB *abbrev.* ◆ faecal occult blood

FOBS *abbrev.* ◆ fractional-orbit bombardment system

FOC *abbrev.* ◆ father of the chapel

foc *abbrev.* ◆ free of charge ◆ free of claims

FoE *abbrev.* ◆ Friends of the Earth

FOFA *abbrev.* ◆ follow-on forces' attack

FOH *abbrev.* ◆ front of house (theatre)

FOI *abbrev.* ◆ Freedom of Information

FOIC *abbrev.* ◆ Flag Officer in Charge

fol. *shortening* ◆ folio ◆ followed ◆ following

FOP *abbrev.* ◆ forward observation post

for. *shortening* ◆ foreign ◆ forestry

Forest *acronym* ◆ Freedom Organization for the Right to Enjoy Smoking Tobacco

Forex *acronym* ◆ foreign exchange

fort. *shortening* ◆ fortification ◆ fortified

Fortran *acronym* ◆ Formula Translation (computer language)

forz. *shortening* ◆ forzando (Italian, = forcing) (music)

fos *abbrev.* ◆ free on ship ◆ free on station

Fosdic *acronym* ◆ film optical sensing device (computer input)

fot *abbrev.* ◆ free of tax

Fox *acronym* ◆ Futures and Options Exchange

FP *abbrev.* ◆ fine paper ◆ fireplug ◆ former pupil ◆ Free Presbyterian ◆ Leicester (British vehicle registration mark)

fp *abbrev.* ◆ fiat pilula (Latin, = let a pill be made) ◆ fiat potio (Latin, = let a drink be made) ◆ fine paper ◆ fireplace ◆ fixed price ◆ footpath ◆ foot-pound ◆ fortepiano (Italian, = loud, soft) (music) ◆ fortepiano (instrument) ◆ freezing point ◆ frontispiece ◆ fully paid

FPA *abbrev.* ◆ Family Planning Association

fpb *abbrev.* ◆ fast patrol boat

FPC *abbrev.* ◆ Family Practitioner Committee

fpc *abbrev.* ◆ family planning clinic ◆ for private circulation

fpm *abbrev.* ◆ feet per minute

FPO *abbrev.* ◆ field post office ◆ Freeport, Bahamas (airport baggage label)

FPS *abbrev.* ◆ Fellow of the Pharmaceutical Society

fps *abbrev.* ◆ feet per second ◆ foot-pound-second ◆ frames per second (cinematography)

FR *abbrev.* ◆ Faeroe Islands (international vehicle registration) ◆ Preston (British vehicle registration mark)

Fr *contraction* ◆ Father ◆ Friar

Fr *symbol* ◆ francium (chemical element)

Fr. *shortening* ◆ France ◆ French ◆ Friday

fr *shortening* ◆ franc (monetary unit)

fr. *shortening* ◆ fragment ◆ frequently ◆ from

FRA *abbrev.* ◆ Frankfurt (airport baggage label)

FRAD *abbrev.* ◆ Fellow of the Royal Academy of Dancing

FRAeS *abbrev.* ◆ Fellow of the Royal Aeronautical Society

FRAI *abbrev.* ◆ Fellow of the Royal Anthropological Institute

FRAM *abbrev.* ◆ Fellow of the Royal Academy of Music

Frame *acronym* ◆ Fund for the Replacement of Animals in Medical Experiments

Franc. *shortening* ◆ Franciscan

Frank. *shortening* ◆ Frankish

FRAS *abbrev.* ◆ Fellow of the Royal Asiatic Society ◆ Fellow of the Royal Astronomical Society

frat. *shortening* ◆ fraternize ◆ fraternity

fraud. *shortening* ◆ fraudulent

FRB *abbrev.* ◆ Federal Reserve Bank (US)

FRBS *abbrev.* ◆ Fellow of the Royal Botanic Society ◆ Fellow of the Royal Society of British Sculptors

FRCA *abbrev.* ◆ Fellow of the Royal College of Art

Fr.-Can. *shortening* ◆ French-Canadian

FRCGP *abbrev.* ◆ Fellow of the Royal College of General Practitioners

FRCM *abbrev.* ◆ Fellow of the Royal College of Music

FRCO *abbrev.* ◆ Fellow of the Royal College of Organists

FOOD ADDITIVES

Many additives are used in food manufacture as preservatives or to improve colour or flavour. The list below gives some of the most commonly used, together with the EC code numbers by which they are identified on ingredient lists.

E102 *tartrazine (colourant)*
E104 *quinoline yellow (colourant)*
E120 *cochineal (colourant)*
E123 *amaranth (colourant)*
E127 *erythrosine (colourant)*
E132 *indigo carmine (colourant)*
E150 *caramel colour (colourant)*
E160(b) *annatto, bixin, norbixin (colourants)*
E210 *benzoic acid (preservative)*
E211 *sodium benzoate (preservative)*
E212 *potassium benzoate (preservative)*
E214 *ethyl 4-hydroxybenzoate (preservative)*
E218 *methyl 4-hydroxybenzoate (preservative)*
E220 *sulphur dioxide (preservative)*
E221 *sodium sulphite (preservative)*
E222 *sodium hydrogen sulphite (preservative)*
E223 *sodium metabisulphite (preservative)*
E226 *calcium sulphite (preservative)*
E249, E252 *potassium nitrate (preservative)*
E250, E251 *sodium nitrate (preservative)*
E310 *propyl gallate (antioxidant)*
E311 *octyl gallate (antioxidant)*
E320 *butylated hydroxanisole (antioxidant)*

E385 *ethylene-diaminetetraacetic acid (antioxidant)*
E407 *carrageenan (stabilizer and thickener)*
E413 *tragacanth (emulsifier, stabilizer, thickener)*
E416 *karaya gum (emulsifier, stabilizer, thickener, binding and filling agent, flavourer)*
E430, E431 *polyoxyethylene stearate (emulsifier and stabilizer; bread freshener)*
E433 *polyoxethylene sorbitan monooleate (emulsifier, moistener)*
E435 *polyoxethylene sorbitan monostearate (emulsifier, stabilizer, moistener)*
E620 *L-glutamic acid (flavour enhancer, salt substitute)*
E621 *monosodium glutamate (flavour enhancer)*
E631 *disodium phosphate (flavour enhancer)*
E924 *potassium bromate (flour improver, also used in brewing)*
E926 *chlorine dioxide (antiseptic, bleach, bactericide, oxidizer, water purifier)*

FRCOG *abbrev.* ◆ Fellow of the Royal College of Obstetricians and Gynaecologists

FRCP *abbrev.* ◆ Fellow of the Royal College of Physicians

FRCPath *abbrev.* ◆ Fellow of the Royal College of Pathologists

FRCPS *abbrev.* ◆ Fellow of the Royal College of Physicians and Surgeons

FRCS *abbrev.* ◆ Fellow of the Royal College of Surgeons

FRCVS *abbrev.* ◆ Fellow of the Royal College of Veterinary Surgeons

FREconS *abbrev.* ◆ Fellow of the Royal Economic Society

Fred *acronym* ◆ Fast Reactor Experiment, Dounreay

FRG *abbrev.* ◆ Federal Republic of Germany

freq. *shortening* ◆ frequent ◆ frequentative

FRHB *abbrev.* ◆ Federation of Registered House Builders

FRGS *abbrev.* ◆ Fellow of the Royal Geographical Society

FRHistS *abbrev.* ◆ Fellow of the Royal Historical Society

FRHS *abbrev.* ◆ Fellow of the Royal Horticultural Society

Fri. *shortening* ◆ Friday

FRIBA *abbrev.* ◆ Fellow of the Royal Society of British Architects

FRICS *abbrev.* ◆ Fellow of the Royal Institution of Chartered Surveyors

FRIPHH *abbrev.* ◆ Fellow of the Royal Institute of Public Health and Hygiene

Fris. *shortening* ◆ Friesland ◆ Frisian

Frl. *shortening* ◆ Fräulein (German, = Miss)

FRMedSoc *abbrev.* ◆ Fellow of the Royal Medical Society

FRMetS *abbrev.* ◆ Fellow of the Royal Meteorological Society

FRMS *abbrev.* ◆ Fellow of the Royal Microscopical Society

FRNS *abbrev.* ◆ Fellow of the Royal Numismatic Society

front. *shortening* ◆ frontispiece

frontis. *shortening* ◆ frontispiece

FRPS *abbrev.* ◆ Fellow of the Royal Photographic Society

frq. *shortening* ◆ frequent

FRS *abbrev.* ◆ Federal Reserve System ◆ Fellow of the Royal Society

Frs. *shortening* ◆ Frisian

FRSA *abbrev.* ◆ Fellow of the Royal Society of Arts

FRSC *abbrev.* ◆ Fellow of the Royal Society of Chemistry

FRSE *abbrev.* ◆ Fellow of the Royal Society of Edinburgh

FRSM *abbrev.* ◆ Fellow of the Royal Society of Medicine

frt *contraction* ◆ freight

frust. *shortening* ◆ frustillatim (Latin, = in small portions)

FRVA *abbrev.* ◆ Fellow of the Rating and Valuation Association

FS *abbrev.* ◆ Fabian Society ◆ Faraday Society ◆ feasibility study ◆ Ferrovie dello Stato (Italian, = State Railways) ◆ financial statement ◆ Flight Sergeant ◆ Free State ◆ Friendly Society ◆ Edinburgh (British vehicle registration mark)

fs *abbrev.* ◆ facsimile ◆ foot-second

FSA *abbrev.* ◆ Fellow of the Society of Antiquaries

FSAA *abbrev.* ◆ Fellow of the Society of Incorporated Accountants and Auditors

FSCA *abbrev.* ◆ Fellow of the Society of Company and Commercial Accountants

FSE *abbrev.* ◆ Fellow of the Society of Engineers

FSG *abbrev.* ◆ Fellow of the Society of Genealogists

FSgt *contraction* ◆ Flight Sergeant

FSH *abbrev.* ◆ follicle-stimulating hormone ◆ full service history

FSIAD *abbrev.* ◆ Fellow of the Society of Industrial Artists and Designers

FSL *abbrev.* ◆ First Sea Lord ◆ Folger Shakespeare Library

FSLN *abbrev.* ◆ Frente Sandinista de Liberación National (Spanish, = Sandinista National Liberation Front) (Nicaragua)

FSS *abbrev.* ◆ Fellow of the Royal Statistical Society

FSSU *abbrev.* ◆ Federated Superannuation Scheme for Universities

FST *abbrev.* ◆ flatter, squarer tube (of TV screens)

FSVA *abbrev.* ◆ Fellow of the Incorporated Society of Valuers and Auctioneers

FT *abbrev.* ◆ Financial Times ◆ full term (pregnancy) ◆ Newcastle upon Tyne (British vehicle registration mark)

Ft *contraction* ◆ forint (Hungarian monetary unit)

ft *contraction* ◆ fiat (Latin, = let there be made) ◆ feint ◆ foot

FTA *abbrev.* ◆ Free Trade Area ◆ Freight Transport Association

FTA Index *abbrev.* ◆ Financial Times Actuaries Share Index

FTAM *abbrev.* ◆ file transfer, access and management

FTASI *abbrev.* ◆ Financial Times Actuaries All-Share Index

FTAT *abbrev.* ◆ Furniture, Timber, and Allied Trades Union

FTB *abbrev.* ◆ first-time buyer

FTBD *abbrev.* ◆ full term, born dead

FTCD *abbrev.* ◆ Fellow of Trinity College, Dublin

FTCL *abbrev.* ◆ Fellow of Trinity College, London

fte *abbrev.* ◆ full-time equivalent

ftg *contraction* ◆ fitting

fth. *shortening* ◆ fathom

fthm *contraction* ◆ fathom

FT Index *abbrev.* ◆ Financial Times Ordinary Share Index

FT-IR *abbrev.* ◆ Fourier-transform infra-red

ft lb *abbrev.* ◆ foot pound

ft mist. *shortening* ◆ fiat mistura (Latin, = let a mixture be made)

FTND *abbrev.* ◆ full term, normal delivery

FT-NMR *abbrev.* ◆ Fourier-transform nuclear magnetic resonance

FT Ord. *abbrev.* ◆ Financial Times Industrial Ordinary Share Index

ft pulv. *shortening* ◆ fiat pulvis (Latin , = let a powder be made)

ft/s *abbrev.* ◆ feet per second

FTSE 100 *abbrev.* ◆ Financial Times Stock Exchange 100-Share Index

FTT *abbrev.* ◆ failure to thrive

fttgs *contraction* ◆ fittings

fttr *contraction* ◆ fitter

FTZ *abbrev.* ◆ Free Trade Zone

FU *abbrev.* ◆ Lincoln (British vehicle registration mark)

fu *abbrev.* ◆ follow-up

FUMIST *abbrev.* ◆ Fellow of the University of Manchester Institute of Science and Technology

FUO *abbrev.* ◆ fever of uncertain origin

fur. *shortening* ◆ furlong ◆ furnished

furn. *shortening* ◆ furnished

fus. *shortening* ◆ fuselage

fut. *shortening* ◆ future ◆ futures

FV *abbrev.* ◆ Frisia Luftverkehr (Dutch, = Frisian Air Transport) (airline baggage code) ◆ Preston (British vehicle registration mark)

FW *abbrev.* ◆ Isles of Scilly Skybus (international civil aircraft marking) ◆ Lincoln (British vehicle registration mark)

FWA *abbrev.* ◆ Family Welfare Association ◆ Free Wales Army

FWAG *abbrev.* ◆ Farming and Wildlife Advisory Group

FWB *abbrev.* ◆ Free-Will Baptists

fwb *abbrev.* ◆ four-wheel braking

FWD *abbrev.* ◆ four-wheel drive ◆ front-wheel drive

fwd *contraction* ◆ forward

fwdg *contraction* ◆ forwarding

fwh *abbrev.* ◆ flexible working hours

fwt *abbrev.* ◆ fair wear and tear

fwt *contraction* ◆ featherweight (boxing)

FX *abbrev.* ◆ Bournemouth (British vehicle registration mark) ◆ sound effects ◆ special effects

Fx *abbrev.* ◆ fracture

fxd *contraction* ◆ fixed ◆ foxed

fxg *contraction* ◆ fixing

FY *abbrev.* ◆ Blackpool (UK postcode) ◆ Liverpool (British vehicle registration mark)

fya *abbrev.* ◆ first-year allowance

fyi *abbrev.* ◆ for your information

FZ *abbrev.* ◆ Belfast (British vehicle registration mark)

fz. *shortening* ◆ forzando (Italian, = forcing) (music)

FZS *abbrev.* ◆ Fellow of the Zoological Society

F-Zug *contraction* ◆ Fernschnellzug (German, = long-distance express train)

G

G *abbrev.* ◆ Gabon (international vehicle registration) ◆ garage ◆ gauss ◆ German ◆ giga- ◆ Glasgow (UK postcode) ◆ gourde (Haitian monetary unit) ◆ Great ◆ Group ◆ guarani (Paraguayan monetary unit) ◆ Gulf ◆ £1000 (slang) ◆ $1000 (slang) ◆ United Kingdom (international civil aircraft marking)

g *abbrev.* ◆ gallon ◆ goal ◆ good ◆ gram ◆ gravitational acceleration ◆ guinea (former UK monetary unit)

G3 *abbrev.* ◆ Group of Three (most powerful Western economies)

G5 *abbrev.* ◆ Group of Five (nations participating in exchange-rate stabilization)

G7 *abbrev.* ◆ Group of Seven (leading industrialized nations)

G10 *abbrev.* ◆ Group of Ten (nations lending money to the IMF)

G24 *abbrev.* ◆ Group of Twenty-Four (industrialized nations)

G77 *abbrev.* ◆ Group of Seventy-Seven (developing nations)

GA *abbrev.* ◆ Gamblers Anonymous ◆ General Agent ◆ general anaesthesia ◆ General Assembly ◆ general average ◆ gestational age ◆ Georgia (US postcode) ◆ Glasgow (British vehicle registration mark)

Ga *contraction* ◆ Georgia

Ga *symbol* ◆ gallium (chemical element)

g/a *abbrev.* ◆ ground to air

GAB *abbrev.* ◆ General Arrangements to Borrow

Gab. *shortening* ◆ Gabon

Gael. *shortening* ◆ Gaelic

Gafta *acronym* ◆ Grain and Free Trade Association

GAI *abbrev.* ◆ General Assembly of International Sports Federations

Gal. *shortening* ◆ Galatians (book of Bible) ◆ County Galway

gal. *shortening* ◆ gallon

gall. *shortening* ◆ gallery

galv. *shortening* ◆ galvanized ◆ galvanometer

Gam. *shortening* ◆ Gambia

G & AE *abbrev.* ◆ general and administrative expenses

G & O *abbrev.* ◆ gas and oxygen

G and S *abbrev.* ◆ Gilbert and Sullivan

g and t *abbrev.* ◆ gin and tonic

GAO *abbrev.* ◆ General Accounting Office (US)

GAP *abbrev.* ◆ great American public ◆ gross agricultural product

gar. *shortening* ◆ garage ◆ garrison

gard. *shortening* ◆ garden

Gasco *acronym* ◆ General Aviation Safety Committee

Gasp *acronym* ◆ Group Against Smog Pollution

gast. *shortening* ◆ gastric

gastroent. *shortening* ◆ gastroenterological ◆ gastroenterology

GATB *abbrev.* ◆ General Aptitude Test Battery

Gatco *acronym* ◆ Guild of Air Traffic Control Officers

Gatt *acronym* ◆ General Agreement on Tariffs and Trade

GAUFCC *abbrev.* ◆ General Assembly of Unitarian and Free Christian Churches

GAV *abbrev.* ◆ gross annual value

GAW *abbrev.* ◆ Global Atmosphere Watch

gaz. *shortening* ◆ gazette ◆ gazetteer

GB *abbrev.* ◆ Gas Board ◆ Girls' Brigade ◆ Glasgow (British vehicle registration mark) ◆ Great Britain ◆ gunboat ◆ United Kingdom (international vehicle registration)

Gb *shortening* ◆ gilbert

gb *abbrev.* ◆ gall bladder

GBA *abbrev.* ◆ Alderney (international vehicle registration) ◆ Governing Bodies Association

GBE *abbrev.* ◆ Dame Grand Cross of the British Empire ◆ Knight Grand Cross of the British Empire

gbe *abbrev.* ◆ gilt bevelled edge

GBG *abbrev.* ◆ Guernsey (international vehicle registration)

GBH *abbrev.* ◆ grievous bodily harm

GBJ *abbrev.* ◆ Jersey (international vehicle registration)

GBM *abbrev.* ◆ Isle of Man (international vehicle registration)

GBNE *abbrev.* ◆ Guild of British Newspaper Editors

gbo *abbrev.* ◆ goods in bad order

g/box *abbrev.* ◆ gearbox

GBP *abbrev.* ◆ great British public

GBZ *abbrev.* ◆ Gibraltar (international vehicle registration)

GC *abbrev.* ◆ Gas Council ◆ gas chromatography ◆ George Cross ◆ Grand Cross ◆ south-west London (British vehicle registration mark)

gc *abbrev.* ◆ gigacycle ◆ going concern ◆ good condition

GCA *abbrev.* ◆ Global Commission on Aids ◆ ground controlled approach (aircraft landing system) ◆ Guatemala (international vehicle registration)

GCapt *abbrev.* ◆ Group Captain

GCB *abbrev.* ◆ Dame Grand Cross of the Order of the Bath ◆ Knight Grand Cross of the Order of the Bath

GCBS *abbrev.* ◆ General Council of British Shipping

GCC *abbrev.* ◆ Game Conservancy Council ◆ Gas Consumers' Council ◆ Gulf Co-operation Council

GCCF *abbrev.* ◆ Governing Council of the Cat Fancy

GCD *abbrev.* ◆ greatest common divisor

GCE *abbrev.* ◆ General Certificate of Education

GCF *abbrev.* ◆ greatest common factor

GCFR *abbrev.* ◆ gas-cooled fast reactor

GCH *abbrev.* ◆ gas central heating ◆ Knight Grand Cross of Hanover

GCHQ *abbrev.* ◆ Government Communications Headquarters

GCI *abbrev.* ◆ ground-controlled interception ◆ Guernsey (airport baggage label)

GCL *abbrev.* ◆ ground-controlled landing

GCLH *abbrev.* ◆ Grand Cross of the Legion of Honour

GCM *abbrev.* ◆ General Court-Martial ◆ greatest common measure ◆ greatest common multiple

GCMG *abbrev.* ◆ Dame Grand Cross of the Order of St Michael and St George ◆ Knight Grand Cross of the Order of St Michael and St George

GCMS *abbrev.* ◆ gas-chromatography mass spectroscopy

GCR *abbrev.* ◆ gas-cooled reactor ◆ ground-controlled radar

GCRN *abbrev.* ◆ General Council and Register of Naturopaths

GCRO *abbrev.* ◆ General Council and Register of Osteopaths

gc/s *abbrev.* ◆ gigacycles per second

GCSE *abbrev.* ◆ General Certificate of Secondary Education

GCR *abbrev.* ◆ gas-cooled reactor ◆ ground-controlled radar

GCMS *abbrev.* ◆ gas chromatography mass spectroscopy

GCVO *abbrev.* ◆ Dame Grand Cross of the Royal Victorian Order ◆ Knight Grand Cross of the Royal Victorian Order

GD *abbrev.* ◆ Glasgow (British vehicle registration mark) ◆ Grand Duchess ◆ Grand Duchy ◆ Grand Duke

Gd *symbol* ◆ gadolinium (chemical element)

gd *contraction* ♦ good
gd. *shortening* ♦ granddaughter
GDBA *abbrev.* ♦ Guide Dogs for the Blind Association
GDC *abbrev.* ♦ General Dental Council
Gde *contraction* ♦ gourde (Haitian monetary unit)
GDN *abbrev.* ♦ Gdansk-Gdynia, Poland (airport baggage label)
gdn *contraction* ♦ garden ♦ guardian
Gdns *contraction* ♦ Gardens
GDP *abbrev.* ♦ gross domestic product
GDPA *abbrev.* ♦ General Dental Practitioners' Association
GDR *abbrev.* ♦ German Democratic Republic (the former East Germany)
Gds *contraction* ♦ Guards
gds *contraction* ♦ goods
Gdsm. *shortening* ♦ Guardsman
gdt *abbrev.* ♦ graphic display terminal
GDU *abbrev.* ♦ graphic display unit
GE *abbrev.* ♦ gastroenterology ♦ Glasgow (British vehicle registration mark) ♦ Guernsey Airlines (airline baggage code)
Ge *symbol* ♦ germanium (chemical element)
ge *abbrev.* ♦ gilt edges
geb. *shortening* ♦ geboren (German, = born)
Gebr. *shortening* ♦ Gebrüder (German, = Brothers)
GEC *abbrev.* ♦ General Electric Company
GED *abbrev.* ♦ general educational development
GEF *abbrev.* ♦ Global Environment Facility
gel. *shortening* ♦ gelatine ♦ gelatinous
Gemcos *pronounced* jem-cos *acronym* ♦ Generalized Message Control System
Gems *acronym* ♦ Global Environment Monitoring System
Gen. *shortening* ♦ General ♦ Genesis (book of Bible)
gen. *shortening* ♦ gender ♦ genealogy ♦ general ♦ genitive ♦ genuine ♦ genus
genit. *shortening* ♦ genital ♦ genitive
Genl *contraction* ♦ General

gent. *shortening* ♦ gentleman
GEO *abbrev.* ♦ geostationary earth orbit
geod. *shortening* ♦ geodesy ♦ geodetic
geog. *shortening* ♦ geographer ♦ geographic ♦ geography
geol. *shortening* ♦ geologic ♦ geologist ♦ geology
geom. *shortening* ♦ geometer ♦ geometric ♦ geometry
GEON *abbrev.* ♦ gyro-erected optical navigation
geophys. *shortening* ♦ geophysical ♦ geophysics
geopol. *shortening* ♦ geopolitical ♦ geopolitics
Georef. *acronym* ♦ World Geographic Reference System
GEOS *abbrev.* ♦ geodetic orbiting satellite
Ger. *shortening* ♦ German ♦ Germany
ger. *shortening* ♦ gerund ♦ gerundive
Gerbil *acronym* ♦ Great Education Reform Bill (GB 1988)
GES *abbrev.* ♦ Global Epidemiological Surveillance and Health Situation (WHO)
Ges. *shortening* ♦ Gesellschaft (German, = company) ♦ Gesellschaft (German, = society)
gest. *shortening* ♦ gestorben (German, = deceased)
Gestapo *acronym* ♦ Geheime Staatspolizei (German, = State Secret Police) (in Nazi Germany and her conquests 1933–45)
GET *abbrev.* ♦ gastric emptying time
GeV *abbrev.* ♦ giga-electron-volt
GEW *abbrev.* ♦ gram-equivalent weight
GF *abbrev.* ♦ General Foods ♦ growth factor ♦ Guinean franc (monetary unit) ♦ Gulf Air (airline baggage code) ♦ south-west London (British vehicle registration mark)
gf *abbrev.* ♦ girlfriend ♦ glass fibre
GFCH *abbrev.* ♦ gas-fired central heating
GFG *abbrev.* ♦ Good Food Guide
GFOF *abbrev.* ♦ Geared Futures and Options Funds

GFR *abbrev.* ◆ German Federal Republic

GFS *abbrev.* ◆ Girls' Friendly Society

GG *abbrev.* ◆ Girl Guides ◆ Glasgow (British vehicle registration mark) ◆ Governor General ◆ Grenadier Guards

gg *abbrev.* ◆ gamma globulin ◆ gas generator

GGA *abbrev.* ◆ Girl Guides' Association

ggd. *shortening* ◆ great-granddaughter

gge *contraction* ◆ garage

ggs. *shortening* ◆ great-grandson

GGSM *abbrev.* ◆ Graduate of Guildhall School of Music

GH *abbrev.* ◆ General Hospital ◆ Ghana (international vehicle registration) ◆ Ghana Airways (airline baggage code) ◆ growth hormone ◆ south-west London (British vehicle registration mark)

GHI *abbrev.* ◆ Good Housekeeping Institute

GHMS *abbrev.* ◆ Graduate in Homeopathic Medicine and Surgery

Ghost *acronym* ◆ global horizontal sounding technique

g/hphr *abbrev.* ◆ gallons per horsepower hour

GHQ *abbrev.* ◆ General Headquarters

g/hr *abbrev.* ◆ gallons per hour

GHRF *abbrev.* ◆ growth hormone releasing factor

GHS *abbrev.* ◆ Girls' High School

GHz *abbrev.* ◆ gigahertz

GI *abbrev.* ◆ gastrointestinal ◆ Gideons International ◆ Government Issue (US slang for ordinary serviceman)

gi *abbrev.* ◆ galvanized iron

gi *shortening* ◆ gill

GIB *abbrev.* ◆ Gibraltar (airport baggage label)

Gib. *shortening* ◆ Gibraltar

GIE *abbrev.* ◆ Graduate of the Institute of Engineers

GIEE *abbrev.* ◆ Graduate of the Institute of Electrical Engineers

GIF *abbrev.* ◆ growth-hormone inhibiting factor

Gift *acronym* ◆ gamete intra-Fallopian transfer

Gigo *acronym* ◆ garbage in, garbage out

GIMechE *abbrev.* ◆ Graduate of the Institution of Mechanical Engineers

Gino *acronym* ◆ graphical input/output

GInstT *abbrev.* ◆ Graduate of the Institute of Transport

GINucE *abbrev.* ◆ Graduate of the Institution of Nuclear Engineers

GIPME *abbrev.* ◆ Global Investigation of Pollution in the Marine Environment

GITB *abbrev.* ◆ Gas Industry Training Board

GJ *abbrev.* ◆ south-west London (British vehicle registration mark)

gj *abbrev.* ◆ gigajoule

GK *abbrev.* ◆ Laker Airways (airline baggage code) ◆ south-west London (British vehicle registration mark)

Gk *contraction* ◆ Greek

gk *abbrev.* ◆ goalkeeper

GKA *abbrev.* ◆ Garter King of Arms

GKN *abbrev.* ◆ Guest, Keen and Nettlefold

GL *abbrev.* ◆ Gloucester (UK postcode) ◆ grande luxe (French, = great luxury) ◆ ground level ◆ Truro (British vehicle registration mark)

Gl. *shortening* ◆ Gloria Patri (Latin, = Glory be to the Father)

gl *contraction* ◆ gill

gl. *shortening* ◆ glass ◆ gloss

g/l *abbrev.* ◆ grams per litre

GLA *abbrev.* ◆ Glasgow (airport baggage label)

Glam. *shortening* ◆ Glamorgan

glam *acronym* ◆ greying, leisured, affluent, married

gland. *shortening* ◆ glandular

Glas. *shortening* ◆ Glasgow ◆ Glaswegian

glauc. *shortening* ◆ glaucoma

glaz. *shortening* ◆ glazed ◆ glazing

GLB *abbrev.* ◆ Girls' Life Brigade

GLC *abbrev.* ◆ gas-liquid

chromatography ♦ Greater London Council

GLCM *abbrev.* ♦ Graduate of the London College of Music ♦ ground-launched cruise missile

Gld *shortening* ♦ guilder (Dutch monetary unit)

Globecom *acronym* ♦ Global Communications System

Glos. *shortening* ♦ Gloucestershire

gloss. *shortening* ♦ glossary

Gloucestr. *shortening* ♦ Gloucestriensis (Latin, = of Gloucester) (bishop's see)

glt *contraction* ♦ gilt

GM *abbrev.* ♦ Air America (airline baggage code) ♦ general manager ♦ General Motors ♦ George Medal ♦ Grand Master ♦ guided missile ♦ Reading (British vehicle registration mark)

gm *contraction* ♦ gram

gm² *abbrev.* ♦ grams per square metre

GMAG *abbrev.* ♦ Genetic Manipulation Advisory Group

G-man *contraction* ♦ Government man (FBI agent)

GMB *abbrev.* ♦ General, Municipal, and Boilermakers Union ♦ Grand Master of the Order of the Bath

gmb *abbrev.* ♦ good merchantable brand

GMBE *abbrev.* ♦ Grand Master of the Order of the British Empire

GmbH *abbrev.* ♦ Gesellschaft mit beschränkter Haftung (German, = limited liability company)

GMC *abbrev.* ♦ General Management Committee ♦ General Medical Council

Gmc *contraction* ♦ Germanic

gmq *abbrev.* ♦ good merchantable quality

GMR *abbrev.* ♦ ground-mapping radar

GMS *abbrev.* ♦ Grant-Maintained Status (of a school funded directly by central Government)

GMSC *abbrev.* ♦ General Medical Services Committee (BMA)

GMST *abbrev.* ♦ Grant-Maintained

Schools Trust ♦ Greenwich Mean Sidereal Time

GMT *abbrev.* ♦ Greenwich Mean Time

GMW *abbrev.* ♦ gram-molecular weight

GMWU *abbrev.* ♦ General and Municipal Workers Union

GN *abbrev.* ♦ Air Gabon (airline baggage code) ♦ Graduate Nurse (US) ♦ south-west London (British vehicle registration mark)

gn *shortening* ♦ guinea (monetary unit)

GNC *abbrev.* ♦ General Nursing Council

gnd *contraction* ♦ ground

GNP *abbrev.* ♦ gross national product

Gnr *contraction* ♦ Gunner

GNVQ *abbrev.* ♦ General National Vocational Qualification

GO *abbrev.* ♦ Gambia Air Shuttle (airline baggage code) ♦ general Office ♦ general order ♦ Group Officer ♦ south-west London (British vehicle registration mark)

GOA *abbrev.* ♦ Genoa (airport baggage label)

goa *abbrev.* ♦ gone on arrival

gob *abbrev.* ♦ good ordinary brand

GOC *abbrev.* ♦ General Officer Commanding

GOC-in-C *abbrev.* ♦ General Officer Commanding-in-Chief

GOCO *abbrev.* ♦ Government-owned, contractor-operated

GOE *abbrev.* ♦ General Ordination Examination

GOM *abbrev.* ♦ Grand Old Man

GOP *abbrev.* ♦ Grand Old Party (US Republican Party) ♦ Gothenburg (airport baggage label)

Gosplan *acronym* ♦ Gosudarstvennaya Planovaya Commissiya (Russian, = State Planning Commission)

Goth. *shortening* ♦ Gothic

gou *shortening* ♦ gourde (Haitian monetary unit)

Gov. *shortening* ♦ Government ♦ Governor

Gov.-Gen. *shortening* ♦ Governor-General

Govt *contraction* ◆ Government

GP *abbrev.* ◆ Gallup Poll ◆ General Practitioner ◆ Gloria Patri (Latin, = glory to the Father) ◆ Government Property ◆ graduated pension ◆ Grand Prix ◆ grande passion ◆ gross profit ◆ south-west London (British vehicle registration mark)

gp *contraction* ◆ group

GPALS *abbrev.* ◆ Global Protection against Limited Strikes

GPC *abbrev.* ◆ General Purposes Committee

gpc *abbrev.* ◆ good physical condition

Gp Capt. *shortening* ◆ Group Captain

gpcd *abbrev.* ◆ gallons per caput per day

Gp Cmdr *contraction* ◆ Group Commander

gpd *abbrev.* ◆ gallons per day

GPDST *abbrev.* ◆ Girls' Public Day School Trust

gph *abbrev.* ◆ gallons per hour

GPh *abbrev.* ◆ Graduate in Pharmacy

GPHI *abbrev.* ◆ Guild of Public Health Inspectors

GPI *abbrev.* ◆ general paralysis of the insane

gpm *abbrev.* ◆ gallons per minute

GPMU *abbrev.* ◆ Graphical, Paper and Media Union

GPO *abbrev.* ◆ General Post Office ◆ Government Printing Office (US)

GPS *abbrev.* ◆ global positioning system ◆ Graduated Pension Scheme

gps *abbrev.* ◆ gallons per second

GPU *abbrev.* ◆ Gosudarstvennoye Politicheskoye Upravlenie (Russian, = State Political Directorate) (Soviet agency for the suppression of espionage and counter-revolution 1922–3)

GQ *abbrev.* ◆ general quarters

GR *abbrev.* ◆ gamma ray ◆ Georgius Rex (Latin, = King George) ◆ Gulielmus Rex (Latin, = King William) ◆ Greece (international vehicle registration)

◆ Newcastle upon Tyne (British vehicle registration mark)

Gr. *shortening* ◆ Greater ◆ Greece ◆ Greek ◆ Grove

gr *shortening* ◆ grain ◆ gram ◆ gross (144)

gr. *shortening* ◆ grade ◆ grammar ◆ grey ◆ gross (including wrappings etc) ◆ ground ◆ group

GRA *abbrev.* ◆ Greyhound Racing Association

Grace *acronym* ◆ group routeing and charging equipment

grad. *shortening* ◆ gradient ◆ grading ◆ gradual ◆ graduate

GradIAE *abbrev.* ◆ Graduate of the Institution of Automobile Engineers

GradIM *abbrev.* ◆ Graduate of the Institute of Metals

GradInstBE *abbrev.* ◆ Graduate of the Institution of British Engineers

GradInstP *abbrev.* ◆ Graduate of the Institute of Physics

GradIPM *abbrev.* ◆ Graduate of the Institute of Personnel Management

GradSE *abbrev.* ◆ Graduate of the Society of Engineers

gram. *shortening* ◆ grammar ◆ grammatical

Gras *acronym* ◆ generally recognized as safe

GRB *abbrev.* ◆ gamma-ray burst ◆ Gas Research Board

GRBI *abbrev.* ◆ Gardeners' Royal Benevolent Institution

Gr. Br. *shortening* ◆ Great Britain

Gr. Brit. *shortening* ◆ Great Britain

GRBS *abbrev.* ◆ Gardeners' Royal Benevolent Society

Gr. Capt. *shortening* ◆ Group Captain

GRCM *abbrev.* ◆ Graduate of the Royal College of Music

GRDF *abbrev.* ◆ Gulf Rapid Deployment Force

GRE *abbrev.* ◆ Guardian Royal Exchange Assurance PLC

GRI *abbrev.* ◆ Georgius Rex Imperator (Latin, = George, King and Emperor)

Grid *acronym* ◆ gay-related immunodeficiency ◆ Global Resource Information Database

GRN *abbrev.* ◆ goods received note

Grn *contraction* ◆ Green

grn *contraction* ◆ green ◆ ground

GRO *abbrev.* ◆ General Register Office (Scotland) ◆ Greenwich Royal Observatory

Gro. *shortening* ◆ Grove

gro *shortening* ◆ gross

GROBDM *abbrev.* ◆ General Register Office of Births, Deaths and Marriages

grp *contraction* ◆ group

grs *contraction* ◆ gross

GRSC *abbrev.* ◆ Graduate of the Royal Society of Chemistry

GRSM *abbrev.* ◆ Graduate of the Royal Schools of Music

GRT *abbrev.* ◆ gross registered tonnage

GRU *abbrev.* ◆ Georgia (international vehicle registration) ◆ Glavnoye Razvedyvatelnoye Upravlenie (Russian, = Central Intelligence Office) (Soviet military intelligence agency)

gry *abbrev.* ◆ gross redemption yield

GRX *abbrev.* ◆ Granada (airport baggage label)

GRZ *abbrev.* ◆ Graz (airport baggage label)

GS *abbrev.* ◆ General Secretary ◆ General Staff ◆ Gold Standard ◆ Grammar School ◆ Luton (British vehicle registration mark)

gs *abbrev.* ◆ grandson ◆ ground speed

gs *contraction* ◆ gauss

GSA *abbrev.* ◆ Girls' School Association

GSC *abbrev.* ◆ gas-solid chromatography

GSD *abbrev.* ◆ General Supply Depot

GSGB *abbrev.* ◆ Geological Survey of Great Britain ◆ Golf Society of Great Britain

GSM *abbrev.* ◆ Garrison Sergeant-Major ◆ General Sales Manager ◆ Guildhall School of Music and Drama

gsm *abbrev.* ◆ good sound merchantable ◆ grams per square metre

GSO *abbrev.* ◆ General Staff Officer

GSOH *abbrev.* ◆ good sense of humour

GSP *abbrev.* ◆ glassfibre-strengthened polyester

GSR *abbrev.* ◆ galvanic skin response

GSS *abbrev.* ◆ geostationary satellite ◆ global surveillance system ◆ Government Statistical Service

GST *abbrev.* ◆ Greenwich Sidereal Time

GSW *abbrev.* ◆ gunshot wound

GT *abbrev.* ◆ gas-tight ◆ gas turbine ◆ Gibraltar Airways (airline baggage code) ◆ gran turismo ◆ gross tonnage ◆ south-west London (British vehicle registration mark)

gt *abbrev.* ◆ gilt top

gt *contraction* ◆ gilt ◆ great

gt. *shortening* ◆ gutta (Latin, = a drop)

GTA *abbrev.* ◆ gas-tungsten arc

Gt Br. *shortening* ◆ Great Britain

Gt Brit. *shortening* ◆ Great Britain

GTC *abbrev.* ◆ General Teaching Council ◆ Government Training Centre

gtc ◆ good till cancelled

GTCL *abbrev.* ◆ Graduate of Trinity College, London

gtd *contraction* ◆ guaranteed

gtee *contraction* ◆ guarantee

GTH *abbrev.* ◆ gonadotrophic hormone

GTI *abbrev.* ◆ Gran Turismo, Injection

GTO *abbrev.* ◆ Gran Turismo Omologato (Italian, = Certified Gran Turismo)

GTR *abbrev.* ◆ Gran Turismo, Racing

gtr *contraction* ◆ greater

GTS *abbrev.* ◆ gas-turbine ship ◆ Gran Turismo, Special ◆ Gran Turismo, Sport

gtt. *shortening* ◆ guttatim (Latin, = a drop at a time)

GU *abbrev.* ◆ gastric ulcer ◆ genito-urinary ◆ Guildford (UK postcode) ◆ south-east London (British vehicle registration mark)

GUA *abbrev.* ◆ Guatemala City (airport baggage label)

guar. *shortening* ◆ guarantee

Guat. *shortening* ◆ Guatemala

Gui *pronounced* goo-i *acronym* ◆ graphics user interface

guil *shortening* ◆ guilder (monetary unit)
Guin. *shortening* ◆ Guinea
gulag *acronym* ◆ Glavnoye Upravleniye
Lagerei (Russian, = Principal
Administrative Camp) (Soviet labour
camp)
GUM *abbrev.* ◆ genito-urinary medicine
◆ Gosudarstvenni Universalni Magazin
(Russian, = Universal State Store)
gun. *shortening* ◆ gunnery ◆ gunpowder
GUS *abbrev.* ◆ Great Universal Stores
GUT *abbrev.* ◆ Grand Unified Theory
guttat. *shortening* ◆ guttatim (Latin, = a
drop at a time)
GUY *abbrev.* ◆ Guyana (international
vehicle registration)
GV *abbrev.* ◆ grande vitesse (French, =
high speed) ◆ Ipswich (British vehicle
registration mark)
gv *abbrev.* ◆ gravimetric volume
GVA *abbrev.* ◆ Geneva (airport baggage
label)
GVH *abbrev.* ◆ graft-versus-host

GVHD *abbrev.* ◆ graft-versus-host disease
Gvt *contraction* ◆ Government
GVW *abbrev.* ◆ gross vehicle weight
GW *abbrev.* ◆ gigawatt ◆ gross weight
◆ south-east London (British vehicle
registration mark)
GWH *abbrev.* ◆ gigawatt-hour
GWP *abbrev.* ◆ gross world product
GWR *abbrev.* ◆ Great Western Railway
Gwyn. *shortening* ◆ Gwynedd
GX *abbrev.* ◆ south-east London (British
vehicle registration mark)
GY *abbrev.* ◆ Guyana Airways (airline
baggage code) ◆ south-east London
(British vehicle registration mark)
Gy *contraction* ◆ gray
gyn. *shortening* ◆ gynaecology
◆ gynaecological
gynaecol. *shortening* ◆ gynaecology
◆ gynaecological
GZ *abbrev.* ◆ Belfast (British vehicle
registration mark)

H

H *abbrev.* ◆ hard (pencil) ◆ hearts (cards) ◆ height ◆ henry ◆ heroin (slang) ◆ hospital ◆ Hungary (international vehicle registration) ◆ hydrant

H *symbol* ◆ hydrogen (chemical element)

h *abbrev.* ◆ hand ◆ hecto- ◆ hot ◆ hour ◆ husband

HA *abbrev.* ◆ Dudley (British vehicle registration mark) ◆ haemagglutination ◆ Harrow (UK postcode) ◆ Hawaiian Airlines (airline baggage code) ◆ Health Authority ◆ high altitude ◆ Historical Association ◆ Hockey Association ◆ Hungary (international civil aircraft marking)

Ha *symbol* ◆ hahnium (chemical element)

ha *abbrev.* ◆ hardy annual ◆ hectare ◆ heir apparent ◆ hoc anno (Latin, = in this year)

HAA *abbrev.* ◆ hepatitis-associated antigen

HAB *abbrev.* ◆ high-altitude bombing

Hab. *shortening* ◆ Habakkuk (book of Bible)

hab. *shortening* ◆ habitat

hab. corp. *shortening* ◆ habeas corpus (Latin, = may you have the body) (writ to present prisoner before judge)

HAC *abbrev.* ◆ high-alumina cement ◆ Honourable Artillery Company

HACSG *abbrev.* ◆ Hyperactive Children's Support Group

had *abbrev.* ◆ hereinafter described

haem. *shortening* ◆ haemoglobin ◆ haemorrhage

HAG *abbrev.* ◆ The Hague (airport baggage label)

Hag. *shortening* ◆ Haggai (book of Bible)

HAI *abbrev.* ◆ haemagglutination inhibition ◆ Health Action International ◆ hospital-acquired infection

HAIL *abbrev.* ◆ Hague Academy of International Law

HAJ *abbrev.* ◆ Hanover (airport baggage label)

HAM *abbrev.* ◆ Hamburg (airport baggage label)

Ham. *shortening* ◆ Hamburg

HAN *abbrev.* ◆ Hanoi (airport baggage label)

Han. *shortening* ◆ Hanover ◆ Hanoverian

h & c *abbrev.* ◆ hot and cold (water)

h & f *abbrev.* ◆ heated and filtered (swimming pool)

h & j *abbrev.* ◆ hyphenation and justification

h & t *abbrev.* ◆ hardened and tempered ◆ hospitalization and treatment

H & W *abbrev.* ◆ Harland and Wolff ◆ Hereford and Worcester

Hants *shortening* ◆ Hampshire (orig. Hantsharing; no point)

HAPA *abbrev.* ◆ Handicapped Adventure Playground Association

Happa *acronym* ◆ Horses and Ponies Protection Association

har. *shortening* ◆ harbour

harm. *shortening* ◆ harmonic ◆ harmony

harp. *shortening* ◆ harpoon

Harv. *shortening* ◆ Harvard

HAS *abbrev.* ◆ Headmasters' Association of Scotland ◆ Health Advisory Service

HASAWA *abbrev.* ◆ Health and Safety at Work Act

Haste *acronym* ◆ Helicopter Ambulance Service to Emergencies

HAT *abbrev.* ◆ housing action trust
◆ housing association trust

haust. *shortening* ◆ haustus (Latin, = draught)

HAV *abbrev.* ◆ Havana (airport baggage label) ◆ hepatitis A virus

haz. *shortening* ◆ hazard ◆ hazardous

HB *abbrev.* ◆ Air Melanesia (airline baggage code) ◆ Cardiff (British vehicle registration mark) ◆ hard black (pencil) ◆ hardy biennial ◆ Switzerland (international civil aircraft marking)

Hb *abbrev.* ◆ haemoglobin

hb *abbrev.* ◆ halfback ◆ handbook ◆ hardback ◆ homing beacon ◆ human being

HBA *abbrev.* ◆ Hobart (airport baggage label)

HbA *abbrev.* ◆ adult haemoglobin

HBAB *abbrev.* ◆ hepatitis B antibody

h'back *abbrev.* ◆ hatchback

HBAg *abbrev.* ◆ hepatitis B antigen

HBC *abbrev.* ◆ Historic Buildings Council ◆ Hudson's Bay Company

HBD *abbrev.* ◆ has been drinking

hbd *abbrev.* ◆ hereinbefore described

hbd *contraction* ◆ hardboard ◆ headboard

HBF *abbrev.* ◆ hepatic blood flow ◆ House-Builders' Federation

HbF *abbrev.* ◆ fetal haemoglobin

HBIG *abbrev.* ◆ hepatitis B immunoglobin

HBJ *abbrev.* ◆ Harcourt Brace Jovanovich

HBLB *abbrev.* ◆ Horse Race Betting Levy Board

HBLV *abbrev.* ◆ human B-lymphotropic virus

HBM *abbrev.* ◆ Her Britannic Majesty ◆ His Britannic Majesty

HBMC *abbrev.* ◆ Historic Buildings and Monuments Commission for England

HBO *abbrev.* ◆ hyperbaric oxygen

h/board *contraction* ◆ hardboard ◆ headboard

H-bomb *contraction* ◆ hydrogen bomb

HBP *abbrev.* ◆ high blood pressure

HBPF *abbrev.* ◆ High Blood Pressure Foundation

hbr *contraction* ◆ harbour

HBS *abbrev.* ◆ Harvard Business School

HbS *abbrev.* ◆ sickle-cell haemoglobin

Hbt *contraction* ◆ Hobart

HBV *abbrev.* ◆ hepatitis B virus

HBWTA *abbrev.* ◆ Home Brewing and Winemaking Trade Association

hby *contraction* ◆ hereby

HC *abbrev.* ◆ Brighton (British vehicle registration mark) ◆ Ecuador (international civil aircraft marking) ◆ Hairdressing Council ◆ Haiti Air International (airline baggage code) ◆ hardcopy ◆ health certificate ◆ Heralds' College ◆ High Commission ◆ High Commissioner ◆ High Court ◆ highly commended ◆ hockey club ◆ Holy Communion ◆ hors concours (French, = outside the competition) ◆ House of Commons ◆ housing corporation

h/c *abbrev.* ◆ held covered

HCAAS *abbrev.* ◆ Homeless Children's Aid and Adoption Society

hcap *contraction* ◆ handicap

HCC *abbrev.* ◆ Housing Consultative Council for England

hcd *abbrev.* ◆ high current density

HC Deb. *abbrev.* ◆ House of Commons Debates

hce *abbrev.* ◆ human-caused error

HCEC *abbrev.* ◆ Hospital Committee of the European Community

HCF *abbrev.* ◆ high carbohydrate and fibre ◆ highest common factor ◆ Honorary Chaplain to the Forces

HCFC *abbrev.* ◆ hydrocholorofluorocarbon

HCG *abbrev.* ◆ human chorionic gonadotrophin

HCGB *abbrev.* ◆ Helicopter Club of Great Britain ◆ Hoverclub of Great Britain

HCH *abbrev.* ◆ hexachlorocyclohexane

HCI *abbrev.* ◆ Hotel and Catering Institute ◆ human–computer interaction ◆ human–computer interface

HCIL *abbrev.* ◆ Hague Conference on International Law

HCITB *abbrev.* ◆ Hotel and Catering Industry Training Board

HCJ *abbrev.* ◆ High Court of Justice

HCO *abbrev.* ◆ Higher Clerical Officer

HCOPIL *abbrev.* ◆ The Hague Conference on Private International Law

hcp *contraction* ◆ handicap

HCPT *abbrev.* ◆ Historic Churches Preservation Trust

HCM *abbrev.* ◆ Her Catholic Majesty ◆ His Catholic Majesty

HCVC *abbrev.* ◆ Historic Commercial Vehicle Club

HCVD *abbrev.* ◆ hypertensive cardiovascular disease

HD *abbrev.* ◆ heavy duty ◆ high density ◆ Hodgkin's Disease ◆ Huddersfield (British vehicle registration mark) ◆ Huddersfield (UK postcode)

hd *abbrev.* ◆ hora decubitus (Latin, = at bedtime)

hd *contraction* ◆ hand ◆ head

HDA *abbrev.* ◆ Hospital Doctors' Association

HDATZ *abbrev.* ◆ high-density air traffic zone

hdbk *contraction* ◆ handbook

HDC *abbrev.* ◆ high-dose chemotherapy ◆ holder in due course

HDD *abbrev.* ◆ head-down display ◆ Higher Dental Diploma ◆ Hyderabad (airport baggage label)

hdg *contraction* ◆ heading

HDK *abbrev.* ◆ husbands don't know

hdkf *contraction* ◆ handkerchief

HDL *abbrev.* ◆ hardware description language ◆ high-density lipoprotein

hdl. *shortening* ◆ handle

HDLC *abbrev.* ◆ high-density lipoprotein cholesterol ◆ high-level data link control

hdle *contraction* ◆ hurdle

hdlg *contraction* ◆ handling

hdlr *contraction* ◆ handler

HDN *abbrev.* ◆ haemolytic disease of the newborn

hdn *contraction* ◆ harden

hdqrs *contraction* ◆ headquarters

HDR *abbrev.* ◆ high dose rate

HDRA *abbrev.* ◆ Henry Doubleday Research Association

HDTV *abbrev.* ◆ high-definition television

HDU *abbrev.* ◆ haemodialysis unit

HDV *abbrev.* ◆ heavy-duty vehicle

hdw. *shortening* ◆ hardwear

hdwd *contraction* ◆ hardwood ◆ headword

HE *abbrev.* ◆ higher education ◆ high explosive ◆ His Eminence ◆ His Excellency ◆ Sheffield (British vehicle registration mark)

He *abbrev.* ◆ helium (chemical element)

HEA *abbrev.* ◆ Health Education Authority

Heb. *shortening* ◆ Hebrew ◆ Hebrews (book of Bible)

Hebr. *shortening* ◆ Hebrew ◆ Hebrews (book of Bible) ◆ Hebrides ◆ Hebridean

HEC *abbrev.* ◆ Health Education Council

Hector *acronym* ◆ heated experimental carbon thermal oscillator reactor

HEF *abbrev.* ◆ high-energy fuel

HEFA *abbrev.* ◆ Human Embryo and Fertilization Authority

HEFC *abbrev.* ◆ Higher Education Funding Council

HEH *abbrev.* ◆ Her Exalted Highness ◆ His Exalted Highness

hei *abbrev.* ◆ high-explosive incendiary

HEIC *abbrev.* ◆ Honourable East India Company

heir app. *shortening* ◆ heir apparent

heir pres. *shortening* ◆ heir presumptive

HEIST *abbrev.* ◆ Further Education Information Services Trust

HEL *abbrev.* ◆ Helsinki (airport baggage label) ◆ high-energy laser

hel. *shortening* ◆ helicopter

HeLa *shortening* ◆ Helen Lake (tumour cell line)

heli. *shortening* ◆ helicopter

Hellen. *shortening* ◆ Hellenic ◆ Hellenism ◆ Hellenistic

helo. *shortening* ◆ helicopter ◆ heliport

Help *acronym* ◆ helicopter electronic landing path

HEO *abbrev.* ◆ Higher Executive Officer

HEOS *abbrev.* ◆ high-ecliptic-inclined-orbit satellite

HER *abbrev.* ◆ Heraklion (airport baggage label)

her. *shortening* ◆ heraldic ◆ heraldry ◆ heres (Latin, = heir)

Herald *acronym* ◆ Highly Enriched Reactor, Aldermaston

herb. *shortening* ◆ herbaceous ◆ herbarium

hered. *shortening* ◆ hereditary ◆ heredity

Hereford. *shortening* ◆ Herefordensis (Latin, = of Hereford)

HERI *abbrev.* ◆ Higher Education Research Institute

herm. *shortening* ◆ hermetic ◆ hermetically

Herts. *pronounced* harts *shortening* ◆ Hertfordshire

HERU *abbrev.* ◆ Higher Education Research Unit

HET *abbrev.* ◆ heavy equipment transporter

heterocl. *shortening* ◆ heteroclite

heterog. *shortening* ◆ heterogeneous

HEU *abbrev.* ◆ highly enriched uranium

heur. *shortening* ◆ heuristic

Hex *acronym* ◆ hexadecimal notation

hex. *shortening* ◆ hexagon ◆ hexagonal

hexag. *shortening* ◆ hexagonal

HF *abbrev.* ◆ hard firm (pencil) ◆ high frequency ◆ Liverpool (British vehicle registration mark)

H/F *abbrev.* ◆ Hlutafjelagid (Icelandic, = limited company)

Hf *symbol* ◆ hafnium (chemical element)

hf *contraction* ◆ half

HFA *abbrev.* ◆ Haifa (airport baggage label)

Hfa *contraction* ◆ Haifa

hf bd *contraction* ◆ half bound

HFC *abbrev.* ◆ high frequency current ◆ hydrofluorocarbon

hf cf *contraction* ◆ half calf (book binding)

hf cl. *shortening* ◆ half cloth (book binding)

hfm *abbrev.* ◆ hold for money

hf mor. *shortening* ◆ half morocco (book binding)

hfr *contraction* ◆ heifer

HFRA *abbrev.* ◆ Honorary Fellow of the Royal Academy

HFRO *abbrev.* ◆ Hill Farming Research Organization

HFS *abbrev.* ◆ heated front seats

HF/st *abbrev.* ◆ heated front seats

Hft *contraction* ◆ Heft (German, = part) (of book)

HG *abbrev.* ◆ Harrogate (UK postcode) ◆ Her Grace ◆ High German ◆ His Grace ◆ Home Guard ◆ Horse Guards ◆ Preston (British vehicle registration mark)

Hg *symbol* ◆ mercury (chemical element)

hgb. *shortening* ◆ haemoglobin

HGCA *abbrev.* ◆ Home Grown Cereals Authority

HGDH *abbrev.* ◆ Her Grand Ducal Highness ◆ His Grand Ducal Highness

HGG *abbrev.* ◆ human gamma-globulin

HGH *abbrev.* ◆ human growth hormone

HGHSC *abbrev.* ◆ Home Grown Herbage Seeds Committee

hgr *contraction* ◆ hangar ◆ hanger

HGTAC *abbrev.* ◆ Home Grown Timber Advisory Committee

HGTMC *abbrev.* ◆ Home Grown Timber Marketing Corporation

HGV *abbrev.* ◆ heavy goods vehicle

HH *abbrev.* ◆ Carlisle (British vehicle registration mark) ◆ double hard (pencil) ◆ Haiti (international civil aircraft marking) ◆ Her Highness ◆ Herren (German, = Messrs) ◆ His Highness ◆ His Holiness ◆ Somali Airlines (airline baggage code)

HHA *abbrev.* ◆ Historic Houses Association

hha *abbrev.* ◆ half-hardy annual
hhb *abbrev.* ◆ half-hardy biennial
hhd *contraction* ◆ hogshead
HHH *abbrev.* ◆ triple hard (pencil)
hhld *contraction* ◆ household
hhp *abbrev.* ◆ half-hardy perennial
HHW *abbrev.* ◆ household hazardous waste
HI *abbrev.* ◆ Dominican Republic (international civil aircraft marking) ◆ Hawaii ◆ Hawaii (US postcode) ◆ Hawaiian Islands ◆ hearing impaired ◆ hic iacet (Latin, = here lies)
HIA *abbrev.* ◆ Housing Improvement Association
hia *abbrev.* ◆ hold in abeyance
HIB *abbrev.* ◆ Herring Industry Board
Hib. *shortening* ◆ Hibernian
Hicat *pronounced* high-cat *acronym* ◆ high-altitude clear air turbulence
HIDB *abbrev.* ◆ Highlands and Islands Development Board
HIE *abbrev.* ◆ Highland and Islands Enterprise
hier. *shortening* ◆ hieroglyphics
HIH *abbrev.* ◆ Her Imperial Highness ◆ His Imperial Highness
HIJ *abbrev.* ◆ Hiroshima (airport baggage label)
Hilac *pronounced* high-lac *acronym* ◆ heavy-ion linear accelerator
HIM *abbrev.* ◆ Her Imperial Majesty ◆ His Imperial Majesty
Hind. *shortening* ◆ Hindi ◆ Hindu ◆ Hindustan ◆ Hindustani
HIS *abbrev.* ◆ hic iacet sepultus (Latin, = here lies buried)
hist. *shortening* ◆ histology ◆ historian ◆ historic ◆ history
histol. *shortening* ◆ histological ◆ histologist ◆ histology
hi-tech. *shortening* ◆ high technology
Hitt. *shortening* ◆ Hittite
HIV *abbrev.* ◆ human immunodeficiency virus
HJ *abbrev.* ◆ Chelmsford (British vehicle registration mark) ◆ Hitler Jugend (German, = Hitler Youth)

HJSC *abbrev.* ◆ Hospital Junior Staff Council (BMA)
HK *abbrev.* ◆ Chelmsford (British vehicle registration mark) ◆ Colombia (international civil aircraft marking) ◆ Hong Kong (international vehicle registration) ◆ House of Keys
HKG *abbrev.* ◆ Hong Kong (airport baggage label)
HKI *abbrev.* ◆ Helen Keller International
HKJ *abbrev.* ◆ Hashemite Kingdom of Jordan (international vehicle registration)
HL *abbrev.* ◆ House of Lords ◆ Korea (international civil aircraft marking) ◆ Sheffield (British vehicle registration mark)
hl *abbrev.* ◆ hectolitre
HLA *abbrev.* ◆ human lymphocyte antigen
HLCas *abbrev.* ◆ House of Lords Cases
HLDeb *abbrev.* ◆ House of Lords Debates
HLE *abbrev.* ◆ high-level exposure
HLG *abbrev.* ◆ Historic Landscapes Group
HLI *abbrev.* ◆ Highland Light Infantry
HLL *abbrev.* ◆ high-level language
h/lmp *contraction* ◆ headlamp
HLNW *abbrev.* ◆ high-level nuclear waste
HLPR *abbrev.* ◆ Howard League for Penal Reform
hlpr *contraction* ◆ helper
HLRW *abbrev.* ◆ high-level radioactive waste
HLS *abbrev.* ◆ Harvard Law School
HLW *abbrev.* ◆ high level waste (radioactive)
HLWW *abbrev.* ◆ headlamp wash and wipe
HM *abbrev.* ◆ central London (British vehicle registration mark) ◆ harbourmaster ◆ hazardous material ◆ headmaster ◆ headmistress ◆ heavy metal (music) ◆ Her Majesty ◆ Her Majesty's ◆ His Majesty ◆ His Majesty's
hm *abbrev.* ◆ hallmark ◆ hectometre
HMA *abbrev.* ◆ Head Masters' Association ◆ high-memory area

HMAC *abbrev.* ◆ Her Majesty's Aircraft Carrier ◆ His Majesty's Aircraft Carrier

HMC *abbrev.* ◆ Her Majesty's Customs ◆ His Majesty's Customs ◆ Headmasters' Conference ◆ Hospital Management Committee ◆ Royal Commission on Historical Manuscripts

HMCG *abbrev.* ◆ Her Majesty's Coast Guard ◆ His Majesty's Coast Guard

HMCIC *abbrev.* ◆ Her Majesty's Chief Inspector of Constabulary ◆ His Majesty's Chief Inspector of Constabulary

HMCIF *abbrev.* ◆ Her Majesty's Chief Inspector of Factories ◆ His Majesty's Chief Inspector of Factories

HMCSC *abbrev.* ◆ Her Majesty's Civil Service Commissioners ◆ His Majesty's Civil Service Commissioners

HMD *abbrev.* ◆ Her Majesty's Destroyer ◆ His Majesty's Destroyer

hmd *contraction* ◆ humid

HMF *abbrev.* ◆ Her Majesty's Forces ◆ His Majesty's Forces

HMFI *abbrev.* ◆ Her Majesty's Factory Inspectorate ◆ His Majesty's Factory Inspectorate

HMG *abbrev.* ◆ Her Majesty's Government ◆ His Majesty's Government

HMHS *abbrev.* ◆ Her Majesty's Hospital Ship ◆ His Majesty's Hospital Ship

HMI *abbrev.* ◆ Her Majesty's Inspector ◆ Her Majesty's Inspectorate (of schools) ◆ His Majesty's Inspector ◆ His Majesty's Inspectorate (of schools) ◆ human-machine interface

HMIC *abbrev.* ◆ Her Majesty's Inspectorate of Constabulary ◆ His Majesty's Inspectorate of Constabulary

HMIP *abbrev.* ◆ Her Majesty's Inspectorate of Pollution ◆ His Majesty's Inspectorate of Pollution

HMIT *abbrev.* ◆ Her Majesty's Inspector of Taxes ◆ His Majesty's Inspector of Taxes

HMLR *abbrev.* ◆ His Majesty's Land Registry

HMML *abbrev.* ◆ Her Majesty's Motor Launch ◆ His Majesty's Motor Launch

HMMS *abbrev.* ◆ Her Majesty's Minesweeper ◆ His Majesty's Minesweeper

HMP *abbrev.* ◆ Her Majesty's Prison ◆ His Majesty's Prison ◆ hoc monumentum posuit (Latin, = erected this monument)

HMS *abbrev.* ◆ Her Majesty's Service ◆ Her Majesty's Ship ◆ His Majesty's Service ◆ His Majesty's Ship

HMSO *abbrev.* ◆ Her Majesty's Stationery Office ◆ His Majesty's Stationery Office

hmstd *contraction* ◆ homestead

HMT *abbrev.* ◆ Her Majesty's Treasury ◆ His Majesty's Treasury

HMV *abbrev.* ◆ His Master's Voice

HMW *abbrev.* ◆ high molecular weight

HN *abbrev.* ◆ Middlesborough (British vehicle registration mark) ◆ NLM-Dutch Airlines (airline baggage code)

hn *abbrev.* ◆ hac nocte (Latin, = tonight)

hn *contraction* ◆ horn

HNC *abbrev.* ◆ Higher National Certificate

HND *abbrev.* ◆ Higher National Diploma

hndbk *contraction* ◆ handbook

hndlg *contraction* ◆ handling

hndlr *contraction* ◆ handler

HNL *abbrev.* ◆ Honolulu (airport baggage label)

hnRNA *abbrev.* ◆ heterogeneous nuclear ribonucleic acid

hnRNP *abbrev.* ◆ heterogeneous nuclear ribnucleoprotein

hnrs *contraction* ◆ honours

HO *abbrev.* ◆ Bournemouth (British vehicle registration mark) ◆ habitual offender ◆ head office ◆ hostilities only

Ho *symbol* ◆ holmium (chemical element)

ho. *shortening* ◆ house

HOCRE *abbrev.* ◆ Home Office Central Research Establishment

HoD *abbrev.* ◆ head of department

H of C *abbrev.* ◆ House of Commons

H of K *abbrev.* ◆ House of Keys
H of L *abbrev.* ◆ House of Lords
H of R *abbrev.* ◆ House of Representatives
Hol. *shortening* ◆ Holland ◆ Holocene
hol. *shortening* ◆ holiday
Holl. *shortening* ◆ Holland
Holland *acronym* ◆ hope our love lasts and never dies
Holmes *acronym* ◆ Home Office large major enquiry system (central crime-investigation computer)
homeo. *shortening* ◆ homeopath ◆ homeopathic ◆ homeopathy
homoeo. *shortening* ◆ homoeopath ◆ homoeopathic ◆ homoeopathy
Hon. *shortening* ◆ honorary ◆ Honourable
Hond. *shortening* ◆ Honduras ◆ Honduran
Hono. *shortening* ◆ Honolulu
hons *contraction* ◆ honours
hon. sec. *shortening* ◆ honorary secretary
hor. *shortening* ◆ horizon ◆ horizontal ◆ horology
hor. dec. *shortening* ◆ hora decubitus (Latin, = at bedtime)
horol. *shortening* ◆ horological ◆ horology
hort. *shortening* ◆ horticultural ◆ horticulture
hortic. *shortening* ◆ horticultural ◆ horticulture
HORU *abbrev.* ◆ Home Office Research Unit
Hos. *shortening* ◆ Hosea (book of Bible)
hosp. *shortening* ◆ hospital
HOT *abbrev.* ◆ Hawk and Owl Trust
Hotol *pronounced* hoe-tol *acronym* ◆ horizontal take-off and landing
HOV *abbrev.* ◆ high-occupancy vehicle
how. *shortening* ◆ howitzer
HP *abbrev.* ◆ Coventry (British vehicle registration mark) ◆ Handley Page ◆ Hemel Hempstead (UK postcode) ◆ Hewlett-Packard ◆ high pressure

◆ High Priest ◆ hire purchase ◆ house physician ◆ Houses of Parliament
hp *abbrev.* ◆ half pay ◆ hardy perennial ◆ heir presumptive ◆ horsepower ◆ hybrid perpetual
HPA *abbrev.* ◆ Hospital Physicists' Association
HPC *abbrev.* ◆ history of present complaint
hpschd *contraction* ◆ harpsichord
HPLC *abbrev.* ◆ high-pressure liquid chromatography
HPPA *abbrev.* ◆ Horses and Ponies Protection Association
HPRU *abbrev.* ◆ Handicapped Persons Research Unit
HPS *abbrev.* ◆ Highland Pony Society ◆ high-pressure steam
HPTA *abbrev.* ◆ Hire Purchase Trade Association
HPV *abbrev.* ◆ human papilloma virus
HQ *abbrev.* ◆ headquarters
HR *abbrev.* ◆ Croatia (international vehicle registration) ◆ Hereford (UK postcode) ◆ Highland Regiment ◆ Home Rule ◆ House of Representatives ◆ human resources ◆ Swindon (British vehicle registration mark)
Hr *contraction* ◆ Herr (German, = Mr)
hr *contraction* ◆ hour
HRC *abbrev.* ◆ high-resolution chromatography
HRCT *abbrev.* ◆ high-resolution computerized tomography
HRE *abbrev.* ◆ Holy Roman Emperor ◆ Holy Roman Empire
HREM *abbrev.* ◆ high-resolution electron microscopy
HRG *abbrev.* ◆ high resolution graphics
HRGC *abbrev.* ◆ high-resolution gas chromatography
HRH *abbrev.* ◆ Her Royal Highness ◆ His Royal Highness
HRIP *abbrev.* ◆ hic requiescit in pace (Latin, = here rests in peace)
HRMS *abbrev.* ◆ high-resolution mass spectrometry

Hrn *contraction* ◆ Herren (German, = Messrs) (on addresses) ◆ Herren (German, = Gentlemen) (as salutation)

HRP *abbrev.* ◆ human remains pouch

HRS *abbrev.* ◆ Human Rights Society

hrsg. *shortening* ◆ herausgegeben (German, = edited) ◆ herausgegeben (German, = published)

HRT *abbrev.* ◆ hormone replacement therapy

HRW *abbrev.* ◆ heated rear window

HS *abbrev.* ◆ Glasgow (British vehicle registration mark) ◆ Hawker Siddley ◆ High School ◆ Home Secretary ◆ hospital ship ◆ house surgeon ◆ Thailand (international civil aircraft marking)

Hs. *shortening* ◆ Handschrift (German, = manuscript)

hs *abbrev.* ◆ hoc sensu (Latin, = in this sense)

HSA *abbrev.* ◆ Humane Slaughter Association ◆ human serum albumin

HSC *abbrev.* ◆ Health and Safety Commission

HSE *abbrev.* ◆ Health and Safety Executive ◆ hic sepultus est (Latin, = here lies buried)

hse *contraction* ◆ house

hsekpr *contraction* ◆ housekeeper

HSDU *abbrev.* ◆ hospital sterilization and disinfection unit

hsg *contraction* ◆ housing

HSH *abbrev.* ◆ Her Serene Highness ◆ His Serene Highness

HSI *abbrev.* ◆ human–system interface ◆ human–system interaction

HSLA *abbrev.* ◆ high strength, low alloy (steel)

HSM *abbrev.* ◆ Her Serene Majesty ◆ His Serene Majesty

HSSU *abbrev.* ◆ hospital sterile supply unit

HST *abbrev.* ◆ High Speed Train

HSV *abbrev.* ◆ herpes simplex virus

HT *abbrev.* ◆ Air Tchad (airline baggage code) ◆ Bristol (British vehicle

registration mark) ◆ heat-treated ◆ heat treatment ◆ high tension ◆ high tide

ht *abbrev.* ◆ half time

ht *contraction* ◆ heat ◆ height

h/t *abbrev.* ◆ half-title

HTA *abbrev.* ◆ Help the Aged

HTB *abbrev.* ◆ high-tension battery

htd *contraction* ◆ heated

htg *contraction* ◆ heating

HTGR *abbrev.* ◆ high-temperature gas-cooled reactor

HTLV *abbrev.* ◆ human T-cell lymphotrophic virus

HTOL *abbrev.* ◆ horizontal take-off and landing

HTR *abbrev.* ◆ high-temperature reactor

htr *contraction* ◆ heater

HTS *abbrev.* ◆ high-temperature superconductor ◆ high-temperature superconductivity ◆ high-tensile steel

Hts *contraction* ◆ Heights

HTT *abbrev.* ◆ heavy tactical transport

HTV *abbrev.* ◆ Harlech Television

ht wkt *contraction* ◆ hit wicket

HU *abbrev.* ◆ Bristol (British vehicle registration mark) ◆ Harvard University ◆ Hull (UK postcode) ◆ Trinidad and Tobago Air Services (airline baggage code)

HUAC *abbrev.* ◆ House of Representatives Un-American Activities Committee (US)

HUD *abbrev.* ◆ head-up display

Hugo *acronym* ◆ Human Genome Organization

hum. *shortening* ◆ human ◆ humane ◆ humanism ◆ humanity ◆ humble ◆ humour ◆ humorous

Humint *acronym* ◆ human intelligence

Humv *pronounced* hum-vee *acronym* ◆ human light vehicle

hund. *shortening* ◆ hundred

Hung. *shortening* ◆ Hungarian ◆ Hungary

Hunts. *shortening* ◆ Huntingdonshire (former UK county)

hur. *shortening* ◆ hurricane

Huridocs *acronym* ◆ International Human Rights Information and Documentation System

Husat *pronounced* hue-sat *acronym* ◆ Human Science and Advanced Technology Research Institute

husb. *shortening* ◆ husbandry

HV *abbrev.* ◆ central London (British vehicle registration mark) ◆ Health Visitor ◆ high velocity ◆ high voltage

HVAC *abbrev.* ◆ heating, ventilation and air conditioning ◆ high-voltage alternating current

HVAR *abbrev.* ◆ high-velocity aircraft rocket

HVDC *abbrev.* ◆ high-voltage direct current

HVEM *abbrev.* ◆ high-voltage electron microscope

HVP *abbrev.* ◆ hydrolysed vegetable protein

HW *abbrev.* ◆ Bristol (British vehicle registration mark) ◆ hazardous waste

hw *abbrev.* ◆ hit wicket (cricket) ◆ hot water

h/w *abbrev.* ◆ herewith ◆ husband and wife

HWL *abbrev.* ◆ high water line

HWLB *abbrev.* ◆ high water, London Bridge

HWM *abbrev.* ◆ high water mark

HWR *abbrev.* ◆ heavy-water reactor

HWS *abbrev.* ◆ hot water system

HWW *abbrev.* ◆ headlamp wash and wipe

hwy *contraction* ◆ highway

HX *abbrev.* ◆ central London (British vehicle registration mark) ◆ Halifax (UK postcode)

HY *abbrev.* ◆ Bristol (British vehicle registration mark)

hyb. *shortening* ◆ hybrid

HYD *abbrev.* ◆ Hyderabad (airport baggage label)

hyd. *shortening* ◆ hydraulic

hyg. *shortening* ◆ hygiene ◆ hygienic

hyp. *shortening* ◆ hypodermic ◆ hypotenuse ◆ hypothesis ◆ hypothetical

hyperb. *shortening* ◆ hyperbole ◆ hyperbolic

HZ *abbrev.* ◆ Saudi Arabia ◆ Tyrone (British vehicle registration mark)

I

I *abbrev.* ◆ independence ◆ independent ◆ institute ◆ island ◆ isle ◆ Italy (international civil aircraft marking) ◆ Italy (international vehicle registration)

I *symbol* ◆ iodine (chemical element)

IA *abbrev.* ◆ Antrim (British vehicle registration mark) ◆ Indian Army ◆ infected area ◆ Iowa (US postcode) ◆ Institute of Actuaries ◆ International Ångström ◆ Iraqi Airways (airline baggage code)

Ia *contraction* ◆ Iowa

IAA *abbrev.* ◆ indoleacetic acid ◆ International Advertising Association

IAAF *abbrev.* ◆ International Amateur Athletic Federation

IAAS *abbrev.* ◆ Incorporated Association of Architects and Surveyors

IAB *abbrev.* ◆ Industrial Advisory Board (OECD) ◆ Inter-American Bank

IABA *abbrev.* ◆ International Association of Aircraft Brokers and Agents

IACA *abbrev.* ◆ Independent Air Carriers' Association

IACB *abbrev.* ◆ International Advisory Committee on Bibliography (Unesco)

IADB *abbrev.* ◆ Inter-American Development Bank

IAEA *abbrev.* ◆ International Atomic Energy Agency

IAF *abbrev.* ◆ International Archery Federation

IAgrE *abbrev.* ◆ Institution of Agricultural Engineers

IAH *abbrev.* ◆ Houston (airport baggage label)

IAHM *abbrev.* ◆ Incorporated Association of Headmasters

IAL *abbrev.* ◆ International Algebraic Language

IAM *abbrev.* ◆ Institute of Administrative Management ◆ Institute of Advanced Motorists

I & D *abbrev.* ◆ incision and drainage

I & O *abbrev.* ◆ intake and output

IANE *abbrev.* ◆ Institute of Advanced Nursing Education

IAPS *abbrev.* ◆ Incorporated Association of Preparatory Schools

IAR *abbrev.* ◆ instruction address register

IARU *abbrev.* ◆ International Amateur Radio Union

IAS *abbrev.* ◆ immediate access store ◆ indicated air speed ◆ instrument approach system

IASA *abbrev.* ◆ International Air Safety Association

iat *abbrev.* ◆ inside air temperature

IATA *abbrev.* ◆ International Air Transport Association

iaw *abbrev.* ◆ in accordance with

IB *abbrev.* ◆ Armagh (British vehicle registration mark) ◆ Iberia Airlines (airline baggage code) ◆ in bond ◆ incendiary bomb ◆ International Baccalaureate ◆ invoice book

ib. *shortening* ◆ ibidem (Latin, = in the same place)

IBA *abbrev.* ◆ Ibadan (airport baggage label) ◆ Independent Broadcasting Authority

IBBR *abbrev.* ◆ interbank bid-rate

IBD *abbrev.* ◆ inflammatory bowel disease

IBE *abbrev.* ◆ Institute of British Engineers ◆ International Bureau of Education

98

IBF *abbrev.* ◆ International Badminton Foundation ◆ International Boxing Foundation

IBG *abbrev.* ◆ interblock gap

IBI *abbrev.* ◆ invoice book, inward

Ibid *acronym* ◆ international bibliographical description

ibid. *shortening* ◆ ibidem (Latin, = in the same place)

IBiol *abbrev.* ◆ Institute of Biology

IBK *abbrev.* ◆ Institute of Bookkeepers

IBM *abbrev.* ◆ intercontinental ballistic missile ◆ International Business Machines

IBMBR *abbrev.* ◆ interbank market bid rate

IBO *abbrev.* ◆ invoice book, outward

IBP *abbrev.* ◆ initial boiling point ◆ Institute of British Photographers

IBRD *abbrev.* ◆ International Bank for Reconstruction and Development

IBS *abbrev.* ◆ irritable bowel syndrome

IBWM *abbrev.* ◆ International Bureau of Weights and Measures

IBZ *abbrev.* ◆ Ibiza (airport baggage label)

IC *abbrev.* ◆ Indian Airlines (airline baggage code) ◆ Industrial Court ◆ integrated circuit ◆ Intelligence Corps ◆ internal combustion

i/c *abbrev.* ◆ in charge ◆ in command

ICA *abbrev.* ◆ Institute of Contemporary Arts ◆ Invalid Care Allowance

Ican *acronym* ◆ International Commission for Air Navigation

ICAO *abbrev.* ◆ International Civil Aviation Organization

ICBD *abbrev.* ◆ International Council of Ballroom Dancing

ICBM *abbrev.* ◆ intercontinental ballistic missile

ICBN *abbrev.* ◆ International Code of Biological Nomenclature

ICBP *abbrev.* ◆ International Council for Bird Preservation

ICC *abbrev.* ◆ International Chamber of Commerce ◆ International Cricket Conference

ICCPR *abbrev.* ◆ International Covenant on Civil and Political Rights

ICD *abbrev.* ◆ International Classification of Diseases

ICE *abbrev.* ◆ Institution of Civil Engineers ◆ internal combustion engine

Ice. *shortening* ◆ Iceland ◆ Icelander ◆ Icelandic

ICF *abbrev.* ◆ International Canoe Federation ◆ International Chess Federation

ICFTU *abbrev.* ◆ International Confederation of Free Trade Unions

IChemE *abbrev.* ◆ Institution of Chemical Engineers

ichth. *shortening* ◆ ichthyology

ichthyol. *shortening* ◆ ichthyologist ◆ ichthyology

Ichthys *acronym* ◆ Iesous Christos, Theou Uios, Soter (Greek, = Jesus Christ, Son of God, Saviour) (a drawing of a fish (*ichthys* in Greek) was a secret identification sign amongst persecuted members of the early Church)

ICI *abbrev.* ◆ Imperial Chemical Industries

ICJ *abbrev.* ◆ International Commission of Jurists ◆ International Court of Justice

ICL *abbrev.* ◆ International Computers Ltd

ICLA *abbrev.* ◆ International Committee on Laboratory Animals

ICN *abbrev.* ◆ in Christi nomine (Latin, = in the name of Christ) ◆ International Council of Nurses

ICNB *abbrev.* ◆ International Code of Nomenclature of Bacteria

ICNCP *abbrev.* ◆ International Code of Nomenclature of Cultivated Plants

ICNV *abbrev.* ◆ International Code of Nomenclature of Viruses

ICO *abbrev.* ◆ International Coffee Organization ◆ Islamic Conference Organization

ICOM *abbrev.* ◆ International Council of Museums

ICOMOS *abbrev.* ◆ International Council on Monuments and Sites

ICPO *abbrev.* ◆ International Criminal Police Organization

ICR *abbrev.* ◆ intelligent character recognition

ICRC *abbrev.* ◆ International Committee of the Red Cross

ICRF *abbrev.* ◆ Imperial Cancer Research Fund

ICRP *abbrev.* ◆ International Commission on Radiological Protection

ICRUM *abbrev.* ◆ International Commission on Radiation Units and Measurements

ICS *abbrev.* ◆ Indian Civil Service ◆ Imperial College of Science and Technology ◆ investors' compensation scheme

ICSA *abbrev.* ◆ Institute of Chartered Secretaries and Administrators

ICSH *abbrev.* ◆ interstitial-cell-stimulating hormone

ICSLS *abbrev.* ◆ International Convention for Safety of Life at Sea

ICSU *abbrev.* ◆ International Council of Scientific Unions

ICTP *abbrev.* ◆ International Centre for Theoretical Physics

ICTU *abbrev.* ◆ Irish Congress of Trade Unions

ICU *abbrev.* ◆ intensive care unit ◆ International Code Use

icw *abbrev.* ◆ in connection with

ICWA *abbrev.* ◆ Institute of Cost and Works Accountants

ICZN *abbrev.* ◆ International Code of Zoological Nomenclature

ID *abbrev.* ◆ Idaho (US postcode) ◆ identification ◆ identity ◆ identity card ◆ infectious diseases ◆ information department ◆ intelligence department ◆ Iraqi dinar (monetary unit)

id. *shortening* ◆ idem (Latin, = the same)

id *abbrev.* ◆ inside diameter

IDA *abbrev.* ◆ International Development Association

Ida. *shortening* ◆ Idaho

IDB *abbrev.* ◆ illicit diamond buyer ◆ illicit diamond buying

IDD *abbrev.* ◆ International Direct Dialling ◆ insulin-dependent diabetes

IDDD *abbrev.* ◆ International Direct Distance Dialling

iden. *shortening* ◆ identification ◆ identify ◆ identity

IDF *abbrev.* ◆ International Dairy Federation ◆ International Dental Federation

IDL *abbrev.* ◆ International Date Line

IDMS *abbrev.* ◆ integrated data management system

IDN *abbrev.* ◆ in Dei nomine (Latin, = in the name of God) ◆ integrated data network

IDP *abbrev.* ◆ integrated data processing ◆ International Driving Permit

IDPM *abbrev.* ◆ Institute of Data Processing Management

IDS *abbrev.* ◆ Income Data services

IDT *abbrev.* ◆ Industrial Design Technology

IE *abbrev.* ◆ Indo-European

ie *abbrev.* ◆ id est (Latin, = that is)

IEA *abbrev.* ◆ International Energy Agency

IEE *abbrev.* ◆ Institution of Electrical Engineers

IEHO *abbrev.* ◆ Institute of Environmental Health Officers

IEM *abbrev.* ◆ inborn error of metabolism

IEng *abbrev.* ◆ Incorporated Engineer

IERE *abbrev.* ◆ Institution of Electronic and Radio Engineers

IEV *abbrev.* ◆ Kiev (airport baggage label)

IF *abbrev.* ◆ intermediate frequency

if *abbrev.* ◆ information feedback

i-f *abbrev.* ◆ in-flight

IFAA *abbrev.* ◆ Independent Financial Advisers Association

IFAD *abbrev.* ◆ International Fund for Agricultural Development

IFAW *abbrev.* ◆ International Fund for Animal Welfare

IFB *abbrev.* ◆ invitation for bid

IFC *abbrev.* ◆ International Finance Corporation

IFE *abbrev.* ◆ intelligent front end

IFIP *abbrev.* ◆ International Federation for Information Processing

IFL *abbrev.* ◆ International Friendship League

IFN *abbrev.* ◆ Ishfahan (airport baggage label)

IFP *abbrev.* ◆ Inkatha Freedom Party (South Africa)

IFR *abbrev.* ◆ instrument flying regulations

IFRB *abbrev.* ◆ International Frequency Registration Board

IFS *abbrev.* ◆ Institute for Fiscal Studies ◆ Irish Free State

IFST *abbrev.* ◆ Institute of Food Science and Technology

IG *abbrev.* ◆ Ilford (UK postcode) ◆ Indo-Germanic ◆ Irish Guards

Ig *abbrev.* ◆ immunoglobulin

ig. *shortening* ◆ ignition

IGA *abbrev.* ◆ International Geographical Association ◆ International Golf Association

IGasE *abbrev.* ◆ Institute of Gas Engineers

IGD *abbrev.* ◆ illicit gold dealer

IGF *abbrev.* ◆ International Gymnastic Federation

IGM *abbrev.* ◆ international grand master (chess)

ign. *shortening* ◆ ignite ◆ ignition ◆ ignotus (Latin, = unknown)

IGO *abbrev.* ◆ intergovernmental organization

IGS *abbrev.* ◆ Imperial General Staff

IGY *abbrev.* ◆ International Geophysical Year

IHC *contraction* ◆ Iesous (Greek, = Jesus) (reproduction of the first three letters of the name as written in Greek capitals)

IHD *abbrev.* ◆ ischaemic heart disease

IHF *abbrev.* ◆ International Hockey Federation

IHP *abbrev.* ◆ indicated horsepower

IHS *contraction* ◆ Iesous (Greek, = Jesus) (reproduction of the first three letters of the name as written in Greek capitals)

IHVE *abbrev.* ◆ Institute of Heating and Ventilation Engineers

IID *abbrev.* ◆ insulin-independent diabetes

IIHF *abbrev.* ◆ International Ice Hockey Federation

IIS *abbrev.* ◆ Institute of Information Scientists

IJ *abbrev.* ◆ Down (British vehicle registration mark)

IKBS *abbrev.* ◆ intelligent knowledge-based system

IKT *abbrev.* ◆ Irkutsk (airport baggage label)

IL *abbrev.* ◆ Fermanagh (British vehicle registration mark) ◆ Illinois (US postcode) ◆ inside left ◆ Institute of Linguists ◆ Israel (international vehicle registration)

il *abbrev.* ◆ inside leg

ILAE *abbrev.* ◆ International League Against Epilepsy

ILD *abbrev.* ◆ interstitial lung disease

ILEA *abbrev.* ◆ Inner London Education Authority

Ill. *shortening* ◆ Illinois

ill. *shortening* ◆ illustrated ◆ illustrator

illegit. *shortening* ◆ illegitimate

illit. *shortening* ◆ illiterate

illum. *shortening* ◆ illuminated ◆ illumination

ILN *abbrev.* ◆ Illustrated London News

ILO *abbrev.* ◆ International Labour Organization

ilo *abbrev.* ◆ in lieu of

ILP *abbrev.* ◆ Independent Labour Party

ILR *abbrev.* ◆ independent local radio

ILS *abbrev.* ◆ instrument landing system

ILW *abbrev.* ◆ intermediate-level waste

IM *abbrev.* ◆ international master (chess) ◆ intramuscular ◆ intramuscularly

imag. *shortening* ◆ imaginary

IMarE *abbrev.* ◆ Institute of Marine Engineers

Imarsat *acronym* ◆ International Maritime Satellite Organization

IMB *abbrev.* ◆ Institute of Marine Biology

IMCO *abbrev.* ◆ Intergovernmental Maritime Consultative Organization

IME *abbrev.* ◆ Institute of Medical Ethics

IMechE *abbrev.* ◆ Institute of Mechanical Engineers

IMet *abbrev.* ◆ Institute of Metals

IMF *abbrev.* ◆ International Monetary Fund

IMinE *abbrev.* ◆ Institution of Mining Engineers

imit. *shortening* ◆ imitation ◆ imitative

IMM *abbrev.* ◆ Institution of Mining and Metallurgy

imm. *shortening* ◆ immediately

immac. *shortening* ◆ immaculate

immed. *shortening* ◆ immediate

immun. *shortening* ◆ immunity ◆ immunization

IMO *abbrev.* ◆ International Maritime Organization ◆ International Miners' Organization

Imp. *shortening* ◆ Imperator (Latin, = Emperor) ◆ Imperatrix (Latin, = Empress) ◆ Imperial

imp. *shortening* ◆ impedance ◆ imperative ◆ imperfect ◆ impersonal ◆ import ◆ important ◆ imported ◆ importer ◆ impression ◆ imprimatur (Latin, = let it be printed) ◆ imprint ◆ improved

imper. *shortening* ◆ imperative

imperf. *shortening* ◆ imperfect ◆ imperforated

impers. *shortening* ◆ impersonal

impf. *shortening* ◆ imperfect

imp gal *shortening* ◆ imperial gallon

imposs. *shortening* ◆ impossible

impreg. *shortening* ◆ impregnate ◆ impregnated ◆ impregnation

improp. *shortening* ◆ improper ◆ improperly

imptd *contraction* ◆ imported

imptr *contraction* ◆ importer

IMR *abbrev.* ◆ infant mortality rate

IMRO *abbrev.* ◆ Investment Management Regulatory Organization

IMS *abbrev.* ◆ Information Management System ◆ Institute of Management Services

IMU *abbrev.* ◆ International Mathematical Union

IMunE *abbrev.* ◆ Institution of Municipal Engineers

IN *abbrev.* ◆ Indiana (US postcode)

In *symbol* ◆ indium (chemical element)

in *shortening* ◆ inch

inaud. *shortening* ◆ inaudible

inaug. *shortening* ◆ inaugurate ◆ inauguration

inbd *contraction* ◆ inboard

Inbucon *acronym* ◆ International Business Consultants

inc. *shortening* ◆ including ◆ inclusive ◆ income ◆ incomplete ◆ incorporated

incho. *shortening* ◆ inchoate

inchoat. *shortening* ◆ inchoative

incid. *shortening* ◆ incidental

incl. *abbrev.* ◆ including ◆ inclusive

incldg *contraction* ◆ including

incls. *shortening* ◆ inclusive

incog. *shortening* ◆ incognito

incomp. *shortening* ◆ incomplete

incompat. *shortening* ◆ incompatible ◆ incompatibility

incorp. *shortening* ◆ incorporated ◆ incorporation

incorr. *shortening* ◆ incorrect

Incpen *acronym* ◆ Industry Committee for Packaging and the Environment

incr. *shortening* ◆ increase ◆ increased ◆ increasing ◆ increment

incumb. *shortening* ◆ incumbent

incun. *shortening* ◆ incunable

IND *abbrev.* ◆ Indianapolis (airport baggage label) ◆ in nomine Dei (Latin, = in the name of God) ◆ India (international vehicle registration)

in d *abbrev.* ◆ in dies (Latin, = each day)

Ind. *shortening* ◆ India ◆ Indian ◆ Indiana

ind. *shortening* ◆ independent ◆ index ◆ indicative ◆ industrial

indecl. *shortening* ◆ indeclinable

indef. *shortening* ◆ indefinite
indep. *shortening* ◆ independence
◆ independent
indic. *shortening* ◆ indicative
indiv. *shortening* ◆ individual
individ. *shortening* ◆ individual
Ind. Meth. *shortening* ◆ Independent
Methodist
Indo-Eur. *shortening* ◆ Indo-European
Indo-Ger. *shortening* ◆ Indo-Germanic
Indon. *shortening* ◆ Indonesia
◆ Indonesian
induc. *shortening* ◆ inductance
◆ induction
indust. *shortening* ◆ industrial
◆ industrialized
INF *abbrev.* ◆ intermediate-range nuclear
forces ◆ International Naturist
Federation
inf. *shortening* ◆ infantry ◆ infectious
◆ inferior ◆ infinitive ◆ influence
◆ informal ◆ information ◆ infra (Latin,
= below) ◆ infusum (Latin, = infusion)
infin. *shortening* ◆ infinitive
infirm. *shortening* ◆ infirmary
infl. *shortening* ◆ influenced
infra dig. *shortening* ◆ infra dignitatem
(Latin, = beneath one's dignity)
Ingo *acronym* ◆ international non-
governmental organization
inhab. *shortening* ◆ inhabitant
INI *abbrev.* ◆ in nomine Iesu (Latin, = in
the name of Jesus)
init. *shortening* ◆ initial ◆ initially
INJ *abbrev.* ◆ in nomine Jesu (Latin, = in
the name of Jesus)
INLA *abbrev.* ◆ Irish National Liberation
Army
in loc. *shortening* ◆ in loco (Latin, = in its
place)
in loc. cit. *abbrev.* ◆ in loco citato (Latin,
= in the place cited)
Inmarsat *acronym* ◆ International
Maritime Satellite
INN *abbrev.* ◆ Innsbruck (airport baggage
label)
inn. *shortening* ◆ innings
inorg. *shortening* ◆ inorganic

INRI *abbrev.* ◆ Jesus Nazarenus Rex
Iudaeorum (Latin, = Jesus of Nazareth,
King of the Jews)
INS *abbrev.* ◆ Immigration and
Naturalization Service (US) ◆ inertial
navigation system ◆ International
News Service
ins. *shortening* ◆ inscription ◆ insert
◆ insulated ◆ insurance
inscr. *shortening* ◆ inscription
insep. *shortening* ◆ inseparable
Inset *acronym* ◆ in-service education and
training
insol. *shortening* ◆ insoluble
insolv. *shortening* ◆ insolvent
insp. *shortening* ◆ inspection ◆ inspector
Inst. *shortening* ◆ Institute ◆ Institution
inst. *shortening* ◆ instant (usual senses)
◆ instant (English, from Latin *instans*,
current, = the present month) (used in
business letters) ◆ instantaneous
◆ instrument
InstAct *acronym* ◆ Institute of Actuaries
InstBE *abbrev.* ◆ Institution of British
Engineers
InstCE *abbrev.* ◆ Institution of Civil
Engineers
InstD *abbrev.* ◆ Institute of Directors
InstF *abbrev.* ◆ Institute of Fuel
InstP *abbrev.* ◆ Institute of Physics
int. *shortening* ◆ interest ◆ interior
◆ interjection ◆ internal ◆ international
◆ interpretation ◆ interval ◆ intransitive
◆ introit
Intelsat *acronym* ◆ International
Telecommunications Satellite
Organization
intens. *shortening* ◆ intensifier
◆ intensive
inter. *shortening* ◆ interjection
◆ intermediate
interj. *shortening* ◆ interjection
internat. *shortening* ◆ international
Interpol *acronym* ◆ International
Criminal Police Organization

interrog. *shortening* ◆ interrogate ◆ interrogation ◆ interrogative ◆ interrogatively

intl *contraction* ◆ international

intr. *shortening* ◆ intransitive

in trans. *shortening* ◆ in transitu (Latin, = in transit)

intrans. *shortening* ◆ intransitive

intro. *shortening* ◆ introduction ◆ introductory

introd. *shortening* ◆ introduction ◆ introductory

INucE *abbrev.* ◆ Institution of Nuclear Engineers

INV *abbrev.* ◆ Inverness (airport baggage label)

Inv. *shortening* ◆ Inverness

inv. *shortening* ◆ invenit (Latin, = designed it) ◆ invented ◆ inventor ◆ invoice

i/o *abbrev.* ◆ input/output

IOB *abbrev.* ◆ Institute of Building

IOC *abbrev.* ◆ International Olympic Committee

IOD *abbrev.* ◆ injured on duty

IOF *abbrev.* ◆ Independent Order of Foresters

IOFB *abbrev.* ◆ intraocular foreign body

IOGT *abbrev.* ◆ Independent Order of Good Templars

IoJ *abbrev.* ◆ Institute of Journalists

IOM *abbrev.* ◆ Institute of Medicine ◆ Isle of Man (airport baggage label) ◆ Isle of Man

Ion. *shortening* ◆ Ionic

IOOF *abbrev.* ◆ Independent Order of Odd Fellows

IOP *abbrev.* ◆ Institute of Painters in Oil Colours ◆ intraocular pressure

IOPCW *abbrev.* ◆ International Organization for the Prohibition of Chemical Weapons

IOR *abbrev.* ◆ Independent Order of Rechabites

IOS *abbrev.* ◆ integrated office system

IOU *abbrev.* ◆ I owe you

IOW. *abbrev.* ◆ Isle of Wight

IP *abbrev.* ◆ india paper ◆ in-patient ◆ instalment plan ◆ International Pharmacopoeia ◆ Ipswich (UK postcode)

IPA *abbrev.* ◆ India Pale Ale ◆ Institute of Practitioners in Advertising ◆ International Phonetic Alphabet ◆ International Phonetic Association ◆ International Publishers' Association

IPARS *abbrev.* ◆ International Programmed Airline Reservation System

IPC *abbrev.* ◆ International Publishing Corporation

IPCC *abbrev.* ◆ Intergovernmental Panel on Climatic Change

IPCS *abbrev.* ◆ Institution of Professional Civil Servants

IPI *abbrev.* ◆ International Press Institute

IPM *abbrev.* ◆ Institute of Personnel Management

INTERNATIONAL CIVIL AIRCRAFT MARKINGS

Only a selection can be given here. Many more will be found in the dictionary.

CF	*Canada*	**JA**	*Japan*	**SX**	*Greece*
CR, CS	*Portugal*	**LN**	*Norway*	**TC**	*Turkey*
D	*Germany*	**N**	*USA*	**VH**	*Australia*
EC	*Spain*	**OE**	*Austria*	**VT**	*India*
EI, EJ	*Ireland*	**OH**	*Finland*	**ZK, ZL, ZM**	*New Zealand*
F	*France*	**OO**	*Belgium*	**ZS, ZT, ZU**	*South Africa*
G	*United Kingdom*	**OY**	*Denmark*		
HB	*Switzerland*	**PH**	*Netherlands*		
I	*Italy*	**SE**	*Sweden*		

ipm *abbrev.* ✦ inches per minute

IPMS *abbrev.* ✦ Institution of Professionals, Managers and Specialists

IPO *abbrev.* ✦ input, processing, output

IPPF *abbrev.* ✦ International Planned Parenthood Federation

ips *abbrev.* ✦ inches per second ✦ instructions per second

IPTPA *abbrev.* ✦ International Professional Tennis Players' Association

IPTS *abbrev.* ✦ International Practical Temperature Scale

IPU *abbrev.* ✦ Interparliamentary Union

IQ *abbrev.* ✦ Caribbean Airways (airline baggage code) ✦ intelligence quotient

iq *abbrev.* ✦ idem quod (Latin, = the same as)

IQA *abbrev.* ✦ Institute of Quality Assurance

IQS *abbrev.* ✦ Institute of Quantity Surveyors

IR *abbrev.* ✦ Industrial Relations ✦ information retrieval ✦ infra red ✦ Inland Revenue ✦ inside right ✦ Iran (international vehicle registration) ✦ Iran Air (airline baggage code) ✦ Iran National Airlines (airline baggage code)

Ir *symbol* ✦ iridium (chemical element)

Ir. *shortening* ✦ Irish

ir *abbrev.* ✦ inside radius

ir. *shortening* ✦ infrared

IRA *abbrev.* ✦ Irish Republican Army

Iran. *shortening* ✦ Iranian

IRBM *abbrev.* ✦ intermediate range ballistic missile

IRC *abbrev.* ✦ International Red Cross

Ire. *shortening* ✦ Ireland

IRF *abbrev.* ✦ International Rowing Federation

IRFB *abbrev.* ✦ International Rugby Football Board

irid. *shortening* ✦ iridescent

IRL *abbrev.* ✦ infra-red remote locking ✦ Ireland (international vehicle registration)

IRN *abbrev.* ✦ Independent Radio News

IRO *abbrev.* ✦ Industrial Relations Officer ✦ Inland Revenue Office ✦ International Refugee Organization

IRQ *abbrev.* ✦ Iraq (international vehicle registration)

irr. *shortening* ✦ irredeemable ✦ irregular

irreg. *shortening* ✦ irregular ✦ irregularly

IRS *abbrev.* ✦ information retrieval system

IS *abbrev.* ✦ Iceland (international vehicle registration) ✦ independent suspension ✦ Industrial Society ✦ information science ✦ internal security

Is. *shortening* ✦ Isaiah (book of Bible) ✦ Island ✦ Isle

Isa. *shortening* ✦ Isaiah (book of Bible)

ISAM *abbrev.* ✦ index sequential access method

ISBN *abbrev.* ✦ International Standard Book Number

ISC *abbrev.* ✦ Imperial Service College ✦ Isles of Scilly (airport baggage label)

ISCh *abbrev.* ✦ Incorporated Society of Chiropodists

ISCM *abbrev.* ✦ International Society for Contemporary Music

ISD *abbrev.* ✦ international subscriber dialling

ISDN *abbrev.* ✦ integrated services digital network

ISH *abbrev.* ✦ Ischia (airport baggage label)

ISI *abbrev.* ✦ International Statistical Institute ✦ Iron and Steel Institute

Isis *acronym* ✦ Independent Schools Information Service

ISK *abbrev.* ✦ Icelandic króna (monetary unit)

isl. *shortening* ✦ island

ISM *abbrev.* ✦ Imperial Service Medal ✦ Incorporated Society of Musicians

ISO *abbrev.* ✦ Imperial Service Order ✦ International Organization for Standardization

ISO7 *abbrev.* ✦ International Organization for Standardization 7-bit code

isol. *shortening* ✦ isolated ✦ isolation

ISQ *abbrev.* ◆ in statu quo (Latin, = unchanged)

ISR *abbrev.* ◆ information storage and retrieval

ISS *abbrev.* ◆ International Social Services

iss. *shortening* ◆ issue ◆ issued

ISSN *abbrev.* ◆ International Standard Serial Number

IST *abbrev.* ◆ insulin shock therapy ◆ Istanbul (airport baggage label)

ISTC *abbrev.* ◆ Institute of Scientific and Technical Communicators ◆ Iron and Steel Trades Confederation

isth. *shortening* ◆ isthmus

IStructE *abbrev.* ◆ Institution of Structural Engineers

ISU *abbrev.* ◆ International Shooting Union ◆ International Skating Union

ISV *abbrev.* ◆ International Scientific Vocabulary

ISVA *abbrev.* ◆ Incorporated Society of Valuers and Auctioneers

ISWG *abbrev.* ◆ Imperial Standard Wire Gauge

IT *abbrev.* ◆ income tax ◆ industrial tribunal ◆ Information Technology ◆ Inner Temple

It. *shortening* ◆ Italian ◆ Italian vermouth ◆ Italy

it. *shortening* ◆ italic

ITA *abbrev.* ◆ Independent Television Authority

ita *abbrev.* ◆ initial teaching alphabet

Ital. *shortening* ◆ Italian

ital. *shortening* ◆ italic

Italy *acronym* ◆ I trust and love you

ITAR *abbrev.* ◆ Information Telegraph Agency of Russia

ITB *abbrev.* ◆ Industry Training Board

ITC *abbrev.* ◆ Imperial Tobacco Company ◆ Independent Television Commission ◆ Industrial Training Council

itc *abbrev.* ◆ installation time and cost

ITF *abbrev.* ◆ International Tennis Federation

itin. *shortening* ◆ itinerary

Itma *acronym* ◆ It's That Man Again (former radio programme)

ITN *abbrev.* ◆ Independent Television News

ITO *abbrev.* ◆ International Trade Organization

ITT *abbrev.* ◆ insulin tolerance test ◆ International Telephone and Telegraph Corporation

ITTF *abbrev.* ◆ International Table Tennis Federation

ITU *abbrev.* ◆ intensive therapy unit ◆ International Telecommunication Union

ITV *abbrev.* ◆ Independent Television

IU *abbrev.* ◆ international unit

IUCD *abbrev.* ◆ intrauterine contraceptive device

IUD *abbrev.* ◆ intrauterine death ◆ intrauterine device

IUGR *abbrev.* ◆ intrauterine growth retardation

IUP *abbrev.* ◆ intrauterine pressure

IUPAC *abbrev.* ◆ International Union of Pure and Applied Chemistry

IUT *abbrev.* ◆ intrauterine transfusion

IV *abbrev.* ◆ British Island Airways (airline baggage code) ◆ interactive video ◆ intravenous ◆ intravenous drip ◆ intravenously ◆ Inverness (UK postcode)

iv *abbrev.* ◆ increased value ◆ invoice value

IVA *abbrev.* ◆ individual voluntary arrangement (in bankruptcy proceedings) ◆ Invalidity Allowance

IVB *abbrev.* ◆ Invalidity Benefit

IVBF *abbrev.* ◆ International Volleyball Federation

IVF *abbrev.* ◆ in-vitro fertilization

IVM *abbrev.* ◆ illuminated vanity mirror

IVR *abbrev.* ◆ International Vehicle Registration

IVT *abbrev.* ◆ intravenous transfusion

IW *abbrev.* ◆ International Air Bahama (airline baggage code) ◆ Isle of Wight ◆ Londonderry (British vehicle registration mark)

IWC *abbrev.* ◆ International Whaling Commission

IWM *abbrev.* ◆ Imperial War Museum

IWW *abbrev.* ◆ Industrial Workers of the World

IX *abbrev.* ◆ Iesous Christos (Greek, = Jesus Christ) (reproduction of the initial letters of the words as written in Greek capitals)

IY *abbrev.* ◆ Yemen Airways (airline baggage code)

IYHF *abbrev.* ◆ International Youth Hostels Federation

IYRU *abbrev.* ◆ International Yacht Racing Union

Iyswim *pronounced* iz-wim *acronym* ◆ if you see what I mean

IZM *abbrev.* ◆ Izmir (airport baggage label)

IZS *abbrev.* ◆ insulin zinc suspension

J

J *abbrev.* ◆ Durham (British vehicle registration mark) ◆ jack (cards) ◆ Japan (international vehicle registration) ◆ joint (of marijuana; slang) ◆ joule ◆ Journal ◆ Judge ◆ Justice

JA *abbrev.* ◆ Jamaica (international vehicle registration) ◆ Japan (international civil aircraft marking) ◆ Judge Advocate ◆ Justice of Appeal ◆ Manchester (British vehicle registration mark)

Jaat *abbrev.* ◆ joint air attack team

JAC *abbrev.* ◆ Joint Advisory Committee (UN)

Jac. *shortening* ◆ Jacobean

Jacari *acronym* ◆ Joint Action Committee Against Racial Interference

JACNE *abbrev.* ◆ Joint Advisory Committee on Nutritional Education

JACT *abbrev.* ◆ Joint Association of Classical Teachers

JAF *abbrev.* ◆ Judge Advocate of the Fleet

JAG *abbrev.* ◆ Judge Advocate General

JAL *abbrev.* ◆ Japan Air Lines (airline baggage code)

Jam. *shortening* ◆ Jamaica ◆ Jamaican ◆ James (book of Bible)

Jan. *shortening* ◆ January

j & wo *abbrev.* ◆ jettison and washing overboard

Janet *acronym* ◆ Joint Academic Network (scholars' computer network)

Jap. *shortening* ◆ Japan ◆ Japanese

Jas. *shortening* ◆ James (book of Bible)

JATCC *abbrev.* ◆ Joint Aviation Telecommunications Coordination Committee

Jato *acronym* ◆ jet-assisted take-off

jaund. *shortening* ◆ jaundice

Jav. *shortening* ◆ Java ◆ Javanese

JB *abbrev.* ◆ joint board ◆ junction box ◆ Reading (British vehicle registration mark)

Jb. *shortening* ◆ Jahrbuch (German , = yearbook)

JBCNS *abbrev.* ◆ Joint Board of Clinical Nursing Studies

Jber. *shortening* ◆ Jahresbericht (German, = annual report)

JBES *abbrev.* ◆ Jodrell Bank Experimental Station

JC *abbrev.* ◆ Bangor (British vehicle registration mark) ◆ Jesus Christ ◆ Jockey Club ◆ Juvenile Court

JCAR *abbrev.* ◆ Joint Commission on Applied Radioactivity

JCB *abbrev.* ◆ J C Bamford (Excavators) Ltd

JCC *abbrev.* ◆ Joint Consultants' Committee ◆ Joint Consultative Committee

JCCBI *abbrev.* ◆ Joint Committee for the Preservation of British Insects

JCHMT *abbrev.* ◆ Joint Committee on Higher Medical Training

JCHST *abbrev.* ◆ Joint Committee on Higher Surgical Training

JCL *abbrev.* ◆ job-control language

JCMC *abbrev.* ◆ Joint Conference on Medical Conventions

JCMD *abbrev.* ◆ Joint Committee on Mobility for the Disabled

JCP *abbrev.* ◆ Japan Communist Party

JCR *abbrev.* ◆ junior common room (in Oxford colleges) ◆ junior combination room (in Cambridge colleges)

JCS *abbrev.* ◆ Jersey Cattle Society of the United Kingdom ◆ Joint Chiefs of Staff

jct. *shortening* ◆ junction

JD *abbrev.* ◆ central London (British vehicle registration mark) ◆ Jordanian dinar (monetary unit)

JDM *abbrev.* ◆ juvenile diabetes mellitus

jds *abbrev.* ◆ job data sheet

JE *abbrev.* ◆ Peterborough (British vehicle registration mark)

JEB *abbrev.* ◆ Joint Examining Board

JECFI *abbrev.* ◆ Joint Expert Committee on Food Irradiation

JED *abbrev.* ◆ Jeddah (airport baggage label)

JER *abbrev.* ◆ Jersey (airport baggage label)

Jer. *shortening* ◆ Jeremiah (book of Bible)

Jessi *acronym* ◆ Joint European Submicron Silicon Initiative

Jet *acronym* ◆ Joint European Torus

jett. *shortening* ◆ jettison

JF *abbrev.* ◆ Leicester (British vehicle registration mark)

JFA *abbrev.* ◆ Jaffa (airport baggage label)

JFET *abbrev.* ◆ junction field-effect transistor

JG *abbrev.* ◆ junior grade ◆ Maidstone (British vehicle registration mark)

Jg. *shortening* ◆ Jahrgang (German, = year's issues) (of magazine etc)

JH *abbrev.* ◆ Reading (British vehicle registration mark)

Jh. *shortening* ◆ Jahresheft (German, = annual volume) ◆ Jahrhundert (German, = century)

jha *abbrev.* ◆ job hazard analysis

JHDA *abbrev.* ◆ Junior Hospital Doctors Association

JI *abbrev.* ◆ Tyrone (British vehicle registration mark)

JIC *abbrev.* ◆ joint industrial council

Jicnars *acronym* ◆ Joint Industry Committee for National Readership Surveys

Jicrar *acronym* ◆ Joint Industry Committee for Radio Audience Research

Jictar *acronym* ◆ Joint Industry Committee for Television Advertising Research

JIT *abbrev.* ◆ just-in-time (stock-control system)

JIU *abbrev.* ◆ Joint Inspection Unit (UN)

JJ *abbrev.* ◆ jaw jerk ◆ Maidstone (British vehicle registration mark)

JK *abbrev.* ◆ Brighton (British vehicle registration mark)

JKH *abbrev.* ◆ Chios (airport baggage label)

jkt *contraction* ◆ jacket

JL *abbrev.* ◆ Japan Air Lines (airline baggage code) ◆ Lincoln (British vehicle registration mark)

JLP *abbrev.* ◆ Juan-les-Pins (airport baggage label)

JM *abbrev.* ◆ Reading (British vehicle registration mark)

JMB *abbrev.* ◆ Joint Matriculation Board

JMC *abbrev.* ◆ Joint Mathematical Council of the United Kingdom

JMK *abbrev.* ◆ Mikonos (airport baggage label)

JMPR *abbrev.* ◆ Joint Meeting on Pesticide Residues (WHO)

JN *abbrev.* ◆ Chelmsford (British vehicle registration mark)

JNB *abbrev.* ◆ Johannesburg (airport baggage label)

jn *contraction* ◆ join ◆ junction

JNC *abbrev.* ◆ Joint Negotiating Committee

jnc. *shortening* ◆ junction

JND *abbrev.* ◆ just noticeable difference

JNF *abbrev.* ◆ Jewish National Fund

jnl *contraction* ◆ journal

jnr *contraction* ◆ junior

jnt stk *contraction* ◆ joint stock

JO *abbrev.* ◆ Oxford (British vehicle registration mark)

joc. *shortening* ◆ jocular

JOD *abbrev.* ◆ juvenile onset diabetes

Jon. *shortening* ◆ Jonah (book of Bible)

Josh. *shortening* ◆ Joshua (book of Bible)

Jovial *acronym* ◆ Jules' Own Version of International Algorithmic Language

JP *abbrev.* ◆ Justice of the Peace ◆ Liverpool (British vehicle registration mark)

jp *abbrev.* ◆ jet propelled ◆ jet propulsion

JPMO *abbrev.* ◆ Jersey Potato Marketing Organization

jps *abbrev.* ◆ jet-propulsion system

jpto *abbrev.* ◆ jet-propelled take-off

JR *abbrev.* ◆ Jacobus Rex (Latin, = King James) ◆ Newcastle upon Tyne (British vehicle registration mark)

jr *contraction* ◆ junior

JRC *abbrev.* ◆ Junior Red Cross

JRS *abbrev.* ◆ Jerusalem (airport baggage label)

JS *abbrev.* ◆ Inverness (British vehicle registration mark) ◆ judicial separation

JSAWC *abbrev.* ◆ Joint Services Amphibious Warfare Centre

JSI *abbrev.* ◆ Skiathos (airport baggage label)

JSP *abbrev.* ◆ Jackson Structure Programming

JSS *abbrev.* ◆ Jacob Sheep Society

JSSC *abbrev.* ◆ Joint Services Staff College

JT *abbrev.* ◆ Bournemouth (British vehicle registration mark)

jt *abbrev.* ◆ joint tenancy

jt *contraction* ◆ joint

JTIDS *abbrev.* ◆ Joint Tactical Information Distribution Systems

JTO *abbrev.* ◆ jump take-off

JTUAC *abbrev.* ◆ Joint Trade Union Advisory Committee

JU *abbrev.* ◆ Leicester (British vehicle registration mark)

JUD *abbrev.* ◆ Juris Utriusque Doctor (Latin, = Doctor of Both Laws) (canon and civil)

Jud. *shortening* ◆ Judges (book of Bible) ◆ Judith (book of Bible)

jud. *shortening* ◆ judicial

Judg. *shortening* ◆ Judges (book of Bible)

Jul. *shortening* ◆ July

Jun. *shortening* ◆ June

jun. *shortening* ◆ junior

junc. *shortening* ◆ junction

junr *contraction* ◆ junior

jurisd. *shortening* ◆ jurisdiction

jurisp. *shortening* ◆ jurisprudence

juss. *shortening* ◆ jussive

juv. *shortening* ◆ juvenile

jux. *shortening* ◆ juxtaposed ◆ juxtaposition

JV *abbrev.* ◆ Jersey European Airways (airline baggage code) ◆ jugular vein ◆ Lincoln (British vehicle registration mark)

JVS *abbrev.* ◆ Jewish Vegetarian and Natural Health Society

JW *abbrev.* ◆ Birmingham (British vehicle registration mark) ◆ Jehovah's Witness

JWB *abbrev.* ◆ Jewish Welfare Board

JWG *abbrev.* ◆ Joint Working Group (between the Roman Catholic Church and the World Council of Churches)

JWPAC *abbrev.* ◆ Joint Waste Paper Advisory Council

JY *abbrev.* ◆ Exeter (British vehicle registration mark) ◆ Jersey European Airways ◆ Jordan (international civil aircraft marking)

Jy *contraction* ◆ jansky ◆ July

JX *abbrev.* ◆ Huddersfield (British vehicle registration mark)

JZ *abbrev.* ◆ Down (British vehicle registration mark)

K

K *abbrev.* ♦ Cambodia (international vehicle registration; orig. Kampuchea) ♦ kaon ♦ Kelvin ♦ kina (Papua New Guinea monetary unit) ♦ King ♦ king (cards, chess) ♦ kip (Laotian monetary unit) ♦ Kirkpatrick (enumeration of Domenico Scarlatti's works) ♦ kitchen ♦ knight (chess) ♦ Köchel (enumeration of Mozart's works) ♦ krona (Swedish monetary unit) ♦ króna (Icelandic monetary unit) ♦ krone (Danish and Norwegian monetary unit) ♦ kwacha (Zambian monetary unit) ♦ kyat (Burmese monetary unit) ♦ Liverpool (British vehicle registration mark) ♦ thousand

K *symbol* ♦ kalium (Latin, = potassium) (chemical element)

k *abbrev.* ♦ kilo- ♦ kilogram ♦ kingdom

KA *abbrev.* ♦ Kilmarnock (UK postcode) ♦ King of Arms ♦ Liverpool (British vehicle registration mark)

KAI *abbrev.* ♦ Keep America Independent

Kan. *shortening* ♦ Kansas

K & B *abbrev.* ♦ kitchen and bathroom

Kadu *acronym* ♦ Kenya African Democratic Union

Kanu *acronym* ♦ Kenya African National Union

Kap. *shortening* ♦ Kapitel (German, = chapter)

KB *abbrev.* ♦ kilobyte ♦ King's Bench ♦ king's bishop (chess) ♦ knight bachelor ♦ Knight of the Order of the Bath ♦ knowledge base ♦ Liverpool (British vehicle registration mark)

KBD *abbrev.* ♦ King's Bench Division

kbd *contraction* ♦ keyboard

KBE *abbrev.* ♦ Knight Commander of the Order of the British Empire

KBL *abbrev.* ♦ Kabul (airport baggage label)

KBP *abbrev.* ♦ king's bishop's pawn (chess)

KBS *abbrev.* ♦ knowledge-based system

kbyte *contraction* ♦ kilobyte

KC *abbrev.* ♦ Kennel Club ♦ King's College ♦ King's Counsel ♦ Liverpool (British vehicle registration mark)

kc *abbrev.* ♦ kilocycle

kcal *shortening* ♦ kilocalorie

KCB *abbrev.* ♦ Knight Commander of the Order of the Bath

K cell *abbrev.* ♦ killer cell

KCK *abbrev.* ♦ Kansas City (airport baggage label)

KCMG *abbrev.* ♦ Knight Commander of the Order of St Michael and St George

Kčs *abbrev.* ♦ koruna československ (Czech, = Czechoslovakian crown) (monetary unit)

kc/s *abbrev.* ♦ kilocycles per second

KCSJ *abbrev.* ♦ Knight Commander of the Order of St John of Jerusalem

KCVO *abbrev.* ♦ Knight Commander of the Royal Victorian Order

KD *abbrev.* ♦ Liverpool (British vehicle registration mark)

kd *abbrev.* ♦ knocked down (disassembled) ♦ Kuwaiti dinar (monetary unit)

KE *abbrev.* ♦ Kenya (international vehicle registration) ♦ kinetic energy ♦ Maidstone (British vehicle registration mark)

keas *abbrev.* ♦ knots equivalent airspeed

Ken. *shortening* ♦ Kentucky

Ker. *shortening* ◆ County Kerry
keV *abbrev.* ◆ kiloelectronvolt
Key *acronym* ◆ keep extending yourself
KF *abbrev.* ◆ Liverpool (British vehicle registration mark)
KFA *abbrev.* ◆ Keep-Fit Association
KG *abbrev.* ◆ Cardiff (British vehicle registration mark) ◆ Knight of the Order of the Garter
kg *abbrev.* ◆ kilogram
kg *contraction* ◆ keg
KGB *abbrev.* ◆ Komitet Gosudarstvennoi Bezopasnosti (Russian, = Committee of State Security) (Soviet espionage and counter-espionage agency 1954–, also responsible for internal security from 1960; continues, with diminished powers, after the collapse of the Soviet system)
kgf *abbrev.* ◆ kilogram-force
KGL *abbrev.* ◆ Kigali (airport baggage label)
Kgl. *shortening* ◆ Königlich (German, = Royal)
KGS *abbrev.* ◆ Kos (airport baggage label)
Kgs *contraction* ◆ Kings (books of Bible)
kgy *contraction* ◆ kilogray
KH *abbrev.* ◆ Hull (British vehicle registration mark)
KHI *abbrev.* ◆ Karachi (airport baggage label)
kHz *contraction* ◆ kilohertz
KIA *abbrev.* ◆ killed in action
kias *abbrev.* ◆ knots indicated airspeed
Kild. *shortening* ◆ County Kildare
Kilk. *shortening* ◆ County Kilkenny
KIM *abbrev.* ◆ Kimberley (airport baggage label)
KIN *abbrev.* ◆ Kingston, Jamaica (airport baggage label)
kind. *shortening* ◆ kindergarten
kingd. *shortening* ◆ kingdom
kit. *shortening* ◆ kitchen
kitch. *shortening* ◆ kitchen

KJ *abbrev.* ◆ knee-jerk ◆ Maidstone (British vehicle registration mark)
kJ *abbrev.* ◆ kilojoule
KK *abbrev.* ◆ Kabushiki Kaisha (Japanese, = Company Ltd) ◆ Maidstone (British vehicle registration mark)
KKK *abbrev.* ◆ Ku-Klux Klan
KKt *abbrev.* ◆ king's knight (chess)
KKtP *abbrev.* ◆ king's knight's pawn (chess)
KL *abbrev.* ◆ Koninklijke Luchtvaart Maatschappij (Dutch, = Royal Dutch Airlines) (airline baggage code) ◆ Kuala Lumpur ◆ Maidstone (British vehicle registration mark)
kl *abbrev.* ◆ kilolitre
KLA *abbrev.* ◆ Kampala (airport baggage label)
KLM *abbrev.* ◆ Koninklijke Luchtvaart Maatschappij (Dutch, = Royal Dutch Airlines) (airline baggage code)
KLS *abbrev.* ◆ kidney, liver, spleen
KM *abbrev.* ◆ Knight of Malta ◆ Maidstone (British vehicle registration mark)
km *abbrev.* ◆ kilometre
km/h *abbrev.* ◆ kilometres per hour
KMT *abbrev.* ◆ Kuomintang (Chinese Nationalist Party)
KN *abbrev.* ◆ king's knight (chess) ◆ kip (Laotian monetary unit) ◆ Maidstone (British vehicle registration mark)
kn. *shortening* ◆ knot (ship's speed) ◆ krona (Swedish monetary unit) ◆ krone (Danish and Norwegian monetary unit)
KNP *abbrev.* ◆ king's knight's pawn (chess)
knt *contraction* ◆ knight
KO *abbrev.* ◆ kick-off ◆ knockout ◆ knock out ◆ Maidstone (British vehicle registration mark)
KOI *abbrev.* ◆ Kirkwall (airport baggage label)

Komintern *acronym*
 ◆ Kommunisticheskii Internatsional
 (Russian, = Communist International)
Komp. *shortening* ◆ Kompanie (German,
 = Company)
Komsomol *acronym*
 ◆ Kommunisticheskii Soyuz Molodezhi
 (Russian, = Communist Union of
 Youth)
Kor. *shortening* ◆ Koran ◆ Korea
 ◆ Korean
KP *abbrev.* ◆ king's pawn (chess)
 ◆ Knight of the Order of St Patrick
 ◆ Maidstone (British vehicle
 registration mark)
KPD *abbrev.* ◆ Kommunistische Partei
 Deutschlands (German, = German
 Communist Party)
kpg *abbrev.* ◆ kilometres per gallon
kph *abbrev.* ◆ kilometres per hour
KPM *abbrev.* ◆ King's Police Medal
KPP *abbrev.* ◆ Keeper of the Privy Purse
kpr *contraction* ◆ keeper
KR *abbrev.* ◆ King's Regulations ◆ king's
 rook (chess) ◆ Maidstone (British
 vehicle registration mark)
Kr *symbol* ◆ krypton (chemical element)
kr. *shortening* ◆ krona (Swedish
 monetary unit) ◆ króna (Icelandic
 monetary unit) ◆ krone (Danish and
 Norwegian monetary unit)
KRL *abbrev.* ◆ knowledge representation
 language
KRP *abbrev.* ◆ king's rook's pawn (chess)
KRT *abbrev.* ◆ Khartoum (airport
 baggage label)
KS *abbrev.* ◆ Kansas (US postcode)
 ◆ Kaposi's sarcoma ◆ King's Scholar
 ◆ King's School
KSh. *shortening* ◆ Kenya shilling
 (monetary unit)
KStJ *abbrev.*

KT *abbrev.* ◆ Kingston-upon-Thames
 ◆ Knight of the Order of the Thistle
 ◆ Knight Templar ◆ Maidstone (British
 vehicle registration mark)
Kt *contraction* ◆ knight (chess)
kt *contraction* ◆ knight ◆ knot (ship's
 speed)
Kt Bach. *shortening* ◆ Knight Bachelor
KU *abbrev.* ◆ Kuwait Airways (airline
 baggage code) ◆ Sheffield (British
 vehicle registration mark)
Ku *symbol* ◆ kurchatovium (chemical
 element)
KUB *abbrev.* ◆ kidney, ureter, bladder
KUL *abbrev.* ◆ Kuala Lumpur (airport
 baggage label)
Kuw. *shortening* ◆ Kuwait ◆ Kuwaiti
KV *abbrev.* ◆ Coventry (British vehicle
 registration mark)
kV *abbrev.* ◆ kilovolt
kVA *abbrev.* ◆ kilovolt-ampere
KW *abbrev.* ◆ Kirkwall (UK postcode)
 ◆ Sheffield (British vehicle registration
 mark)
kW *abbrev.* ◆ kilowatt
kwac *acronym* ◆ keyword and context
kWh *abbrev.* ◆ kilowatt-hour
KWI *abbrev.* ◆ Kuwait (airport baggage
 label)
kwic *acronym* ◆ keyword in context
kwoc *acronym* ◆ keyword out of context
KWT *abbrev.* ◆ Kuwait (international
 vehicle registration)
KX *abbrev.* ◆ Luton (British vehicle
 registration mark)
KY *abbrev.* ◆ Kentucky (US postcode)
 ◆ Kirkcaldy (UK postcode) ◆ Sheffield
 (British vehicle registration mark)
Ky *contraction* ◆ Kentucky
ky. *shortening* ◆ kyat (Burmese monetary
 unit)
KZ *abbrev.* ◆ Antrim (British vehicle
 registration mark) ◆ killing zone

L

L *abbrev.* ◆ Lake ◆ lambert ◆ large (clothing size) ◆ Latin ◆ learner ◆ lecturer ◆ left ◆ lempira (Honduran monetary unit) ◆ Liberal ◆ Licentiate ◆ live (electrical wiring) ◆ Liverpool (UK postcode) ◆ Loch ◆ Lough ◆ Luxembourg (international vehicle registration)

l *abbrev.* ◆ laevorotatory ◆ large ◆ late ◆ latitude ◆ league ◆ leasehold ◆ left ◆ length ◆ libra (Latin, = pound) (obsolete) ◆ line ◆ lira (Italian monetary unit) ◆ litre ◆ low

LA *abbrev.* ◆ Lancaster (UK postcode) ◆ Latin America ◆ Latin American ◆ left atrium ◆ Legislative Assembly ◆ Library Association ◆ Licensing Act ◆ Literate in Arts ◆ local anaesthetic ◆ local authority ◆ Los Angeles ◆ Louisiana (US postcode) ◆ north-west London (British vehicle registration mark)

La *symbol* ◆ lanthanum (chemical element)

La. *shortening* ◆ Lane ◆ Louisiana

la *abbrev.* ◆ low altitude

LAA *abbrev.* ◆ light anti-aircraft

LAB *abbrev.* ◆ Legal Aid Board ◆ low-altitude bombing

Lab. *shortening* ◆ Labour ◆ Labrador ◆ Labradorean

lab. *shortening* ◆ label ◆ laboratory

Labbs *acronym* ◆ Ladies' Association of British Barbershop Singers

LAC *abbrev.* ◆ leading aircraftsman ◆ Landscape Advisory Committee ◆ Licentiate of the Apothecaries' Company

lac. *shortening* ◆ lacquer

Laces *acronym* ◆ London Airport Cargo Electronic Processing Scheme

Laconiq *acronym* ◆ laboratory computer on-line inquiry

Lacs *acronym* ◆ League Against Cruel Sports

LACW *abbrev.* ◆ leading aircraftswoman

LAD *abbrev.* ◆ language acquisition device

ladar *acronym* ◆ laser detection and ranging

ladp *contraction* ◆ ladyship

LAdv *abbrev.* ◆ Lord Advocate

lag. *shortening* ◆ lagoon

LAIA *abbrev.* ◆ Latin American Integration Association

LAM *abbrev.* ◆ London Academy of Music

Lam. *shortening* ◆ Lamarck ◆ Lamentations

lam. *shortening* ◆ laminated ◆ lamination

Lamda *acronym* ◆ London Academy of Music and Dramatic Art

lan *acronym* ◆ local area network

Lancs. *shortening* ◆ Lancashire

l & d *abbrev.* ◆ loans and discounts ◆ loss and damage

l & w *abbrev.* ◆ living and well

lang. *shortening* ◆ language

Lantirn *acronym* ◆ low-altitude navigation and targeting infrared system

Lap. *shortening* ◆ Lapland ◆ Lappish

LAPES *abbrev.* ◆ low-altitude parachute extraction system

LAO *abbrev.* ◆ Laos (international vehicle registration)

LAR *abbrev.* ◆ Libya (international vehicle registration) ◆ limit address register

laryngol. *shortening* ◆ laryngologist ◆ laryngology

LAS *abbrev.* ◆ Las Vegas (airport baggage label) ◆ League of Arab States ◆ Legal Aid Society

Lat. *shortening* ◆ Latin ◆ Latvia ◆ Latvian

lat. *shortening* ◆ lateral ◆ latissimus dorsi (a back muscle) ◆ latitude

LATCC *abbrev.* ◆ London Air Traffic Control Centre

Lats *acronym* ◆ long-acting thyroid stimulator

LAUK *abbrev.* ◆ Library Association of the United Kingdom

Lautro *acronym* ◆ Life Assurance and Unit Trust Regulatory Organization

LAV *abbrev.* ◆ light-armoured vehicle

LAX *abbrev.* ◆ Los Angeles (airport baggage label)

lax. *shortening* ◆ laxative

LB *abbrev.* ◆ late bottled (wines) ◆ Liberia (international vehicle registration) ◆ north-west London (British vehicle registration mark)

lb *abbrev.* ◆ left back (football) ◆ leg before wicket (cricket) ◆ leg bye (cricket)

lb *shortening* ◆ libra (Latin, = pound) (weight)

LBA *abbrev.* ◆ Leeds (airport baggage label)

LBC *abbrev.* ◆ London Broadcasting Company

LBdr *abbrev.* ◆ Lance Bombardier

LBF *abbrev.* ◆ liver blood flow

lbf *abbrev.* ◆ pound force

lb-ft *abbrev.* ◆ pound-foot

LBH *abbrev.* ◆ length, breadth, height

LBL *abbrev.* ◆ lymphoblastic lymphoma

LBO *abbrev.* ◆ leveraged buy-out

LBS *abbrev.* ◆ London Business School

lbw *abbrev.* ◆ leg before wicket (cricket)

LC *abbrev.* ◆ landing craft ◆ letter of credit ◆ Library of Congress ◆ Loganair (airline baggage code) ◆ Lord

Chamberlain ◆ Lord Chancellor ◆ Lutheran Council of Great Britain ◆ north-west London (British vehicle registration mark)

lc *abbrev.* ◆ left centre ◆ letter of credit ◆ loco citato (Latin, = in the place cited) ◆ lower case (non-capital letter)

LCB *abbrev.* ◆ Lord Chief Baron

LCC *abbrev.* ◆ Legalize Cannabis Campaign ◆ life-cycle costing ◆ London County Council

LCCC *abbrev.* ◆ Library of Congress Catalogue Card

LCD *abbrev.* ◆ liquid crystal display ◆ Lord Chamberlain's Department ◆ Lord Chancellor's Department ◆ lowest common denominator

LCDT *abbrev.* ◆ London Contemporary Dance Theatre

LCE *abbrev.* ◆ Licentiate in Civil Engineering ◆ London Commodity Exchange

LCF *abbrev.* ◆ Law Centres Federation

LCGB *abbrev.* ◆ Locomotive Club of Great Britain

LCH *abbrev.* ◆ London Clearing House

LCh *abbrev.* ◆ Licentiatus Chirurgiae (Latin, = Licentiate in Surgery) ◆ Lord Chancellor

LChir *abbrev.* ◆ Licentiatus Chirurgiae (Latin, = Licentiate in Surgery)

LCJ *abbrev.* ◆ Lord Chief Justice

LCM *abbrev.* ◆ London College of Music ◆ lowest common multiple

LCP *abbrev.* ◆ last complete programme ◆ Licentiate of the College of Preceptors ◆ London College of Printing

LCpl *abbrev.* ◆ Lance Corporal

LCPS *abbrev.* ◆ Licentiate of the College of Physicians and Surgeons

LCS *abbrev.* ◆ London Co-operative Society

LCST *abbrev.* ◆ Licentiate of the College of Speech Therapists

LD *abbrev.* ◆ Lady Day ◆ Laus Deo (Latin, = praise be to God) ◆ lethal dosage ◆ Liberal Democrat ◆ Libyan dinar (monetary unit) ◆ Llandrindod

Wells (UK postcode) ✦ low density
✦ Low Dutch ✦ north-west London
(British vehicle registration mark)

L/D *abbrev.* ✦ letter of deposit

Ld *contraction* ✦ Lord

ld *contraction* ✦ load

Lda *contraction* ✦ Limitada (Portuguese,
Spanish, = Limited)

LDC *abbrev.* ✦ less developed country

ldc *abbrev.* ✦ long-distance call

LDDC *abbrev.* ✦ London Docklands
Development Corporation

LDE *abbrev.* ✦ Lourdes (airport baggage
label)

LDentSc *abbrev.* ✦ Licentiate in Dental
Science

Ldg *contraction* ✦ Leading

ldg *contraction* ✦ landing ✦ loading
✦ lodging

ldge *contraction* ✦ lodge

ldk *contraction* ✦ lower deck

LDL *abbrev.* ✦ low-density lipoprotein

LDN *abbrev.* ✦ less developed nation

LDOS *abbrev.* ✦ Lord's Day Observance
Society

LDP *abbrev.* ✦ long-distance path

ldp *contraction* ✦ ladyship ✦ lordship

LDR *abbrev.* ✦ Liberal, Democratic and
Reform Group (European Parliament)

ldr *contraction* ✦ leader ✦ ledger ✦ lodger

ldry *contraction* ✦ laundry

LDS *abbrev.* ✦ Latter-Day Saints ✦ laus
Deo semper (Latin, = praise be to God
always) ✦ Licentiate in Dental Surgery

LDSc *abbrev.* ✦ Licentiate in Dental
Science

LDV *abbrev.* ✦ Local Defence Volunteers

LDWA *abbrev.* ✦ Long Distance Walkers'
Association

LE *abbrev.* ✦ Leicester (UK postcode)
✦ London Electricity ✦ north-west
London (British vehicle registration
mark)

Le *contraction* ✦ leone (Sierra Leonean
monetary unit)

LEA *abbrev.* ✦ local education authority

Leap *acronym* ✦ Life Education for the
Autistic Person

Leb. *shortening* ✦ Lebanese ✦ Lebanon

lect. *shortening* ✦ lecture ✦ lecturer

LED *abbrev.* ✦ light-emitting diode

leg. *shortening* ✦ legal ✦ legate ✦ legation
✦ legato (Italian, = joined) (music)
✦ legislation ✦ legislative ✦ legislature

legg. *shortening* ✦ leggiero (Italian, =
light) (music)

legis. *shortening* ✦ legislation
✦ legislative ✦ legislature

LEH *abbrev.* ✦ Le Havre (airport baggage
label)

Leicester. *shortening* ✦ Leicesteriensis
(Latin , = of Leicester)

Leics. *shortening* ✦ Leicestershire

Leit. *shortening* ✦ County Leitrim

LEJ *abbrev.* ✦ Leipzig (airport baggage
label)

lem *acronym* ✦ lunar excursion module

Lenta *acronym* ✦ London Enterprise
Agency

Lepra *acronym* ✦ Leprosy Relief
Association

LESS *abbrev.* ✦ least-cost estimating and
scheduling

lev *acronym* ✦ lunar excursion vehicle

Lev. *shortening* ✦ Leviticus (book of
Bible)

Levit. *shortening* ✦ Leviticus (book of
Bible)

lex. *shortening* ✦ lexicon

lexicog. *shortening* ✦ lexicographer
✦ lexicographical ✦ lexicography

LF *abbrev.* ✦ line feed ✦ low frequency
✦ north-west London (British vehicle
registration mark)

lf *contraction* ✦ leaf

LFC *abbrev.* ✦ Lutheran Free Church

lfc *abbrev.* ✦ low-frequency current

LFD *abbrev.* ✦ least fatal dose ✦ low fat
diet

LG *abbrev.* ✦ Chester (British vehicle
registration mark) ✦ Life Guards ✦ Low
German

lg. *shortening* ✦ large

LGBC *abbrev.* ✦ Local Government
Boundary Commission for England

LGCM *abbrev.* ◆ Lesbian and Gay Christian Movement

lge *contraction* ◆ large

LGEB *abbrev.* ◆ Local Government Examinations Board

LGer *abbrev.* ◆ Low German

LGG *abbrev.* ◆ Liège (airport baggage label)

LGM *abbrev.* ◆ little green men

LGR *abbrev.* ◆ leasehold ground rent

LGSM *abbrev.* ◆ Licentiate of the Guildhall School of Music

lgth *contraction* ◆ length

LGU *abbrev.* ◆ Ladies' Golf Union

LH *abbrev.* ◆ Lufthansa German Airlines (airline baggage code) ◆ luteinizing hormone ◆ north-west London (British vehicle registration mark)

L/H *abbrev.* ◆ leasehold

lh *abbrev.* ◆ left half ◆ left hand

LHA *abbrev.* ◆ local health authority ◆ Lord High Admiral

lhb *abbrev.* ◆ left half-back

lhd *abbrev.* ◆ left-hand drive

LHE *abbrev.* ◆ Lahore (airport baggage label)

l/hld *contraction* ◆ leasehold

LHMC *abbrev.* ◆ London Hospital Medical College

LHS *abbrev.* ◆ left-hand side

LI *abbrev.* ◆ light infantry ◆ Lincoln's Inn

Li *symbol* ◆ lithium (chemical element)

LIA *abbrev.* ◆ Life Insurance Association

Lib. *shortening* ◆ Liberal ◆ Liberia ◆ Liberian ◆ Libya ◆ Libyan

lib. *shortening* ◆ liber (Latin, = book) ◆ librarian ◆ library ◆ liberation ◆ libretto

lib. cat. *shortening* ◆ library catalogue

Lib. Cong. *shortening* ◆ Library of Congress

Lib. Dem. *shortening* ◆ Liberal Democrat

Lib.-Lab. *shortening* ◆ Liberal-Labour

Libid *acronym* ◆ London Inter-Bank Bid Rate

Libor *acronym* ◆ London Inter-Bank Offered Rate

lic. *shortening* ◆ licence ◆ licensed

Lidar *acronym* ◆ light detection and ranging

LIE *abbrev.* ◆ loss of independent existence

Lieut. *shortening* ◆ Lieutenant

Liffe *pronounced* liffy or life *acronym* ◆ London International Financial Futures Exchange

Lifo *acronym* ◆ last in, first out

lighthse *contraction* ◆ lighthouse

Lilo *acronym* ◆ last in, last out

Lim. *shortening* ◆ County Limerick

lim. *shortening* ◆ limit

lin. *shortening* ◆ lineal ◆ linear

Linac *acronym* ◆ linear accelerator

Lincoln. *shortening* ◆ Lincolniensis (Latin, = of Lincoln)

Lincs. *shortening* ◆ Lincolnshire

ling. *shortening* ◆ linguistics

Linn. *shortening* ◆ Linnaean ◆ Linnaeus

LInstP *abbrev.* ◆ Licentiate of the Institute of Physics

LIP *abbrev.* ◆ life insurance policy

Lips *acronym* ◆ logical inferences per second

liq. *shortening* ◆ liquid ◆ liquor

LIS *abbrev.* ◆ Lisbon (airport baggage label)

Lisc *acronym* ◆ Library and Information Services Council

LISM *abbrev.* ◆ Licentiate of the Incorporated Society of Musicians

Lisp *acronym* ◆ List Processing (computer programming language)

LIT *abbrev.* ◆ Little Rock (airport baggage label)

lit. *shortening* ◆ literal ◆ literally ◆ literary ◆ literature ◆ litre ◆ little ◆ liturgy

Lit. *abbrev.* ◆ lire italiane (Italian, = Italian lire) (monetary unit)

lit. crit. *shortening* ◆ literary criticism

Lith. *shortening* ◆ Lithuania ◆ Lithuanian

lith. *shortening* ◆ lithograph ◆ lithography

litho. *shortening* ◆ lithograph ◆ lithography

lithog. *shortening* ◆ lithograph ◆ lithography

lithol. *shortening* ◆ lithology
lit. hum. *shortening* ◆ litterae humaniores (Latin, = more humane letters) (Oxford honours degree in Greek, Latin, Ancient History and Philosophy)
LittB *abbrev.* ◆ Litterarum Baccalaureus (Latin, = Bachelor of Letters)
LittD *abbrev.* ◆ Litterarum Doctor (Latin, = Doctor of Letters)
liturg. *shortening* ◆ liturgical
liv. *shortening* ◆ livraison (French, = delivery)
LJ *abbrev.* ◆ Bournemouth (British vehicle registration mark) ◆ Lord Justice ◆ Sierra Leone Airways (airline baggage code)
lj *abbrev.* ◆ life jacket
LJA *abbrev.* ◆ Lady Jockeys' Association
LK *abbrev.* ◆ north-west London (British vehicle registration mark)
lkd *contraction* ◆ locked
lkg *contraction* ◆ locking
lkge *contraction* ◆ leakage
lkr *contraction* ◆ locker
LL *abbrev.* ◆ Late Latin ◆ Law Latin ◆ Llandudno (UK postcode) ◆ Lord Lieutenant ◆ Low Latin ◆ north-west London (British vehicle registration mark)
L/L *abbrev.* ◆ Lutlang (Norwegian, = Limited)
LLB *abbrev.* ◆ Legum Baccalaureus (Latin, = Bachelor of Laws)
LLCM *abbrev.* ◆ Licentiate of the London College of Music
LLD *abbrev.* ◆ Legum Doctor (Latin, = Doctor of Laws)
lli *abbrev.* ◆ latitude and longitude indicator
LLL *abbrev.* ◆ low-level logic
LLM *abbrev.* ◆ Legum Magister (Latin, = Master of Laws)
LLNW *abbrev.* ◆ low-level nuclear waste
LLRW *abbrev.* ◆ low-level radioactive waste
LLW *abbrev.* ◆ Lilongwe (airport baggage label) ◆ low-level waste

LM *abbrev.* ◆ Licentiate in Midwifery ◆ Lord Mayor ◆ lunar module ◆ north-west London (British vehicle registration mark)
Lm *abbrev.* ◆ Maltese lira (monetary unit)
lm *shortening* ◆ lumen
lmd *contraction* ◆ leafmould
LME *abbrev.* ◆ London Metal Exchange
LMP *abbrev.* ◆ last menstrual period
LMRCP *abbrev.* ◆ Licentiate in Midwifery of the Royal College of Physicians
LMS *abbrev.* ◆ Latin Mass Society ◆ local management of schools ◆ London Missionary Society
LMSR *abbrev.* ◆ London, Midland and Scottish Railway
LMSSA *abbrev.* ◆ Licentiate in Medicine and Surgery of the Society of Apothecaries
LMT *abbrev.* ◆ length, mass, time
LMX *abbrev.* ◆ London Market Excess of Loss (insurance)
LN *abbrev.* ◆ Libyan Arab Airlines (airline baggage code) ◆ Lincoln (UK postcode) ◆ north-west London (British vehicle registration mark) ◆ Norway (international civil aircraft marking)
ln *abbrev.* ◆ logarithmus naturalis (Latin, = natural logarithm)
£neg. *shortening* ◆ salary negotiable
LNER *abbrev.* ◆ London and North-Eastern Railway
LNG *abbrev.* ◆ liquefied natural gas
lnge *contraction* ◆ lounge
LNLC *abbrev.* ◆ Ladies' Naval Luncheon Club
LNS *abbrev.* ◆ land navigation system
LO *abbrev.* ◆ liaison officer ◆ north-west London (British vehicle registration mark)
LOA *abbrev.* ◆ leave of absence
loa *abbrev.* ◆ length overall
LOB *abbrev.* ◆ Location of Offices Bureau
loc *abbrev.* ◆ lines of communication
loc. *shortening* ◆ local ◆ location ◆ locative

loc. cit. *shortening* ◆ loco citato (Latin, = at the reference already given)

locn *contraction* ◆ location

L of C *abbrev.* ◆ Library of Congress ◆ line of communication

L of N *abbrev.* ◆ League of Nations

Loft *acronym* ◆ low-frequency radio telescope

log *shortening* ◆ logarithm

LOI *abbrev.* ◆ Loyal Orange Institution

Lola *acronym* ◆ library on-line acquisition

LON *abbrev.* ◆ London (airport baggage label)

lon. *shortening* ◆ longitude

Lond. *shortening* ◆ London

Londin. *shortening* ◆ Londiniensis (Latin, = of London)

Long. *shortening* ◆ County Longford

long. *shortening* ◆ longitude

longl *contraction* ◆ longitudinal

Lonrho *acronym* ◆ London and Rhodesian Mining and Land Company Ltd

loq. *shortening* ◆ loquitur (Latin, = speaks)

LOS *abbrev.* ◆ Lagos (airport baggage label) ◆ line of sight ◆ loss of signal

LOT *abbrev.* ◆ Polske Linie Lotnicze (Polish, = Polish Airlines)

LP *abbrev.* ◆ Labour party ◆ Lady Provost ◆ large paper ◆ Liberal Party ◆ life policy ◆ long-playing record ◆ Lord Provost ◆ low pressure ◆ north-west London (British vehicle registration mark)

lp *contraction* ◆ lordship

LPB *abbrev.* ◆ La Paz (airport baggage label)

LPC *abbrev.* ◆ Lord President of the Council

LPG *abbrev.* ◆ liquefied petroleum gas

lpi *abbrev.* ◆ lines per inch

LPL *abbrev.* ◆ Liverpool (airport baggage label)

lpm *abbrev.* ◆ lines per millimetre ◆ lines per minute

LPO *abbrev.* ◆ London Philharmonic Orchestra

L'pool *abbrev.* ◆ Liverpool

LPS *abbrev.* ◆ Lord Privy Seal

LPU *abbrev.* ◆ Low Pay Unit

LQ *abbrev.* ◆ letter quality

lqdr *contraction* ◆ liquidator

LR *abbrev.* ◆ Land Registry ◆ Latvia (international vehicle registration) ◆ Lloyd's Register ◆ north-west London (British vehicle registration mark)

Lr *symbol* ◆ lawrencium (chemical element)

lr *shortening* ◆ lira (Italian monetary unit) ◆ lower

LRAD *abbrev.* ◆ Licentiate of the Royal Academy of Dancing

LRAM *abbrev.* ◆ Licentiate of the Royal Academy of Music

LRB *abbrev.* ◆ London Residuary Body

LRC *abbrev.* ◆ London Rowing Club

LRCM *abbrev.* ◆ Licentiate of the Royal College of Music

LRCP *abbrev.* ◆ Licentiate of the Royal College of Physicians

LRCS *abbrev.* ◆ Licentiate of the Royal College of Surgeons

LRCVS *abbrev.* ◆ Licentiate of the Royal College of Veterinary Surgeons

LRS *abbrev.* ◆ Land Registry Stamp

LRSC *abbrev.* ◆ Licentiate of the Royal Society of Chemistry

LRSM *abbrev.* ◆ Licentiate of the Royal Schools of Music

LRT *abbrev.* ◆ London Regional Transport

LS *abbrev.* ◆ Edinburgh (British vehicle registration mark) ◆ Law Society ◆ Leading Seaman ◆ Leeds (UK postcode) ◆ Lesotho (international vehicle registration) ◆ Linnaean Society ◆ loco sigilli (Latin, = in place of a seal) ◆ London Sinfonietta ◆ long shot ◆ loudspeaker

ls *abbrev.* ◆ left side ◆ lump sum

LSA *abbrev.* ◆ Learning Support Assistant ◆ Licentiate of the Society of Apothecaries

LSB *abbrev.* ◆ least significant bit

lsc *abbrev.* ◆ loco supra citato (Latin, = in the place cited above)

LSCS *abbrev.* ◆ lower segment Caesarian section

LSD *abbrev.* ◆ lysergic acid diethylamide

£sd *abbrev.* ◆ librae, solidi, denarii (Latin, = pounds, shillings, pence)

lsd *abbrev.* ◆ least significant digit

LSE *abbrev.* ◆ London School of Economics and Political Science ◆ London Stock Exchange ◆ Lorinser sport exhaust

lse *contraction* ◆ lease

LSgt *abbrev.* ◆ Lance Sergeant

LSHTM *abbrev.* ◆ London School of Hygiene and Tropical Medicine

LSI *abbrev.* ◆ Labour and Socialist International ◆ large-scale integration

LSJ *abbrev.* ◆ London School of Journalism

LSO *abbrev.* ◆ London Symphony Orchestra

LSS *abbrev.* ◆ life support system

LSW *abbrev.* ◆ lights spray and wipe

LT *abbrev.* ◆ Lithuania (international vehicle registration) ◆ local time ◆ locum tenens ◆ London Transport ◆ long ton ◆ low temperature ◆ low tension ◆ north-west London (British vehicle registration mark) ◆ Turkish lira (monetary unit)

Lt *contraction* ◆ Lieutenant

LTA *abbrev.* ◆ Lawn Tennis Association ◆ lighter than air

LTB *abbrev.* ◆ London Tourist Board

ltb *abbrev.* ◆ low-tension battery

LTBT *abbrev.* ◆ Limited Test Ban Treaty

LTC *abbrev.* ◆ lawn tennis club

Lt Cdr *contraction* ◆ Lieutenant Commander

LTCL *abbrev.* ◆ Licentiate of Trinity College of Music, London

Lt Col. *shortening* ◆ Lieutenant Colonel

Lt Com. *shortening* ◆ Lieutenant Commander

Ltd *contraction* ◆ Limited

LTE *abbrev.* ◆ London Transport Executive

Lt Gen. *shortening* ◆ Lieutenant General

Lt Gov. *shortening* ◆ Lieutenant Governor

LTH *abbrev.* ◆ luteotropic hormone

LTh *abbrev.* ◆ Licentiate in Theology

lth. *shortening* ◆ leather

lthr *contraction* ◆ leather

lt inf. *shortening* ◆ light infantry

LTM *abbrev.* ◆ Licentiate in Tropical Medicine ◆ long-term memory

LTN *abbrev.* ◆ Luton (airport baggage label)

LTO *abbrev.* ◆ Leading Torpedo Operator

LTOM *abbrev.* ◆ London Traded Options Market

LTQ *abbrev.* ◆ Le Touquet (airport baggage label)

LtRN *abbrev.* ◆ Lieutenant, Royal Navy

LU *abbrev.* ◆ lock-up ◆ Luton (UK postcode) ◆ north-west London (British vehicle registration mark)

Lu *symbol* ◆ lutetium (chemical element)

lu *shortening* ◆ lumen

lub. *shortening* ◆ lubricant ◆ lubricate ◆ lubrication

lubr. *shortening* ◆ lubricant ◆ lubricate ◆ lubrication

LUD *abbrev.* ◆ leather-upholstered dashboard

LUM *abbrev.* ◆ lunar excursion module

lum. *shortening* ◆ luminous

LUN *abbrev.* ◆ Lusaka (airport baggage label)

l/up *contraction* ◆ lock-up

LUT *abbrev.* ◆ launcher umbilical tower

Luth. *shortening* ◆ Lutheran

LUX *abbrev.* ◆ Luxembourg (airport baggage label)

Lux. *shortening* ◆ Luxembourg ◆ Luxembourger

lux. *shortening* ◆ luxurious ◆ luxury

LuxF *abbrev.* ◆ Luxembourg franc (monetary unit)

LV *abbrev.* ◆ Argentine Republic (international civil aircraft marking) ◆ El Al Israel Airlines (airline baggage code) ◆ left ventricle ◆ Liverpool (British vehicle registration mark) ◆ luncheon voucher

Lv *contraction* ◆ lev (Bulgarian monetary unit)

lv *abbrev.* ◆ low voltage

LVA *abbrev.* ◆ Licensed Victuallers' Association

LVS *abbrev.* ◆ Licentiate in Veterinary Science

LW *abbrev.* ◆ lightweight ◆ long wave ◆ low water ◆ north-west London (British vehicle registration mark)

LWA *abbrev.* ◆ London Weighting Allowance

LW & S *abbrev.* ◆ lights wipe and spray

lwb *abbrev.* ◆ long wheel-base

LWL *abbrev.* ◆ length at waterline ◆ load waterline

LWM *abbrev.* ◆ low water mark

LWR *abbrev.* ◆ light-water reactor

LWT *abbrev.* ◆ London Weekend Television

LX *abbrev.* ◆ electrical ◆ electrics ◆ Luxembourg (international civil aircraft marking) ◆ technical staff who work on lighting and sound ◆ north-west London (British vehicle registration mark)

lx *abbrev.* ◆ lux

LXR *abbrev.* ◆ Luxor (airport baggage label)

LXS *abbrev.* ◆ Lemnos (airport baggage label)

LXX *abbrev.* ◆ Septuagint (Greek translation of the Old Testament said to have been undertaken by 70 (in Roman numerals lxx) scholars)

lxxx *abbrev.* ◆ love and kisses (before signature of letter)

LY *abbrev.* ◆ El Al Israel Airlines (airline baggage code) ◆ north-west London (British vehicle registration mark)

LZ *abbrev.* ◆ Armagh (British vehicle registration mark) ◆ Bulgaria (international civil aircraft marking)

M

M *abbrev.* ◆ Malta (international vehicle registration) ◆ Manchester (UK postcode) ◆ medium (clothing size) ◆ mega- ◆ Member ◆ metronome (with pulse value) ◆ monetary aggregate ◆ Monday ◆ million ◆ Monsieur (French, = Mr) ◆ Motorway

m *abbrev.* ◆ maiden over (cricket) ◆ male ◆ mark (German monetary unit) ◆ married ◆ masculine ◆ mass ◆ medium ◆ metre ◆ mile ◆ mille- ◆ million ◆ minim (liquid measure) ◆ minute ◆ month ◆ morning

MA *abbrev.* ◆ Chester (British vehicle registration mark) ◆ Magyar Legikolekedesi Vallat (Hungarian, = Hungarian Airlines) (airline baggage code) ◆ Massachusetts (US postcode) ◆ Master of Arts ◆ Mathematical Association ◆ menstrual age ◆ mental age ◆ Military Academy ◆ Morocco (international vehicle registration) ◆ Museums Association

mA *abbrev.* ◆ milliampere

m/a *abbrev.* ◆ my account

MAA *abbrev.* ◆ Madras (airport baggage label) ◆ Master at Arms ◆ Motor Agents' Association

MAB *abbrev.* ◆ monoclonal antibody

MABP *abbrev.* ◆ mean arterial blood pressure

MAC *abbrev.* ◆ maximum allowable concentration ◆ multiplex analogue components

Mac. *shortening* ◆ Macao

MACC *abbrev.* ◆ military aid to the civilian community

Macc. *shortening* ◆ Maccabees (books of Bible)

Maced. *shortening* ◆ Macedonia ◆ Macedonian

mach. *shortening* ◆ machine ◆ machinery ◆ machinist

macroecon. *shortening* ◆ macroeconomics

MAD *abbrev.* ◆ Madrid (airport baggage label) ◆ major affective disorder

Mad *acronym* ◆ magnetic anomaly detection ◆ mutual assured destruction

Mad. *shortening* ◆ Madeira

mad *abbrev.* ◆ maintenance, assembly and disassembly

Madag. *shortening* ◆ Madagascar

MADO *abbrev.* ◆ Member of the Association of Dispensing Opticians

mag. *shortening* ◆ magazine

MA(Econ) *abbrev.* ◆ Master of Arts in Economics

MA(Ed) *abbrev.* ◆ Master of Arts in Education

maest. *shortening* ◆ maestoso (Italian, = majestic) (music)

MAG *abbrev.* ◆ Motorcycle Action Group

Mag. *shortening* ◆ Magnificat (canticle)

mag. *shortening* ◆ magazine ◆ magnetic

magg. *shortening* ◆ maggiore (Italian, = major) (type of musical scale)

maglev *acronym* ◆ magnetically levitated ◆ magnetic levitation

magn. *shortening* ◆ magnetic ◆ magnetism

magnif. *shortening* ◆ magnificent

MAgr *abbrev.* ◆ Master of Agriculture

mah. *shortening* ◆ mahogany

mahog. *shortening* ◆ mahogany

MAIB *abbrev.* ◆ Marine Accident Investigation Board

maint. *shortening* ◆ maintenance

mais. *shortening* ◆ maisonette

MAIU *abbrev.* ◆ Marine Accident Investigation Unit

Maj. *shortening* ◆ Major

maj. *shortening* ◆ major ◆ majority

Maj.-Gen. *shortening* ◆ Major-General

MAL *abbrev.* ◆ Malaysia (international vehicle registration)

Mal. *abbrev.* ◆ Malachi (book of Bible) ◆ Malaysia ◆ Malaysian ◆ Malta ◆ Maltese

mall. *shortening* ◆ malleable

MAN *abbrev.* ◆ Manchester (airport baggage label)

Man. *shortening* ◆ Manila ◆ Manitoba

man. *shortening* ◆ manual ◆ manufacture

mand. *shortening* ◆ mandamus (Latin, = we send) (sort of writ) ◆ mandatory ◆ mandolin

M & B *abbrev.* ◆ May and Baker ◆ Mills and Boon

M & E *abbrev.* ◆ music and effects

Man. Dir. *shortening* ◆ Managing Director

M & G *abbrev.* ◆ Mercantile and General (insurance company)

m & r *abbrev.* ◆ maintenance and repairs

M & S *abbrev.* ◆ Marks and Spencer PLC

m & s *abbrev.* ◆ maintenance and supply

Man. Ed. *shortening* ◆ Managing Editor

manf. *shortening* ◆ manufacture ◆ manufactured ◆ manufacturer

Manit. *shortening* ◆ Manitoba

man. op. *shortening* ◆ manually operated

man. pr. *shortening* ◆ mane primo (Latin, = first thing in the morning)

Mans *contraction* ◆ Mansions

manuf. *shortening* ◆ manufacture ◆ manufactured ◆ manufacturer

MAO *abbrev.* ◆ Master of Arts, Obstetrics

MAP *abbrev.* ◆ mean arterial pressure ◆ medical aid post

MAppArts *abbrev.* ◆ Master in Applied Arts

MAppSc *abbrev.* ◆ Master in Applied Science

Mar *abbrev.* ◆ memory address register

Mar. *shortening* ◆ March

mar. *shortening* ◆ marimba ◆ marine ◆ maritime ◆ married

marc *acronym* ◆ machine-readable cataloguing

marc. *shortening* ◆ marcato (Italian, = marked)

MArch *abbrev.* ◆ Master of Architecture

MArchE *abbrev.* ◆ Master of Architectural Engineering

march. *shortening* ◆ marchioness

marg. *shortening* ◆ margarine ◆ margin ◆ marginal

marit. *shortening* ◆ maritime

mar. lic. *shortening* ◆ marriage licence

marq. *shortening* ◆ marquis

mart. *shortening* ◆ martyr

marv *acronym* ◆ manoeuvrable re-entry vehicle

MAS *abbrev.* ◆ Master of Agricultural Science ◆ Master of Applied Science ◆ Medical Advisory Service

mas. *shortening* ◆ masculine

MASc *abbrev.* ◆ Master of Agricultural Science ◆ Master of Applied Science

masc. *shortening* ◆ masculine

maser *acronym* ◆ microwave amplification by stimulated emission of radiation

MASH *abbrev.* ◆ Mobile Army Surgical Hospital (US)

Mass. *abbrev.* ◆ Massachusetts

Masta *acronym* ◆ Medical Advisory Service for Travellers Abroad

mat. *shortening* ◆ maternity ◆ matinée ◆ matins ◆ matrix ◆ maturity

math. *shortening* ◆ mathematical ◆ mathematics (US)

maths *contraction* ◆ mathematics

Matt. *shortening* ◆ Matthew (book of Bible)

matts *acronym* ◆ multiple airborne target trajectory system

MATV *abbrev.* ◆ master antenna television

Maur. *shortening* ◆ Mauritius

Mau. Re *contraction* ◆ Mauritian rupee (monetary unit)

MAW *abbrev.* ◆ medium assault weapon

max. *shortening* ◆ maxim ◆ maximum

MAYC *abbrev.* ◆ Methodist Association of Youth Clubs

Mayo *shortening* ◆ County Mayo

MB *abbrev.* ◆ Chester (British vehicle registration mark) ◆ Maternity Benefit ◆ Medicinae Baccalaureus (Latin, = Bachelor of Medicine) ◆ megabyte

mb *abbrev.* ◆ millibar

MBA *abbrev.* ◆ Master of Business Administration

mbar *contraction* ◆ millibar

MBC *abbrev.* ◆ Mountain Bike Club

mbc *abbrev.* ◆ maximum breathing capacity

MBCS *abbrev.* ◆ Member of the British Computer Society

MBD *abbrev.* ◆ minimal brain dysfunction

MBE *abbrev.* ◆ Member of the Order of the British Empire

MBF *abbrev.* ◆ Musicians' Benevolent Fund

MBFR *abbrev.* ◆ Mutual Balanced Force Reduction

mbH *abbrev.* ◆ mit beschränkter Haftung (German, = Ltd)

MBK *abbrev.* ◆ missing, believed killed

MBI *abbrev.* ◆ management buy-in

MBIFD *abbrev.* ◆ Member of the British Institute of Funeral Directors

MBL *abbrev.* ◆ menstrual blood loss

MBO *abbrev.* ◆ management buy-out ◆ management by objectives

MBP *abbrev.* ◆ mean blood pressure

MBR *abbrev.* ◆ memory buffer register

mbr *contraction* ◆ member

MBS *abbrev.* ◆ Manchester Business School

MBSc *abbrev.* ◆ Master of Business Science

MBT *abbrev.* ◆ main battle tank

Mbyte *contraction* ◆ megabyte

MC *abbrev.* ◆ Magister Chirurgiae (Latin, = Master of Surgery) ◆ magistrates' court ◆ marriage certificate ◆ Master of Ceremonies ◆ medical certificate ◆ Member of Congress ◆ Member of Council ◆ Military Cross ◆ Monaco (international vehicle registration) ◆ Monte Carlo (international civil aircraft marking) ◆ Morse Code ◆ north-east London (British vehicle registration mark)

m/c *abbrev.* ◆ motor cycle

MCA *abbrev.* ◆ monetary compensatory amounts ◆ Motor Cycle Association ◆ multiple classification analysis

MCANW *abbrev.* ◆ Medical Campaign Against Nuclear Weapons

MCB *abbrev.* ◆ memory control block ◆ Metric Conversion Board

mcb *abbrev.* ◆ miniature circuit breaker

MCC *abbrev.* ◆ Marylebone Cricket Club ◆ Maxwell Communications Corporation ◆ Motor Caravanners' Club

MCCA *abbrev.* ◆ Minor Counties Cricket Association

MCCU *abbrev.* ◆ mobile coronary care unit

MCE *abbrev.* ◆ Master of Chemical Engineering ◆ Master of Civil Engineering

MCGA *abbrev.* ◆ multicolour graphics array

MCH *abbrev.* ◆ mean corpuscular haemoglobin

MCh *abbrev.* ◆ Magister Chirurgiae (Latin, = Master of Surgery)

MCHC *abbrev.* ◆ mean corpuscular haemoglobin concentration

MChD *abbrev.* ◆ Magister Chirurgiae Dentalis (Latin, = Master of Dental Surgery)

MChE *abbrev.* ◆ Master of Chemical Engineering

MChemEng *abbrev.* ◆ Master of Chemical Engineering

MChir *abbrev.* ◆ Magister Chirurgiae (Latin, = Master of Surgery)

MChOrth *abbrev.* ◆ Magister Chirurgiae Orthopaedicae

MChS *abbrev.* ◆ Member of the Society of Chiropodists

MCIOB *abbrev.* ◆ Member of the Chartered Institute of Building

MCIS *abbrev.* ◆ Member of the Institute of Chartered Secretaries and Administrators

MCL *abbrev.* ◆ Master of Civil Law

MCM *abbrev.* ◆ Monte Carlo (airport baggage label)

MCom *abbrev.* ◆ Master of Commerce

MComm *abbrev.* ◆ Master of Commerce

MCOphth *abbrev.* ◆ Member of the College of Ophthalmologists

MCP *abbrev.* ◆ male chauvinist pig ◆ Member of the College of Preceptors

MCPO *abbrev.* ◆ Master Chief Petty Officer

MCPS *abbrev.* ◆ Mechanical Copyright Protection Society ◆ Member of the College of Physicians and Surgeons

mcq *abbrev.* ◆ multiple-choice question

MCR *abbrev.* ◆ Middle Common Room ◆ mobile control room

MCS *abbrev.* ◆ Marine Conservation Society ◆ Master of Commercial Science ◆ Military College of Science

Mc/s *abbrev.* ◆ megacycles per second

MCSP *abbrev.* ◆ Member of the Chartered Society of Physiotherapy

MCST *abbrev.* ◆ Member of the College of Speech Therapists

MCT *abbrev.* ◆ Muscat (airport baggage label)

MCU *abbrev.* ◆ medium close-up (photography)

MCV *abbrev.* ◆ mean corpuscular volume

MCW *abbrev.* ◆ modulated continuous wave

MD *abbrev.* ◆ main droite (French, = right hand) ◆ malicious damage ◆ Managing Director ◆ mano destra (Italian, = right hand) ◆ market day ◆ Maryland (US postcode) ◆ Medellín (airport baggage label) ◆ Medicinae Doctor (Latin, = Doctor of Medicine) ◆ mentally

deficient ◆ Middle Dutch ◆ muscular dystrophy ◆ musical director ◆ north-east London (British vehicle registration mark)

Md *contraction* ◆ Maryland

Md *symbol* ◆ mendelevium (chemical element)

MDA *abbrev.* ◆ Muscular Dystrophy Association

mda *abbrev.* ◆ monochrome display adaptor

MDC *abbrev.* ◆ more developed country

Mddx *contraction* ◆ Middlesex

MDentSc *abbrev.* ◆ Master of Dental Science

MDF *abbrev.* ◆ Manic Depression Fellowship

MDL *abbrev.* ◆ Mandalay (airport baggage label)

Mdlle *contraction* ◆ Mademoiselle (French, = Miss)

Mdm. *shortening* ◆ Madame (French, = Mrs)

MDMA *abbrev.* ◆ methylene-dioxymethamphetamine (the hallucinogenic drug Ecstasy)

mdnt *contraction* ◆ midnight

MDR *abbrev.* ◆ memory data register ◆ minimum daily requirement

MDS *abbrev.* ◆ Master of Dental Surgery

MDSc *abbrev.* ◆ Master of Dental Science

MD/st *contraction* ◆ memory-adjusted driver's seat

MDT *abbrev.* ◆ mean down time

MDU *abbrev.* ◆ Medical Defence Union

MDu *abbrev.* ◆ Middle Dutch

ME *abbrev.* ◆ Maine (US postcode) ◆ Master of Engineering ◆ mechanical engineer ◆ Medway (UK postcode) ◆ Methodist Episcopal ◆ Middle East ◆ Middle English ◆ mining engineer ◆ Most Excellent ◆ myalgic encephalomyelitis ◆ north-east London (British vehicle registration mark)

Me *contraction* ◆ Maine

me *abbrev.* ◆ marbled edges

meas. *shortening* ◆ measure ◆ measurement

Meath *shortening* ◆ County Meath
MEB *abbrev.* ◆ Melbourne (airport baggage label)
MEC *abbrev.* ◆ Member of the Executive Council ◆ Methodist Episcopal Church ◆ minimum effective concentration
MEc *abbrev.* ◆ Master of Economics
mech. *shortening* ◆ mechanic ◆ mechanical ◆ mechanics ◆ mechanism
MEcon *abbrev.* ◆ Master of Economics
MED *abbrev.* ◆ Medina (airport baggage label) ◆ minimum effective dose
MEd *abbrev.* ◆ Master of Education
Med. *shortening* ◆ Mediterranean
med. *shortening* ◆ medal ◆ medallist ◆ medical ◆ medicine ◆ medieval ◆ medium
Medit. *shortening* ◆ Mediterranean
Medlars *acronym* ◆ Medical Literature Analysis and Retrieval System
MEE *abbrev.* ◆ Master of Electrical Engineering
Melan. *shortening* ◆ Melanesia ◆ Melanesian
Mem. *shortening* ◆ Member
mem. *shortening* ◆ memoir ◆ memorandum ◆ memorial ◆ memory
Mencap *acronym* ◆ Royal Society for Mentally Handicapped Children and Adults
MEng *abbrev.* ◆ Master of Engineering
menst. *shortening* ◆ menstrual ◆ menstruation
mensur. *shortening* ◆ mensuration
ment. *shortening* ◆ mental ◆ mention ◆ mentioned
mentd *contraction* ◆ mentioned
MEP *abbrev.* ◆ Member of the European Parliament
mep *abbrev.* ◆ mean effective pressure
Mer. *shortening* ◆ Merionethshire
mer. *shortening* ◆ meridian ◆ meridional
merc. *shortening* ◆ mercantile
Merlin *acronym* ◆ Multi-Element Radio-Linked Interferometer Network
MERU *abbrev.* ◆ Maharishi European Research University

MESc *abbrev.* ◆ Master of Engineering Science
Messrs *contraction* ◆ Messieurs (French) (used as a plural of *Mr*)
Met. *shortening* ◆ Metropolitan Opera House (New York) ◆ Metropolitan Police (London)
met. *shortening* ◆ metallic ◆ metallurgical ◆ metallurgist ◆ metallurgy ◆ metaphor ◆ metaphoric ◆ metaphysics ◆ meteorological ◆ metronome
metall. *shortening* ◆ metallurgical ◆ metallurgy
metaph. *shortening* ◆ metaphor ◆ metaphoric ◆ metaphysical ◆ metaphysics
meteor. *shortening* ◆ meteorological ◆ meteorology
meteorol. *shortening* ◆ meteorological ◆ meteorology
Meth. *shortening* ◆ Methodist
m et n *abbrev.* ◆ mane et nocte (Latin, = morning and night)
metsat *acronym* ◆ meteorological satellite
MeV *abbrev.* ◆ mega-electron-volt
MEW *abbrev.* ◆ microwave early warning system
MEX *abbrev.* ◆ Mexico (international vehicle registration) ◆ Mexico City (airport baggage label)
Mex. *shortening* ◆ Mexican ◆ Mexico
MEZ *abbrev.* ◆ mitteleuropäische Zeit (German, = Central European Time)
MF *abbrev.* ◆ machine finished ◆ medium frequency ◆ Middle French ◆ multi-frequency ◆ north-east London (British vehicle registration mark)
M/F *abbrev.* ◆ male or female
mF *abbrev.* ◆ microfarad
mf *abbrev.* ◆ mezzo-forte (Italian, = medium-loud) (music)
MFA *abbrev.* ◆ Master of Fine Arts ◆ Multi-Fibre Arrangement
MFARCS *abbrev.* ◆ Member of the Faculty of Anaesthetists of the Royal College of Surgeons
MFD *abbrev.* ◆ minimum fatal dose

mfd *contraction* ◆ manufactured
mfg *contraction* ◆ manufacturing
MFH *abbrev.* ◆ Master of Foxhounds
◆ mobile field hospital
MFHom *abbrev.* ◆ Member of the Faculty
of Homeopathy
MFlem *abbrev.* ◆ Middle Flemish
mflops *pronounced* em-flops *acronym*
◆ million floating-point operations per
second
MFM *abbrev.* ◆ modified frequency
modulation
MFN *abbrev.* ◆ most favoured nation
MFr *abbrev.* ◆ Middle French
mfr *contraction* ◆ manufacturer
mft *contraction* ◆ mistura fiat (Latin, = let
a mixture be made)
mfv *abbrev.* ◆ motor fleet vehicle
MG *abbrev.* ◆ machine-gun ◆ main
gauche (French, = left hand) ◆ Major-
General ◆ Morris Garages ◆ north-east
London (British vehicle registration
mark)
Mg *symbol* ◆ magnesium (chemical
element)
mg *abbrev.* ◆ milligram
mgawd *abbrev.* ◆ make good all works
disturbed
MGB *abbrev.* ◆ Ministerstvo
Gosudarstvennoi Bezopasnosti
(Russian, = Ministry for State Security)
(Soviet espionage and counter-
espionage agency, also responsible for
prisoner-of-war camps and the
ideological supervision of the Soviet
military and of satellite states 1946–53)
MGC *abbrev.* ◆ Marriage Guidance
Council
mgd *abbrev.* ◆ million gallons per day
MGlam *abbrev.* ◆ Mid Glamorgan
MGM *abbrev.* ◆ Metro-Goldwyn-Mayer
◆ mobile guided missile
mgmt *shortening* ◆ management
MGN *abbrev.* ◆ Mirror Group
Newspapers
MGQ *abbrev.* ◆ Mogadishu (airport
baggage label)

Mgr *contraction* ◆ Monseigneur
◆ Monsignor
mgr *shortening* ◆ manager
MH *abbrev.* ◆ Malaysian Airline System
(airline baggage code) ◆ marital history
◆ Master of Horse ◆ Master of Hounds
◆ north-east London (British vehicle
registration mark)
mH *abbrev.* ◆ millihenry
MHA *abbrev.* ◆ Member of the House of
Assembly ◆ Methodist Homes for the
Aged
MHC *abbrev.* ◆ major histocompatibility
complex
MHD *abbrev.* ◆ magnetic hydrodynamic
MHE *abbrev.* ◆ Master of Home
Economics
MHG *abbrev.* ◆ Middle High German
MHK *abbrev.* ◆ Member of the House of
Keys
MHLG *abbrev.* ◆ Ministry of Housing and
Local Government
MHortSc *abbrev.* ◆ Master of
Horticultural Science
MHR *abbrev.* ◆ Member of the House of
Representatives
MHRA *abbrev.* ◆ Modern Humanities
Research Association
MHS *abbrev.* ◆ medical history sheet
◆ message handling system
MHTGR *abbrev.* ◆ modular high-
temperature gas-cooled reactor
MHW *abbrev.* ◆ mean high water
MHz *abbrev.* ◆ megahertz
MI *abbrev.* ◆ medical inspection
◆ Michigan (US postcode) ◆ Military
Intelligence (UK state security and
counter-espionage service) ◆ mounted
infantry ◆ myocardial infarction
mi. *shortening* ◆ mile
MI5 *abbrev.* ◆ Military Intelligence 5
(popular title for UK state security
service; official use ceased 1964)
MI6 *abbrev.* ◆ Military Intelligence 6
(popular title for UK state counter-
espionage service; official use ceased
1964)
MIA *abbrev.* ◆ missing in action

MIAA & S *abbrev.* ◆ Member of the Incorporated Institute of Auctioneers and Surveyors

Mic. *shortening* ◆ Micah (book of Bible)

mic. *shortening* ◆ mica

MICE *abbrev.* ◆ Member of the Institution of Civil Engineers

Mich. *shortening* ◆ Michaelmas ◆ Michigan

MIChemE *abbrev.* ◆ Member of the Institute of Chemical Engineers

MICR *abbrev.* ◆ magnetic ink character recognition

Micro *acronym* ◆ Multinational Initiative for the Use of Computers in Research Organizations

Micro. *shortening* ◆ Micronesia ◆ Micronesian

microbiol. *shortening* ◆ microbiology

micros. *shortening* ◆ microscopic ◆ microscopy

MICU *abbrev.* ◆ mobile intensive care unit

MID *abbrev.* ◆ minimum infective dose

mid. *shortening* ◆ middle

Midas *acronym* ◆ Missile Defence Alarm System

Middx *contraction* ◆ Middlesex

Midi *acronym* ◆ musical instrument digital interface

MIEE *abbrev.* ◆ Member of the Institution of Electrical Engineers

MIF *abbrev.* ◆ migration inhibition factor ◆ Miners' International Federation

MIG *abbrev.* ◆ mortgage indemnity guarantee

MiG *abbrev.* ◆ Mikoyan and Gurevich (designers of Soviet warplane)

MIGasE *abbrev.* ◆ Member of the Institution of Gas Engineers

MIL *abbrev.* ◆ Member of the Institute of Linguists ◆ Milan (airport baggage label)

mil. *shortening* ◆ mileage ◆ military

milit. *shortening* ◆ military

MIMechE *abbrev.* ◆ Member of the Institution of Mechanical Engineers

MIMinE *abbrev.* ◆ Member of the Institution of Mining Engineers

min. *shortening* ◆ minimum ◆ mining ◆ minister ◆ ministry ◆ minor ◆ minute

mineral. *shortening* ◆ mineralogical ◆ mineralogy

Minn. *shortening* ◆ Minnesota

MInstD *abbrev.* ◆ Member of the Institute of Directors

MInstP *abbrev.* ◆ Member of the Institute of Physics

MIP *abbrev.* ◆ marine insurance policy ◆ monthly investment plan

mip *abbrev.* ◆ mean indicated pressure

MIPA *abbrev.* ◆ Member of the Institute of Practitioners of Advertising

MIPM *abbrev.* ◆ Member of the Institute of Personnel Management

mips *acronym* ◆ millions of instructions per second

MIR *abbrev.* ◆ mortgage interest relief

Miras *acronym* ◆ mortgage interest relief at source

MIRV *abbrev.* ◆ multiple independently targeted re-entry vehicle

MIS *abbrev.* ◆ Management Information System

misc. *shortening* ◆ miscellaneous ◆ miscellany

MISD *abbrev.* ◆ multiple instruction, single data stream

Miss. *shortening* ◆ Mississippi

mist. *shortening* ◆ mistura (Latin, = mixture)

mistrans. *shortening* ◆ mistranslation

MIStructE *abbrev.* ◆ Member of the Institution of Structural Engineers

MIT *abbrev.* ◆ Massachusetts Institute of Technology

mitts *acronym* ◆ minutes of telecommunications traffic

MIU *abbrev.* ◆ Maharishi International University

mixt. *shortening* ◆ mixture

MJ *abbrev.* ◆ Luton (British vehicle registration mark) ◆ megajoule

MJI *abbrev.* ◆ Member of the Institute of Journalists

MJQ *abbrev.* ◆ Modern Jazz Quartet

MK *contraction* ◆ Air Mauritius (airline baggage code) ◆ Malawi kwacha (monetary unit) ◆ mark (enumeration of design variants of car etc) ◆ Milton Keynes (UK postcode) ◆ north-east London (British vehicle registration mark)

mk *contraction* ◆ mark (German monetary unit) ◆ markka (Finnish monetary unit)

mks *abbrev.* ◆ metre-kilogram-second

mksa *abbrev.* ◆ metre-kilogram-second-ampere

mkt *contraction* ◆ market

ML *abbrev.* ◆ Licentiate in Midwifery ◆ medieval Latin ◆ Motherwell (UK postcode) ◆ north-east London (British vehicle registration mark)

ml *abbrev.* ◆ millilitre

MLA *abbrev.* ◆ Member of the Legislative Assembly ◆ Modern Language Association ◆ Valetta (airport baggage label)

MLC *abbrev.* ◆ mixed lymphocyte culture

MLD *abbrev.* ◆ mean lethal dose ◆ minimum lethal dose

MLF *abbrev.* ◆ multilateral force

MLG *abbrev.* ◆ Middle Low German

mlg. *shortening* ◆ mileage

MLibSc *abbrev.* ◆ Master of Library Science

MLitt *abbrev.* ◆ Magister Litterarum (Latin, = Master of Letters)

Mlle *contraction* ◆ Mademoiselle (French, = Miss)

MLR *abbrev.* ◆ minimum lending rate ◆ mixed lymphocyte reaction

MLRS *abbrev.* ◆ multiple launch rocket system

MLS *abbrev.* ◆ Master of Library Science ◆ Member of the Linnean Society

MLSO *abbrev.* ◆ Medical Laboratory Scientific Officer

MLV *abbrev.* ◆ murine leukaemia virus

MLW *abbrev.* ◆ Monrovia (airport baggage label)

MM *abbrev.* ◆ Maelzel's metronome (with pulse value) ◆ Military Medal ◆ mucus membrane ◆ north-east London (British vehicle registration mark) ◆ Sociedad Aeronautica Medellín (airline baggage code)

mm *abbrev.* ◆ millimetre

MMA *abbrev.* ◆ Malmö (airport baggage label)

MMath *abbrev.* ◆ Master of Mathematics

MMB *abbrev.* ◆ Milk Marketing Board

MMC *abbrev.* ◆ Monopolies and Mergers Commission

MME *abbrev.* ◆ Master of Mechanical Engineering ◆ Middlesborough (airport baggage label)

Mme *contraction* ◆ Madame (French, = Mrs)

MMed *abbrev.* ◆ Master of Medicine

MMet *abbrev.* ◆ Master of Metallurgy

MMetE *abbrev.* ◆ Master of Metallurgical Engineering

mmf *abbrev.* ◆ magnetomotive force

MMG *abbrev.* ◆ medium machine gun

mmHg *abbrev.* ◆ millimetre of mercury (unit of pressure)

MMI *abbrev.* ◆ man–machine interface

3M *abbrev.* ◆ Minnesota Mining and Manufacturing Company

mmol *abbrev.* ◆ millimole

MMP *abbrev.* ◆ Military Mounted Police

MMQ *abbrev.* ◆ mimimum manufacturing quantity

MMR *abbrev.* ◆ mass miniature radiography ◆ measles, mumps and rubella

MMU *abbrev.* ◆ memory management unit

MMus *abbrev.* ◆ Master of Music

MN *abbrev.* ◆ Master of Nursing ◆ Merchant Navy ◆ Minnesota (US postcode)

Mn *symbol* ◆ manganese (chemical element)

MNAD *abbrev.* ◆ Multinational Airborne Division (Nato)

MNC *abbrev.* ◆ multinational company

MND *abbrev.* ◆ motor neurone disease

MNE *abbrev.* ✦ Mentone (airport baggage label)

MNL *abbrev.* ✦ Manila (airport baggage label)

MNR *abbrev.* ✦ marine nature reserve

Mnr *contraction* ✦ Mijnheer (Dutch, = Mr)

MNSc *abbrev.* ✦ Master of Nursing Science

MNurs *abbrev.* ✦ Master of Nursing

MO *abbrev.* ✦ mass observation ✦ Medical Officer ✦ Meteorological Office ✦ Missouri (US postcode) ✦ modus operandi (Latin, = way of working) ✦ money order ✦ Reading (British vehicle registration mark)

Mo *symbol* ✦ molybdenum (chemical element)

Mo. *shortening* ✦ Missouri

mo. *shortening* ✦ month

MOC *abbrev.* ✦ Mozambique (international vehicle registration)

MOA *abbrev.* ✦ memorandum of agreement

MOBS *abbrev.* ✦ multiple orbit bombardment system

MOD *abbrev.* ✦ mail order department ✦ Ministry of Defence

mod. *shortening* ✦ model ✦ moderate ✦ moderato (Italian, = moderate) (music) ✦ modern ✦ modernized ✦ modernization ✦ modification

modem *acronym* ✦ modulator-demodulator

MOH *abbrev.* ✦ Master of Otter Hounds ✦ Medical Officer of Health

mol. *shortening* ✦ molecular ✦ molecule

mol. wt *contraction* ✦ molecular weight

Moma *acronym* ✦ Museum of Modern Art

Momi *acronym* ✦ Museum of the Moving Image

moms *acronym* ✦ mervaerdiomsaetningsskat (Danish, = VAT) ✦ mervardesomsattningsskatt (Swedish, = VAT)

Mon. *shortening* ✦ Monaco ✦ Monday ✦ Monegasque ✦ Monmouthshire

mon. *shortening* ✦ monastery ✦ monastic ✦ monetary

Monag. *shortening* ✦ County Monaghan

Mong. *shortening* ✦ Mongolia ✦ Mongolian

Mont. *shortening* ✦ Montana ✦ Montgomeryshire

MOR *abbrev.* ✦ middle-of-the-road (of broadcast music)

Mor. *shortening* ✦ Moroccan ✦ Morocco

mor. *shortening* ✦ morendo (Italian, = dying) (music) ✦ morocco (binding)

Mori *acronym* ✦ Market and Opinion Research Institute

morn. *shortening* ✦ morning

morph. *shortening* ✦ morphological ✦ morphology

morphol. *shortening* ✦ morphological ✦ morphology

mor. sol. *shortening* ✦ more solito (Latin, = in the usual way)

mort. *shortening* ✦ mortal ✦ mortality ✦ mortar ✦ mortgage ✦ mortuary

MOS *abbrev.* ✦ metal oxide semiconductor

MOT *abbrev.* ✦ Ministry of Transport

mot. *shortening* ✦ motor ✦ motorized

MOU *abbrev.* ✦ memorandum of understanding

mous *acronym* ✦ multiple occurrence of unexplained symptoms

Mouse *acronym* ✦ minimum orbital unmanned satellite of the earth

mov. *shortening* ✦ movimento (Italian, = motion) (music)

Move *acronym* ✦ Men over Violence (offering counselling etc to wife-batterers)

MOW *abbrev.* ✦ Moscow (airport baggage label) ✦ Movement for the Ordination of Women

MP *abbrev.* ✦ Member of Parliament ✦ Metropolitan Police ✦ Military Police ✦ mounted police ✦ north-east London (British vehicle registration mark)

mp *abbrev.* ✦ mezzo-piano (Italian, = moderately quiet) (music) ✦ melting-point

MPAA *abbrev.* ◆ Motion Picture Association of America

MPAGB *abbrev.* ◆ Modern Pentathlon Association of Great Britain

MPB *abbrev.* ◆ male pattern baldness

MPC *abbrev.* ◆ maximum permissible concentration ◆ Metropolitan Police Commissioner

MPD *abbrev.* ◆ maximum permissible dose

MPE *abbrev.* ◆ Master of Physical Education ◆ maximum permissible exposure (to radiation) ◆ maximum possible error

mpg *abbrev.* ◆ miles per gallon

MPh *abbrev.* ◆ Master of Philosophy

mph *abbrev.* ◆ miles per hour

MPharm *abbrev.* ◆ Master of Pharmacy

MPhil *abbrev.* ◆ Master of Philosophy

MPI *abbrev.* ◆ maximum permissible intake ◆ Max Planck Institute

MPL *abbrev.* ◆ maximum permissible level

MPLA *abbrev.* ◆ Movimento Popolar de Libertação de Angola (Portuguese, = Popular Movement for the Liberation of Angola)

mpm *abbrev.* ◆ metres per minute

MPS *abbrev.* ◆ Member of the Pharmaceutical Society ◆ Member of the Philological Society

mps *abbrev.* ◆ metres per second

MPsych *abbrev.* ◆ Master of Psychology

MPU *abbrev.* ◆ Medical Practitioners Union

mpu *abbrev.* ◆ microprocessor unit

MPV *abbrev.* ◆ multipurpose vehicle

Mpy *contraction* ◆ Maatschappij (Dutch, = Company)

Mqe *contraction* ◆ Martinique

MR *abbrev.* ◆ Air Mauretanie (airline baggage code) ◆ magnetic resonance ◆ map reference ◆ Master of the Rolls ◆ Mauritian rupee (monetary unit) ◆ mental retardation ◆ metabolic rate ◆ motivational research ◆ Swindon (British vehicle registration mark)

Mr *pronounced* mis-ter *contraction* ◆ Master (former title of adult men, now supplanted by its abbreviation, which is pronounced as shown)

MRA *abbrev.* ◆ Moral Rearmament

MRAeS *abbrev.* ◆ Member of the Royal Aeronautical Society

MRAF *abbrev.* ◆ Marshal of the Royal Air Force

MRAS *abbrev.* ◆ Member of the Royal Asiatic Society ◆ Member of the Royal Astronomical Society

MRBM *abbrev.* ◆ medium range ballistic missile

MRC *abbrev.* ◆ Medical Research Council

MRCA *abbrev.* ◆ multirole combat aircraft

MRCGP *abbrev.* ◆ Member of the Royal College of General Practitioners

MRCOG *abbrev.* ◆ Member of the Royal College of Obstetricians and Gynaecologists

MRCP *abbrev.* ◆ Member of the Royal College of Physicians

MRCS *abbrev.* ◆ Member of the Royal College of Surgeons

MRCVS *abbrev.* ◆ Member of the Royal College of Veterinary Surgeons

MRD *abbrev.* ◆ minimal residual disease

MRE *abbrev.* ◆ Master of Religious Education ◆ Meals Ready to Eat ◆ Microbiological Research Establishment

MRe *contraction* ◆ Mauritian Rupee (monetary unit)

MRG *abbrev.* ◆ Minority Rights Group

MRGS *abbrev.* ◆ Member of the Royal Geographical Society

MRI *abbrev.* ◆ magnetic resonance imaging

MRICS *abbrev.* ◆ Member of the Royal Institution of Chartered Surveyors

MRM *abbrev.* ◆ mechanically recovered meat

mRNA *abbrev.* ◆ messenger ribonucleic acid

mrp *abbrev.* ◆ manufacturer's recommended price

mrrp *abbrev.* ✦ manufacturer's recommended retail price

MRS *abbrev.* ✦ Marseilles (airport baggage label)

Mrs *pronounced* miss-is *contraction* ✦ Mistress (former title of married women, now supplanted by its contraction, which is pronounced as shown)

MRSC *abbrev.* ✦ Member of the Royal Society of Chemistry

MRSM *abbrev.* ✦ Member of the Royal Society of Medicine

MRU *abbrev.* ✦ Mauritius (airport baggage label)

MRV *abbrev.* ✦ multiple re-entry vehicle

MS *abbrev.* ✦ Edinburgh (British vehicle registration mark) ✦ Egyptair (airline baggage code) ✦ mano sinistra (Italian, = left hand) ✦ manuscript ✦ mass spectrometry ✦ Master of Science ✦ Master of Surgery ✦ Mauritius (international vehicle registration) ✦ Mississippi (US postcode) ✦ multiple sclerosis

Ms *contraction* ✦ Miss ✦ Mrs (designed to blur the marital information contained in *Miss* and *Mrs*)

ms *abbrev.* ✦ millisecond

m/s *abbrev.* ✦ metres per second

MSA *abbrev.* ✦ Master of Agricultural Science ✦ motorway service area

MSAgr *abbrev.* ✦ Master of Science in Agriculture

MSArch *abbrev.* ✦ Master of Science in Architecture

MSB *abbrev.* ✦ most significant bit

MSBA *abbrev.* ✦ Master of Science in Business Administration

MSBus *abbrev.* ✦ Master of Science in Business

MSC *abbrev.* ✦ Manpower Services Commission

MSc *abbrev.* ✦ Master of Science

msc *abbrev.* ✦ moved, seconded and carried

MScAg *abbrev.* ✦ Master of Science in Agriculture

MSCE *abbrev.* ✦ Master of Science in Civil Engineering

MScChemE *abbrev.* ✦ Master of Science in Chemical Engineering

MSCI Index *abbrev.* ✦ Morgan Stanley Capital International World Index

MScMed *abbrev.* ✦ Master of Medical Science

MS-DOS *abbrev.* ✦ MicroSoft Disk-Operating System

MSF *abbrev.* ✦ Manufacturing, Science and Finance Union ✦ Master of Science in Forestry ✦ Médecins sans Frontières ✦ medium standard frequency

MSG *abbrev.* ✦ monosodium glutamate

msg. *shortening* ✦ message

Msgr *contraction* ✦ Monsignor

msgr *contraction* ✦ messenger

MSH *abbrev.* ✦ Master of Stag Hounds

MSI *abbrev.* ✦ medium-scale integration

MSIAD *abbrev.* ✦ Member of the Society of Industrial Artists and Designers

MSIE *abbrev.* ✦ Master of Science in Industrial Engineering

MSL *abbrev.* ✦ mean sea-level

MSM *abbrev.* ✦ Meritorious Service Medal

MSN *abbrev.* ✦ Master of Science in Nursing

MSR *abbrev.* ✦ manual sun roof

MSQ *abbrev.* ✦ Minsk (airport baggage label)

MSS *abbrev.* ✦ mass storage system ✦ Master of Social Science

MST *abbrev.* ✦ Maastricht (airport baggage label) ✦ mean survival time ✦ Mountain Standard Time

MSt *abbrev.* ✦ Master of Studies

MSU *abbrev.* ✦ mid-stream specimen of urine

msv *abbrev.* ✦ millisievert

MSW *abbrev.* ✦ magnetic surface wave ✦ Medical Social Worker

MSY *abbrev.* ✦ maximum sustainable yield ✦ New Orleans (airport baggage label)

MT *abbrev.* ✦ machine translation ✦ mean time ✦ Mechanical Transport ✦ Middle

Temple ◆ Montana (US postcode)
◆ north-east London (British vehicle
registration mark)
Mt *abbrev.* ◆ metical (Mozambique
monetary unit)
Mt *contraction* ◆ Mount
mt *abbrev.* ◆ megaton ◆ metric ton
mt. *shortening* ◆ mountain
MTB *abbrev.* ◆ motor torpedo-boat
MTBF *abbrev.* ◆ mean time between
failures
MTD *abbrev.* ◆ maximum tolerated dose
◆ moving target detector
mtd *contraction* ◆ mounted
mtg *contraction* ◆ meeting
mtgd *contraction* ◆ mortgaged
mtge *contraction* ◆ mortgage
mtgee *contraction* ◆ mortgagee
mtgor *contraction* ◆ mortgagor
MTh *abbrev.* ◆ Master of Theology
mth *contraction* ◆ month
MTI *abbrev.* ◆ moving target indicator
MTM *abbrev.* ◆ methods time
measurement
MTTR *abbrev.* ◆ mean time to repair
MU *abbrev.* ◆ China Eastern Airlines
(airline baggage code) ◆ Mothers'
Union ◆ Musicians' Union ◆ north-east

London (British vehicle registration
mark)
m/u *abbrev.* ◆ make-up
MUC *abbrev.* ◆ Munich (airport baggage
label)
MUF *abbrev.* ◆ maximum usable
frequency
Mufti *acronym* ◆ Minimum Use of Force
Tactical Intervention
mun. *shortening* ◆ municipal ◆ munitions
mus. *shortening* ◆ music ◆ musical
◆ museum
MusB *abbrev.* ◆ Musicae Baccalaureus
(Latin, = Bachelor of Music)
MusD *abbrev.* ◆ Musicae Doctor (Latin, =
Doctor of Music)
mut. *shortening* ◆ mutual
MV *abbrev.* ◆ south-east London (British
vehicle registration mark)
mV *abbrev.* ◆ millivolt
mv *abbrev.* ◆ market value ◆ merchant
vessel ◆ motor vessel ◆ muzzle velocity
MVD *abbrev.* ◆ Ministervo Vrytrennikh
Del (Russian , = Ministry of Internal
Affairs) (Soviet agency for internal
security 1946–60) ◆ Montevideo
(airport baggage label)

SOME MUSIC ABBREVIATIONS

This panel lists those abbreviations most commonly found by players and singers,
together with a practical explanation of their meaning. There is no space here to
give the Italian words from which they are derived, but they are all listed at the
appropriate entries in the dictionary, along with many other terms from music
and the arts.

A	*alto*	**DS**	*from the sign (for repeat etc)*	**pizz.**	*plucked*
accel.	*getting faster*			**pp**	*very soft*
AS	*to the sign (for repeat etc)*	**f**	*loud*	**rall.**	*slowing*
		ff	*very loud*	**rit.**	*held back*
B	*bass*	**leg.**	*smooth*	**sfz.**	*emphasized*
bar.	*baritone*	**maest.**	*majestic*	**S**	*soprano*
cresc.	*getting louder*	**mf**	*fairly loud*	**sost.**	*held*
DC	*from the top (for repeat etc)*	**mov.**	*speed*	**T**	*tenor*
		mp	*fairly quiet*	**ten.**	*tenuto*
decresc.	*getting softer*	**p**	*quiet*	**unis.**	*unison*
dim.	*getting softer*	**pianiss.**	*very quiet*	**vs**	*turn over quickly*

MVO *abbrev.* ◆ Member of the Royal Victorian Order

MVSc *abbrev.* ◆ Master of Veterinary Science

mvmt *contraction* ◆ movement

MW *abbrev.* ◆ Malawi (international vehicle registration) ◆ medium wave ◆ megawatt ◆ Swindon (British vehicle registration mark)

mW *abbrev.* ◆ milliwatt

MWF *abbrev.* ◆ Medical Women's Federation

MWGM *abbrev.* ◆ Most Worshipful Grand Master (freemasonry)

MWh *abbrev.* ◆ megawatt hour

mwh *abbrev.* ◆ milliwatt hour

MX *abbrev.* ◆ Mexicana de Aviación (airline baggage code) ◆ missile experimental ◆ south-east London (British vehicle registration mark)

Mx *contraction* ◆ Middlesex

mx *abbrev.* ◆ maxwell

MY *abbrev.* ◆ Air Mali (airline baggage code) ◆ south-east London (British vehicle registration mark)

my *abbrev.* ◆ million years

my. *shortening* ◆ myopia ◆ myopic

myc. *shortening* ◆ mycological ◆ mycology

mycol. *shortening* ◆ mycological ◆ mycology

myob *abbrev.* ◆ mind your own business

myth. *shortening* ◆ mythical ◆ mythological ◆ mythology

mythol. *shortening* ◆ mythological ◆ mythology

MZ *abbrev.* ◆ Belfast (British vehicle registration mark)

MZM *abbrev.* ◆ metical (Mozambique monetary unit)

N

N *abbrev.* ◆ knight (chess) ◆ naira (Nigerian monetary unit) ◆ national ◆ navy ◆ neutral (electrical wiring) ◆ newton ◆ ngultrum (Bhutanese monetary unit) ◆ Norse ◆ north ◆ northern ◆ north London (UK postcode) ◆ Norway (international vehicle registration) ◆ nuclear ◆ United States of America (international civil aircraft marking)

N *symbol* ◆ nitrogen (chemical element)

n *abbrev.* ◆ indefinite number ◆ name ◆ nano- ◆ natus (Latin, = born) ◆ nephew ◆ neuter ◆ new ◆ nominative ◆ noon ◆ note ◆ noun ◆ number

NA *abbrev.* ◆ Manchester (British vehicle registration mark) ◆ Netherlands Antilles (international vehicle registration) ◆ North America

Na *symbol* ◆ natrium (Latin, = sodium) (chemical element)

n/a *abbrev.* ◆ no account ◆ not applicable ◆ not available

NAACP *abbrev.* ◆ National Association for the Advancement of Colored People (US)

NAAFA *abbrev.* ◆ National Association to Aid Fat Americans

Naafi *acronym* ◆ Navy, Army and Air Force Institutes

NAAS *abbrev.* ◆ National Agricultural Advisory Scheme

NABC *abbrev.* ◆ National Association of Boys' Clubs

NAC *abbrev.* ◆ National Association for the Childless

NACAB *abbrev.* ◆ National Association of Citizens' Advice Bureaux

Nacods *acronym* ◆ National Association of Colliery Overmen, Deputies and Shotfirers

Nacro *acronym* ◆ National Association for the Care and Resettlement of Offenders

NAD *abbrev.* ◆ no abnormality detected ◆ no appreciable difference ◆ not on active duty

NAEA *abbrev.* ◆ National Association of Estate Agents

NAEW *abbrev.* ◆ Nato Airborne Early Warning

NAFD *abbrev.* ◆ National Association of Funeral Directors

nag *abbrev.* ◆ net annual gain

NAGC *abbrev.* ◆ National Association for Gifted Children

NAGS *abbrev.* ◆ National Allotments and Gardens Society

Nah. *shortening* ◆ Nahum (book of Bible)

Nahat *acronym* ◆ National Association of Health Authorities and Trusts

NAHT *abbrev.* ◆ National Association of Head Teachers

NAI *abbrev.* ◆ non-accidental injury

Nairu *acronym* ◆ non-accelerating inflation rate of unemployment

Nalgo *acronym* ◆ National and Local Government Officers' Association

NAm *abbrev.* ◆ North America ◆ North American

N & Q *abbrev.* ◆ Notes and Queries

n & v *abbrev.* ◆ nausea and vomiting

NAO *abbrev.* ◆ National Audit Office

NAP *abbrev.* ◆ Naples (airport baggage label)

Nap *acronym* ◆ National Association of the Paralysed

NAPF *abbrev.* ◆ National Association of Pension Funds

Napo *acronym* ◆ National Association of Probation Officers

NAPV *abbrev.* ◆ National Association of Prison Visitors

NAS *abbrev.* ◆ Nassau (airport baggage label) ◆ National Academy of Sciences (US) ◆ National Adoption Society ◆ Noise Abatement Society

Nasa *acronym* ◆ National Aeronautics and Space Administration (US)

NAS/UWT *abbrev.* ◆ National Association of Schoolmasters/Union of Women Teachers

nat. *acronym* ◆ national ◆ nationalist ◆ native ◆ natural ◆ natus (Latin, = born)

NATFHE *abbrev.* ◆ National Association of Teachers in Further and Higher Education

Natlas *acronym* ◆ National Testing Laboratory Accreditation Scheme

Nato *acronym* ◆ North Atlantic Treaty Organization

Natsopa *acronym* ◆ National Society of Operative Printers, Graphical and Media Personnel (orig. Printers and Assistants)

Nattke *acronym* ◆ National Association of Television, Theatrical and Kinematographic Employees

NatWest *acronym* ◆ National Westminster Bank PLC

NAU *abbrev.* ◆ Nauru (international vehicle registration)

naut. *shortening* ◆ nautical

NAV *abbrev.* ◆ net asset value

nav. *shortening* ◆ naval ◆ navigable ◆ navigation ◆ navigator

NAVS *abbrev.* ◆ National Anti-Vivisection Society

navsat *acronym* ◆ navigational satellite

NAWB *abbrev.* ◆ National Association of Workshops for the Blind

NAYC *abbrev.* ◆ Youth Clubs UK (orig. National Association of Youth Clubs)

Naypic *acronym* ◆ National Association of Young People in Care

NAYT *abbrev.* ◆ National Association of Youth Theatres

Nazi *shortening* ◆ Nationalsozialist (German, = National Socialist) (National Socialist German Workers' Party, led by Hitler 1920–45)

NB *abbrev.* ◆ Manchester (British vehicle registration mark) ◆ Nebraska (US postcode) ◆ New Brunswick ◆ North Britain ◆ North British ◆ nota bene (Latin, = note carefully)

Nb *symbol* ◆ niobium (chemical element)

nb *abbrev.* ◆ no ball

NBA *abbrev.* ◆ Net Book Agreement

NBC *abbrev.* ◆ National Broadcasting Company (US) ◆ nuclear, biological and chemical (warfare)

nbg *abbrev.* ◆ no bloody good

NBI *abbrev.* ◆ National Benevolent Institution

NBL *abbrev.* ◆ National Book League

nbl *abbrev.* ◆ not bloody likely

NBO *abbrev.* ◆ Nairobi (airport baggage label)

NBR *abbrev.* ◆ National Buildings Record

NBRI *abbrev.* ◆ National Building Research Institute

NBTS *abbrev.* ◆ National Blood Transfusion Service

nbv *abbrev.* ◆ net book value

NC *abbrev.* ◆ Manchester (British vehicle registration mark) ◆ National Certificate ◆ National Curriculum ◆ Nature Conservancy ◆ North Carolina (US postcode)

nc *abbrev.* ◆ numerical control ◆ numerically controlled

n/c *abbrev.* ◆ no charge

NCA *abbrev.* ◆ National Childminding Association ◆ National Cricket Association

nca *abbrev.* ◆ no copies available

NCB *abbrev.* ◆ National Coal Board ◆ no-claim bonus

NCBW *abbrev.* ◆ nuclear, chemical and biological warfare

NCC *abbrev.* ◆ National Computing Centre Ltd ◆ National Consumer Council ◆ National Curriculum Council ◆ Nature Conservancy Council

NCCL *abbrev.* ◆ National Council for Civil Liberties

ncd *abbrev.* ◆ no can do

NCDL *abbrev.* ◆ National Canine Defence League

NCE *abbrev.* ◆ Nice (airport baggage label)

NCL *abbrev.* ◆ National Carriers Ltd ◆ Newcastle (airport baggage label)

NCO *abbrev.* ◆ non-commissioned officer

NCP *abbrev.* ◆ National Car Parks Ltd

NCPS *abbrev.* ◆ non-contributory pension scheme

NCR *abbrev.* ◆ National Cash Register Company Ltd

ncr *abbrev.* ◆ no carbon required

NCRL *abbrev.* ◆ National Chemical Research Laboratory

NCT *abbrev.* ◆ National Childbirth Trust

NCU *abbrev.* ◆ National Communications Union ◆ National Cyclists' Union

ncup *abbrev.* ◆ no commission until paid

ncv *abbrev.* ◆ no commercial value

NCVO *abbrev.* ◆ National Council for Voluntary Organizations

NCVQ *abbrev.* ◆ National Council for Vocational Qualifications

ND *abbrev.* ◆ Manchester (British vehicle registration mark) ◆ National Debt ◆ National Diploma ◆ North Dakota (US postcode)

Nd *symbol* ◆ neodymium (chemical element)

nd *abbrev.* ◆ no date ◆ not dated ◆ not drawn ◆ nothing doing

NDak *abbrev.* ◆ North Dakota

NDE *abbrev.* ◆ near-death experience

NDH *abbrev.* ◆ Delhi (airport baggage label)

NDL *abbrev.* ◆ Norddeutscher Lloyd

NDP *abbrev.* ◆ net domestic product

NDR *abbrev.* ◆ Norddeutscher Rundfunk (German, = North German Radio)

NDT *abbrev.* ◆ non-destructive testing

NE *abbrev.* ◆ Manchester (British vehicle registration mark) ◆ Nebraska (US postcode) ◆ Newcastle upon Tyne (UK postcode) ◆ New England ◆ north-east

Ne *symbol* ◆ neon (chemical element)

ne *abbrev.* ◆ not essential ◆ not exceeding

n/e *abbrev.* ◆ new edition ◆ no effects (no funds) ◆ not entered

NEB *abbrev.* ◆ National Enterprise Board ◆ New English Bible

Neb. *abbrev.* ◆ Nebraska

Nebr. *abbrev.* ◆ Nebraska

NEC *abbrev.* ◆ National Executive Committee ◆ National Exhibition Centre

nec *abbrev.* ◆ not elsewhere classified

nec. *shortening* ◆ necessary

necr. *shortening* ◆ necrosis

NEDC *abbrev.* ◆ National Economic Development Council

Neddy *acronym* ◆ National Economic Development Council

Nedo *acronym* ◆ National Economic Development Office

NEF *abbrev.* ◆ National Energy Foundation

neg. *shortening* ◆ negative ◆ negatively ◆ negotiable ◆ negotiation

NEH *abbrev.* ◆ National Endowment for the Humanities

Neh. *shortening* ◆ Nehemiah (book of Bible)

NEL *abbrev.* ◆ National Engineering Laboratory

nem. con. *shortening* ◆ nemine contradicente (Latin, = without objection)

nem. diss. *shortening* ◆ nemine dissentiente (Latin, = unanimously)

neol. *shortening* ◆ neologism

NEP *abbrev.* ◆ Nepal (international vehicle registration)

Nep. *shortening* ◆ Nepal ◆ Nepali

Nerc *shortening* ◆ National English Rabbit Club ◆ Natural Environment Research Council

Neris *acronym* ◆ National Educational Resources Information Service

NES *abbrev.* ◆ National Eczema Society

nes *abbrev.* ◆ not elsewhere specified

net *abbrev.* ◆ not earlier than

Neth. *shortening* ◆ Netherlands

n et m *abbrev.* ◆ nocte et mane (Latin, = night and morning)

neurol. *shortening* ◆ neurological ◆ neurology

neut. *shortening* ◆ neuter ◆ neutral

Nev. *shortening* ◆ Nevada

news. *shortening* ◆ newsagent

NF *abbrev.* ◆ Manchester (British vehicle registration mark) ◆ National Front ◆ Nationale Front (German, = National Front) ◆ no funds ◆ noise factor ◆ Norman French ◆ Northern French

nf *abbrev.* ◆ no fool ◆ noun feminine

NFA *abbrev.* ◆ National Federation of Anglers

nfa *abbrev.* ◆ no further action

NFBPM *abbrev.* ◆ National Federation of Builders' and Plumbers' Merchants

NFC *abbrev.* ◆ National Freight Consortium

nfc *abbrev.* ◆ not favourably considered

NFER *abbrev.* ◆ National Foundation for Educational Research

NFFC *abbrev.* ◆ National Film Finance Corporation

Nfld *contraction* ◆ Newfoundland

NFMS *abbrev.* ◆ National Federation of Music Societies

nfr *abbrev.* ◆ no further requirements

nfs *abbrev.* ◆ not for sale

NFSC *abbrev.* ◆ National Federation of Football Supporters' Clubs

NFSE *abbrev.* ◆ National Federation of Self-Employed

NFT *abbrev.* ◆ National Film Theatre

NFTS *abbrev.* ◆ National Film and Television School

NFU *abbrev.* ◆ National Farmers' Union

NFWI *abbrev.* ◆ National Federation of Women's Institutes

NFYFC *abbrev.* ◆ National Federation of Young Farmers' Clubs

NG *abbrev.* ◆ National Gallery ◆ National Guard (US) ◆ Norwich (British vehicle registration mark) ◆ Nottingham (UK postcode)

ng *abbrev.* ◆ no good ◆ not given

NGA *abbrev.* ◆ National Graphical Association

NGC *abbrev.* ◆ New General Catalogue (listing all stars etc known in 1888)

NGNP *abbrev.* ◆ nominal gross national product

NGO *abbrev.* ◆ nongovernmental organization

NGRC *abbrev.* ◆ National Greyhound Racing Club

NGU *abbrev.* ◆ non-gonococcal urethritis

NH *abbrev.* ◆ National Hunt ◆ New Hampshire (US postcode) ◆ Manchester (British vehicle registration mark)

NHBRC *abbrev.* ◆ National House-Builders' Registration Certificate ◆ National House-Builders' Registration Council

NHF *abbrev.* ◆ National Hairdressers' Federation

NHI *abbrev.* ◆ National Health Insurance

NHMF *abbrev.* ◆ National Heritage Memorial Fund

nhp *abbrev.* ◆ nominal horsepower

NHR *abbrev.* ◆ National Hunt Rules

NHS *abbrev.* ◆ National Health Service

NI *abbrev.* ◆ National Insurance ◆ Nicaraguan Airlines (airline baggage code) ◆ Northern Ireland

Ni *symbol* ◆ nickel (chemical element)

NIC *abbrev.* ◆ National Insurance contributions ◆ Nicaragua (international vehicle registration) ◆ Nicosia (airport baggage label)

Nic. *shortening* ◆ Nicaragua ◆ Nicaraguan

nic *abbrev.* ◆ newly industrialized country ◆ not in contract

Nicar. *shortening* ◆ Nicaragua ◆ Nicaraguan

NICEC *abbrev.* ◆ National Institute for Careers Education and Counselling

NICEIC *abbrev.* ◆ National Inspection Council for Electrical Installation Contracting

Nicu *acronym* ◆ neonatal intensive care unit

NIESR *abbrev.* ◆ National Institute of Economic and Social Research

Nig. *shortening* ◆ Nigeria ◆ Nigerian

NII *abbrev.* ◆ Nuclear Installations Inspectorate

nimby *acronym* ◆ not in my back yard

NIMH *abbrev.* ◆ National Institute of Mental Health

NIMR *abbrev.* ◆ National Institute for Medical Research

NIRC *abbrev.* ◆ National Industrial Relations Court

NIre *abbrev.* ◆ Northern Ireland

Nirex *shortening* ◆ Nuclear Industry Radioactive Waste Executive

NIS *abbrev.* ◆ New Israeli Shekel (monetary unit)

nis *abbrev.* ◆ not in stock

NIT *abbrev.* ◆ negative income tax

NJ *abbrev.* ◆ Brighton (British vehicle registration mark) ◆ New Jersey (US postcode)

NJAC *abbrev.* ◆ National Joint Advisory Council

NJC *abbrev.* ◆ National Joint Council

NJCC *abbrev.* ◆ National Joint Consultative Committee

NJNC *abbrev.* ◆ National Joint Negotiating Committee

NK *abbrev.* ◆ Luton (British vehicle registration mark) ◆ natural killer

NKGB *abbrev.* ◆ Narodny Komissariat Gosudarstvennoi Bezopasnosti (Russian, = People's Commissariat of State Security) (Soviet espionage and counter-espionage agency 1941–6)

NKr *abbrev.* ◆ Norwegian krone (monetary unit)

NKVD *abbrev.* ◆ Narodny Komissariat Vnutrennikh Del (Russian, = People's Commissariat for Internal Affairs) (Soviet agency for the suppression of espionage and counter-revolution

1934–41, and for internal security only 1941–6)

NL *abbrev.* ◆ Air Liberia (airline baggage code) ◆ Netherlands (international vehicle registration) ◆ Newcastle upon Tyne (British vehicle registration mark)

NLB *abbrev.* ◆ National Library for the Blind

NLB & D *abbrev.* ◆ National League of the Blind and Disabled

NLF *abbrev.* ◆ National Liberation Front

nln *abbrev.* ◆ no longer needed

NLP *abbrev.* ◆ natural language processing

NLQ *abbrev.* ◆ near letter quality (printer characters)

nlt *abbrev.* ◆ not later than ◆ not less than

NM *abbrev.* ◆ Luton (British vehicle registration mark) ◆ New Mexico (US postcode)

nm *abbrev.* ◆ nanometre ◆ nautical mile ◆ nocte et mane ◆ noun masculine

n/m *abbrev.* ◆ not married

nmc *abbrev.* ◆ no more credit

NMex *abbrev.* ◆ New Mexico

NMR *abbrev.* ◆ nuclear magnetic resonance

nmt *abbrev.* ◆ not more than

NMTF *abbrev.* ◆ National Market Traders' Federation

NN *abbrev.* ◆ Northampton (UK postcode) ◆ Nottingham (British vehicle registration mark)

nnd *abbrev.* ◆ neonatal death

NNE *abbrev.* ◆ north-north-east

NNEB *abbrev.* ◆ National Nursery Examination Board

NNHT *abbrev.* ◆ Nuffield Nursing Homes Trust

NNI *abbrev.* ◆ Noise and Number Index (aircraft noise)

NNT *abbrev.* ◆ nuclear non-proliferation treaty

NNW *abbrev.* ◆ north-north-west

NO *abbrev.* ◆ Chelmsford (British vehicle registration mark) ◆ natural order

no *abbrev.* ◆ not out (cricket)

no *contraction* ◆ numero (Italian, = number)

NOC *abbrev.* ◆ National Olympic Committee

NOD *abbrev.* ◆ Naval Ordnance Department

nohp *abbrev.* ◆ not otherwise herein provided

nok *abbrev.* ◆ next of kin

nol. pros. *shortening* ◆ nolle prosequi (Latin, = to be unwilling to proceed) (formula for plaintiff's abandonment of case)

nom. *shortening* ◆ nominal ◆ nomination ◆ nominative

nom. cap. *shortening* ◆ nominal capital

nomin. *shortening* ◆ nominal ◆ nominative

noncom. *shortening* ◆ noncommissioned ◆ nonconformist

non rep. *shortening* ◆ non repetatur (Latin, = let it not be repeated)

non seq. *shortening* ◆ non sequitur (Latin, = it does not follow) (logically)

nonstd *contraction* ◆ nonstandard

NOP *abbrev.* ◆ National Opinion Poll

nop *abbrev.* ◆ not otherwise provided

NOPWC *abbrev.* ◆ National Old People's Welfare Council

NOR *abbrev.* ◆ nucleolar-organizing region

Nor. *shortening* ◆ Norman ◆ North ◆ Norwegian ◆ Norway

Norf. *shortening* ◆ Norfolk

Norm. *shortening* ◆ Norman

norm. *shortening* ◆ normal

Northants ◆ Northamptonshire

Northumb. *shortening* ◆ Northumberland

Norvic. *shortening* ◆ Norvicensis (Latin, = of Norwich)

Norw. *shortening* ◆ Norway ◆ Norwegian

NOTB *abbrev.* ◆ National Ophthalmic Treatment Board

Notts. *shortening* ◆ Nottinghamshire

Nov. *shortening* ◆ November

NP *abbrev.* ◆ National Park ◆ National Power PLC ◆ net profit ◆ new paragraph ◆ Newport, Gwent (UK postcode) ◆ Notary Public ◆ Worcester (British vehicle registration mark)

Np *symbol* ◆ neptunium (chemical element)

np *abbrev.* ◆ net personalty ◆ net proceeds ◆ nisi prius (Latin, = unless previously) ◆ nomen proprium (Latin, = its own name) (labelling direction to pharmacist) ◆ no place of publication

NPA *abbrev.* ◆ Newspaper Publishers' Assocation

NPD *abbrev.* ◆ Nationaldemokratische Partei Deutschlands (German, = National Democratic Party of Germany)

npf *abbrev.* ◆ not provided for

NPFA *abbrev.* ◆ National Playing Fields Association

NPG *abbrev.* ◆ National Portrait Gallery

NPHT *abbrev.* ◆ Nuffield Provincial Hospitals Trust

NPL *abbrev.* ◆ National Physical Laboratory

npo *abbrev.* ◆ nil per os (Latin, = nothing by mouth)

npv *abbrev.* ◆ net present value

NR *abbrev.* ◆ Leicester (British vehicle registration mark) ◆ North Riding (former division of Yorkshire) ◆ Norwich (UK postcode)

Nr *contraction* ◆ Nummer (German, = number)

nr *contraction* ◆ near

NRA *abbrev.* ◆ National Rifle Association ◆ National Rivers Authority

nra *abbrev.* ◆ never refuse anything

NRDC *abbrev.* ◆ National Research Development Corporation

NRDS *abbrev.* ◆ neonatal respiratory distress syndrome

NREM *abbrev.* ◆ non-rapid eye movement

NRPB *abbrev.* ◆ National Radiological Protection Board

NRS *abbrev.* ◆ National Rose Society

NRs *abbrev.* ◆ Nepalese rupees (monetary unit)

nrv *abbrev.* ◆ net realizable value

NS *abbrev.* ◆ Glasgow (British vehicle registration mark) ◆ new series ◆ New Style ◆ Nova Scotia

ns *abbrev.* ◆ nanosecond ◆ near side ◆ non smoker ◆ not significant ◆ not specified

n/s *abbrev.* ◆ news-sheet ◆ not sufficient

NSA *abbrev.* ◆ National Skating Association

NSAID *abbrev.* ◆ non-steroidal anti-inflammatory drug

NSB *abbrev.* ◆ National Savings Bank

NSC *abbrev.* ◆ National Safety Council ◆ National Security Council (US)

NSCR *abbrev.* ◆ National Society for Cancer Relief

NSD *abbrev.* ◆ nominal standard dose ◆ normal spontaneous delivery

NSDAP *abbrev.* ◆ Nationalsozialistische Deutsche Arbeiterpartei (German, = National Socialist German Workers' Party) (led by Hitler 1920–45)

NSF *abbrev.* ◆ National Science Foundation ◆ not sufficient funds

NSFGB *abbrev.* ◆ National Ski Federation of Great Britain

NSG *abbrev.* ◆ nonstatutory guidelines (to the education National Curriculum)

NSGT *abbrev.* ◆ Non-Selfgoverning Territory

NSL *abbrev.* ◆ National Sporting League

NSPCA *abbrev.* ◆ National Society for the Prevention of Cruelty to Animals

NSPCC *abbrev.* ◆ National Society for the Prevention of Cruelty to Children

nspf *abbrev.* ◆ not specifically provided for

NSRA *abbrev.* ◆ National Small-Bore Rifle Association

NSS *abbrev.* ◆ National Secular Society Ltd

NSTP *abbrev.* ◆ Nuffield Science Teaching Project

NSU *abbrev.* ◆ non-specific urethritis

NSW *abbrev.* ◆ New South Wales

NT *abbrev.* ◆ National Theatre ◆ National Trust ◆ New Testament ◆ Northern Territory ◆ no trumps (cards) ◆ Shrewsbury (British vehicle registration mark)

NTA *abbrev.* ◆ National Training Award

nth *contraction* ◆ north

ntp *abbrev.* ◆ normal temperature and pressure ◆ no title page

NTS *abbrev.* ◆ National Trust for Scotland

nts *abbrev.* ◆ not to scale

NTVLRO *abbrev.* ◆ National Television Licence Records Office

nt wt *contraction* ◆ net weight

NU *abbrev.* ◆ name unknown ◆ Nottingham (British vehicle registration mark) ◆ number unobtainable

Nu. *abbrev.* ◆ ngultrum (Bhutanese monetary unit)

NUAAW *abbrev.* ◆ National Union of Agricultural and Allied Workers

nuc. *shortening* ◆ nuclear

NUCPS *abbrev.* ◆ National Union of Civil and Public Servants

NUGMW *abbrev.* ◆ National Union of General and Municipal Workers

NUI *abbrev.* ◆ National University of Ireland

NUIW *abbrev.* ◆ National Union of Insurance Workers

NUJ *abbrev.* ◆ National Union of Journalists

NUJMB *abbrev.* ◆ Northern Universities Joint Matriculation Board

NUM *abbrev.* ◆ National Union of Mineworkers

Num. *shortening* ◆ Numbers (book of Bible)

num. *shortening* ◆ numerous

Numast *acronym* ◆ National Union of Marine, Aviation and Shipping Transport Officers

Numb. *shortening* ◆ Numbers (book of Bible)

numis. *shortening* ◆ numismatic ◆ numismatics ◆ numismatist

Nupe *pronounced* new-pee *acronym*
♦ National Union of Public Employees

NUR *abbrev.* ♦ National Union of Railwaymen

NUS *abbrev.* ♦ National Union of Seamen ♦ National Union of Students

NUT *abbrev.* ♦ National Union of Teachers

NUTG *abbrev.* ♦ National Union of Townswomens' Guilds

NV *abbrev.* ♦ Naamloze Vennootschap (Dutch, = Limited Company) ♦ Nevada (US postcode) ♦ new version ♦ non-vintage ♦ Northampton (British vehicle registration mark)

nv *abbrev.* ♦ non-voting

n/v *abbrev.* ♦ non-vintage

NVALA *abbrev.* ♦ National Viewers' and Listeners' Association

nvd *abbrev.* ♦ no value declared

NVQ *abbrev.* ♦ National Vocational Qualification

NW *abbrev.* ♦ Leeds (British vehicle registration mark) ♦ north-west ♦ north-west London (UK postcode)

NWT *abbrev.* ♦ Northwest Territories

NX *abbrev.* ♦ Dudley (British vehicle registration mark)

NY *abbrev.* ♦ Cardiff (British vehicle registration mark) ♦ New York (US postcode)

NYC *abbrev.* ♦ New York City

NYD *abbrev.* ♦ not yet diagnosed

NYO *abbrev.* ♦ National Youth Orchestra

NYSE *abbrev.* ♦ New York Stock Exchange

NYT *abbrev.* ♦ National Youth Theatre

NZ *abbrev.* ♦ Londonderry (British vehicle registration mark) ♦ New Zealand ♦ New Zealand (international vehicle registration)

NZBC *abbrev.* ♦ New Zealand Broadcasting Corporation

O

O *abbrev.* ◆ Office ◆ Order (of monks etc) ◆ ordinary

O *symbol* ◆ oxygen (chemical element)

o *abbrev.* ◆ ottava (Italian, = octave) (music)

OA *abbrev.* ◆ Birmingham (British vehicle registration mark) ◆ office automation ◆ Olympic Airways (airline baggage code) ◆ operations analysis ◆ osteoarthritis

oa *abbrev.* ◆ overall

o/a *abbrev.* ◆ on account of

OAD *abbrev.* ◆ obstructive airways disease

O & C *abbrev.* ◆ Oxford and Cambridge

o & c *abbrev.* ◆ onset and course

O & G *abbrev.* ◆ obstetrics and gynaecology

O & M *abbrev.* ◆ organization and methods

oao *abbrev.* ◆ off and on ◆ one and only

OAP *abbrev.* ◆ old-age pensioner

Oapec *pronounced* oh-ay-pek *acronym* ◆ Organization of Arab Petroleum-Exporting Countries

OAS *abbrev.* ◆ on active service ◆ Organization of American States

OAT *abbrev.* ◆ outside air temperature

OATG *abbrev.* ◆ outside air temperature gauge

OAU *abbrev.* ◆ Organization of African Unity

OB *abbrev.* ◆ Birmingham (British vehicle registration mark) ◆ obstetrics ◆ old boy ◆ outside broadcast ◆ Peru (international civil aircraft marking)

ob. *shortening* ◆ obiit (Latin, = died) ◆ oboe

o/b *abbrev.* ◆ on or before

Obad. *shortening* ◆ Obadiah (book of Bible)

obb. *shortening* ◆ obbligato (Italian, = essential) (of solo part etc)

ÖBB *abbrev.* ◆ Österreichische Bundesbahnen (German, = Austrian Federal Railways)

OBC *abbrev.* ◆ on-board computer

OBD *abbrev.* ◆ organic brain disease

obdt *contraction* ◆ obedient

OBE *abbrev.* ◆ Officer of the Order of the British Empire ◆ out-of-the-body experience

obit. *shortening* ◆ obituary

obj. *shortening* ◆ object ◆ objective ◆ objection

obl. *shortening* ◆ oblique ◆ oblong

obs. *shortening* ◆ obscure ◆ observation ◆ observatory ◆ obsolete

obsol. *shortening* ◆ obsolescent ◆ obsolete

obstet. *shortening* ◆ obstetrics

OC *abbrev.* ◆ Birmingham (British vehicle registration mark) ◆ Officer Commanding ◆ Officer in Charge ◆ oral contraceptive ◆ original cover (stamp collecting)

oc *abbrev.* ◆ office copy ◆ only child

o/c *abbrev.* ◆ overcharge

Ocas *acronym* ◆ Organization of Central American States

occas. *shortening* ◆ occasional

OCD *abbrev.* ◆ obsessive compulsive disorder

OCelt *abbrev.* ◆ Old Celtic

OCF *abbrev.* ◆ Officiating Chaplain to the Forces

OCR *abbrev.* ◆ optical character recognition

OCSC *abbrev.* ◆ Office of the Civil Service Commissioners

Oct. *shortening* ◆ October

oct. *shortening* ◆ octave ◆ octavo

Octu *acronym* ◆ Officer Cadet Training Unit

OD *abbrev.* ◆ Exeter (British vehicle registration mark) ◆ Lebanon (international civil aircraft marking) ◆ Officer of the Day ◆ Old Dutch ◆ Ordnance Datum ◆ overdose ◆ overdraft ◆ overdrawn

od *abbrev.* ◆ outer diameter

o/d *abbrev.* ◆ on demand

ODA *abbrev.* ◆ Overseas Development Administration

ODan *abbrev.* ◆ Old Danish

ODC *abbrev.* ◆ Order of Discalced Carmelites

ODS *abbrev.* ◆ Odessa (airport baggage label)

OE *abbrev.* ◆ Austria (international civil aircraft marking) ◆ Birmingham (British vehicle registration mark) ◆ Old English ◆ Old Etonian

Oe *abbrev.* ◆ oersted

oe *abbrev.* ◆ omissions excepted

OECD *abbrev.* ◆ Organization for Economic Co-operation and Development

OED *abbrev.* ◆ Oxford English Dictionary

OEM *abbrev.* ◆ original equipment manufacturer

OF *abbrev.* ◆ Birmingham (British vehicle registration mark) ◆ Oddfellow ◆ oil-fired ◆ Old French

Off. *shortening* ◆ County Offaly

off. *shortening* ◆ office ◆ officer ◆ official ◆ officinal

Offer *acronym* ◆ Office of Electricity Regulation

Ofgas *acronym* ◆ Office of Gas Supply

Oflag. *shortening* ◆ Offizierlager (German, = officers' prison camp)

OFM *abbrev.* ◆ Ordo Fratrum Minorum (Latin, = Order of Minor Friars) (Franciscans)

OFr *abbrev.* ◆ Old French

OFris *abbrev.* ◆ Old Frisian

OFS *abbrev.* ◆ Orange Free State

Ofsted *acronym* ◆ Office for Standards in Education

OFT *abbrev.* ◆ Office of Fair Trading

Oftel *acronym* ◆ Office of Telecommunications

Ofwat *acronym* ◆ Office of Water Services

OG *abbrev.* ◆ Birmingham (British vehicle registration mark)

og *abbrev.* ◆ original gravity (beer strength) ◆ original gum (stamp collecting) ◆ own goal (football)

OGael *abbrev.* ◆ Old Gaelic

OGM *abbrev.* ◆ Ordinary General Meeting

Ogpu *acronym* ◆ Obyedinyonnoye Gosudarstvennoye Politicheskoye Upravleniye (Russian, = United State Political Directorate) (Soviet agency for the suppression of espionage and counter-revolution 1923–34)

OH *abbrev.* ◆ Birmingham (British vehicle registration mark) ◆ Finland (international civil aircraft marking) ◆ Ohio (US postcode)

oh *abbrev.* ◆ office hours ◆ omni hora (Latin , = every hour)

OHC *abbrev.* ◆ overhead camshafts

OHG *abbrev.* ◆ Old High German

OHMS *abbrev.* ◆ On Her Majesty's Service ◆ On His Majesty's Service

ohp *abbrev.* ◆ overhead projector

OHS *abbrev.* ◆ Occupational Health Service

OHV *abbrev.* ◆ overhead valves

OI *abbrev.* ◆ Belfast (British vehicle registration mark)

OIcel *abbrev.* ◆ Old Icelandic

OILC *abbrev.* ◆ Offshore Industry Liaison Committee

OIEO *abbrev.* ◆ offers in excess of

OIr *abbrev.* ◆ Old Irish

OIRO *abbrev.* ◆ offers in the region of

OIRT *abbrev.* ◆ Organisation Internationale de Radiodiffusion et

Télévision (French, = International Radio and Television Organization)

OJ *abbrev.* ◆ Birmingham (British vehicle registration mark)

Ojocs *acronym* ◆ overnight declaration of jockeys (horse-racing)

OK *abbrev.* ◆ Birmingham (British vehicle registration mark) ◆ Czechoslovak Airlines (airline baggage code) ◆ Czechoslovakia (international civil aircraft marking) ◆ satisfactory ◆ Oklahoma (US postcode)

Okla. *shortening* ◆ Oklahoma

OL *abbrev.* ◆ Birmingham (British vehicle registration mark) ◆ Oldham (UK postcode) ◆ on-line ◆ outside left

OLG *abbrev.* ◆ Old Low German

O/licence *contraction* ◆ off licence

o'lkng *contraction* ◆ overlooking

OLRT *abbrev.* ◆ on-line real time

OM *abbrev.* ◆ Birmingham (British vehicle registration mark) ◆ Order of Merit

om *abbrev.* ◆ omni mane (Latin, = every morning)

omc *abbrev.* ◆ operation and maintenance costs

omn. hor. *shortening* ◆ omni hora (Latin, = every hour)

omn. noct. *shortening* ◆ omni nocte (Latin, = every night)

omo *abbrev.* ◆ one-man operation (buses)

OMR *abbrev.* ◆ optical mark reader

OMRS *abbrev.* ◆ Orders and Medals Research Society

OMS *abbrev.* ◆ Omsk (airport baggage label)

oms *abbrev.* ◆ output per man shift

ON *abbrev.* ◆ Birmingham (British vehicle registration mark) ◆ Old Norse

on *abbrev.* ◆ omni nocte (Latin, = every night)

ONC *abbrev.* ◆ Ordinary National Certificate

OND *abbrev.* ◆ Ordinary National Diploma ◆ other neurological disorders

ONF *abbrev.* ◆ Old Norman French

ono *abbrev.* ◆ or near offer

Ont. *shortening* ◆ Ontario

ONTR *abbrev.* ◆ orders not to resuscitate

OO *abbrev.* ◆ Belgium (international civil aircraft marking) ◆ Chelmsford (British vehicle registration mark)

o/o *abbrev.* ◆ on order ◆ offers over

oop *abbrev.* ◆ out-of-pocket (expenses etc)

oot *abbrev.* ◆ out-of-town

ONCE AN ABBREVIATION . . .

Many words started their lives as convenient abbreviations of other longer words or groups of words, and have over the years become so popular that they have replaced the longer term, which may as a result pass completely out of use, or only be employed in the most formal contexts. A few examples of such words are given below: since they are no longer considered to be abbreviations, they will not be found in the dictionary.

amp	*ampere*	**meths**	*methylated spirits*	**quin**	*quintuplet*
bike	*bicycle*			**radar**	*radio detection and ranging*
bra	*brassiere*	**perk**	*perquisite*		
bus	*omnibus*	**perm**	*permanent wave*	**recap**	*recapitulation*
disco	*discotheque*	**plane**	*aeroplane*	**scuba**	*self-contained underwater breathing apparatus*
exam	*examination*	**polio**	*poliomyelitis*		
fridge	*refrigerator*	**pram**	*perambulator*		
laser	*light amplification by stimulated emission of radiation*	**Prom**	*Promenade Concert*	**taxi**	*taximeter cab*
		pub	*public house*		
		quad	*quadruplet*		

OP *abbrev.* ✦ Birmingham (British vehicle registration mark) ✦ observation point ✦ observation post ✦ opposite prompt (actor's position on stage) ✦ Ordo Praedicatorum (Latin, = Order of Preachers) (Dominicans) ✦ outpatient

op *abbrev.* ✦ open-plan ✦ other people ✦ out of print ✦ over proof

op. *shortening* ✦ opera ✦ operation ✦ operator ✦ opposite ✦ optical ✦ opus

OPB *abbrev.* ✦ Occupational Pensions Board

op. cit. *shortening* ✦ opere citato (Latin, = in the work cited)

OPCS *abbrev.* ✦ Office of Population, Censuses and Surveys

OPD *abbrev.* ✦ Outpatient Department

Opec *acronym* ✦ Organization of Petroleum-Exporting Countries

OPO *abbrev.* ✦ Oporto (airport baggage label)

opp. *shortening* ✦ oppose ✦ opposed ✦ opposite

opt. *abbrev.* ✦ optative ✦ optic ✦ optical ✦ optimal ✦ optime (Latin, = excellently) ✦ optimum ✦ optional

OPV *abbrev.* ✦ oral poliomyelitis vaccine

OR *abbrev.* ✦ official receiver ✦ operating room ✦ operational research ✦ Oregon (US postcode) ✦ other ranks ✦ Portsmouth (British vehicle registration mark)

or *abbrev.* ✦ owner's risk

or. *shortening* ✦ oriental

Oracle *acronym* ✦ optional reception of announcements by coded line electronics

orb *abbrev.* ✦ owner's risk of breakage

orch. *shortening* ✦ orchestra ✦ orchestrated

ord *abbrev.* ✦ owner's risk of damage

ord. *shortening* ✦ ordained ✦ order ✦ ordinal ✦ ordinary ✦ ordnance

Oreg. *shortening* ✦ Oregon

orf *abbrev.* ✦ owner's risk of fire

org. *shortening* ✦ organ ✦ organic ✦ organism ✦ organist ✦ organization ✦ organized

orig. *shortening* ✦ origin ✦ original ✦ originally ✦ originate ✦ originated

ORK *abbrev.* ✦ Cork (airport baggage label)

Ork. *shortening* ✦ Orkney Islands

ORL *abbrev.* ✦ otorhinolaryngology (treatment of the ear, nose and throat)

orl *abbrev.* ✦ owner's risk of leakage

ornithol. *shortening* ✦ ornithology

ORT *abbrev.* ✦ oral rehydration therapy

Orth. *shortening* ✦ Orthodox

ORTF *abbrev.* ✦ Organisation de Radio et Télévision Française (French, = French Radio and Television Organization)

ortho. *shortening* ✦ orthopaedic

OS *abbrev.* ✦ Austrian Airlines (airline baggage code) ✦ Glasgow (British vehicle registration mark) ✦ Old Saxon ✦ Old Style ✦ Ordinary Seaman ✦ Ordnance Survey ✦ out of stock ✦ outsize

Os *symbol* ✦ osmium (chemical element)

os *abbrev.* ✦ only son

o/s *abbrev.* ✦ out of stock ✦ outstanding

OSA *abbrev.* ✦ Official Secrets Act ✦ Ordo Sancti Augustini (Latin, = Order of Saint Augustine) (Augustinians)

OSax *abbrev.* ✦ Old Saxon

OSB *abbrev.* ✦ Ordo Sancti Benedicti (Latin, = Order of Saint Benedict) (Benedictines)

OScand *abbrev.* ✦ Old Scandinavian

Oscar *abbrev.* ✦ Organization for Sickle Cell Anaemia Research

OSF *abbrev.* ✦ Ordo Sancti Francisci (Latin, = Order of Saint Francis) (Franciscans)

OSFC *abbrev.* ✦ Ordo Sancti Francisci Cappuchinorum (Latin, = Cappuchin Order of Saint Francis) (Cappuchins)

OSCH *abbrev.* ✦ off-peak storage central heating

OSI *abbrev.* ✦ Open Systems Interconnection

OSJ *abbrev.* ✦ on a secret journey

OSl *abbrev.* ✦ Old Slavonic

OSM *abbrev.* ✦ Ordo Servorum Beatae Virginis Mariae (Latin, = Order of the Servants of the Blessed Virgin Mary) (Servites)

osp *abbrev.* ♦ obiit sine prole (Latin, = died without issue) ♦ off-street parking

OST *abbrev.* ♦ Ostend (airport baggage label)

OStJ *abbrev.* ♦ Officer of the Order of St John of Jerusalem

OSw *abbrev.* ♦ Old Swedish

OT *abbrev.* ♦ occupational therapy ♦ Old Testament ♦ operating theatre ♦ overtime ♦ Portsmouth (British vehicle registration mark)

OTB *abbrev.* ♦ off-track betting

OTC *abbrev.* ♦ Officers' Training Corps ♦ over-the-counter

OTE *abbrev.* ♦ on-target earnings ♦ or the equivalent

OTeut *abbrev.* ♦ Old Teutonic

OTG *abbrev.* ♦ outside temperature gauge

OTT *abbrev.* ♦ over the top

ott. *shortening* ♦ ottava (Italian, = octave) (music)

OTU *abbrev.* ♦ operational training unit

OU *abbrev.* ♦ Bristol (British vehicle registration mark) ♦ the Open University ♦ Oxford University

Ouds *pronounced* owds *acronym* ♦ Oxford University Dramatic Society

OUP *abbrev.* ♦ Oxford University Press

OV *abbrev.* ♦ Birmingham (British vehicle registration mark)

ovc *abbrev.* ♦ other valuable consideration

overlkg *contraction* ♦ overlooking

ovno *abbrev.* ♦ or very near offer

OW *abbrev.* ♦ Portsmouth (British vehicle registration mark)

own. *shortening* ♦ owner

OX *abbrev.* ♦ Birmingham (British vehicle registration mark) ♦ Oxford (UK postcode)

Oxbridge *contraction* ♦ Oxford and Cambridge

Oxf. *shortening* ♦ Oxford

Oxfam *acronym* ♦ Oxford Committee for Famine Relief

Oxon. *shortening* ♦ Oxonia (Latin, = Oxford) (used as the county abbreviation) ♦ Oxoniensis (Latin, = of Oxford) (used with degrees and in bishop's signature)

OY *abbrev.* ♦ Denmark (international civil aircraft marking) ♦ north-west London (British vehicle registration mark)

OZ *abbrev.* ♦ Belfast (British vehicle registration mark)

oz *abbrev.* ♦ onza (Italian, = ounce)

oz ap. *shortening* ♦ apothecaries' ounce

oz av. *shortening* ♦ avoirdupois ounce

oz T *abbrev.* ♦ troy ounce

P

P *abbrev.* ◆ parking ◆ pawn (chess) ◆ peta- ◆ Portugal (international vehicle registration)

P *symbol* ◆ phosphorus (chemical element)

p *abbrev.* ◆ new penny (British monetary unit) ◆ page ◆ paragraph ◆ participle ◆ passive ◆ past ◆ per ◆ perennial ◆ peseta (Spanish monetary unit) ◆ peso (monetary unit) ◆ piano (Italian, = softly) (music) ◆ pico- ◆ positive ◆ proton

PA *abbrev.* ◆ Guildford (British vehicle registration mark) ◆ Paisley (UK postcode) ◆ Panama (international vehicle registration) ◆ Pan-American World Airways Incorporated (airline baggage code) ◆ Pedestrians' Association ◆ Pennsylvania (US postcode) ◆ pernicious anaemia ◆ personal appearance ◆ personal assistant ◆ Piper Aircraft ◆ power amplifier ◆ press agent ◆ Press Association ◆ programme assistant ◆ Protestant Alliance ◆ Psoriasis Association ◆ public address system ◆ publicity agent ◆ Publishers' Association ◆ pulmonary artery

Pa *shortening* ◆ pascal

Pa *symbol* ◆ protactinium (chemical element)

Pa. *shortening* ◆ Pennsylvania

pa *abbrev.* ◆ participial adjective ◆ per annum

p/a *abbrev.* ◆ private account

pa. *shortening* ◆ past

PABIAC *abbrev.* ◆ Paper and Board Industry Advisory Committee

Pabla *acronym* ◆ problem analysis by logical approach

PABX *abbrev.* ◆ private automatic branch exchange

PAC *abbrev.* ◆ Pan Africanist Congress ◆ Permanent Agricultural Committee (ILO) ◆ Public Accounts Committee

Pac. *shortening* ◆ Pacific

PACA *abbrev.* ◆ Public Art Commissions Agency

Pace *acronym* ◆ Parental Alliance for Choice in Education ◆ peformance and cost evaluation ◆ Police and Criminal Evidence Act ◆ Polytechnic Association for Continuing Education ◆ Protestant and Catholic Encounter

Pacif. *shortening* ◆ Pacific

PAD *abbrev.* ◆ packet assembler/disassembler ◆ payable after death

PADT *abbrev.* ◆ Public Art Development Trust

paediat. *shortening* ◆ paediatrician ◆ paediatrics

paf *abbrev.* ◆ puissance au frein (French, = brake horsepower)

PAGB *abbrev.* ◆ Poultry and Egg Producers' Association of Great Britain

Pain *acronym* ◆ Parents Against Injustice

PAK *abbrev.* ◆ Pakistan (international vehicle registration)

Pak. *shortening* ◆ Pakistan ◆ Pakistani

PAL *abbrev.* ◆ phase alternation line (colour TV system)

palaeog. *shortening* ◆ palaeographic ◆ palaeography

palaeontol. *shortening* ◆ palaeontological ◆ palaeontology

PAM *abbrev.* ◆ pulse-amplitude modulation

pam. *shortening* ◆ pamphlet
pamph. *shortening* ◆ pamphlet
PAMR *abbrev.* ◆ Public Access Mobile Radio
Pan *acronym* ◆ Pesticides Action Network
Pan. *shortening* ◆ Panama ◆ Panamanian
pan. *shortening* ◆ panchromatic
Panaftel *acronym* ◆ Pan-African Telecommunications Network
PanAm *acronym* ◆ Pan-American World Airways Incorporated
PanCan *acronym* ◆ Panama Canal
P & G *abbrev.* ◆ Procter and Gamble
p & l *abbrev.* ◆ profit and loss
P & O *abbrev.* ◆ Peninsular and Oriental Steamship Navigation Company
p & p *abbrev.* ◆ postage and packing
PANN *abbrev.* ◆ Professional Association of Nursery Nurses
PAP *abbrev.* ◆ Port au Prince (airport baggage label)
Pap. *shortening* ◆ Papua ◆ Papuan
PAR *abbrev.* ◆ Paris (airport baggage label) ◆ precision approach radar
par *abbrev.* ◆ planed all round (timber)
par. *shortening* ◆ paragraph ◆ parallel ◆ parish
Para. *shortening* ◆ Paraguay ◆ Paraguayan

para. *shortening* ◆ parachute ◆ paragraph
parab. *shortening* ◆ parabola
par. aff. *shortening* ◆ pars affecta (Latin, = the injured part)
parch. *shortening* ◆ parchment
paren. *shortening* ◆ parenthesis
park. *shortening* ◆ parking
parl. *shortening* ◆ parliament ◆ parliamentary
part. *shortening* ◆ partial ◆ participation ◆ participial ◆ participle ◆ particle ◆ partition
part. aeq. *shortening* ◆ partes aequales (Latin, = equal portions)
PARU *abbrev.* ◆ post-anaesthetic recovery unit
PAS *abbrev.* ◆ public address system
pas *abbrev.* ◆ power assisted steering
Pascal *acronym* ◆ Programme appliqué à la sélection et la compilation automatique de la littérature (French, = Program applied to the selection and automatic compilation of literature)
Pasok *acronym* ◆ Panellenion Sozialistikon Kinema (Greek, = Panhellenic Socialist Movement)
Pass. *shortening* ◆ Passover
pass. *shortening* ◆ passive
PAT *abbrev.* ◆ planned activities time ◆ Professional Association of Teachers

---

PAPER SIZES

These are the international standard sizes for sheets of paper. The A series is used for writing paper, books, etc; the B series for posters. Each successive sheet is the size of the previous one folded in half.

A0	*841 × 1189 mm*	**B0**	*1000 × 1414 mm*
A1	*594 × 841 mm*	**B1**	*707 × 1000 mm*
A2	*420 × 594 mm*	**B2**	*500 × 707 mm*
A3	*297 × 420 mm*	**B3**	*353 × 500 mm*
A4	*210 × 297 mm*	**B4**	*250 × 353 mm*
A5	*148 × 210 mm*	**B5**	*176 × 250 mm*
A6	*105 × 148 mm*	**B6**	*125 × 176 mm*
A7	*74 × 105 mm*	**B7**	*88 × 125 mm*
A8	*52 × 74 mm*	**B8**	*62 × 88 mm*
A9	*37 × 52 mm*	**B9**	*44 × 62 mm*
A10	*26 × 37 mm*	**B10**	*31 × 44 mm*

pat. *shortening* ◆ patent ◆ patented

Pata. *shortening* ◆ Patagonia
◆ Patagonian

path. *shortening* ◆ pathological
◆ pathology

pathol. *shortening* ◆ pathological
◆ pathology

Pat. Off. *shortening* ◆ Patent Office

pat. pend. *shortening* ◆ patent pending

PAU *abbrev.* ◆ Pan American Union

pav. *shortening* ◆ pavilion

PAX *abbrev.* ◆ private automatic
exchange

pax *abbrev.* ◆ per annum, exclusive (of
rent net of Council Tax, water rates, etc)

PAYE *abbrev.* ◆ pay as you earn ◆ pay as
you enter

PAYP *abbrev.* ◆ pay as you play (of golf
club etc membership)

PAYV *abbrev.* ◆ pay as you view

PB *abbrev.* ◆ Guildford (British vehicle
registration mark) ◆ passbook
◆ Pharmacopoeia Britannica
◆ Plymouth Brethren ◆ power brakes
◆ Prayer Book

Pb *symbol* ◆ plumbum (Latin, = lead)
(chemical element)

pb *abbrev.* ◆ paperback

p/b *abbrev.* ◆ purpose-built ◆ push-
button

pba *abbrev.* ◆ poor bloody assistant

PBFA *abbrev.* ◆ Provincial Booksellers'
Fairs Association

PBI *abbrev.* ◆ Peace Brigades
International ◆ poor bloody infantry

pbk *contraction* ◆ paperback

PBM *abbrev.* ◆ permanent benchmark

PBMA *abbrev.* ◆ Plastic Bath
Manufacturers' Association

pbr *abbrev.* ◆ payment by results

PBS *abbrev.* ◆ Public Broadcasting
Service (US)

PBT *abbrev.* ◆ President of the Board of
Trade

pbt *abbrev.* ◆ profit before tax

pbuh *abbrev.* ◆ peace be upon him

PBX *abbrev.* ◆ private branch exchange

PC *abbrev.* ◆ Fiji Air (airline baggage
code) ◆ Guildford (British vehicle
registration mark) ◆ Panama Canal
◆ Parish Council ◆ Peace Corps
◆ personal computer ◆ Plaid Cymru
(Welsh, = Party of Wales) ◆ Police
Constable ◆ Political Correctness
◆ Politically Correct ◆ postcard ◆ Press
Council ◆ Privy Councillor

pc *abbrev.* ◆ parsec ◆ per cent ◆ post
cibum (Latin, = after food)

p/c *abbrev.* ◆ petty cash ◆ prices current

PCA *abbrev.* ◆ Parliamentary
Commissioner for Administration
(official title of Ombudsman)
◆ Parochial Clergy Association ◆ Police
Complaints Authority ◆ Professional
Cycling Association

PCAS *abbrev.* ◆ Polytechnics Central
Admissions System

PCB *abbrev.* ◆ polychlorinated biphenyl
◆ post-coital bleeding

pcb *abbrev.* ◆ petty cash book ◆ printed
circuit board

PCC *abbrev.* ◆ parochial church council
◆ Press Complaints Commission
◆ Professional Conduct Committee
(disciplinary body of BMA) ◆ Puerto
Rico (airport baggage label)

PCCS *abbrev.* ◆ Primate Captive Care
Society

pce *contraction* ◆ piece

pcf *abbrev.* ◆ pounds per cubic foot

PCFC *abbrev.* ◆ Polytechnics and
Colleges Funding Council

PCFRE *abbrev.* ◆ Professional Council
for Religious Education

PCGG *abbrev.* ◆ Primary Care Group in
Gynaecology

PCI *abbrev.* ◆ Pax Christi International

pci *abbrev.* ◆ pounds per cubic inch

PCID *abbrev.* ◆ Pontifical Council for
Inter-Religious Dialogue

PCIFC *abbrev.* ◆ Permanent Commission
of the International Fisheries
Convention

PCIJ *abbrev.* ◆ Permanent Court of
International Justice

PCIS *abbrev.* ◆ Period Cottage Improvement Society

PCL *abbrev.* ◆ printer control language

pcm *abbrev.* ◆ per calendar month ◆ pulse code modulation

PCMA *abbrev.* ◆ Plastic Crate Manufacturers' Association ◆ Potato Chip Manufacturers' Association

PCN *abbrev.* ◆ personal communications network

PCOCA *abbrev.* ◆ Parti-Colour Oriental Cat Association

PCOD *abbrev.* ◆ polycystic ovary disease

PCP *abbrev.* ◆ pentachlorophenol ◆ phencyclidine (angel dust) ◆ Pneumocystis carinii pneumonia

PCPCU *abbrev.* ◆ Pontifical Council for Promoting Christian Unity

PCPI *abbrev.* ◆ Parent Co-operative Preschools International ◆ Permanent Committee on Patent Information (WIPO)

PCR *abbrev.* ◆ politically correct retailing ◆ polymerase chain reaction

PCS *abbrev.* ◆ Principal Clerk of Session

pct *contraction* ◆ percent

PCTE *abbrev.* ◆ portable common tool environment

PCV *abbrev.* ◆ passenger-carrying vehicle

PCWPC *abbrev.* ◆ Permanent Committee of the World Petroleum Congress

PCZ *abbrev.* ◆ Panama Canal Zone

PD *abbrev.* ◆ Guildford (British vehicle registration mark) ◆ preventive detention ◆ public domain

Pd *symbol* ◆ palladium (chemical element)

pd *abbrev.* ◆ per diem (Latin, = each day) ◆ postage due ◆ postdated

pd *contraction* ◆ paid

p/d *abbrev.* ◆ price–dividend (ratio etc)

PDC *abbrev.* ◆ Population Documentation Center (UN)

pdi *abbrev.* ◆ pre-delivery inspection

PDL *abbrev.* ◆ page description language

PDN *abbrev.* ◆ public data network

pdn *contraction* ◆ production

pdq *abbrev.* ◆ pretty damn quick

PDRA *abbrev.* ◆ postdoctoral research assistant

PDRE *abbrev.* ◆ People's Democratic Republic of Ethiopia

PDRY *abbrev.* ◆ People's Democratic Republic of the Yemen

PDS *abbrev.* ◆ Parkinson's Disease Society of the United Kingdom

PDSA *abbrev.* ◆ People's Dispensary for Sick Animals

PE *abbrev.* ◆ Guildford (British vehicle registration mark) ◆ People Express (airline baggage code) ◆ Peru (international vehicle registration) ◆ Peterborough (UK postcode) ◆ phase-encoded ◆ physical education ◆ Protestant Episcopal

pe *abbrev.* ◆ personal estate ◆ plastic explosive

p/e *abbrev.* ◆ price–earnings (ratio etc)

PEA *abbrev.* ◆ Physical Education Association of Great Britain and Northern Ireland

PEAB *abbrev.* ◆ Professional Engineers' Appointments Bureau

PEC *abbrev.* ◆ Protestant Episcopal Church

pec *acronym* ◆ photoelectric cell

PED *abbrev.* ◆ Emergency Preparedness and Disaster Relief Co-ordination Office

Ped. *shortening* ◆ pedal

PEF *abbrev.* ◆ European Pentecostal Fellowship ◆ Palestine Exploration Fund

PEI *abbrev.* ◆ Prince Edward Island

PEK *abbrev.* ◆ Beijing (airport baggage label)

Pembs. *shortening* ◆ Pembrokeshire

PEN *abbrev.* ◆ Penang (airport baggage label)

Pen *acronym* ◆ International Association of Poets, Playwrights, Editors, Essayists and Novelists

pen. *shortening* ◆ penal ◆ penetrate ◆ peninsula

Penn. *shortening* ◆ Pennsylvania

Pent. *shortening* ◆ Pentateuch (books of Bible) ◆ Pentecost

penthse *contraction* ◆ penthouse

Pep *acronym* ◆ personal equity plan ◆ political and economic planning

PER *abbrev.* ◆ Professional and Executive Recruitment ◆ Professional Employment Register

Per. *shortening* ◆ Persia ◆ Persian

per. *shortening* ◆ period ◆ person

PERA *abbrev.* ◆ Production Engineering Research Association of Great Britain

per ann. *shortening* ◆ per annum

perc. *shortening* ◆ percussion

perd. *shortening* ◆ perdendosi (Italian, = vanishing) (music)

perdend. *shortening* ◆ perdendosi (Italian, = vanishing) (music)

perf. *shortening* ◆ perfect ◆ perforated (stamp collecting) ◆ performance ◆ performed ◆ performer

perh. *shortening* ◆ perhaps

peri. *shortening* ◆ perigee

perm. *shortening* ◆ permanent

PERME *abbrev.* ◆ Propellants, Explosives and Rocket Motor Establishment

perp. *shortening* ◆ perpendicular

per pro. *shortening* ◆ per procurationem (Latin, = through the agency of)

Pers. *shortening* ◆ Persia ◆ Persian

pers. *shortening* ◆ person ◆ personal

persp. *shortening* ◆ perspective

pert *acronym* ◆ programme evaluation and review technique

pert. *shortening* ◆ pertaining

Peruv. *shortening* ◆ Peruvian

Pes. *shortening* ◆ peseta (Spanish monetary unit)

PESGB *abbrev.* ◆ Petroleum Exploration Society of Great Britain

Pest *acronym* ◆ Pressure for Economic and Social Toryism

PET *abbrev.* ◆ polyethylene terephthalate ◆ pre-eclamptic toxaemia

pet *acronym* ◆ positron emission tomography

Pet. *shortening* ◆ Peter (books of Bible)

petn *contraction* ◆ petition

petr. *shortening* ◆ petrification

Petras *acronym* ◆ Polytechnic Educational Resources Advisory Service

Petriburg. *shortening* ◆ Petriburgensis (Latin, = of Peterborough)

petrochem. *shortening* ◆ petrochemical

petrog. *shortening* ◆ petrography

petrol. *shortening* ◆ petrology ◆ petrological

PF *abbrev.* ◆ Guildford (British vehicle registration mark) ◆ Pagan Federation ◆ Patriotic Front ◆ Procurator Fiscal

Pf. *shortening* ◆ pfennig (German monetary unit)

pF *abbrev.* ◆ picofarad

pf *abbrev.* ◆ piano e forte (Italian, = soft and then loud) (music) ◆ più forte (Italian, = louder) (music) ◆ public funding

pf *contraction* ◆ proof

pf. *shortening* ◆ perfect ◆ pianoforte (instrument)

PFA *abbrev.* ◆ Popular Flying Association ◆ Professional Footballers' Association

PFB *abbrev.* ◆ preformed beam

PFC *abbrev.* ◆ polychlorinated fluorocarbon

pfc *abbrev.* ◆ passed flying college

PFLO *abbrev.* ◆ Popular Front for the Liberation of Oman

PFLP *abbrev.* ◆ Popular Front for the Liberation of Palestine

PFLT *abbrev.* ◆ People's Front of Liberation Tigers (Sri Lankan separatist terrorists)

PFM *abbrev.* ◆ pulse frequency modulation

PFMA *abbrev.* ◆ Pet Food Manufacturers Association

PFP *abbrev.* ◆ personal financial planning

PFPUT *abbrev.* ◆ Pension Fund Property Unit Trust

PFR *abbrev.* ◆ prototype fast reactor

PFSF *abbrev.* ◆ Parents for Safe Food

PG *abbrev.* ◆ Guildford (British vehicle registration mark) ◆ Parental Guidance (film censorship classification) ◆ paying guest ◆ postgraduate

Pg. *shortening* ◆ Portugal ◆ Portuguese

pg. *shortening* ◆ page

PGA *abbrev.* ◆ Power Generation Association ◆ Prison Governors' Association ◆ Professional Golfers' Association

PGCE *abbrev.* ◆ Postgraduate Certificate in Education

PgDn *contraction* ◆ page down (computer key)

PGDRS *abbrev.* ◆ psychogeriatric dependency rating scale

PGF *abbrev.* ◆ polypeptide growth factor

PGG *abbrev.* ◆ Professional Gardeners' Guild

PGL *abbrev.* ◆ persistent generalized lymphadenopathy

PGM *abbrev.* ◆ Past Grand Master ◆ precision guided missile

pgt *abbrev.* ◆ per gross ton

PgUp *contraction* ◆ page up (computer key)

PH *abbrev.* ◆ Guildford (British vehicle registration mark) ◆ Netherlands (international civil aircraft marking) ◆ Perth (UK postcode) ◆ Polynesian Airlines ◆ previous history

pH *abbrev.* ◆ potential of hydrogen ions (measure of soil acidity)

ph *shortening* ◆ phot

ph. *shortening* ◆ phone

Phab *acronym* ◆ Physically Handicapped and Able Bodied

PharB *abbrev.* ◆ Pharmaciae Baccalaureus (Latin, = Bachelor of Pharmacy)

PharD *abbrev.* ◆ Pharmaciae Doctor (Latin, = Doctor of Pharmacy)

PharM *abbrev.* ◆ Pharmaciae Magister (Latin, = Master of Pharmacy)

pharm. *shortening* ◆ pharmaceutical ◆ pharmacist ◆ pharmacology ◆ pharmacopoeia ◆ pharmacy

pharmacol. *shortening* ◆ pharmacology ◆ pharmacological

PharmB *abbrev.* ◆ Pharmaciae Baccalaureus (Latin, = Bachelor of Pharmacy)

PharmD *abbrev.* ◆ Pharmaciae Doctor (Latin, = Doctor of Pharmacy)

PhB *abbrev.* ◆ Philosophiae Baccalaureus (Latin, = Bachelor of Philosophy)

PHC *abbrev.* ◆ pharmaceutical chemist ◆ primary health care

PHCA *abbrev.* ◆ Private Hire Car Association

PhD *abbrev.* ◆ Philosophiae Doctor (Latin, = Doctor of Philosophy)

PHI *abbrev.* ◆ permanent health insurance ◆ Public Health Inspector

Phil. *shortening* ◆ Philharmonic ◆ Philippians (book of Bible) ◆ philippines

phil. *shortening* ◆ philological ◆ philology ◆ philosophical ◆ philosophy

Philem. *shortening* ◆ Philemon (book of Bible)

philol. *shortening* ◆ philological ◆ philology

philos. *shortening* ◆ philosophical ◆ philosophy

PhL *abbrev.* ◆ Licentiate in Philosophy

PHLS *abbrev.* ◆ Public Health Laboratory Service

PHLSB *abbrev.* ◆ Public Health Laboratory Service Board

PhM *abbrev.* ◆ Philosophiae Magister (Latin, = Master of Philosophy)

phon. *shortening* ◆ phonetic ◆ phonetics

phonet. *shortening* ◆ phonetic ◆ phonetics

phonog. *shortening* ◆ phonography

phonol. *shortening* ◆ phonology

phot. *shortening* ◆ photographic ◆ photography

photog. *shortening* ◆ photographic ◆ photography

photom. *shortening* ✦ photometric
✦ photometry
php *abbrev.* ✦ pounds per horsepower
phr. *shortening* ✦ phrase
phrenol. *shortening* ✦ phrenological
✦ phrenology
PHRG *abbrev.* ✦ Parliamentary Human
Rights Group
PHSA *abbrev.* ✦ Provincial Hospital
Services Association
PHWR *abbrev.* ✦ pressurized heavy
water reactor
phys. *shortening* ✦ physical ✦ physician
✦ physics ✦ physiological ✦ physiology
physiog. *shortening* ✦ physiognomy
physiol. *shortening* ✦ physiological
✦ physiologist ✦ physiology
PI *abbrev.* ✦ parainfluenza virus
✦ Performers and Artists for Nuclear
Disarmament International
✦ Philippine Islands ✦ Phillipine
Republic (international civil aircraft
marking) ✦ Privacy International
✦ programmed instruction
PIA *abbrev.* ✦ Pakistan International
Airlines ✦ Personal Investment
Authority
PIAC *abbrev.* ✦ Petroleum Industry
Advisory Council
pianiss. *shortening* ✦ pianissimo (Italian,
= very softly)
PIB *abbrev.* ✦ Petroleum Information
Bureau ✦ Prices and Incomes Board
Pibor *pronounced* pee-bore *acronym*
✦ Paris Interbank Offered Rate
PIBS *abbrev.* ✦ permanent interest-
bearing share
PIC *abbrev.* ✦ Poultry Industry
Conference ✦ programmable interrupt
controller
PICC *abbrev.* ✦ Provisional International
Computation Centre
pic. *shortening* ✦ piccolo
pict. *shortening* ✦ pictorial
PICUTPC *abbrev.* ✦ Permanent and
International Committee of
Underground Town Planning and
Construction

PICV *abbrev.* ✦ Permanent International
Commission of Viticulture
PID *abbrev.* ✦ pelvic inflammatory
disease ✦ personal identification device
✦ prolapsed intervertebral disc (slipped
disc)
Pids *acronym* ✦ primary immune
deficiency syndrome
PIFA *abbrev.* ✦ Packaging and Industrial
Films Association
PIH *abbrev.* ✦ Paintings in Hospitals
✦ pregnancy-induced hypertension
pik *abbrev.* ✦ payment in kind
PIL *abbrev.* ✦ Pest Infestation Laboratory
pil *abbrev.* ✦ payment in lieu
pil. *shortening* ✦ pilula (Latin, = pill)
Pill *acronym* ✦ programmed instruction
language learning
Pim *acronym* ✦ personal information
manager
PIME *abbrev.* ✦ Pontificium Institutum
pro Missionibus Externis (Latin, =
Pontifical Institute for Foreign
Missions)
PIMS *abbrev.* ✦ profit impact of market
strategy
PIN *acronym* ✦ personal identification
number
Pinc *acronym* ✦ property income
certificate
pinx. *shortening* ✦ pinxit (Latin, = painted
it)
PIRA *abbrev.* ✦ Paper and Board, Printing
and Packaging Industries Research
Association
PITB *abbrev.* ✦ Petroleum Industry
Training Board
pizz. *shortening* ✦ pizzicato (Italian, =
plucked)
PJ *abbrev.* ✦ Curaçao (international civil
aircraft marking) ✦ Guildford (British
vehicle registration mark) ✦ Presiding
Judge ✦ Probate Judge
PK *abbrev.* ✦ Guildford (British vehicle
registration mark) ✦ Pakistan
International (airline baggage code)
Pk *contraction* ✦ Park

pk *abbrev.* ◆ personal knowledge
◆ psychokinesis
pk *contraction* ◆ pack
PKC *abbrev.* ◆ Phuket (airport baggage label)
pkg *contraction* ◆ packing
pkge *contraction* ◆ package
pkt *contraction* ◆ packet
PKTF *abbrev.* ◆ Printing and Kindred Trades Federation
PKU *abbrev.* ◆ phenylketonuria
pkwy *contraction* ◆ parkway
PL *abbrev.* ◆ Aero Peru (airline baggage code) ◆ Guildford (British vehicle registration mark) ◆ patrol leader (scouting) ◆ Plymouth (UK postcode) ◆ Poet Laureate ◆ Poland (international vehicle registration) ◆ Primrose League ◆ Public Library
PL/1 *abbrev.* ◆ Programming Language 1
Pl. *shortening* ◆ Place
pl. *shortening* ◆ place ◆ plate (book illustration) ◆ plural
p/l *abbrev.* ◆ profit and loss
PLA *abbrev.* ◆ Port of London Authority ◆ Private Libraries Association ◆ programmable logic array
Plan *acronym* ◆ People's Liberation Army of Namibia
plat. *shortening* ◆ platform ◆ platoon
Plato *acronym* ◆ Programmed Logic for Automatic Teaching Operation
PLC *abbrev.* ◆ Public Limited Company
PLCW & TWU *abbrev.* ◆ Power Loom Carpet Weavers' and Textile Workers' Union
plen. *shortening* ◆ plenipotentiary
PLF *abbrev.* ◆ Palestine Liberation Front
plf *contraction* ◆ plaintiff
PLH *abbrev.* ◆ Plymouth (airport baggage label)
PL/M *abbrev.* ◆ Programming Language for Microcomputers
PLO *abbrev.* ◆ Palestine Liberation Organization
PLP *abbrev.* ◆ Parliamentary Labour Party
PLR *abbrev.* ◆ public lending right

Pl. Sgt *contraction* ◆ platoon sergeant
plsnt *contraction* ◆ pleasant
PLSS *abbrev.* ◆ portable life-support system
plup. *shortening* ◆ pluperfect
plur. *shortening* ◆ plural
PM *abbrev.* ◆ Guildford (British vehicle registration mark) ◆ Paymaster ◆ Past Master ◆ Postmaster ◆ Prime Minister ◆ Provost-Marshal
Pm *symbol* ◆ promethium (chemical element)
pm *abbrev.* ◆ post meridiem (Latin, = after noon) ◆ post-mortem ◆ premium ◆ premolar
PMA *abbrev.* ◆ paramethoxyamphetamine (hallucinogenic drug)
PMBX *abbrev.* ◆ private manual branch exchange
PMDA *abbrev.* ◆ Pianoforte Manufacturers' and Distributors' Association
PMG *abbrev.* ◆ Paymaster-General ◆ Postmaster-General
PME *abbrev.* ◆ Portsmouth (airport baggage label)
PMH *abbrev.* ◆ previous medical history
pmh *abbrev.* ◆ per man-hour
PMI *abbrev.* ◆ Pensions Management Institute
pmk *contraction* ◆ postmark
PMMS *abbrev.* ◆ Plainsong and Medieval Music Society
PMO *abbrev.* ◆ Palermo (airport baggage label) ◆ Principal Medical Officer
pmr *contraction* ◆ paymaster
PMRAFNS *abbrev.* ◆ Princess Mary's Royal Air Force Nursing Service
PMS *abbrev.* ◆ premenstrual syndrome
PMT *abbrev.* ◆ photomechanical transfer ◆ premenstrual tension
pmt *contraction* ◆ payment
PMU *abbrev.* ◆ Pontifical Missionary Union
PN *abbrev.* ◆ Brighton (British vehicle registration mark) ◆ postnatal
pn *abbrev.* ◆ promissory note

PNA *abbrev.* ◆ Psychiatric Nurses' Association

PND *abbrev.* ◆ postnatal depression

PNdB *abbrev.* ◆ perceived noise decibel

PNEU *abbrev.* ◆ Parents' National Education Union

PNG *abbrev.* ◆ Papua New Guinea ◆ Papua New Guinea (international vehicle registration)

png *abbrev.* ◆ persona non grata (Latin, = unacceptable person) (diplomat rejected by government of host country)

PNH *abbrev.* ◆ Phnom Penh (airport baggage label)

PNLA *abbrev.* ◆ Palestine National Liberation Army

PNLM *abbrev.* ◆ Palestine National Liberation Movement

pnr *abbrev.* ◆ prior notice required

PNS *abbrev.* ◆ parasympathetic nervous system

pnxt *contraction* ◆ pinxit (Latin, = painted it)

PO *abbrev.* ◆ Petty Officer ◆ Pilot Officer ◆ Portsmouth (British vehicle registration mark) ◆ Portsmouth (UK postcode) ◆ Postal Order ◆ Post Office

Po *symbol* ◆ polonium (chemical element)

po *abbrev.* ◆ per os (Latin, = through the mouth)

POA *abbrev.* ◆ Prison Officers' Association

POD *abbrev.* ◆ port of debarkation

pod *abbrev.* ◆ pay on delivery

POE *abbrev.* ◆ port of embarkation ◆ port of entry

poet. *shortening* ◆ poetic ◆ poetry

POEU *abbrev.* ◆ Post Office Engineering Union

POL *abbrev.* ◆ Patent Office Library ◆ petrol, oil and lubricants

pol *abbrev.* ◆ problem-oriented language

Pol. *shortening* ◆ Poland ◆ Polish

pol. *shortening* ◆ polar ◆ polarized ◆ police ◆ political ◆ politics

Polis *acronym* ◆ Parliamentary On-Line Information Service

polit. *shortening* ◆ political ◆ politics

poll. *shortening* ◆ pollution

POM *abbrev.* ◆ prescription-only medicine

POP *abbrev.* ◆ point of purchase ◆ Post Office Preferred (envelope sizes)

pop *abbrev.* ◆ plaster of Paris

pop. *shortening* ◆ popular ◆ popularly ◆ population

POPA *abbrev.* ◆ Property Owners' Protection Association

Popin *acronym* ◆ Population Information Network

Poplab *contraction* ◆ International Programme of Laboratories for Population Statistics

por *abbrev.* ◆ pay on receipt ◆ pay on return

por. *shortening* ◆ porosity ◆ porous ◆ portion

Port. *shortening* ◆ Portugal ◆ Portuguese

port. *shortening* ◆ portable ◆ portrait ◆ portraiture

POS *abbrev.* ◆ point of sale ◆ Port-of-Spain (airport baggage label)

pos. *shortening* ◆ position ◆ positive ◆ possession ◆ possessive

Posas *contraction* ◆ Patent Office Search and Advisory Service

posn *contraction* ◆ position

poss. *shortening* ◆ possession ◆ possessive ◆ possible ◆ possibly

posslq *pronounced* poss-el-cue *acronym* ◆ person of opposite sex sharing living quarters

Post *acronym* ◆ Parliamentary Office of Science and Technology ◆ point-of-sale terminal

posth. *shortening* ◆ posthumous

posthum. *shortening* ◆ posthumously

postn *contraction* ◆ position

pot. *shortening* ◆ potential

poul. *shortening* ◆ poultry

POUNC *abbrev.* ◆ Post Office Users' National Council

pov *abbrev.* ◆ point of view ◆ privately owned vehicle

POW *abbrev.* ◆ Prince of Wales ◆ prisoner of war

Powagod *acronym* ◆ Prince of Wales' Advisory Group on Disability

PP *abbrev.* ◆ Brazil (international civil aircraft marking) ◆ Luton (British vehicle registration mark) ◆ parish priest ◆ past president ◆ present pupil

pp *abbrev.* ◆ past participle ◆ per person ◆ per procurationem (Latin, = through the agency of) ◆ pianissimo (Italian, = very quietly) (music) ◆ planning permission ◆ post paid ◆ post prandium (Latin, = after dinner) ◆ privately printed

PPA *abbrev.* ◆ Pre-School Playgroups Association

ppb *abbrev.* ◆ paper, printing and binding ◆ parts per billion

ppc *abbrev.* ◆ progressive patient care ◆ prospective parliamentary candidate

ppd *contraction* ◆ prepaid

PPE *abbrev.* ◆ Philosophy, Politics and Economics

PPH *abbrev.* ◆ post-partum haemorrhage

ppi *abbrev.* ◆ plan-position indicator (radar)

PPITB *abbrev.* ◆ Printing and Publishing Industry Training Board

pple *contraction* ◆ participle

PPM *abbrev.* ◆ peak programme meter

ppm *abbrev.* ◆ pages per minute ◆ parts per million

PPMA *abbrev.* ◆ Produce Packaging and Marketing Association

PPN *abbrev.* ◆ public packet network

PPP *abbrev.* ◆ personal pension plan ◆ Private Patients' Plan ◆ Psychology, Philosophy and Physiology

ppp *abbrev.* ◆ pianississimo (Italian, = extremely quietly) (music)

pppm *abbrev.* ◆ per person per month

pppn *abbrev.* ◆ per person per night

PPR *abbrev.* ◆ printed paper rate

PPRA *abbrev.* ◆ Past President of the Royal Academy

PPS *abbrev.* ◆ Parliamentary Private Secretary ◆ pelvic pain syndrome ◆ post postscriptum (Latin, = after the postscript) ◆ Principal Private Secretary

PPU *abbrev.* ◆ Peace Pledge Union

PQ *abbrev.* ◆ parliamentary question ◆ Parti Québecois (advocating French-language separatism) ◆ Province of Quebec

pq *abbrev.* ◆ previous question

UNITED KINGDOM POSTCODES

The United Kingdom is divided into 120 principal postcode areas, which are indicated by the letter or letters that precede the first numeral in the postcode of any address: all of them are listed in this dictionary at their alphabetical place. This panel shows the postcodes of some of the principal towns and cities of the UK.

AB	*Aberdeen*	**EC**	*east central London*	**OX**	*Oxford*
B	*Birmingham*	**EH**	*Edinburgh*	**SE**	*south-east London*
BA	*Bath*	**G**	*Glasgow*	**SO**	*Southampton*
BD	*Bradford*	**L**	*Liverpool*	**SW**	*south-west London*
BS	*Bristol*	**LS**	*Leeds*	**W**	*west London*
BT	*Belfast*	**M**	*Manchester*	**WC**	*west central London*
CB	*Cambridge*	**N**	*north London*	**YO**	*York*
CF	*Cardiff*	**NE**	*Newcastle upon Tyne*		
CV	*Coventry*	**NW**	*north-west London*		
E	*east London*				

PR *abbrev.* ✦ Bournemouth (British vehicle registration mark) ✦ Philippine Airlines (airline baggage code) ✦ Pipe Roll ✦ press release ✦ Preston (UK postcode) ✦ prize ring ✦ proportional representation ✦ public relations ✦ Puerto Rico

Pr *symbol* ✦ praseodymium (chemical element)

pr *abbrev.* ✦ per rectum (Latin, = by way of the rectum)

pr *contraction* ✦ pair ✦ per

Pr. *shortening* ✦ Prince ✦ Provençal

pr. *shortening* ✦ present ✦ price ✦ priest

PRA *abbrev.* ✦ President of the Royal Academy

PRB *abbrev.* ✦ Pre-Raphaelite Brotherhood

PRC *abbrev.* ✦ post Romam conditam (Latin, = after the foundation of Rome)

preb. *shortening* ✦ prebend ✦ prebendary

prec. *shortening* ✦ preceding ✦ precentor ✦ precision

Precis *acronym* ✦ preserved context index system

pred. *shortening* ✦ predicate ✦ predicative ✦ predicatively

predic. *shortening* ✦ predicate ✦ predicative ✦ predicatively

pref. *shortening* ✦ preface ✦ prefect ✦ preferably ✦ preference ✦ preferred ✦ prefix

prehist. *shortening* ✦ prehistoric ✦ prehistory

prej. *shortening* ✦ prejudice

prel. *shortening* ✦ prelude

prelim. *shortening* ✦ preliminary

prem. *shortening* ✦ premature ✦ premium

premed. *shortening* ✦ premedication

prems *contraction* ✦ premises

prep. *shortening* ✦ preparation ✦ preparatory ✦ preposition

PREP *abbrev.* ✦ post-registration education and practice (for nurses)

Pres. *shortening* ✦ Presbyterian

pres. *shortening* ✦ present ✦ president ✦ presidential ✦ presumed ✦ presumptive

Presb. *shortening* ✦ Presbyterian

press. *shortening* ✦ pressure

pret. *shortening* ✦ preterite

prev. *shortening* ✦ previous ✦ previously

PRF *abbrev.* ✦ pulse repetition frequency

prf *contraction* ✦ proof

PRG *abbrev.* ✦ Prague (airport baggage label)

PRI *abbrev.* ✦ Penal Reform International ✦ Plastics and Rubber Institute

PRIBA *abbrev.* ✦ President of the Royal Institute of British Architects

prim. *shortening* ✦ primary ✦ primate ✦ primer ✦ primitive

primip. *shortening* ✦ primipara (Latin, = woman who has given birth for the first time)

prin. *shortening* ✦ principal ✦ principality ✦ principle

princ. *shortening* ✦ principal ✦ principality ✦ principle

print. *shortening* ✦ printed ✦ printing

prism. *shortening* ✦ prismatic

priv. *shortening* ✦ private ✦ privative

PRJ *abbrev.* ✦ Capri (airport baggage label)

prm *abbrev.* ✦ personal radiation monitor

prn *abbrev.* ✦ pro re nata (Latin, = as the situation may require)

PRO *abbrev.* ✦ Public Record Office ✦ public relations officer

pro-am *acronym* ✦ professional-amateur

prob. *shortening* ✦ probability ✦ probable ✦ probably ✦ probate ✦ problem

proc. *shortening* ✦ procedure ✦ proceedings ✦ process ✦ proctor

prod. *shortening* ✦ produce ✦ produced ✦ producer ✦ product ✦ production

prof. *shortening* ✦ professional ✦ professor

Pr of Man. *shortening* ✦ Prayer of Manasses (book of Bible)

prog. *shortening* ✦ prognosis ✦ program ✦ programme ✦ progress ✦ progressive

proj. *shortening* ◆ project ◆ projectile ◆ projection ◆ projector

prol. *shortening* ◆ prologue

Prolog *acronym* ◆ Programming in Logic (programming language)

Prom *acronym* ◆ programmable read-only memory

prom. *shortening* ◆ prominent ◆ promontory ◆ promotion

pron. *shortening* ◆ pronominal ◆ pronoun ◆ pronounced ◆ pronunciation

Prop *acronym* ◆ Preservation of the Rights of Prisoners

prop. *shortening* ◆ proper ◆ properly ◆ property ◆ proportion ◆ proportional ◆ proposition ◆ proprietary ◆ proprietor

pros. *shortening* ◆ prosody

prosc. *shortening* ◆ proscenium

prost. *shortening* ◆ prostate

Prot. *shortening* ◆ Protestant

prot. *shortening* ◆ protectorate

pro tem. *shortening* ◆ pro tempore (Latin, = for the moment)

Prov. *shortening* ◆ Proverbs (book of Bible)

prov. *shortening* ◆ proverb ◆ province ◆ provincial ◆ provisional ◆ provost

prox. *shortening* ◆ proximo (Latin, = in the next) (month)

prox. acc. *shortening* ◆ proxime accessit (Latin, = came closest) (of runner-up in competition etc)

prox. luc. *shortening* ◆ proxima luce (Latin, = on the preceding day)

PRP *abbrev.* ◆ performance-related pay

PRR *abbrev.* ◆ pulse repetition rate

PRS *abbrev.* ◆ Performing Rights Society ◆ President of the Royal Society ◆ Protestant Reformation Society

PRs *abbrev.* ◆ Pakistani rupees (monetary unit)

PRTC *abbrev.* ◆ Princess Royal Trust for Carers

Pru *shortening* ◆ Prudential Assurance Company

PS *abbrev.* ◆ Aberdeen (British vehicle registration mark) ◆ Parliamentary Secretary ◆ Pastel Society ◆ Permanent Secretary ◆ Pharmaceutical Society of Great Britain ◆ Philological Society ◆ Physical Society ◆ Police Sergeant ◆ postscript ◆ private secretary ◆ Privy

---

ADVERTSPEAK 2: Property

Many futile viewing-trips can be saved if you can break the code of the initial advertisement. This dictionary contains a wide selection of property-seller's abbreviations, from which I have selected for this box those common ones which are the least user-friendly.

b	*bathroom*	**ftb**	*first-time buyer*	**osp**	*off-street parking*
bs	*building society*	**gch**	*gas central heating*	**pax**	*per annum, exclusive*
c & c	*carpets and curtains*			**pb**	*purpose-built*
df	*double-fronted*	**gfch**	*gas fired central heating*	**pp**	*planning permission*
dg	*double-glazed; double glazing*	**k**	*kitchen*	**ptr**	*porter*
es	*en suite*	**lh**	*leasehold*	**sc**	*self-catering; self-contained*
fch	*full central heating*	**lu**	*lock-up*		
ff	*fixtures and fittings; fully fitted; fully furnished*	**op**	*open plan*	**sof**	*share of freehold*
		osch	*overnight storage central heating*	**uf**	*unfurnished*
fh	*freehold*				

Seal ◆ prompt side (actor's position on stage)

Ps. *shortening* ◆ Psalm ◆ Psalms (book of Bible)

ps. *shortening* ◆ pseudonym

PSA *abbrev.* ◆ Pickles and Sauces Association ◆ Pisa (airport baggage label) ◆ Property Services Agency ◆ Public Services Authority

PSAC *abbrev.* ◆ Production Statistics Advisory Committee

PSB *abbrev.* ◆ Prayer Book Society

PSBR *abbrev.* ◆ Public Sector Borrowing Requirement

PSC *abbrev.* ◆ Pipe Smokers' Council

psc *abbrev.* ◆ passed staff college

PSD *abbrev.* ◆ Port Said (airport baggage label)

PSDA *abbrev.* ◆ Paper Sack Development Association

PSDR *abbrev.* ◆ Public Sector Debt Repayment

PSE *abbrev.* ◆ psychological stress evaluator (sort of lie detector)

pseud. *shortening* ◆ pseudonym

psf *abbrev.* ◆ per square foot

PSGB *abbrev.* ◆ Pharmaceutical Society of Great Britain

PSI *abbrev.* ◆ Policy Studies Institute

psi *abbrev.* ◆ pounds per square inch

PSIF *abbrev.* ◆ Prison Service Industries and Farms

PSIS *abbrev.* ◆ Permanent Secretaries' Committee on the Intelligence Services

psk *abbrev.* ◆ phase shift keying

PSL *abbrev.* ◆ Perth (airport baggage label) ◆ private sector liquidity ◆ public sector loan

PSM *abbrev.* ◆ product sales manager

PSN *abbrev.* ◆ packet switching network

PSO *abbrev.* ◆ principal scientific officer

PSPS *abbrev.* ◆ Paddle Steamer Preservation Society

PSS *abbrev.* ◆ packet switching system ◆ Partially Sighted Society

PST *abbrev.* ◆ Pacific Standard Time

PSTN *abbrev.* ◆ public switched telephone network

PSU *abbrev.* ◆ power supply unit

PSV *abbrev.* ◆ public service vehicle

PSW *abbrev.* ◆ psychiatric social worker

PSY *abbrev.* ◆ Port Stanley (airport baggage label)

psych. *shortening* ◆ psychic ◆ psychiatry ◆ psychology

psychoanal. *shortening* ◆ psychoanalysis ◆ psychoanalytic

psychol. *shortening* ◆ psychological ◆ psychologist ◆ psychology

PT *abbrev.* ◆ Brazil (international civil aircraft marking) ◆ Newcastle upon Tyne (British vehicle registration mark) ◆ part time ◆ physical training ◆ physiotherapist ◆ postal telegraph ◆ post town ◆ pupil teacher ◆ purchase tax

Pt *contraction* ◆ Point ◆ Port

Pt *symbol* ◆ platinum (chemical element)

pt *abbrev.* ◆ past tense ◆ pro tempore (Latin, = for the moment)

pt *contraction* ◆ part ◆ payment ◆ pint ◆ point

PTA *abbrev.* ◆ Parent-Teacher Association ◆ Passenger Transport Authority ◆ Piano Tuners' Association ◆ prior to admission

pta *contraction* ◆ peseta (Spanish monetary unit)

PTBT *abbrev.* ◆ partial test-ban treaty

PTD *abbrev.* ◆ permanent total disability

PTE *abbrev.* ◆ Passenger Transport Executive

Pte *contraction* ◆ Private

PTFE *abbrev.* ◆ polytetrafluoroethylene

Ptg. *shortening* ◆ Portugal ◆ Portuguese

PTH *abbrev.* ◆ parathyroid hormone

PTI *abbrev.* ◆ public tool interface

PTIA *abbrev.* ◆ Pet Trade and Industry Association

PTM *abbrev.* ◆ pulse–time modulation

PTN *abbrev.* ◆ public telephone network

ptnr *contraction* ◆ partner

PTO *abbrev.* ◆ please turn over ◆ Public Telecommunications Operator ◆ Public Trustee Office

ptr *contraction* ◆ porter ◆ printer

PTS *abbrev.* ◆ Philatelic Traders' Society

PTSD *abbrev.* ◆ post-traumatic stress disorder

PTT *abbrev.* ◆ Posts, Telegraphs and Telephones (national communications organization in various countries)

pt-tm. *shortening* ◆ part-time

PTU *abbrev.* ◆ Plumbing Trades Union

PTUF *abbrev.* ◆ Professional Tennis Umpires' Federation

ptw *abbrev.* ◆ per thousand words

PTY *abbrev.* ◆ Panama City (airport baggage label)

Pty *contraction* ◆ proprietary (Australian and South African equivalent of Ltd)

PTx *abbrev.* ◆ parathyroidectomy

PU *abbrev.* ◆ Chelmsford (British vehicle registration mark) ◆ passed urine ◆ peptic ulcer ◆ polyurethane ◆ processing unit

Pu *symbol* ◆ plutonium (chemical element)

pub. *shortening* ◆ public ◆ publication ◆ published

publ. *shortening* ◆ publicity ◆ publisher ◆ publishing

pud *abbrev.* ◆ pick-up and delivery

PUFA *abbrev.* ◆ polyunsaturated fatty acids

pulv. *shortening* ◆ pulvis (Latin, = powder)

pums *abbrev.* ◆ permanently unfit for military service

pun. *shortening* ◆ punishment

punct. *shortening* ◆ punctuation

PUO *abbrev.* ◆ pyrexia of uncertain origin ◆ pyrexia of unknown origin

purch. *shortening* ◆ purchase

purp. *shortening* ◆ purple

PUS *abbrev.* ◆ Parliamentary Under-Secretary ◆ Permanent Under-Secretary

pus *abbrev.* ◆ permanently unfit for service

PUVA *abbrev.* ◆ psoralen plus ultra-violet A (treatment for psoriasis)

PV *abbrev.* ◆ Ipswich (British vehicle registration mark)

pv *abbrev.* ◆ per vaginam (Latin, = by way of the vagina)

PVA *abbrev.* ◆ polyvinyl acetate

PVC *abbrev.* ◆ polyvinyl chloride

PVD *abbrev.* ◆ peripheral vascular disease

PVFS *abbrev.* ◆ post-viral fatigue syndrome

PVOA *abbrev.* ◆ Passenger Vehicle Operators' Association

PVS *abbrev.* ◆ persistent vegetative state

pvt *abbrev.* ◆ pressure, volume, temperature

Pvt. *shortening* ◆ Private

pvte *contraction* ◆ private

PW *abbrev.* ◆ Norwich (British vehicle registration mark) ◆ Policewoman ◆ power windows

pw *abbrev.* ◆ per week

PWA *medi* ◆ person with Aids

PWC *abbrev.* ◆ Postwar Credits

PWD *abbrev.* ◆ Public Works Department

PWG *abbrev.* ◆ Permanent Working Group of European Junior Hospital Doctors

PWLB *abbrev.* ◆ Public Works Loan Board

PWM *abbrev.* ◆ pulse width modulation

PWPS *abbrev.* ◆ Pure Water Preservation Society

PWR *abbrev.* ◆ pressurized water reactor

pwr *contraction* ◆ power

pwt *contraction* ◆ pennyweight

PX *abbrev.* ◆ physical examination ◆ Portsmouth (British vehicle registration mark) ◆ private exchange

px *abbrev.* ◆ part exchange

pxt *contraction* ◆ pinxit (Latin, = painted it)

PY *abbrev.* ◆ Middlesborough (British vehicle registration mark) ◆ Paraguay (international vehicle registration) ◆ Surinam Airways (airline baggage code)

PYO *abbrev.* ◆ pick your own
pyrotech. *shortening* ◆ pyrotechnical ◆ pyrotechnics
PZ *abbrev.* ◆ Belfast (British vehicle registration mark) ◆ Lineas Aéreas Paraguayas (airline baggage code) ◆ Surinam (international civil aircraft marking)
PZE *abbrev.* ◆ Penzance (airport baggage label)

Q

Q *abbrev.* ◆ Qatar (international vehicle registration) ◆ quality ◆ quantity ◆ quartermaster ◆ Quarto (early Shakespeare text) ◆ Quebec ◆ Queen ◆ queen (cards, chess) ◆ Queensland ◆ question ◆ quetzal (Guatemalan monetary unit)

q *abbrev.* ◆ quark ◆ quart ◆ quarter ◆ query ◆ quintal ◆ quire

QA *abbrev.* ◆ quality assurance ◆ quarters allowance

qa *abbrev.* ◆ quick assembly

QAB *abbrev.* ◆ Queen Anne's Bounty

QADS *abbrev.* ◆ quality assurance data system

QAIMNS *abbrev.* ◆ Queen Alexandra's Imperial Military Nursing Service

Qaly *acronym* ◆ quality-adjusted life year (used in cost–benefit assessment of possible treatments)

Q & A *abbrev.* ◆ question and answer

Qantas *acronym* ◆ Queensland and Northern Territory Aerial Service (Australian international airline)

QARANC *abbrev.* ◆ Queen Alexandra's Royal Army Nursing Corps

QARNNS *abbrev.* ◆ Queen Alexandra's Royal Naval Nursing Service

QB *abbrev.* ◆ Quebecair (airline baggage code) ◆ Queen's Bench ◆ queen's bishop (chess)

QBD *abbrev.* ◆ Queen's Bench Division

QBI *abbrev.* ◆ quite bloody impossible

Q-boat *contraction* ◆ query-boat (ship with hidden guns, and thus of uncertain status)

QBP *abbrev.* ◆ queen's bishop's pawn (chess)

QC *abbrev.* ◆ Air Zaire (airline baggage code) ◆ Queen's Counsel

qc *abbrev.* ◆ quality control

QCD *abbrev.* ◆ quantum chromodynamics

QCE *abbrev.* ◆ quality control engineering

qck *contraction* ◆ quick

QCT *abbrev.* ◆ quality control technology

qds *abbrev.* ◆ quater die sumendus (Latin, = to be taken four times a day)

QE *abbrev.* ◆ Air Tahiti (airline baggage code)

qe *abbrev.* ◆ quod est (Latin, = which is)

QE2 *abbrev.* ◆ Queen Elizabeth the Second (ship)

QED *abbrev.* ◆ quantum electrodynamics ◆ quod erat demonstrandum (Latin, = which was to be proved)

QEF *abbrev.* ◆ quod erat faciendum (Latin, = which was to be done)

QEH *abbrev.* ◆ Queen Elizabeth Hall

QEI *abbrev.* ◆ quod erat inveniendum (Latin, = which was to be found)

QF *abbrev.* ◆ quick-firing

QFD *abbrev.* ◆ quantum flavourdynamics

QFSM *abbrev.* ◆ Queen's Fire Service Medal

QG *abbrev.* ◆ Quartermaster General

QGM *abbrev.* ◆ Queen's Gallantry Medal

QH *abbrev.* ◆ West African Airways (airline baggage code)

qh *abbrev.* ◆ quaque hora (Latin, = every hour)

QI *abbrev.* ◆ quartz-iodine

qid *abbrev.* ◆ quater in die (Latin, = four times a day)

Qisam *acronym* ◆ queued indexed sequential access method

qk *contraction* ◆ quick

QKt *abbrev.* ◆ queen's knight (chess)

QKtP *abbrev.* ◆ queen's knight's pawn (chess)

QL *abbrev.* ◆ Lesotho Airways (airline baggage code) ◆ query language

ql *abbrev.* ◆ quantum libet (Latin, = as much as you please)

ql *contraction* ◆ quintal

Qld *contraction* ◆ Queensland

qlty *contraction* ◆ quality

qly *contraction* ◆ quarterly

QM *abbrev.* ◆ Air Malawi (airline baggage code) ◆ Quartermaster ◆ quantum mechanics

qm *abbrev.* ◆ quaque mane (Latin, = each morning)

QMess *abbrev.* ◆ Queen's Messenger

QMG *abbrev.* ◆ Quartermaster-General

Qmr *contraction* ◆ Quartermaster

QMS *abbrev.* ◆ Quartermaster-Sergeant

Qn *contraction* ◆ Queen

QN *abbrev.* ◆ queen's knight (chess)

qn *abbrev.* ◆ quaque nocte (Latin, = each night)

qn *contraction* ◆ question ◆ quotation

QNI *abbrev.* ◆ Queen's Nursing Institute

QNP *abbrev.* ◆ queen's knight's pawn (chess)

qns *abbrev.* ◆ quantity not sufficient

qnt *contraction* ◆ quintet

qnty *contraction* ◆ quantity

QP *abbrev.* ◆ queen's pawn (chess)

qp *abbrev.* ◆ quantum placet (Latin, = as much as you wish)

QPM *abbrev.* ◆ Queen's Police Medal

QPR *abbrev.* ◆ Queen's Park Rangers

QPS *abbrev.* ◆ Quaker Peace and Service

qq. hor. *shortening* ◆ quaque hora (Latin, = each hour)

QR *abbrev.* ◆ queen's rook (chess) ◆ Qatari riyal (monetary unit)

qr *contraction* ◆ quarter ◆ quire

QRA *abbrev.* ◆ quick reaction alert

QRP *abbrev.* ◆ queen's rook's pawn

qrs *contraction* ◆ quarters

QS *abbrev.* ◆ quarter sessions ◆ Queen's Scholar

qs *abbrev.* ◆ quantum sufficit (Latin, = enough) ◆ quadraphonic stereo

QSO *abbrev.* ◆ quasi-stellar object

QSS *abbrev.* ◆ quasi-stellar radio source

QSTOL *abbrev.* ◆ quiet short take-off and landing

qt *contraction* ◆ quart

QT *pronounced* kew-tee *acronym* ◆ quiet (in the phrase 'on the QT')

qt. *shortening* ◆ quantity

qtly *contraction* ◆ quarterly

qto *contraction* ◆ quarto

QTOL *abbrev.* ◆ quiet take-off and landing

qtr *contraction* ◆ quarter

qty *contraction* ◆ quantity

QU *abbrev.* ◆ Uganda Airlines (airline baggage code)

Qu. *abbrev.* ◆ Queen ◆ question

qu. *abbrev.* ◆ quart ◆ quarter ◆ quarterly ◆ question

quad. *shortening* ◆ quadrilateral ◆ quadrant ◆ quadraphonic ◆ quadruple

qual. *shortening* ◆ qualification ◆ qualitative ◆ quality

qualgo *acronym* ◆ quasi-autonomous local government organization

qualn *contraction* ◆ qualification

quango *acronym* ◆ quasi-autonomous non-governmental organization

quant. *shortening* ◆ quantitative ◆ quantity

quant. suff. *shortening* ◆ quantum sufficit (Latin, = enough)

quar. *shortening* ◆ quart ◆ quarter ◆ quarterly

quart. *shortening* ◆ quarter ◆ quarterly

quasar *acronym* ◆ quasi-stellar object

quat. *shortening* ◆ quaternary ◆ quattuor (Latin, = four)

QUB *abbrev.* ◆ Queen's University of Belfast

Que. *shortening* ◆ Quebec
ques. *shortening* ◆ question
quint. *shortening* ◆ quintuplicate
quor. *shortening* ◆ quorum
quot. *shortening* ◆ quotation ◆ quoted
quotid. *shortening* ◆ quotidie (Latin, = daily)
qv *abbrev.* ◆ quantum vis (Latin, = as much as you wish) ◆ quod vide (Latin, = which see)

qwerty *acronym* ◆ standard keyboard layout of typewriter etc (from sequence of top-row keys from left)
qwl *abbrev.* ◆ quality of working life
QY *abbrev.* ◆ Aero Virgin Islands (airline baggage code)
qy *contraction* ◆ query
QZ *abbrev.* ◆ Zambia Airways (airline baggage code)
qz *contraction* ◆ quartz

ACADEMIC QUALIFICATIONS

The list below gives 30 of those most frequently seen on letter-headings and brass plates. The dictionary contains hundreds more, and new ones seem to appear every day.

BA *Bachelor of Arts*	**FCCA** *Fellow of the Chartered Association of Certified Accountants*
BChir *Bachelor of Surgery*	
BD *Bachelor of Divinity*	
BEd *Bachelor of Education*	**FRIBA** *Fellow of the Royal Institute of British Architects*
BLitt *Bachelor of Letters*	
BMus *Bachelor of Music*	**FRS** *Fellow of the Royal Society*
BPhil *Bachelor of Philosophy*	**LLB** *Bachelor of Laws*
BSc *Bachelor of Science*	**LRAM** *Licentiate of the Royal Academy of Music*
CertEd *Certificate in Education*	
DCL *Doctor of Civil Law*	**LTCL** *Licentiate of Trinity College of Music, London*
DD *Doctor of Divinity*	
DLitt *Doctor of Letters*	**MA** *Master of Arts*
DMus *Doctor of Music*	**MB** *Bachelor of Medicine*
DPhil *Doctor of Philosophy*	**MBA** *Master of Business Administration*
DRCOG *Diploma of the Royal College of Obstetricians and Gynaecologists*	
	MD *Doctor of Medicine*
FBOA *Fellow of the British Optical Association*	**MRCGP** *Member of the Royal College of General Practitioners*
	PGCE *Postgraduate Certificate in Education*
FCA *Fellow of the Institute of Chartered Accountants*	
	RA *Royal Academician*

R

R *abbrev.* ◆ Rabbi ◆ railway ◆ rand (South African monetary unit) ◆ Réaumur (temperature scale) ◆ recipe (Latin, = take) ◆ Rector ◆ Regina (Latin, = Queen) ◆ reply ◆ Republican ◆ response (liturgical) ◆ return (train etc ticket) ◆ reverse ◆ Rex (Latin, = King) ◆ right ◆ River ◆ Röntgen ◆ rook (chess) ◆ rouble (monetary unit of Belorussia, Kirghizia, Russia, Tajikstan and Uzbekistan) ◆ Royal ◆ run (cricket etc) ◆ rupee (Indian monetary unit)

r *abbrev.* ◆ radius ◆ rear ◆ recto ◆ right ◆ rises (of sun) ◆ run

R18 *abbrev.* ◆ Restricted 18 (film censorship classification denoting material that may only be exhibited on, or distributed from, premises to which no one under the age of 18 is admitted)

RA *abbrev.* ◆ Nottingham (British vehicle registration mark) ◆ Racecourse Association ◆ Ramblers' Association ◆ Rear Admiral ◆ Referees' Association ◆ Republic of Argentina (international vehicle registration) ◆ rheumatoid arthritis ◆ right atrium ◆ Royal Academician ◆ Royal Academy ◆ Royal Artillery ◆ Royal Nepal Airlines (airline baggage code) ◆ Rural Action

Ra *symbol* ◆ radium (chemical element)

RAA *abbrev.* ◆ Royal Academy of Arts

RAAF *abbrev.* ◆ Royal Auxiliary Air Force

rabb. *shortening* ◆ rabbinical

RABDF *abbrev.* ◆ Royal Association of British Dairy Farmers

RABI *abbrev.* ◆ Royal Agricultural Benevolent Institution

RAC *abbrev.* ◆ Royal Agricultural College ◆ Royal Armoured Corps ◆ Royal Automobile Club

Race *acronym* ◆ rapid automatic checkout equipment

RAD *abbrev.* ◆ reflex anal dilatation ◆ Royal Academy of Dancing

rad. *shortening* ◆ radar ◆ radiator ◆ radical ◆ radio ◆ radius ◆ radix

Rada *acronym* ◆ Royal Academy of Dramatic Art

Radar *acronym* ◆ Royal Association for Disability and Rehabilitation

RADC *abbrev.* ◆ Royal Army Dental Corps

RADD *abbrev.* ◆ Royal Association in Aid of the Deaf and Dumb

RAdm *abbrev.* ◆ Rear Admiral

radmon *acronym* ◆ radiological monitoring

RAE *abbrev.* ◆ Royal Aerospace Establishment

RAEC *abbrev.* ◆ Royal Army Educational Corps

RAeroC *abbrev.* ◆ Royal Aero Club

RAeS *abbrev.* ◆ Royal Aeronautical Society

RAF *abbrev.* ◆ Royal Air Force

RAFA *abbrev.* ◆ Royal Air Forces Association

RAFBF *abbrev.* ◆ Royal Air Force Benevolent Fund

RAFES *abbrev.* ◆ Royal Air Force Educational Service

RAFMS *abbrev.* ◆ Royal Air Force Medical Services

RAFR *abbrev.* ◆ Royal Air Force Regiment

RAFRO *abbrev.* ◆ Royal Air Force Reserve of Officers

RAFSC *abbrev.* ◆ Royal Air Force Staff College ◆ Royal Air Force Strike Command

RAFVR *abbrev.* ◆ Royal Air Force Volunteer Reserve

RAH *abbrev.* ◆ Royal Albert Hall

RAI *abbrev.* ◆ Radiotelevisione Italiana (Italian, = Italian Radio and Television) (orig. Radio Audizione Italiane) ◆ Royal Anthropological Institute ◆ Royal Archaeological Institute

Rajar *acronym* ◆ Radio Joint Audience Research

RAK *abbrev.* ◆ Marrakesh (airport baggage label)

rall. *shortening* ◆ rallentando (Italian, = slowing) (music)

RAM *abbrev.* ◆ Royal Academy of Music

RAM *acronym* ◆ random access memory

ram *abbrev.* ◆ relative atomic mass

ramb. *shortening* ◆ rambler (rose)

RAMC *abbrev.* ◆ Royal Army Medical Corps

R & A *abbrev.* ◆ Royal and Ancient (Scottish golf club)

R & B *abbrev.* ◆ rhythm and blues

r & cc *abbrev.* ◆ riot and civil commotion

R & D *abbrev.* ◆ research and development

R & E *abbrev.* ◆ research and engineering

R & I *abbrev.* ◆ Regina et Imperatrix (Latin, = Queen and Empress) ◆ Rex et Imperator (Latin, = King and Emperor)

r & m *abbrev.* ◆ reliability and marketing ◆ reports and memoranda

R & R *abbrev.* ◆ rescue and resuscitation ◆ rest and recreation ◆ rock and roll

R & VA *abbrev.* ◆ Rating and Valuation Association

RAOB *abbrev.* ◆ Royal Antediluvian Order of Buffaloes

RAOC *abbrev.* ◆ Royal Army Ordnance Corps

rap. *shortening* ◆ rapid

RAPC *abbrev.* ◆ Royal Army Pay Corps

Rapid *acronym* ◆ Register for the Ascertainment and Prevention of Inherited Diseases

RARDE *abbrev.* ◆ Royal Armament Research and Development Establishment

RARO *abbrev.* ◆ Regular Army Reserve of Officers

RAS *abbrev.* ◆ Royal Agricultural Society ◆ Royal Asiatic Society ◆ Royal Astronomical Society

RASC *abbrev.* ◆ Royal Army Service Corps

rat. *shortening* ◆ rateable

Rato *acronym* ◆ rocket-assisted take-off

RAuxAF *abbrev.* ◆ Royal Auxiliary Air Force

RAVC *abbrev.* ◆ Royal Army Veterinary Corps

RAWC *abbrev.* ◆ Radioactive Waste Co-ordinating Committee

RAX *abbrev.* ◆ rural automatic exchange

RB *abbrev.* ◆ Nottingham (British vehicle registration mark) ◆ reconnaissance bomber ◆ Republic of Botswana (international vehicle registration) ◆ Rifle Brigade ◆ Royal Ballet ◆ Syrian Arab Airlines (airline baggage code)

Rb *symbol* ◆ rubidium (chemical element)

rb *abbrev.* ◆ right back

RBA *abbrev.* ◆ Retail Book, Stationery and Allied Trades Employees Association ◆ Royal Society of British Artists

RBC *abbrev.* ◆ red blood cell

RBE *abbrev.* ◆ relative biological effectiveness (of radiation treatment)

r/belt *contraction* ◆ rear seat-belt

RBG *abbrev.* ◆ Royal Botanic Gardens (Kew)

RBI *abbrev.* ◆ request better information

RBL *abbrev.* ◆ Royal British Legion

rbl *contraction* ◆ rouble (monetary unit of Belorussia, Kirghizia, Russia, Tajikstan and Uzbekistan)

RBNA *abbrev.* ◆ Royal British Nurses' Association

RBS *abbrev.* ✦ Rare Breeds Society ✦ Royal Botanical Society ✦ Royal Society of British Sculptors

RBST *abbrev.* ✦ Rare Breeds Survival Trust

RBT *abbrev.* ✦ random breath-testing

RC *abbrev.* ✦ Nottingham (British vehicle registration mark) ✦ radio/cassette player ✦ red cell (blood) ✦ red corpuscle ✦ Red Cross ✦ reversed charge (phone call) ✦ Rifle Club ✦ Roman Catholic ✦ Royal Commission ✦ Republic of China (international vehicle registration for Taiwan)

rc *abbrev.* ✦ reinforced concrete

RCA *abbrev.* ✦ République Centafricaine (French, = Central African Republic) (international vehicle registration) ✦ Radio Corporation of America ✦ Royal College of Art ✦ Rural Crafts Association

RCB *abbrev.* ✦ Republic of the Congo (Brazzaville) (international vehicle registration)

RCC *abbrev.* ✦ Roman Catholic Church

RCCh *abbrev.* ✦ Roman Catholic Church

RCD *abbrev.* ✦ residual current device

rcd *contraction* ✦ received

RCDS *abbrev.* ✦ Royal College of Defence Studies

RCF *abbrev.* ✦ Redundant Churches Fund

RCGP *abbrev.* ✦ Royal College of General Practitioners

RCH *abbrev.* ✦ Republic of Chile (international vehicle registration)

RCHM *abbrev.* ✦ Royal Commission on Historical Manuscripts ✦ Royal Commission on Historical Monuments

RCI *abbrev.* ✦ Radiochemical Inspectorate

rci *abbrev.* ✦ radar coverage indicator

RCJ *abbrev.* ✦ Royal Courts of Justice

RCM *abbrev.* ✦ radar countermeasures ✦ Regimental Court Martial ✦ Royal College of Midwives ✦ Royal College of Music

RCMP *abbrev.* ✦ Royal Canadian Mounted Police

RCN *abbrev.* ✦ Royal College of Nursing

RCO *abbrev.* ✦ Royal College of Organists

RCOG *abbrev.* ✦ Royal College of Obstetricians and Gynaecologists

RCP *abbrev.* ✦ Revolutionary Communist Party ✦ Royal College of Physicians ✦ Royal College of Preceptors

RCPath *abbrev.* ✦ Royal College of Pathologists

RCPB *abbrev.* ✦ Revolutionary Communist Party of Great Britain

RCPsych *abbrev.* ✦ Royal College of Psychiatrists

rcpt *contraction* ✦ receipt

RCR *abbrev.* ✦ Royal College of Radiologists

RCRP *abbrev.* ✦ Rape Counselling and Research Project

RCS *abbrev.* ✦ Royal Choral Society ✦ Royal College of Science ✦ Royal College of Surgeons ✦ Royal Commonwealth Society ✦ Royal Corps of Signals

RCSC *abbrev.* ✦ Radio Components Standardization Committee

RCT *abbrev.* ✦ randomized clinical trial ✦ regimental combat team ✦ remote-control transmitter ✦ Royal Corps of Transport

RCU *abbrev.* ✦ remote control unit

rcvr *contraction* ✦ receiver

RCVS *abbrev.* ✦ Royal College of Veterinary Surgeons

RD *abbrev.* ✦ Reading (British vehicle registration mark) ✦ Reserve Decoration ✦ refer to drawer ✦ Rural Dean

Rd *contraction* ✦ Road

rd *contraction* ✦ rutherford

RDA *abbrev.* ✦ Riding for the Disabled Association ✦ recommended daily allowance ✦ recommended dietary allowance

rd & d *abbrev.* ◆ research, development and demonstration

rd & e *abbrev.* ◆ research, development and engineering

RDAT *abbrev.* ◆ rotary-head digital audio tape

RDB *abbrev.* ◆ Royal Danish Ballet

RDBMS *abbrev.* ◆ relational database management system

RDC *abbrev.* ◆ Rural Development Commission ◆ Rural District Council

rdd *abbrev.* ◆ required delivery date

RDF *abbrev.* ◆ radio direction-finding ◆ rapid deployment force ◆ refuse-derived fuel

rDNA *abbrev.* ◆ recombinant deoxyribonucleic acid

rdr *contraction* ◆ radar

RDS *abbrev.* ◆ radio data system (automatic tuning) ◆ Research Defence Society ◆ respiratory distress syndrome

rdt & e *abbrev.* ◆ research, development, testing and engineering

RDX *abbrev.* ◆ Research Department Explosive (cyclonite)

rdy *contraction* ◆ ready

RDZ *abbrev.* ◆ radiation danger zone

RE *abbrev.* ◆ Reformed Episcopal ◆ religious education ◆ Royal Engineers ◆ Royal Exchange ◆ Royal Society of Painter-Printmakers (orig. Royal Society of Painter-Etchers and Engravers) ◆ Stoke-on-Trent (British vehicle registration mark)

Re *contraction* ◆ rupee (Indian monetary unit)

Re *symbol* ◆ rhenium (chemical element)

Réau. *shortening* ◆ Réaumur (temperature scale)

React *acronym* ◆ Research, Education and Aid for Children with Potentially Terminal Illness

Rear-Adm. *shortening* ◆ Rear-Admiral

REC *abbrev.* ◆ Recife (airport baggage label) ◆ regional electricity company

rec. *shortening* ◆ receipt ◆ received ◆ reception (room) ◆ recipe ◆ recipe (Latin, = take) ◆ recognized

◆ recommended ◆ record ◆ recorded ◆ recreation

recd *contraction* ◆ received

recep. *shortening* ◆ reception (room)

recept. *shortening* ◆ reception (room)

recip. *shortening* ◆ reciprocal

recit. *shortening* ◆ recitativo (Italian, = recitative)

recmd *contraction* ◆ recommended

recon. *shortening* ◆ reconditioned ◆ reconsign

recond. *shortening* ◆ reconditioned

REconS *abbrev.* ◆ Royal Economic Society

recpt *contraction* ◆ receipt

recpt. *shortening* ◆ reception (room)

Rect. *shortening* ◆ Rector ◆ Rectory

rect. *shortening* ◆ rectangle ◆ rectangular

red. *shortening* ◆ redeemable ◆ reduced ◆ reduction

redup. *shortening* ◆ reduplicate ◆ reduplication

redupl. *shortening* ◆ reduplicate ◆ reduplication

Ref. *shortening* ◆ Reformation

ref. *shortening* ◆ refer ◆ referee ◆ reference ◆ referred ◆ reformed

refash. *shortening* ◆ refashion ◆ refashioned

Ref. Ch. *shortening* ◆ Reformed Church

refd *contraction* ◆ refund

refl. *shortening* ◆ reflection ◆ reflective ◆ reflex ◆ reflexive

Ref. Pres. *shortening* ◆ Reformed Presbyterian

refurb. *shortening* ◆ refurbished

REG *abbrev.* ◆ Reggio di Calabria (airport baggage label)

Reg. *shortening* ◆ Regent ◆ Regina (Latin, = Queen) ◆ Regius (Latin, = King's)

reg. *shortening* ◆ regiment ◆ region ◆ register ◆ registered ◆ registrar ◆ registry ◆ regular ◆ regulation

regd *contraction* ◆ registered

Reg. Gen. *shortening* ◆ Registrar General

regt *contraction* ◆ regiment

reinf. *shortening* ◆ reinforced

reinfmt *contraction* ◆ reinforcement

rej. *shortening* ✦ reject
REK *abbrev.* ✦ Reykjavik (airport baggage label)
rel. *shortening* ✦ related ✦ relating ✦ relation ✦ relative ✦ religion ✦ religious
relig. *shortening* ✦ religion ✦ religious
rel. pron. *shortening* ✦ relative pronoun
REM *acronym* ✦ rapid eye movement
rem. *shortening* ✦ remark ✦ remission ✦ remit ✦ remittance
REMC *abbrev.* ✦ Radio and Electronics Measurements Committee
Reme *pronounced* ree-mee *acronym* ✦ Royal Electrical and Mechanical Engineers
Ren. *shortening* ✦ Renaissance
Renfe *acronym* ✦ Red Nacional de Ferrocarriles Españoles (Spanish, = Spanish National Railway Network)
rep. *shortening* ✦ repair ✦ repeat ✦ repertory ✦ repetatur (Latin, = let it be repeated) ✦ report ✦ representative ✦ republic ✦ republican
repl. *shortening* ✦ replace ✦ replacement
repo. *shortening* ✦ repossess ✦ repossession
repr. *shortening* ✦ representative ✦ reprint
repro. *shortening* ✦ reproduced ✦ reproduction
rept *contraction* ✦ receipt ✦ report
repub. *shortening* ✦ republic ✦ republican ✦ republish

req. *shortening* ✦ request ✦ required ✦ requisition
reqd *contraction* ✦ required
RES *abbrev.* ✦ Royal Economic Society ✦ Royal Entomological Society
res. *shortening* ✦ research ✦ reservation ✦ reserve ✦ residence ✦ resident ✦ residential ✦ resigned ✦ resolution
resid. *shortening* ✦ residential ✦ residual
resig. *shortening* ✦ resignation
resp. *shortening* ✦ respective ✦ respiration ✦ responsibility
rest. *shortening* ✦ restaurant ✦ restoration ✦ restored ✦ restricted
rest'nt *contraction* ✦ restaurant
ret. *shortening* ✦ retained ✦ retired ✦ returned
retd *contraction* ✦ retained ✦ retired ✦ returned
R et I *abbrev.* ✦ Regina et Imperatrix (Latin, = Queen and Empress) ✦ Rex et Imperator (Latin, = King and Emperor)
retnr *contraction* ✦ retainer
Rev. *shortening* ✦ Revelation (book of Bible) ✦ Reverend
rev. *shortening* ✦ revenue ✦ reverse ✦ review ✦ revised ✦ revision ✦ revolution
Revd *contraction* ✦ Reverend
rev/min *shortening* ✦ revolutions per minute
Revolt *acronym* ✦ Rural England Versus Overhead Live Transmissions

---

COUNTIES IN THE REPUBLIC OF IRELAND

Car.	*County Carlow*	**Leix**	*County Leix*	**Ros.**	*County Roscommon*
Cav.	*County Cavan*	**Lim.**	*County Limerick*		
Clare	*County Clare*			**Sligo**	*County Sligo*
Cork	*County Cork*	**Long.**	*County Longford*	**Tipp.**	*County Tipperary*
Don.	*County Donegal*			**Wat.**	*County Waterford*
Dub.	*County Dublin*	**Louth**	*County Louth*	**Westmeath**	*County Westmeath*
Gal.	*County Galway*	**Mayo**	*County Mayo*		
Ker.	*County Kerry*	**Meath**	*County Meath*	**Wex.**	*County Wexford*
Kild.	*County Kildare*	**Monag.**	*County Monaghan*	**Wick.**	*County Wicklow*
Kilk.	*County Kilkenny*				
Leit.	*County Leitrim*	**Off.**	*County Offaly*		

rev/s *shortening* ◆ revolutions per second
rew. *shortening* ◆ reward ◆ rewired
◆ rewiring
RF *abbrev.* ◆ République Française
(French, = French Republic)
◆ Rockefeller Foundation ◆ rugby
football ◆ Stoke-on-Trent (British
vehicle registration mark)
Rf *symbol* ◆ rutherfordium (chemical
element)
rf *abbrev.* ◆ radio frequency ◆ range
finder ◆ rapid fire
rf. *shortening* ◆ rinforzando (Italian, =
reinforcing)
RFA *abbrev.* ◆ Royal Fleet Auxiliary
◆ Rugby Fives Association
RFAC *abbrev.* ◆ Royal Fine Art
Commission
RFC *abbrev.* ◆ Royal Flying Corps
◆ Rugby Football Club
RFD *abbrev.* ◆ radio frequency device
◆ reporting for duty
RFL *abbrev.* ◆ Rugby Football League
RFH *abbrev.* ◆ Royal Festival Hall
RFI *abbrev.* ◆ radio-frequency
interference
RFQ *abbrev.* ◆ request for quotation
RFR *abbrev.* ◆ Royal Fleet Reserve
RFS *abbrev.* ◆ rear-facing seat ◆ Registry
of Friendly Societies ◆ Royal Forestry
Society
RFSU *abbrev.* ◆ Rugby Football Schools
Union
RFTF *abbrev.* ◆ Retail Fruit Trade
Federation
RFU *abbrev.* ◆ Rugby Football Union
rfz. *shortening* ◆ rinforzando (Italian, =
reinforcing)
RG *abbrev.* ◆ Newcastle upon Tyne
(British vehicle registration mark)
◆ Reading (UK postcode) ◆ Republic of
Guinea (international vehicle
registration)
RGB *abbrev.* ◆ red-green-blue (colour-
transmission system)
rge *contraction* ◆ range
RGG *abbrev.* ◆ Royal Grenadier Guards

RGN *abbrev.* ◆ Rangoon (airport baggage
label) ◆ Registered General Nurse
RGNP *abbrev.* ◆ real gross national
product
RGO *abbrev.* ◆ Royal Greenwich
Observatory
RGR *abbrev.* ◆ Rio Grande (airport
baggage label)
RGS *abbrev.* ◆ Royal Geographical
Society
rgt *contraction* ◆ regiment
rgtl *contraction* ◆ regimental
RGV *abbrev.* ◆ remote guidance vehicle
RH *abbrev.* ◆ Air Zimbabwe (airline
baggage code) ◆ Hull (British vehicle
registration mark) ◆ Redhill (UK
postcode) ◆ Republic of Haiti
(international vehicle registration)
◆ Royal Highness
Rh *abbrev.* ◆ Rhesus (blood group)
Rh *symbol* ◆ rhodium (chemical element)
rh *abbrev.* ◆ right half (football) ◆ right
hand
RHA *abbrev.* ◆ Regional Health
Authority ◆ Road Haulage Association
◆ Royal Horse Artillery
RHB *abbrev.* ◆ Regional Hospital Board
RHD *abbrev.* ◆ right hand drive
RHE *abbrev.* ◆ Rheims (airport baggage
label)
RHEL *abbrev.* ◆ Rutherford High Energy
Laboratory
rheo. *shortening* ◆ rheostat
rhet. *shortening* ◆ rhetoric ◆ rhetorical
RHF *abbrev.* ◆ Royal Highland Fusiliers
RHG *abbrev.* ◆ Royal Horse Guards
RHHI *abbrev.* ◆ Royal Hospital and
Home for Incurables
RHistS *abbrev.* ◆ Royal Historical Society
RHM *abbrev.* ◆ Rank Hovis McDougall
RHO *abbrev.* ◆ Rhodes (airport baggage
label)
rhomb. *shortening* ◆ rhomboid
◆ rhombus
rhp *abbrev.* ◆ rated horsepower
RHQ *abbrev.* ◆ regimental headquarters
RHR *abbrev.* ◆ rear head-restraints
◆ Royal Highland Regiment

RHS *abbrev.* ◆ Robin Hood Society ◆ Royal Highland Show ◆ Royal Historical Society ◆ Royal Horticultural Society ◆ Royal Humane Society

rhs *abbrev.* ◆ right-hand side ◆ round-headed screw

RHT *abbrev.* ◆ Railway Heritage Trust

RHV *abbrev.* ◆ Burkina (international vehicle registration; orig. République de Haute-Volta) ◆ Registered Health Visitor

RI *abbrev.* ◆ Railway Inspectorate ◆ Regina et Imperatrix (Latin, = Queen and Empress) ◆ religious instruction ◆ Republic of Indonesia (international vehicle registration) ◆ Rex et Imperator (Latin, = King and Emperor) ◆ Rhode Island (US postcode) ◆ Rotary International ◆ Royal Institute of Painters in Water Colours ◆ Royal Institution

ri *abbrev.* ◆ refractive index

Riba *acronym* ◆ Royal Institute of British Architects

RIC *abbrev.* ◆ Radio Industry Council ◆ Royal Institute of Chemistry ◆ Royal Irish Constabulary

RICA *abbrev.* ◆ Research Institute for Consumer Affairs

RICS *abbrev.* ◆ Royal Institution of Chartered Surveyors

RIE *abbrev.* ◆ recognized investment exchange

RIF *abbrev.* ◆ reduction in force

RIGS *abbrev.* ◆ regionally important geological site

RILC *abbrev.* ◆ Racing Industry Liaison Committee

Rilko *acronym* ◆ Research into Lost Knowledge Organization

RIIA *abbrev.* ◆ Royal Institute of International Affairs

RIM *abbrev.* ◆ République Islamique de Mauretanie (French, = Islamic Republic of Mauretania) (international vehicle registration)

Rimnet *acronym* ◆ Radioactive Incident Monitoring Network

RIO *abbrev.* ◆ Rio di Janeiro (airport baggage label)

RIOP *abbrev.* ◆ Royal Institute of Oil Painters

RIP *abbrev.* ◆ requiescat in pace (Latin, = may he rest in peace) ◆ requiescant in pace (Latin, = may they rest in peace)

rip. *shortening* ◆ ripieno (Italian, = filled up) (indicating music for extra players)

RIPA *abbrev.* ◆ Royal Institute of Public Administration

RIPHH *abbrev.* ◆ Royal Institute of Public Health and Hygiene

RIS *abbrev.* ◆ Research Information Service

Risc *acronym* ◆ reduced instruction set computer

RIT *abbrev.* ◆ Rorschach Inkblot Test

rit. *shortening* ◆ ritardando (Italian, = slowing down) (music)

riten. *shortening* ◆ ritenuto (Italian, = held back) (music)

riv. *shortening* ◆ river

RJ *abbrev.* ◆ Manchester (British vehicle registration mark) ◆ Royal Jordanian Airlines (airline baggage code)

RJE *abbrev.* ◆ remote job entry

RJET *abbrev.* ◆ remote job entry terminal

RK *abbrev.* ◆ north-west London (British vehicle registration mark) ◆ religious knowledge

RKO *abbrev.* ◆ Radio-Keith-Orpheum (former US film production and distribution company)

RL *abbrev.* ◆ Aerolineas Niceraguenses (airline baggage code) ◆ reference library ◆ Republic of Lebanon (international vehicle registration) ◆ Rugby League ◆ Truro (British vehicle registration mark)

RLC *abbrev.* ◆ Royal Logistic Corps

RLF *abbrev.* ◆ Royal Literary Fund

RLO *abbrev.* ◆ Returned Letter Office

RLPO *abbrev.* ◆ Royal Liverpool Philharmonic Orchestra

RLPS *abbrev.* ◆ Royal Liverpool Philharmonic Society

Rls *contraction* ◆ rial (Iranian monetary unit)

RLSS *abbrev.* ◆ Royal Life Saving Society

rly *contraction* ◆ railway

RM *abbrev.* ◆ Carlisle (British vehicle registration mark) ◆ Republic of Madagascar (international vehicle registration) ◆ Resident Magistrate ◆ Romford (UK postcode) ◆ Royal Mail ◆ Royal Marines

rm *contraction* ◆ ream ◆ room

RMA *abbrev.* ◆ Royal Military Academy ◆ Royal Musical Association

RMCM *abbrev.* ◆ Royal Manchester College of Music

RMCS *abbrev.* ◆ Royal Miltary College of Science

RMetS *abbrev.* ◆ Royal Meteorological Society

RMFVR *abbrev.* ◆ Royal Marine Forces Volunteer Reserves

RMI *abbrev.* ◆ Rimini (airport baggage label)

RMM *abbrev.* ◆ Republic of Mali (international vehicle registration)

RMN *abbrev.* ◆ Registered Mental Nurse

RMO *abbrev.* ◆ Resident Medical Officer

RMP *abbrev.* ◆ Royal Marine Police ◆ Royal Military Police

RMR *abbrev.* ◆ Royal Marines Reserve

RMS *abbrev.* ◆ Royal Medical Society ◆ Royal Microscopical Society ◆ Royal Society of Miniature Painters

rms *abbrev.* ◆ root-mean-square

RMSchMus *abbrev.* ◆ Royal Marines School of Music

RMSM *abbrev.* ◆ Royal Military School of Music

RMT *abbrev.* ◆ National Union of Rail, Maritime and Transport Workers

RN *abbrev.* ◆ Preston (British vehicle registration mark) ◆ Registered Nurse ◆ Republic of Niger ◆ Republic of Niger (international vehicle registration) ◆ Royal Navy

Rn *symbol* ◆ radon (chemical element)

rn *abbrev.* ◆ reception nil

RNA *abbrev.* ◆ ribonucleic acid ◆ Romantic Novelists' Association ◆ Royal Naval Association

RNAS *abbrev.* ◆ Royal Naval Air Service

RNase *contraction* ◆ ribonuclease

r'n'b *abbrev.* ◆ rhythm and blues

RNBS *abbrev.* ◆ Royal Naval Benevolent Society

RNBT *abbrev.* ◆ Royal Naval Benevolent Trust

RNC *abbrev.* ◆ Royal Naval College

RNCM *abbrev.* ◆ Royal Northern College of Music

RNEC *abbrev.* ◆ Royal Naval Engineering College

Rnf. *shortening* ◆ Renfrewshire (former Scottish county)

RNHA *abbrev.* ◆ Registered Nursing Home Association

RNHU *abbrev.* ◆ Royal National Homing Union

RNIB *abbrev.* ◆ Royal National Institute for the Blind

RNID *abbrev.* ◆ Royal National Institute for the Deaf

RNLI *abbrev.* ◆ Royal National Lifeboat Institution

RNMDSF *abbrev.* ◆ Royal National Mission to Deep Sea Fishermen

RNMH *abbrev.* ◆ Registered Nurse for the Mentally Handicapped

RNMS *abbrev.* ◆ Royal Naval Medical School

RNR *abbrev.* ◆ Royal Naval Reserve

r'n'r *abbrev.* ◆ rock and roll

RNRS *abbrev.* ◆ Royal National Rose Society

RNS *abbrev.* ◆ Royal Numismatic Society

RNSC *abbrev.* ◆ Royal Naval Staff College

RNSR *abbrev.* ◆ Royal Naval Special Reserve

RNSS *abbrev.* ◆ Royal Naval Scientific Service

RNT *abbrev.* ◆ Royal National Theatre

RNTE *abbrev.* ◆ Royal Naval Training Establishment

RNTU *abbrev.* ◆ Royal Naval Training Unit

RNVR *abbrev.* ◆ Royal Naval Volunteer Reserve

RNXS *abbrev.* ◆ Royal Naval Auxiliary Service

RO *abbrev.* ◆ Luton (British vehicle registration mark) ◆ Returning Officer ◆ Romania (international vehicle registration) ◆ Royal Observatory

ro *contraction* ◆ recto ◆ run out (cricket)

ROA *abbrev.* ◆ Racehorse Owners' Association ◆ Record of Achievement ◆ return on assets

ROAR *abbrev.* ◆ right of admission reserved

ROC *abbrev.* ◆ return on capital ◆ Royal Observer Corps

ROE *abbrev.* ◆ return on equity ◆ Royal Observatory, Edinburgh

ROF *abbrev.* ◆ Royal Ordnance Factory

Roffen. *shortening* ◆ Roffensis (Latin, = of Rochester)

ROH *abbrev.* ◆ Royal Opera House (Covent Garden)

ROI *abbrev.* ◆ return on investment ◆ Royal Institute of Oil Painters

ROK *abbrev.* ◆ Republic of Korea ◆ Republic of Korea (international vehicle registration)

ROM *abbrev.* ◆ Rome (airport baggage label) ◆ rupture of membranes

ROM *acronym* ◆ read-only memory

Rom. *shortening* ◆ Romance ◆ Romans (book of Bible)

rom. *shortening* ◆ roman (typeface)

RORC *abbrev.* ◆ Royal Ocean Racing Club

ro-ro *acronym* ◆ roll-on, roll-off (sort of ferry)

Ros. *shortening* ◆ County Roscommon

Rosco *acronym* ◆ Road Operators' Safety Council

Rose *acronym* ◆ Research Open Systems in Europe

ROSL *abbrev.* ◆ Royal Overseas League

RoSPA *acronym* ◆ Royal Society for the Prevention of Accidents

ROT *abbrev.* ◆ registered occupational therapist ◆ rule of thumb

rot. *shortening* ◆ rotary

ROU *abbrev.* ◆ Republic of Uruguay ◆ Republic of Uruguay (international vehicle registration)

rout. *shortening* ◆ routine

ROV *abbrev.* ◆ remotely-operated vehicle ◆ Rostov (airport baggage label)

ROW *abbrev.* ◆ right of way ◆ Rights of Women

Rox. *shortening* ◆ Roxburghshire (former Scottish county)

RP *abbrev.* ◆ Northampton (British vehicle registration mark) ◆ Received Pronunciation ◆ recommended price ◆ Reformed Presbyterian ◆ Regius Professor ◆ reply paid ◆ reprint ◆ Republic of the Philippines (international vehicle registration) ◆ retinitis pigmentosa ◆ Royal Society of Portrait Painters

Rp *abbrev.* ◆ rupiah (Indonesian monetary unit)

rp *abbrev.* ◆ reception poor

RPA *abbrev.* ◆ Rationalist Press Association ◆ Record of Personal Achievement ◆ Registered Plumbers' Association

RPB *abbrev.* ◆ recognized professional body ◆ Republic of Benin (international vehicle registration)

RPC *abbrev.* ◆ Royal Pioneer Corps

RPE *abbrev.* ◆ Reformed Protestant Episcopal

RPG *abbrev.* ◆ Report Program Generator ◆ rocket-propelled grenade ◆ role-playing game

rph *abbrev.* ◆ revolutions per hour

RPhilS *abbrev.* ◆ Royal Philharmonic Society

RPI *abbrev.* ◆ retail price index

RPM *abbrev.* ◆ resale price maintenance ◆ retail price maintenance

rpm *abbrev.* ◆ revolutions per minute

RPMS *abbrev.* ◆ Royal Postgraduate Medical School

RPN *abbrev.* ◆ Registered Psychiatric Nurse ◆ reverse Polish notation

RPO *abbrev.* ◆ Royal Philharmonic Orchestra

RPP *abbrev.* ◆ retropubic prostatectomy

RPQ *abbrev.* ◆ request for price quotation

RPRA *abbrev.* ◆ Royal Pigeon Racing Association

RPS *abbrev.* ◆ Radiological Protection Service ◆ Royal Philharmonic Society ◆ Royal Photographic Society

rps *abbrev.* ◆ revolutions per second

RPSGB *abbrev.* ◆ Royal Pharmaceutical Society of Great Britain

RPSL *abbrev.* ◆ Royal Philatelic Society, London

RPT *abbrev.* ◆ registered physiotherapist

rpt *shortening* ◆ repeat ◆ report

RPV *abbrev.* ◆ remotely piloted vehicle

RQ *abbrev.* ◆ Maldives International Airlines (airline baggage code) ◆ regraded quality (tyres) ◆ remoulded quality (tyres) ◆ request for quotation ◆ respiratory quotient

RQMS *abbrev.* ◆ Regimental Quartermaster-Sergeant

rqmt *contraction* ◆ requirement

RR *abbrev.* ◆ Nottingham (British vehicle registration mark) ◆ Remington Rand ◆ Right Reverend ◆ Rolls-Royce

r/r *abbrev.* ◆ roof rails

RRA *abbrev.* ◆ Royal Regiment of Artillery

RRB *abbrev.* ◆ Race Relations Board

RRC *abbrev.* ◆ Edinburgh (British vehicle registration mark) ◆ Road Runners' Club

RRF *abbrev.* ◆ Rapid Reaction Force

rRNA *abbrev.* ◆ ribosomal ribonucleic acid

RRP *abbrev.* ◆ recommended retail price

RS *abbrev.* ◆ Aberdeen (British vehicle registration mark) ◆ Received Standard (of educated speech) ◆ Royal Society

rs *abbrev.* ◆ right side

r/s *abbrev.* ◆ rejection slip

RSA *abbrev.* ◆ Republic of South Africa ◆ Royal Society of Arts ◆ Royal Society for the Encouragement of Arts, Manufactures, and Commerce

RSAMD *abbrev.* ◆ Royal Scottish Academy of Music and Drama

RSC *abbrev.* ◆ Royal Shakespeare Company ◆ Royal Society of Chemistry

RSCDS *abbrev.* ◆ Royal Scottish Country Dance Society

RSCM *abbrev.* ◆ Royal School of Church Music

RSCN *abbrev.* ◆ Registered Sick Children's Nurse

rsdntl *contraction* ◆ residential

RSE *abbrev.* ◆ Received Standard English

RSFSR *abbrev.* ◆ Russian Soviet Federative Socialist Republic (official Soviet title (1920–91) of Russia)

RSG *abbrev.* ◆ rates-support grant ◆ regional seat of government ◆ Royal Scots Greys

RSGB *abbrev.* ◆ Radio Society of Great Britain

RSI *abbrev.* ◆ repetitive strain injury

RSJ *abbrev.* ◆ rolled steel joist

RSL *abbrev.* ◆ Royal Society of Literature

RSM *abbrev.* ◆ Regimental Sergeant-Major ◆ Republic of San Marino (international vehicle registration) ◆ Royal School of Mines ◆ Royal Society of Medicine ◆ Royal Society of Musicians of Great Britain

RSNC *abbrev.* ◆ Royal Society for Nature Conservation

RSNO *abbrev.* ◆ Royal Scottish National Orchestra

RSNT *abbrev.* ◆ Railway Staffs National Tribunal

rsp *abbrev.* ◆ rain stopped play (cricket)

RSPB *abbrev.* ◆ Royal Society for the Protection of Birds

RSPBA *abbrev.* ◆ Royal Scottish Pipe Band Association

RSPCA *abbrev.* ◆ Royal Society for the Prevention of Cruelty to Animals

RSPP *abbrev.* ◆ Royal Society of Portrait Painters

RSPS *abbrev.* ◆ Royal Scottish Pipers' Society

RSRE *abbrev.* ◆ Royal Signals and Radar Establishment

RSS *abbrev.* ◆ Regiae Societatis Socius (Latin, = Fellow of the Royal Society)

R/st *contraction* ◆ rear seat

rst *abbrev.* ◆ radio/stereo

RSTM & H *abbrev.* ◆ Royal Society of Tropical Medicine and Hygiene

RSV *abbrev.* ◆ Revised Standard Version (translation of Bible)

RSVP *abbrev.* ◆ répondez s'il vous plaît (French, = please reply)

RSWC *abbrev.* ◆ right side up with care

RT *abbrev.* ◆ Ipswich (British vehicle registration mark) ◆ radio telephone ◆ room temperature

rt *contraction* ◆ right

RTA *abbrev.* ◆ reciprocal trade agreement ◆ road traffic accident

rtb *abbrev.* ◆ return to base

rtd *contraction* ◆ retired ◆ returned

rtd ht *contraction* ◆ retired hurt (cricket)

RTDS *abbrev.* ◆ real time data system

RTE *abbrev.* ◆ Radio Telefis Éireann (Gaelic, = Irish Radio and Television) ◆ real time execution

rte *contraction* ◆ route

Rtecs *pronounced* ar-tex *acronym* ◆ Registry of Toxic Effects of Chemical Substances

RTF *abbrev.* ◆ Radiodiffusion-Télévision Française (French, = French Radio and Television Broadcasting Company)

Rt Hon. *shortening* ◆ Right Honourable

RTI *abbrev.* ◆ respiratory tract infection ◆ Round Table International

RTITB *abbrev.* ◆ Road Transport Industry Training Board

RTK *abbrev.* ◆ right to know

RTL *abbrev.* ◆ real time language

RTM *abbrev.* ◆ Rotterdam (airport baggage label)

rtn *contraction* ◆ retain ◆ return

RTOL *abbrev.* ◆ reduced take-off and landing

RTP *abbrev.* ◆ room temperature and pressure

RTPI *abbrev.* ◆ Royal Town Planning Institute

RTR *abbrev.* ◆ Royal Tank Regiment

Rt Rev. *shortening* ◆ Right Reverend

Rt Revd *contraction* ◆ Right Reverend

RTS *abbrev.* ◆ Religious Tract Society ◆ Royal Television Society

RTSA *abbrev.* ◆ Retail Standards Association

RTTC *abbrev.* ◆ Road Time Trials Council (cycling)

rtu *abbrev.* ◆ returned to unit

rtw *abbrev.* ◆ ready to wear

RTYC *abbrev.* ◆ Royal Thames Yacht Club

RTZ *abbrev.* ◆ Rio Tinto Zinc Corporation Ltd

RU *abbrev.* ◆ Bournemouth (British vehicle registration mark) ◆ Republic of Burundi (international vehicle registration; orig. Ruanda-Urundi) ◆ Rugby Union

Ru *symbol* ◆ ruthenium (chemical element)

Ru. *shortening* ◆ Russia ◆ Russian

RUC *abbrev.* ◆ Republic of Cameroon (international vehicle registration; orig. République Unie du Cameroun) ◆ Royal Ulster Constabulary

RUCR *abbrev.* ◆ Royal Ulster Constabulary Reserve

Rug *acronym* ◆ restricted users group

RUH *abbrev.* ◆ Riyadh (airport baggage label)

Rukba *acronym* ◆ Royal United Kingdom Beneficent Association

RUR *abbrev.* ◆ Royal Ulster Regiment

Rural *acronym* ◆ Society for the Responsible Use of Resources in Agriculture and on the Land

RUS *abbrev.* ◆ Russia (international vehicle registration)

Rus. *shortening* ◆ Russia ◆ Russian

RUSI *abbrev.* ◆ Royal United Services Institute for Defence Studies

RUSM *abbrev.* ◆ Royal United Service Museum

Russ. *shortening* ◆ Russia ◆ Russian

Rut. *shortening* ◆ Rutland (former English county)

RV *abbrev.* ◆ Portsmouth (British vehicle registration mark) ◆ rateable value ◆ Revised Version (translation of Bible) ◆ right ventricle

rv *abbrev.* ◆ rendezvous

RVC *abbrev.* ◆ Royal Veterinary College

RVSVP *abbrev.* ◆ répondez vite, s'il vous plaît (French, = please reply quickly)

RW *abbrev.* ◆ Coventry (British vehicle registration mark) ◆ Right Worshipful ◆ Right Worthy ◆ runway

r/w *abbrev.* ◆ read/write

Rw. *shortening* ◆ Rwanda ◆ Rwandan

RWA *abbrev.* ◆ Race Walking Association ◆ Rwanda (international vehicle registration)

RWD *abbrev.* ◆ radioactive waste disposal

rwd *abbrev.* ◆ rear wheel drive

RWF *abbrev.* ◆ Royal Welch Fusiliers

RWFCS *abbrev.* ◆ Red and White Friesian Cattle Society

RWIC *abbrev.* ◆ Rioja Wine Information Centre

RWM *abbrev.* ◆ radioactive waste management

RWMAC *abbrev.* ◆ Radioactive Waste Management Advisory Committee

RWP *abbrev.* ◆ Rawalpindi (airport baggage label)

RWS *abbrev.* ◆ Royal Society of Painters in Water Colours

rwy *contraction* ◆ railway

RX *abbrev.* ◆ Reading (British vehicle registration mark) ◆ Republic of Panama (international civil aircraft marking)

RY *abbrev.* ◆ Air Rwanda (airline baggage code) ◆ Leicester (British vehicle registration mark)

ry *contraction* ◆ railway

RYA *abbrev.* ◆ Royal Yachting Association

RYS *abbrev.* ◆ Royal Yacht Squadron

RZ *abbrev.* ◆ Antrim (British vehicle registration mark) ◆ Arab International Airlines (airline baggage code)

RZS *abbrev.* ◆ Royal Zoological Society

S

S *abbrev.* ◆ Sabbath ◆ Saint ◆ Saturday ◆ schilling (Austrian monetary unit) ◆ school ◆ segno (Italian, = sign) (music) ◆ September ◆ Sheffield (UK postcode) ◆ siemens ◆ Signor (Italian, = Mr) ◆ slow ◆ small (clothing size) ◆ Society ◆ soprano ◆ south ◆ spades (cards) ◆ square ◆ stokes ◆ summer ◆ sun ◆ Sunday ◆ Sweden (international vehicle registration)

S *symbol* ◆ sulphur (chemical element)

S4C *abbrev.* ◆ Sianel 4 Cymru (Welsh, = Channel 4 Wales)

s *abbrev.* ◆ second ◆ section ◆ semi- ◆ series ◆ sets (of sun) ◆ shilling (former British monetary unit) ◆ singular ◆ sister ◆ son ◆ substantive ◆ succeeded ◆ suit

SA *abbrev.* ◆ Aberdeen (British vehicle registration mark) ◆ Salvation Army ◆ Saudi Arabia ◆ Saudi Arabia (international vehicle registration) ◆ Saudi Arabian ◆ sex-appeal ◆ small arms ◆ Sociedad Anónima (Spanish, = PLC) ◆ Società Anonima (Italian, = PLC) ◆ Société Anonyme (French, = PLC) ◆ Society of Antiquaries ◆ Society of Arts ◆ Soil Association ◆ South Africa ◆ South African ◆ South African Airways (airline baggage code) ◆ South America ◆ South American ◆ South Australia ◆ South Australian ◆ Sturm Abteilung (German, = Storm Detachment) (paramilitary wing of Nazi party 1921–34) ◆ Swansea (UK postcode) ◆ subsistence allowance

sa *abbrev.* ◆ secundum artem (Latin, = in the standard way) ◆ semiannual

s/a *abbrev.* ◆ subject to acceptance ◆ subject to approval

SAA *abbrev.* ◆ Scottish Archery Association ◆ small arms ammunition ◆ South African Airways ◆ Systems Application Architecture (software operating system)

SAAA *abbrev.* ◆ Scottish Amateur Athletic Association

Saab *pronounced* sarb *acronym* ◆ Svensk Aeroplan Aktiebolag (Swedish, = Swedish Aeroplane Company) (car and aircraft manufacturer)

Saabs *acronym* ◆ Scottish Action Against Blood Sports

SAAD *abbrev.* ◆ small-arms ammunition depot

SAB *abbrev.* ◆ Scientific Advisory Board ◆ soprano, alto, bass

sab. *shortening* ◆ sabbath ◆ sabbatarian ◆ sabbatical

SABA *abbrev.* ◆ Scottish Amateur Boxing Association

sabbat. *shortening* ◆ sabbatical

SABC *abbrev.* ◆ Scottish Association of Boys' Clubs ◆ South African Broadcasting Corporation

Sabena *acronym* ◆ Société Anonyme Belge d'Exploitation de la Navigation Aérienne (French, = Belgian Company for the Development of Air Travel) (Belgian international airline)

Sabic *acronym* ◆ Society for the Advancement of Brain-Injured Children

sabo. *shortening* ◆ sabotage

SAC *abbrev.* ◆ Post Office Stamp Advisory Committee ◆ Sacramento (airport baggage label) ◆ Scottish Arts

Council ◆ Scottish Automobile Club
◆ Senior Aircraftman ◆ Strategic Air
Command (US)

SACAB *abbrev.* ◆ Scottish Association of
Citizens' Advice Bureaux

SACHR *abbrev.* ◆ Standing Advisory
Commission on Human Rights

SACRO *abbrev.* ◆ Scottish Association
for the Care and Resettlement of
Offenders

Sacu *acronym* ◆ Society for the
Promotion of Anglo-Chinese
Understanding

SACW *abbrev.* ◆ Senior Aircraftwoman

SAD *abbrev.* ◆ seasonal affective disorder

Sad *acronym* ◆ Scottish Action on
Dementia ◆ Scottish Association for the
Deaf

Sadi *acronym* ◆ Society of Approved
Driving Instructors

sae *abbrev.* ◆ stamped addressed
envelope ◆ self-addressed envelope

SAEF *abbrev.* ◆ Stock Exchange
Automatic Execution Facility

SAF *abbrev.* ◆ Santa Fe (airport baggage
label) ◆ Scottish Athletic Federation

SAFA *abbrev.* ◆ Scottish Amateur
Football Association

SAfr *abbrev.* ◆ South Africa ◆ South
African

SAfrD *abbrev.* ◆ South African Dutch
(Afrikaans)

SAFU *abbrev.* ◆ Scottish Amateur
Fencing Union

SAGA *abbrev.* ◆ Scottish Amateur
Gymnastics Association

SAGB *abbrev.* ◆ Schizophrenia
Association of Great Britain
◆ Spiritualist Association of Great
Britain

Sagga *acronym* ◆ Scout and Guide
Graduate Association

SAH *abbrev.* ◆ subarachnoid
haemorrhage ◆ Supreme Allied
Headquarters

SAHC *abbrev.* ◆ Scottish Association of
Health Councils

SAHGB *abbrev.* ◆ Society of Architectural
Historians of Great Britain

SAHR *abbrev.* ◆ Society of Army
Historical Research

SAIC *abbrev.* ◆ Scottish Agricultural
Improvement Council

SAISSA *abbrev.* ◆ Scottish Amateur Ice
Speed Skating Association

SAL *abbrev.* ◆ San Salvador (airport
baggage label)

sal. *shortening* ◆ salary

Salop *shortening* ◆ Salopia (Latin, =
Shropshire)

SALRC *abbrev.* ◆ Society for Assistance
to Ladies in Reduced Circumstances

Salt *acronym* ◆ Scottish Association for
Language Teaching ◆ Strategic Arms
Limitation Talks ◆ Strategic Arms
Limitation Treaty

Salv. *shortening* ◆ Salvador
◆ Salvadorean

salv. *shortening* ◆ salvage

SAM *abbrev.* ◆ Scottish Aids Monitor

SAm *abbrev.* ◆ South America ◆ South
American

sam *acronym* ◆ surface-to-air missile

Sam. *shortening* ◆ Samuel (books of
Bible)

SAMA *abbrev.* ◆ Scottish Amateur Music
Association

SAmer *abbrev.* ◆ South America ◆ South
American

SAMH *abbrev.* ◆ Scottish Association for
Mental Health

san. *shortening* ◆ sanitary

Sana *acronym* ◆ Scottish Anglers'
National Association

Sand *acronym* ◆ Scotland Against
Nuclear Dumping

s & d *abbrev.* ◆ search and destroy ◆ song
and dance

s & f *abbrev.* ◆ stock and fixtures

s & fa *abbrev.* ◆ shipping and forwarding
agents

s & h *abbrev.* ◆ shipping and handling

S and M *abbrev.* ◆ sadism and
masochism

s & m *abbrev.* ◆ sausages and mash ◆ stock and machinery

Sands *acronym* ◆ Stillbirth and Neonatal Death Society

S and T *abbrev.* ◆ signalling and telecommunications

s & t *abbrev.* ◆ supply and transport

S & TA *abbrev.* ◆ Salmon and Trout Association

Sane *acronym* ◆ Schizophrenia: A National Emergency

SANFP *abbrev.* ◆ Scottish Association for Natural Family Planning

sanit. *shortening* ◆ sanitary ◆ sanitation

sanrs *abbrev.* ◆ subject to approval—no risks

Sans. *shortening* ◆ Sanskrit

Sansk. *shortening* ◆ Sanskrit

SAO *abbrev.* ◆ São Paulo (airport baggage label)

sap *abbrev.* ◆ soon as possible

SAPC *abbrev.* ◆ Scottish Accident Prevention Council

sapfu *abbrev.* ◆ surpassing all previous fuck-ups

SAPT *abbrev.* ◆ Scottish Association for Public Transport

SAR *abbrev.* ◆ South African Republic ◆ synthetic aperture radar

Sar. *shortening* ◆ Sardinia ◆ Sardinian

sar *abbrev.* ◆ search and rescue

SARA *abbrev.* ◆ Scottish Amateur Rowing Association ◆ Scottish Anti-Racist Alliance

Sarl *acronym* ◆ Société à Responsabilité Limitée (French, = Ltd)

SARM *abbrev.* ◆ Scottish Anti-Racist Movement

Sarsat *acronym* ◆ Search and Rescue Satellite (for maritime disasters etc)

Sarum. *shortening* ◆ Sarumensis (Latin, = of Salisbury)

SAS *abbrev.* ◆ Società in accomandita semplice (Italian, = Ltd) ◆ Societatis Antiquariorum Socius (Latin, = Fellow of the Society of Antiquaries) ◆ Special Air Service

Sasa *acronym* ◆ Scottish Amateur Snooker Association ◆ Scottish Amateur Swimming Association

SASF *abbrev.* ◆ Salvation Army Students' Fellowship

Sask. *shortening* ◆ Saskatchewan

SASO *abbrev.* ◆ Senior Air Staff Officer

SASR *abbrev.* ◆ Special Air Service Regiment

SASV *abbrev.* ◆ Scottish Association for the Speaking of Verse

SAT *abbrev.* ◆ South Australia Time

SAt *abbrev.* ◆ South Atlantic

Sat *acronym* ◆ Standard Assessment Task

Sat. *shortening* ◆ Saturday

sat. *shortening* ◆ satellite ◆ saturated

SATB *abbrev.* ◆ soprano, alto, tenor, bass

Satco *acronym* ◆ signal automatic air-traffic control system

Satips *acronym* ◆ Society of Assistant Teachers in Preparatory Schools

satn *contraction* ◆ saturation

Satro *acronym* ◆ Science and Technology Regional Organization

SAus *abbrev.* ◆ South Australia ◆ South Australian

SAV *abbrev.* ◆ sale at valuation ◆ stock at valuation

Save *acronym* ◆ Save Britain's Heritage

SAVS *abbrev.* ◆ Scottish Anti-Vivisection Society

sax. *shortening* ◆ saxophone

SAYE *abbrev.* ◆ Save as You Earn

SAW *abbrev.* ◆ Scottish Association of Writers ◆ surface acoustic wave

SAWA *abbrev.* ◆ Scottish Amateur Wrestling Association

SAY *abbrev.* ◆ Salisbury, Zimbabwe (airport baggage label)

SAYC *abbrev.* ◆ Scottish Association of Youth Clubs

SAYE *abbrev.* ◆ save as you earn

SB *abbrev.* ◆ Glasgow (British vehicle registration mark) ◆ Savings Bank ◆ selection board ◆ sick bay ◆ simultaneous broadcast ◆ smooth

bore ◆ Special Branch (police)
◆ stillbirth

Sb *symbol* ◆ stibium (Latin, = antimony)
(chemical element)

sb *abbrev.* ◆ single-breasted

sb *contraction* ◆ stilb

sb. *shortening* ◆ substantive

SBA *abbrev.* ◆ School of Business
Administration ◆ Scottish Basketball
Association ◆ sick bay attendant

SBAC *abbrev.* ◆ Society of British
Aerospace Companies

SBB *abbrev.* ◆ Schweizerische
Bundesbahn (German, = Swiss Federal
Railways)

SBBNF *abbrev.* ◆ Ship and Boat Builders'
National Federation

SBC *abbrev.* ◆ single-board computer

SBGI *abbrev.* ◆ Society of British Gas
Industries

SBH *abbrev.* ◆ Scottish Board of Health

SBJ *abbrev.* ◆ Simla (airport baggage
label)

SBL *abbrev.* ◆ Society of Biblical
Literature

SBN *abbrev.* ◆ Standard Book Number

SBP *abbrev.* ◆ systolic blood pressure

SBPR *abbrev.* ◆ Society for Back Pain
Research

SBR *abbrev.* ◆ strict bed rest

SBS *abbrev.* ◆ sick building syndrome
◆ Special Boat Service

SBSA *abbrev.* ◆ Scottish Board Sailing
Association

SBSB *abbrev.* ◆ Society of British Snuff
Blenders

SBTD *abbrev.* ◆ Society of British Theatre
Designers

SBU *abbrev.* ◆ Scottish Badminton Union
◆ strategic business unit

SC *abbrev.* ◆ Edinburgh (British vehicle
registration mark) ◆ sailing club
◆ Schools Council ◆ Security Council
(UN) ◆ Signal Corps ◆ Social Club
◆ South Carolina (US postcode)
◆ Special Constable ◆ Sports Club
◆ Staff College ◆ standing committee
◆ structural change ◆ subcutaneous

Sc *symbol* ◆ scandium (chemical
element)

Sc. *abbrev.* ◆ Scandinavia ◆ Scandinavian
◆ Scotland ◆ Scottish

sc *abbrev.* ◆ small capitals

sc. *shortening* ◆ scale ◆ scene ◆ science
◆ scientific ◆ scilicet (Latin, = namely)
◆ scruple (former apothecaries' weight)
◆ sculpsit (Latin, = carved it)

s/c *abbrev.* ◆ self-catering ◆ self-
contained

SCA *abbrev.* ◆ Scottish Canoe
Association ◆ Scottish Chess
Association ◆ Scottish Council on
Alcohol ◆ Scottish Croquet Association
◆ sickle-cell anaemia ◆ Suez Canal
Authority

Scaarf *acronym* ◆ Scottish Combined
Action Against Racism and Fascism

Scafa *acronym* ◆ Scottish Child and
Family Alliance

SCAHT *abbrev.* ◆ Scottish Churches
Architectural Heritage Trust

SCAN *abbrev.* ◆ suspected child abuse
and neglect

Scan. *shortening* ◆ Scandinavia
◆ Scandinavian

Scand. *shortening* ◆ Scandinavia
◆ Scandinavian

SCAR *abbrev.* ◆ Scientific Committee on
Antarctic Research

Scarf *acronym* ◆ Sickle Cell Anaemia
Research Foundation

SCB *abbrev.* ◆ Solicitors' Complaints
Bureau ◆ Speedway Control Board
(motor-cycle racing)

ScB *abbrev.* ◆ Scientiae Baccalaureus
(Latin, = Bachelor of Science)

SCBU *abbrev.* ◆ special care baby unit

SCC *abbrev.* ◆ Scottish Churches Council
◆ Scottish Consumer Council ◆ Sea
Cadet Corps

scc *abbrev.* ◆ single column centimetre

SCCA *abbrev.* ◆ Scottish Consumer
Credit Association ◆ Society of
Company and Commercial
Accountants

SCCL *abbrev.* ♦ Scottish Council for Civil Liberties

SCD *abbrev.* ♦ Scottish Council on Disability

ScD *abbrev.* ♦ Scientiae Doctor (Latin, = Doctor of Science)

SCDC *abbrev.* ♦ Schools Curriculum Development Committee

SCE *abbrev.* ♦ Scottish Certificate of Education

SCEC *abbrev.* ♦ Scottish Community Education Council

SCF *abbrev.* ♦ Save the Children Fund

scf *abbrev.* ♦ standard cubic feet

scfh *abbrev.* ♦ standard cubic feet per hour

scfd *abbrev.* ♦ standard cubic feet per day

Sc. Gael. *shortening* ♦ Scottish Gaelic

SCGB *abbrev.* ♦ Ski Club of Great Britain

Sch. *shortening* ♦ Schilling (Austrian monetary unit)

sch. *shortening* ♦ schedule (taxation system) ♦ scholar ♦ school ♦ schooner

schem. *shortening* ♦ schematic

scherz. *shortening* ♦ scherzando (Italian, = joking) (music)

schol. *shortening* ♦ scholar ♦ scholarship ♦ scholiast ♦ scholium

sci. *shortening* ♦ science ♦ scientific

sci *abbrev.* ♦ single column inch

SCIAF *abbrev.* ♦ Scottish Catholic International Aid Fund

Scid *acronym* ♦ Scotland's Campaign against Irresponsible Drivers ♦ severe combined immunodeficiency disease

sci. fa. *shortening* ♦ scire facias (Latin, = make him aware) (sort of writ)

scil. *shortening* ♦ scilicet (Latin, = you may understand)

SCL *abbrev.* ♦ Scottish Central Library ♦ Student of Civil Law

SCLC *abbrev.* ♦ Scottish Child Law Centre

SCM *abbrev.* ♦ State Certified Midwife ♦ Student Christian Movement

ScM *abbrev.* ♦ Scientiae Magister (Latin, = Master of Science)

SCMA *abbrev.* ♦ Stilton Cheese Manufacturers' Association

SCMAC *abbrev.* ♦ Scottish Catholic Marriage Advisory Council

SCNI *abbrev.* ♦ Sports Council for Northern Ireland

Scobec *acronym* ♦ Scottish Business Education Council

Scolag *acronym* ♦ Scottish Legal Action Group

Sconul *acronym* ♦ Standing Conference of National and University Libraries

Scot. *shortening* ♦ Scotland ♦ Scottish

Scotvec *acronym* ♦ Scottish Vocational Education Council

SCP *abbrev.* ♦ single-cell protein

SCPS *abbrev.* ♦ Society of Civil and Public Servants

SCR *abbrev.* ♦ senior common room (in Oxford colleges) ♦ senior combination room (in Cambridge colleges) ♦ sequence control register

scr. *shortening* ♦ scruple (former apothecaries' weight)

Scram *acronym* ♦ Scottish Campaign to Resist the Atomic Menace

SCRE *abbrev.* ♦ Scottish Council for Racial Equality ♦ Scottish Council for Research in Education

Scream *acronym* ♦ Society for the Control and Registration of Estate Agents and Mortgage Brokers

script. *shortening* ♦ scripture ♦ scriptural

SCRE *abbrev.* ♦ Scottish Council for Research in Education

Script. *shortening* ♦ Scriptural ♦ Scripture

SCS *abbrev.* ♦ Scottish Crime Squad

SCSI *abbrev.* ♦ small computer systems interface

SCU *abbrev.* ♦ Scottish Cricket Union ♦ Scottish Cyclists' Union ♦ Special Care Unit

SCUA *abbrev.* ♦ Scottish Conservative and Unionist Association ♦ Suez Canal Users' Association

sculp. *shortening* ♦ sculpsit (Latin, = carved it) ♦ sculptor ♦ sculpture

sculpt. *shortening* ◆ sculptor ◆ sculpture
SCV *abbrev.* ◆ Stato della Città del Vaticano (Italian, = Vatican City State)
SCY *abbrev.* ◆ Truro, Scilly Isles (British vehicle registration mark)
SD *abbrev.* ◆ Air Sudan (airline baggage code) ◆ Glasgow (British vehicle registration mark) ◆ senile dementia ◆ South Dakota (US postcode) ◆ structural description ◆ Swaziland (international vehicle registration)
sd *abbrev.* ◆ semi-detached ◆ sine die (Latin, = without a day) (fixed for the business to be transacted) ◆ special delivery ◆ stage door ◆ standard deviation
SDA *abbrev.* ◆ Scottish Darts Association ◆ Scottish Development Agency ◆ Seventh Day Adventist ◆ Social Democratic Alliance
SDak *abbrev.* ◆ South Dakota
SDA *abbrev.* ◆ Scottish Development Agency
SDAT *abbrev.* ◆ senile dementia of the Alzheimer type
S-DAT *abbrev.* ◆ stationary digital audio tape
SDCGB *abbrev.* ◆ Square Dance Callers of Great Britain
SDD *abbrev.* ◆ Scottish Development Department ◆ subscriber direct dialling
SDG *abbrev.* ◆ soli Deo gloria (Latin, = glory be to God alone)
SDI *abbrev.* ◆ Strategic Defense Initiative
SDLP *abbrev.* ◆ Social Democratic and Labour Party (Northern Ireland)
SDMJ *abbrev.* ◆ September, December, March, June (for quarterly payments)
SDO *abbrev.* ◆ senior duty officer
SDP *abbrev.* ◆ Social Democratic Party ◆ social, domestic and pleasure (motor insurance)
SDR *abbrev.* ◆ special despatch rider ◆ special drawing right ◆ Suddeutscher Rundfunk (German, = South German Radio)
SDTU *abbrev.* ◆ Sign and Display Trades Union

SDUK *abbrev.* ◆ Society for the Diffusion of Useful Knowledge
SE *abbrev.* ◆ Aberdeen (British vehicle registration mark) ◆ Scottish Enterprise ◆ Society of Engineers ◆ south-east ◆ south-east London (UK postcode) ◆ south-eastern ◆ Stock Exchange
Se *symbol* ◆ selenium (chemical element)
se *abbrev.* ◆ standard error
SEA *abbrev.* ◆ Seattle (airport baggage label) ◆ South-East Asia
Seac *acronym* ◆ Schools Examinations and Assessment Council ◆ South-East Asia Command
Seaq *acronym* ◆ Stock Exchange Automated Quotations
Seato *acronym* ◆ South-East Asia Treaty Organization
SEC *abbrev.* ◆ Scottish Evangelistic Crusade ◆ Secondary Examinations Council
sec *shortening* ◆ secant ◆ second
sec. *shortening* ◆ secondary ◆ secretary ◆ section ◆ security
Secam *acronym* ◆ Séquentiel Couleur à Mémoire (French, = colour sequence by memory) (French and Russian colour television system)
Sec.-Gen. *shortening* ◆ Secretary-General
sec. leg. *shortening* ◆ secundam legem (Latin, = according to the law)
sec. nat. *shortening* ◆ secundam naturam (Latin, = according to nature)
sec. reg. *shortening* ◆ secundum regulam (Latin, = according to the rule)
sect. *shortening* ◆ section
secy *contraction* ◆ secretary
SED *abbrev.* ◆ Scottish Education Department
sed. *shortening* ◆ sedative ◆ sediment
sedtn *contraction* ◆ sedimentation
See *acronym* ◆ Save Eyes Everywhere (British Council for the Prevention of Blindness)
SEF *abbrev.* ◆ Shipbuilding Employers' Federation
seg. *shortening* ◆ segment ◆ segregate

SEG *abbrev.* ◆ socioeconomic grade

SEIS *abbrev.* ◆ submarine escape immersion suit

seismol. *shortening* ◆ seismological ◆ seismology

SEL *abbrev.* ◆ Seoul (airport baggage label)

sel. *shortening* ◆ selected ◆ selection

SEM *abbrev.* ◆ scanning electron microscope

Sem. *shortening* ◆ Semitic

sem. *shortening* ◆ semester ◆ semicolon ◆ seminary

se(m) *abbrev.* ◆ standard error (of the mean)

semp. *shortening* ◆ sempre (Italian, = always) (music)

s/empl. *shortening* ◆ self-employed

SEN *abbrev.* ◆ Special Educational Needs ◆ State Enrolled Nurse

sen. *shortening* ◆ senate ◆ senator ◆ senior ◆ senza (Italian, = without)

S en C *abbrev.* ◆ Sociedad en Comandita (Spanish, = limited partnership) ◆ Société en Commandite (French, = limited partnership)

Sennac *acronym* ◆ Special Educational Needs National Advisory Council

senr *contraction* ◆ senior

sent. *shortening* ◆ sentence

SEO *abbrev.* ◆ Senior Executive Officer ◆ Senior Experimental Officer ◆ Society of Education Officers

seoo *abbrev.* ◆ sauf erreurs ou omissions (French, = errors and omissions excepted)

Sep. *shortening* ◆ September

sep. *shortening* ◆ sepal ◆ separate ◆ separation

Sepa *acronym* ◆ Scottish Environment Protection Agency

sepn *contraction* ◆ separation

Sept. *shortening* ◆ September ◆ Septuagint

seq. *shortening* ◆ sequel ◆ sequence ◆ sequens (Latin, = following)

seq. luce *contraction* ◆ sequenti luce (Latin, = on the following day)

ser. *shortening* ◆ serial ◆ series ◆ serine ◆ sermon ◆ service

Serb. *shortening* ◆ Serbia ◆ Serbian

Serc *acronym* ◆ Science and Engineering Research Council

Serg. *shortening* ◆ Sergeant

Sergt *contraction* ◆ Sergeant

Serl *acronym* ◆ Services Electronics Research Laboratory

Serps *acronym* ◆ State Earnings-Related Pension Scheme

serv. *shortening* ◆ service

SES *abbrev.* ◆ Scientific Exploration Society ◆ socioeconomic status

sess. *shortening* ◆ session

SET *abbrev.* ◆ selective employment tax

Seti *acronym* ◆ search for extra-terrestrial intelligence

sev. *shortening* ◆ several ◆ severe

sew. *shortening* ◆ sewer ◆ sewage ◆ sewerage

Sexag. *shortening* ◆ Sexagesima

sext. *shortening* ◆ sextant

SF *abbrev.* ◆ Edinburgh (British vehicle registration mark) ◆ Finland (international vehicle registration) ◆ science fiction ◆ signal frequency ◆ Sinn Fein ◆ Society of Friends

sf *abbrev.* ◆ sinking fund ◆ sub finem (Latin, = towards the end)

sf. *shortening* ◆ sforzando (Italian, = strengthening) (music)

SFA *abbrev.* ◆ Scottish Football Association ◆ Securities and Futures Authority ◆ Small Farmers' Association ◆ Sweet Fanny Adams

SFBMS *abbrev.* ◆ Small Farm Business Management Scheme

SFC *abbrev.* ◆ specific fuel consumption

SFD *abbrev.* ◆ small for dates

sfgd *contraction* ◆ safeguard

SFHEA *abbrev.* ◆ Scottish Further and Higher Education Association

SFL *abbrev.* ◆ Scottish Football League ◆ sequenced flashing lights (on airport runway)

sfm *abbrev.* ◆ surface feet per minute

SFO *abbrev.* ◆ San Francisco (airport baggage label) ◆ Senior Flag Officer ◆ Serious Fraud Office

SFr *abbrev.* ◆ Swiss franc (monetary unit)

SFSR *abbrev.* ◆ Socialist Federation of Soviet Republics

SFU *abbrev.* ◆ suitable for upgrade (on airline tickets)

sfz. *shortening* ◆ sforzando (Italian, = strengthening) (music)

SG *abbrev.* ◆ Edinburgh (British vehicle registration mark) ◆ Seaman Gunner ◆ selon grandeur (French, = according to size) (price indication on menus etc) ◆ Secretary General ◆ Showmens' Guild of Great Britain ◆ Society of Genealogists ◆ Solicitor-General ◆ Stevenage (UK postcode) ◆ Surgeon General

sg *abbrev.* ◆ specific gravity ◆ steel girder

sg. *shortening* ◆ singular

SGA *abbrev.* ◆ Scottish Games Association ◆ small for gestational age ◆ Society of Graphic Art

SGBI *abbrev.* ◆ Schoolmistresses' and Governesses' Benevolent Institution

SgC *abbrev.* ◆ Surgeon Captain

Sg. Cr *contraction* ◆ Surgeon Commander

sgd *contraction* ◆ signed

sgdg *abbrev.* ◆ sans garantie du gouvernement (French, = without government guarantee) (on French patents)

SGF *abbrev.* ◆ Scottish Grocers' Federation

SGHWR *abbrev.* ◆ steam-generating heavy water reactor

sgl. *shortening* ◆ single

SGlam *abbrev.* ◆ South Glamorgan

SgLCr *abbrev.* ◆ Surgeon Lieutenant-Commander

sgle *contraction* ◆ single

SGM *abbrev.* ◆ Sea Gallantry Medal

SGML *abbrev.* ◆ Standardized Generalized Mark-up Language

SGN *abbrev.* ◆ Saigon (airport baggage label)

SGP *abbrev.* ◆ Singapore (international vehicle registration)

SgRA *abbrev.* ◆ Surgeon Rear-Admiral

Sgt *contraction* ◆ Sergeant

SGT *abbrev.* ◆ Society of Glass Technology

Sgt Maj. *shortening* ◆ Sergeant Major

SGTS *abbrev.* ◆ Scottish Gaelic Texts Society

SGU *abbrev.* ◆ Scottish Gliding Union ◆ Scottish Golf Union

SgVA *abbrev.* ◆ Surgeon Vice-Admiral

SH *abbrev.* ◆ Edinburgh (British vehicle registration mark) ◆ sexual harassment ◆ southern hemisphere

sh *abbrev.* ◆ scrum half (rugby football) ◆ second-hand ◆ shit-house

sh. *shortening* ◆ shall ◆ share ◆ sheet ◆ shilling (former British monetary unit)

s/h *abbrev.* ◆ shorthand

SHA *abbrev.* ◆ Scottish Hockey Association ◆ Secondary Heads' Association ◆ Shanghai (airport baggage label) ◆ Special Health Authority

Shac *acronym* ◆ Shelter Housing Aid Centre

Shact *acronym* ◆ Scottish Housing Associations Charitable Trust

Shaef *pronounced* shayf *acronym* ◆ Supreme Headquarters, Allied Expeditionary Forces (World War II)

Shape *acronym* ◆ Supreme Headquarters, Allied Powers Europe (Nato)

shd *contraction* ◆ should

S/HE *abbrev* ◆ Sundays and holidays excepted

s/he *contraction* ◆ she or he

SHEFC *abbrev.* ◆ Scottish Higher Education Funding Council

Sheffield. *shortening* ◆ Sheffieldensis (Latin, = of Sheffield)

Shet. *shortening* ◆ Shetland Islands

SHEx *abbrev.* ◆ Sundays and holidays excepted

shf *abbrev.* ◆ superhigh frequency

SHGF *abbrev.* ◆ Scottish Hang-Gliding Federation

SHHD *abbrev.* ◆ Scottish Home and Health Department

shipmt *contraction* ◆ shipment

s/hist. *shortening* ◆ service history (of car etc)

shm *abbrev.* ◆ simple harmonic motion

SHMIS *abbrev.* ◆ Society of Headmasters of Independent Schools

SHMO *abbrev.* ◆ Senior Hospital Medical Officer

SHMIS *abbrev.* ◆ Society of Headmasters and Headmistresses of Independent Schools

SHO *abbrev.* ◆ Senior House Officer

shoran *acronym* ◆ short-range navigation

shp *abbrev.* ◆ shaft horsepower ◆ single-flowered hardy perennial (rose)

shpg *contraction* ◆ shipping

shpt *contraction* ◆ shipment

SHQ *abbrev.* ◆ supreme headquarters

shr. *shortening* ◆ share

shrap. *shortening* ◆ shrapnel

SHRG *abbrev.* ◆ Scottish Homosexual Rights Group

Shrops. *shortening* ◆ Shropshire

SHS *abbrev.* ◆ Societatis Historicae Socius (Latin, = Fellow of the Historical Society) ◆ Scottish History Society ◆ Shire Horse Society ◆ Social History Society of the United Kingdom

sht *abbrev.* ◆ single-flowered hybrid tea (rose)

sht *contraction* ◆ sheet

shtg. *shortening* ◆ shortage

SHU *abbrev.* ◆ Scottish Hockey Union

shv *abbrev.* ◆ sub hac voce (Latin, = under this word)

SHW *abbrev.* ◆ safety, health and welfare

shwr *contraction* ◆ shower

SI *abbrev.* ◆ seriously ill ◆ Smithsonian Institution ◆ Socialist International ◆ statutory instrument ◆ Système International d'Unités (French, = International Units System)

Si *symbol* ◆ silicon (chemical element)

si *abbrev.* ◆ sum insured

SIA *abbrev.* ◆ Securities Industry Association ◆ Society of Investment Analysts ◆ Spinal Injuries Association

SIAD *abbrev.* ◆ Society of Industrial Artists and Designers

SIB *abbrev.* ◆ Securities and Investments Board ◆ self-injurious behaviour ◆ Shipbuilding Industry Board ◆ Special Investigations Branch (police)

Sib. *shortening* ◆ Siberia ◆ Siberian

SIBH *abbrev.* ◆ Society for the Interpretation of Britain's Heritage

Sibor *acronym* ◆ Singapore Inter-Bank Offered Rate

SIC *abbrev.* ◆ Standard Industrial Classification

Sic. *shortening* ◆ Sicilian ◆ Sicily

sic. *shortening* ◆ siccus (Latin, = dry)

SICAV *abbrev.* ◆ Société d'Investissement à Capital Variable (French, = unit trust)

sid *abbrev.* ◆ sudden ionospheric disturbance

Sids *acronym* ◆ sudden infant death syndrome

SIG *abbrev.* ◆ special interest group

Sig. *abbrev.* ◆ Signor (Italian, = Mr)

sig. *shortening* ◆ signal ◆ signetur (Latin, = let it be labelled) ◆ signature ◆ significant

SIGBI *abbrev.* ◆ Soroptomist International of Great Britain and Ireland

sigill. *shortening* ◆ sigillum (Latin, = seal)

sigint *acronym* ◆ signals intelligence

Sigmn *contraction* ◆ Signalman

sign. *shortening* ◆ signature

signif. *shortening* ◆ significant ◆ signifier

sig. nom. pro. *shortening* ◆ signa nomine proprio (Latin, = label with the correct title)

SigO *abbrev.* ◆ Signals Officer

SIH *abbrev.* ◆ Society for Italic Handwriting

SIM *abbrev.* ◆ self-inflicted mutilation

sim. *shortening* ◆ similar ◆ simile

Sima *acronym* ♦ Scientific Instrument Manufacturers' Association of Great Britain

Simca *acronym* ♦ Société Industrielle de Mécanique et Carrosserie Automobiles (French, = Car Engine and Coachbuilding Company) (French car manufacturers)

simd *abbrev.* ♦ single instruction, multiple data

SIMG *abbrev.* ♦ Societas Internationalis Medicinae Generalis (Latin, = International Society of General Medicine)

SIMM *abbrev.* ♦ single in-line memory module

SIN *abbrev.* ♦ Singapore (airport baggage label)

sin *shortening* ♦ sine

sing. *shortening* ♦ singular ♦ singulorum (Latin, = of each) (ingredient)

Sing. *shortening* ♦ Singapore ♦ Singaporean

sio *abbrev.* ♦ serial input/output

sipo *acronym* ♦ serial in, parallel out

SIPS *abbrev.* ♦ side impact protection system

Sir. *shortening* ♦ Sirach (book of Bible)

SIS *abbrev.* ♦ Satellite Information Services ♦ Secret Intelligence Service

SISD *abbrev.* ♦ Scottish Information Service for the Disabled

Sister *acronym* ♦ Special Institutions for Scientific and Technical Education and Research

sit. *shortening* ♦ situated ♦ situation

SITC *abbrev.* ♦ Standard International Trade Classification

Sitpro *acronym* ♦ Simpler Trade Procedures Board (orig. Simplification of International Trade Procedures)

sitt. *shortening* ♦ sitting room

sit. vac. *shortening* ♦ situation vacant

SIW *abbrev.* ♦ self-inflicted wound

SIWA *abbrev.* ♦ Scottish Inland Waterways Association

SJ *abbrev.* ♦ Glasgow (British vehicle registration mark) ♦ Society of Jesus (Jesuits)

sj *abbrev.* ♦ sub judice (Latin, = under trial)

SJAA *abbrev.* ♦ St John Ambulance Association

SJAB *abbrev.* ♦ St John Ambulance Brigade

SJBI *abbrev.* ♦ Scottish Joint Breast-Feeding Initiative

SJC *abbrev.* ♦ standing joint committee

SJCRE *abbrev.* ♦ Scottish Joint Committee on Religious Education

SJF *abbrev.* ♦ Scottish Judo Federation

SJJ *abbrev.* ♦ Sarajevo (airport baggage label)

SK *abbrev.* ♦ Inverness (British vehicle registration mark) ♦ Sealed Knot ♦ Skandinavian Airlines (airline baggage code) ♦ Stockport (UK postcode)

sk. *shortening* ♦ sketch

SKC *abbrev.* ♦ Scottish Kennel Club

SKD *abbrev.* ♦ Samarkand (airport baggage label)

SKFA *abbrev.* ♦ Scottish Keep Fit Association

SKG *abbrev.* ♦ Salonika (airport baggage label)

Skm *contraction* ♦ Stockholm

SKr *abbrev.* ♦ Swedish krona (monetary unit)

Skr. *shortening* ♦ Sanskrit

Skt *contraction* ♦ Sanskrit

SL *abbrev.* ♦ Dundee (British vehicle registration mark) ♦ sea level ♦ Sergeant-at-Law ♦ Slough (UK postcode) ♦ Sierra Leone ♦ Solicitor at Law ♦ Squadron Leader

sl. *shortening* ♦ slightly

SLA *abbrev.* ♦ School Libraries Association ♦ Scottish Library Association

Slade *acronym* ♦ Society of Lithographic Artists, Designers, Engravers and Process Workers

Slam *acronym* ◆ stand-off land-attack missile

Slar *acronym* ◆ side-looking airborne radar

SLAS *abbrev.* ◆ Society for Latin American Studies

Slash *acronym* ◆ Scottish Local Authorities Special Housing Group

Slav. *shortening* ◆ Slavonic

SLBM *abbrev.* ◆ submarine-launched ballistic missile

SLC *abbrev.* ◆ Salt Lake City (airport baggage label) ◆ Scottish Land Court ◆ Scottish Law Commission ◆ Surgeon Lieutenant-Commander

SLCM *abbrev.* ◆ sea-launched cruise missile

SLD *abbrev.* ◆ self-locking device ◆ Social and Liberal Democrats

sld *contraction* ◆ sailed ◆ sealed ◆ sold

SLDP *abbrev.* ◆ Social and Liberal Democratic Party

SLdr *abbrev.* ◆ Squadron Leader

SLE *abbrev.* ◆ systemic lupus erythematosus

S-level *contraction* ◆ Scholarship Level ◆ Special Level

SLF *abbrev.* ◆ Scottish Landowners' Federation

slf *abbrev.* ◆ straight line frequency

SLGA *abbrev.* ◆ Scottish Ladies' Golfing Association

SLLA *abbrev.* ◆ Scottish Ladies' Lacrosse Association

SLM *abbrev.* ◆ ship-launched missile

SLMC *abbrev.* ◆ Scottish Ladies' Mountaineering Club

SLO *abbrev.* ◆ senior liaison officer ◆ Slovenia

SLOA *abbrev.* ◆ Steam Locomotive Operators' Association

SLP *abbrev.* ◆ Scottish Labour Party

slp *abbrev.* ◆ sine legitima prole (Latin, = without legitimate issue)

SLR *abbrev.* ◆ single-lens reflex ◆ self-loading rifle ◆ Sri Lanka rupee (monetary unit)

SLRS *abbrev.* ◆ Sexual Law Reform Society

SLTA *abbrev.* ◆ Scottish Lawn Tennis Association ◆ Scottish Licensed Trade Association

SLV *abbrev.* ◆ Society of Licensed Victuallers ◆ space launch vehicle ◆ standard launch vehicle

sly *contraction* ◆ slowly

SM *abbrev.* ◆ Glasgow (British vehicle registration mark) ◆ sado-masochism ◆ sado-masochist ◆ sales manager ◆ Scientiae Magister (Master of Science) ◆ Sergeant-Major ◆ stage manager ◆ stipendiary magistrate ◆ strategic missile ◆ Surgeon Major ◆ Sutton (UK postcode) ◆ systolic murmur

Sm *symbol* ◆ samarium (chemical element)

sm. *shortening* ◆ small

SMAC *abbrev.* ◆ Standing Medical Advisory Committee (NHS)

SMATV *abbrev.* ◆ satellite master antenna television

SMBF *abbrev.* ◆ Scottish Musicians' Benevolent Fund

SMBG *abbrev.* ◆ self-monitoring of blood glucose

SMC *abbrev.* ◆ School Meals Campaign ◆ Scottish Mountaineering Club ◆ Scottish Museums Council

SMD *abbrev.* ◆ senile macular degeneration ◆ surface-mounted device

SME *abbrev.* ◆ Sancta Mater Ecclesia (Latin, = Holy Mother Church) ◆ Suriname (international vehicle registration)

SMetO *abbrev.* ◆ Senior Meteorological Officer

SMG *abbrev.* ◆ submachine-gun

SMGC *abbrev.* ◆ Scottish Marriage Guidance Council

SMI *abbrev.* ◆ Samos (airport baggage label)

Smith. Inst. *shortening* ◆ Smithsonian Institution

SML *abbrev.* ◆ Science Museum Library

sml *abbrev.* ◆ small, medium, large (range of clothing etc sizes)

sml *contraction* ◆ small

SMM *abbrev.* ◆ Sancta Mater Maria (Latin, = Holy Mother Mary)

SMMB *abbrev.* ◆ Scottish Milk Marketing Board

SMMT *abbrev.* ◆ Society of Motor Manufacturers and Traders

SMO *abbrev.* ◆ Senior Medical Officer

SMP *abbrev.* ◆ Statutory Maternity Pay

smp *abbrev.* ◆ sine mascula prole (Latin, = without male issue)

SMR *abbrev.* ◆ standard metabolic rate ◆ standard mortality rate

SMRC *abbrev.* ◆ Scottish Motor Racing Club

SMRE *abbrev.* ◆ Safety in Mines Research Establishment

SMS *abbrev.* ◆ Shipwrecked Mariners' Society

SMTA *abbrev.* ◆ Scottish Motor Trade Association

SMTF *abbrev.* ◆ Scottish Milk Trade Federation

SMTWTFS *abbrev.* ◆ Sunday Monday Tuesday Wednesday Thursday Friday Saturday

SMWS *abbrev.* ◆ Scottish Malt Whisky Society

SN *abbrev.* ◆ Dundee (British vehicle registration mark) ◆ Sabena (airline baggage code) ◆ Senegal (international vehicle registration) ◆ Swindon (UK postcode)

Sn *symbol* ◆ stannum (Latin, = tin) (chemical element)

sn *abbrev.* ◆ secundum naturam (Latin, = according to nature) ◆ sine nomine (Latin, = without name) ◆ sub nomine (Latin, = under the name)

s/n *abbrev.* ◆ serial number ◆ service number ◆ signal-to-noise (ratio)

SNA *abbrev.* ◆ Scottish Netball Association ◆ Systems Network Architecture (software operating system)

snafu *acronym* ◆ situation normal—all fucked up

Snap *acronym* ◆ Shelter Neighbourhood Action Project ◆ systems for auxiliary nuclear power

SNBTS *abbrev.* ◆ Scottish National Blood Transfusion Service

SNCFB *abbrev.* ◆ Société Nationale de Chemins de Fer Belges (French, = Belgian National Railway Company)

SNCF *abbrev.* ◆ Société Nationale des Chemins de Fer Français (French, = French National Railway Company)

SNF *abbrev.* ◆ solids, non-fat

SNFU *abbrev.* ◆ Scottish National Farmers' Union

SNG *abbrev.* ◆ synthetic natural gas

SNH *abbrev.* ◆ Scottish National Heritage

snig *acronym* ◆ sustainable noninflationary growth

SNLA *abbrev.* ◆ Scottish National Liberation Army

snlr *abbrev.* ◆ services no longer required

SNLV *abbrev.* ◆ strategic nuclear launch vehicle

SNN *abbrev.* ◆ Shannon (airport baggage label)

SNO *abbrev.* ◆ Scottish National Orchestra ◆ Senior Naval Officer ◆ Senior Nursing Officer

SNP *abbrev.* ◆ Scottish National Party

SNR *abbrev.* ◆ signal-to-noise ratio ◆ Society for Nautical Research

snr *contraction* ◆ senior

SNSC *abbrev.* ◆ Scottish National Ski Council

SNSS *abbrev.* ◆ School Natural Science Society

SNU *abbrev.* ◆ Spiritualists' National Union

Snug *acronym* ◆ Scottish Network Users' Group

SO *abbrev.* ◆ Aberdeen (British vehicle registration mark) ◆ Scottish Office ◆ Signal Officer ◆ Somalia (international vehicle registration) ◆ Southampton (UK postcode) ◆ special order ◆ Staff Officer ◆ standing order

♦ Stationery Office ♦ sub-office
♦ symphony orchestra

so *abbrev.* ♦ seller's option ♦ shipping order

SOA *abbrev.* ♦ Scottish Orienteering Association

SoA *abbrev.* ♦ Society of Authors

soa *abbrev.* ♦ state of the art

SOAS *abbrev.* ♦ School of Oriental and African Studies

SOB *abbrev.* ♦ shortness of breath

sob *abbrev.* ♦ silly old bastard ♦ son of a bitch

SOBHD *abbrev.* ♦ Scottish Official Board of Highland Dancing

SOC *abbrev.* ♦ Scottish Ornithologists' Club

soc. *shortening* ♦ social ♦ socialist ♦ society

sociol. *shortening* ♦ sociological ♦ sociologist ♦ sociology

SOCO *abbrev.* ♦ scene-of-crime officer

socy *contraction* ♦ society

SOE *abbrev.* ♦ Special Operations Executive (World War II)

SOED *abbrev.* ♦ Scottish Office Education Department ♦ Shorter Oxford English Dictionary

SOF *abbrev.* ♦ share of freehold ♦ Sofia (airport baggage label)

S of S *abbrev.* ♦ Secretary of State ♦ Song of Solomon *or* Song of Songs (book of Bible)

S of III Ch. *shortening* ♦ Song of the Three Children (book of Bible)

Sogat *acronym* ♦ Society of Graphical and Allied Trades

SOH *abbrev.* ♦ sense of humour

Sol. *shortening* ♦ Song of Solomon (book of Bible)

sol. *shortening* ♦ solicitor ♦ soluble ♦ solution

Sol.-Gen. *shortening* ♦ Solicitor-General

soln *contraction* ♦ solution

solr *contraction* ♦ solicitor

solv. *shortening* ♦ solve (Latin, = dissolve) ♦ solvent

SOM *abbrev.* ♦ Society of Occupational Medicine

Som. *shortening* ♦ Somerset

SON *abbrev.* ♦ Spear of the Nation (former military wing of the African National Congress)

SOP *abbrev.* ♦ significant other person ♦ standard operating procedure ♦ sum of products

sop. *shortening* ♦ soprano

soph. *shortening* ♦ sophomore

SOR *abbrev.* ♦ sale or return

Sorg *acronym* ♦ Stratospheric Ozone Review Group

SOS *abbrev.* ♦ save our souls (international radio distress signal; the letters were chosen as the clearest to transmit and receive in Morse code)

SoS *abbrev.* ♦ Secretary of State

sos *abbrev.* ♦ si opus sit (Latin, = if necessary)

sost. *shortening* ♦ sostenuto (Italian, = sustained)

SOT *abbrev.* ♦ stay-on tab

Soton *contraction* ♦ Southampton

SOU *abbrev.* ♦ Southampton (airport baggage label)

Southwark. *shortening* ♦ Southwarkensis (Latin, = of Southwark)

Southwell. *shortening* ♦ Southwellensis (Latin, = of Southwell)

SOV *abbrev.* ♦ subject-object-verb

Sov. *shortening* ♦ Soviet

sov *abbrev.* ♦ shut-off valve

sov. *shortening* ♦ sovereign

Soweto *acronym* ♦ Southwestern Townships (South Africa)

SP *abbrev.* ♦ Dundee (British vehicle registration mark) ♦ Salisbury (UK postcode) ♦ Socialist Party ♦ starting price (horse-race betting) ♦ submarine patrol

Sp. *shortening* ♦ Spain ♦ Spanish

sp *abbrev.* ♦ self-propelled ♦ sine prole (Latin, = without issue) ♦ stop payment

sp. *shortening* ♦ species ♦ specimen ♦ speed ♦ spelling

SPA *abbrev.* ◆ Scottish Pipers' Association ◆ Scottish Pistol Association ◆ Scottish Publishers' Association

SpA *abbrev.* ◆ Società per Azioni (Italian, = PLC)

Spab *acronym* ◆ Society for the Protection of Ancient Buildings

Spac *acronym* ◆ Standing Pharmaceutical Advisory Committee (NHS)

spac. *shortening* ◆ spacious

Span. *shortening* ◆ Spaniard ◆ Spanish

Spana *acronym* ◆ Society for the Protection of Animals in North Africa

sparc *acronym* ◆ scalable processor architecture

SPBA *abbrev.* ◆ Scottish Pipe Band Association

SPBP *abbrev.* ◆ Society for the Preservation of Birds of Prey

SPBW *abbrev.* ◆ Society for the Preservation of Beers from the Wood

SPC *abbrev.* ◆ Southern Pacific Commission ◆ stored program control

SPCK *abbrev.* ◆ Society for Promoting Christian Knowledge

spd *contraction* ◆ speed (of vehicle gearbox) ◆ subject to permission to deal

SPDA *abbrev.* ◆ single-premium deferred annuity

SPE *abbrev.* ◆ Society for Pure English

Spec *acronym* ◆ South Pacific Bureau for Economic Co-operation

spec. *shortening* ◆ special ◆ specific ◆ specifically ◆ specification ◆ speculation

specif. *shortening* ◆ specific ◆ specifically ◆ specification

Spect *acronym* ◆ single photon emission computed tomography

SPES *abbrev.* ◆ South Place Ethical Society

Spet *acronym* ◆ single photon emission tomography

SPF *abbrev.* ◆ sun protection factor

SPG *abbrev.* ◆ Society for the Propagation of the Gospel ◆ Special Patrol Group

SPGA *abbrev.* ◆ Scottish Professional Golfers' Association

SPGB *abbrev.* ◆ Socialist Party of Great Britain

sp. gr. *shortening* ◆ specific gravity

spirit. *shortening* ◆ spiritoso (Italian, = lively) (music)

SPKC *abbrev.* ◆ Small Pig Keepers' Council

spl *abbrev.* ◆ sine prole legitima (Latin, = without legitimate issue)

spm *abbrev.* ◆ sine prole mascula (Latin, = without male issue)

SPMO *abbrev.* ◆ Senior Principal Medical Officer

SPMU *abbrev.* ◆ Society of Professional Musicians in Ulster

SPNM *abbrev.* ◆ Society for the Promotion of New Music

SPNR *abbrev.* ◆ Society for the Promotion of Nature Reserves

SPOA *abbrev.* ◆ Scottish Prison Officers' Association

Spoof *acronym* ◆ Society for the Perpetration of Outrageous Farces

s/pool *contraction* ◆ swimming pool

Spore *acronym* ◆ Society for the Preservation of the Rain-Forest Environment

SPP *abbrev.* ◆ sub-pubic prostatectomy

SPQR *abbrev.* ◆ Senatus Populusque Romanus (Latin, = Senate and people of Rome) ◆ small profits and quick returns

SPR *abbrev.* ◆ Society for Psychical Research ◆ strategic petroleum reserve

Spr *contraction* ◆ Sapper

spr. *shortening* ◆ spring ◆ sprung

Spr *contraction* ◆ Sapper

SPRC *abbrev.* ◆ Society for the Prevention and Relief of Cancer

SPRI *abbrev.* ◆ Scott Polar Research Institute

Sprint *acronym* ◆ solid-propellant rocket-intercept missile

sprl *abbrev.* ◆ Société de Personnes à Responsabilité Limitée (French, = Ltd)

SPS *abbrev.* ◆ Scottish Painters' Society

sps *abbrev.* ◆ sine prole superstite (Latin, = without surviving offspring)

SPSO *abbrev.* ◆ Senior Principal Scientific Officer

SPU *abbrev.* ◆ Split (airport baggage label)

Spuc *acronym* ◆ Society for the Protection of the Unborn Child

SPVD *abbrev.* ◆ Society for the Prevention of Venereal Disease

sp. vol. *shortening* ◆ specific volume

SQ *abbrev.* ◆ Singapore Airlines (airline baggage code)

sq *abbrev.* ◆ stereophonic-quadraphonic

sq. *shortening* ◆ sequens (Latin, = following) ◆ squadron ◆ square

SQA *abbrev.* ◆ software quality assurance

sq cm *shortening* ◆ square centimetre

sqd *contraction* ◆ squad

sq ft *shortening* ◆ square foot

sq in *shortening* ◆ square inch

sq km *shortening* ◆ square kilometre

SQL *abbrev.* ◆ standard query language ◆ structured query language

sq m *shortening* ◆ square metre

sq mi *shortening* ◆ square mile

sq mm *shortening* ◆ square millimetre

SQMS *abbrev.* ◆ Staff Quartermaster Sergeant

sqn *contraction* ◆ squadron

Sqn Ldr *contraction* ◆ Squadron Leader

SqnQMS *abbrev.* ◆ Squadron Quartermaster Sergeant

SqnSM *abbrev.* ◆ Squadron Sergeant Major

SqO *abbrev.* ◆ Squadron Officer

squid *abbrev.* ◆ superconducting quantum interference device

sq yd *shortening* ◆ square yard

SR *abbrev.* ◆ Dundee (British vehicle registration mark) ◆ Saudi Arabian riyal (monetary unit) ◆ Saunders Roe ◆ Senior Registrar ◆ Southern Region ◆ Sunderland (UK postcode) ◆ Swissair (airline baggage code)

Sr *abbrev.* ◆ Señor (Spanish, = Mr) ◆ Sir ◆ Sister

Sr *symbol* ◆ strontium (British vehicle registration mark)

sr *abbrev.* ◆ self-raising

sr *contraction* ◆ senior

sr *shortening* ◆ steradian

s/r *abbrev.* ◆ sale or return

SRA *abbrev.* ◆ Snail Racing Association ◆ Squash Rackets Association

Sra *contraction* ◆ Senhora (Portuguese, = Mrs) ◆ Señora (Spanish, = Mrs)

SRA *abbrev.* ◆ Squash Rackets Association

SRAM *acronym* ◆ static random access memory

Sram *acronym* ◆ short-range attack missile

SRAP *abbrev.* ◆ Scottish Rent Assessment Panel

SRBM *abbrev.* ◆ short range ballistic missile

SRC *abbrev.* ◆ Science Research Council ◆ Sociedad Regolar Collectiva (Spanish, = partnership) ◆ Student Representative Council

srcc *abbrev.* ◆ strikes, riots and civil commotion

SRCh *abbrev.* ◆ State Registered Chiropodist

SRCN *abbrev.* ◆ State Registered Children's Nurse

SRDE *abbrev.* ◆ Signals Research and Development Establishment

SRE *abbrev.* ◆ Sancta Romana Ecclesia (Latin, = Holy Roman Church)

SRG *abbrev.* ◆ Strategic Research Group

SRHE *abbrev.* ◆ Society for Research into Higher Education

SRIS *abbrev.* ◆ Science Reference Information Service

Srl *abbrev.* ◆ Società a Responsabilità Limitata (Italian, = Ltd)

SRI *abbrev.* ◆ Saudi Arabian riyal (monetary unit)

SRM *abbrev.* ◆ short-range missile

SRMN *abbrev.* ◆ State Registered Mental Nurse

SRN *abbrev.* ◆ State Registered Nurse

sRNA *abbrev.* ◆ soluble ribonuleic acid

SRO *abbrev.* ◆ Scottish Record Office ◆ self-regulatory organization ◆ single room occupancy ◆ standing room only ◆ statutory rules and orders

s/roof *contraction* ◆ sun roof

SRP *abbrev.* ◆ Society of Recorder Players ◆ State Registered Physiotherapist ◆ suggested retail price

SRPA *abbrev.* ◆ Squash Rackets Professional Association

SRPS *abbrev.* ◆ Scottish Railway Preservation Society

SRR *abbrev.* ◆ Society for Research in Rehabilitation

SRS *abbrev.* ◆ Scottish Record Society ◆ Societatis Regiae Sodalis (Latin, = Fellow of the Royal Society)

Srta *contraction* ◆ Senhorita (Portuguese, = Miss) ◆ Señorita (Spanish, = Miss)

SRU *abbrev.* ◆ Scottish Rugby Union

SRWS *abbrev.* ◆ Scottish Rights of Way Society

SS *abbrev.* ◆ Aberdeen (British vehicle registration mark) ◆ Secretary of State ◆ Schutzstaffel (German, = protection group) (Nazi special police force, orig. (1925) party paramilitaries and Hitler's bodyguard; later in charge of captured countries and concentration camps; also (Waffen SS) the title of special shock troops in the German army 1940–5) ◆ screw steamer ◆ Social Security ◆ Southend-on-Sea (UK postcode) ◆ Spastics Society ◆ steamship ◆ surface to surface (of missile etc)

ss *contraction* ◆ semis (Latin, = half)

ss. *shortening* ◆ subsection

SSA *abbrev.* ◆ Scottish Schoolmasters' Association ◆ Scottish Skateboard Association ◆ Society of Scottish Artists ◆ standard spending assessment

SSAC *abbrev.* ◆ Scottish Sub-Aqua Club ◆ Social Security Advisory Committee

SSAE *abbrev.* ◆ stamped self-addressed envelope

SSAFA *abbrev.* ◆ Soldiers', Sailors', and Airmen's Families Association

SSAP *abbrev.* ◆ Statement of Standard Accounting Practice

SSC *abbrev.* ◆ Scottish Ski Club ◆ Scottish Sports Council ◆ short service commission ◆ Solicitor to the Supreme Court

SSD *abbrev.* ◆ Sanctissimus Dominus (Latin, = the most holy lord) (the Pope) ◆ Social Services Department

SSE *abbrev.* ◆ south-south-east

SSEC *abbrev.* ◆ Secondary Schools Examinations Council

SSEES *abbrev.* ◆ School of Slavonic and East European Studies

SSEG *abbrev.* ◆ Scottish Solar Energy Group

SSF *abbrev.* ◆ Society of St Francis

SSFA *abbrev.* ◆ Scottish Schools' Football Association

SSGBP *abbrev.* ◆ Society of Snuff Grinders, Blenders and Purveyors

S/Sgt *contraction* ◆ Staff Sergeant

SSHA *abbrev.* ◆ Scottish Special Housing Association

SSHC *abbrev.* ◆ Society to Support Home Confinement

SSI *abbrev.* ◆ site of scientific interest ◆ Social Services Inspectorate

SSJE *abbrev.* ◆ Society of St John the Evangelist (Cowley Fathers)

SSLH *abbrev.* ◆ Society for the Study of Labour History

SSM *abbrev.* ◆ Saturday, Sunday, Monday ◆ Staff Sergeant-Major ◆ surface to surface missile

SSMH *abbrev.* ◆ Scottish Society for the Mentally Handicapped

SSN *abbrev.* ◆ severely subnormal ◆ standard serial number

SSO *abbrev.* ◆ Senior Supply Officer

SSP *abbrev.* ◆ Scottish Socialist Party ◆ statutory sick pay

SSPCA *abbrev.* ◆ Scottish Society for the Prevention of Cruelty to Animals

SSPWB *abbrev.* ◆ Scottish Society for the Protection of Wild Birds

SSR *abbrev.* ◆ Soviet Socialist Republic

SSRA *abbrev.* ◆ Scottish Squash Rackets Association

SSRC *abbrev.* ◆ Social Science Research Council

SSRI *abbrev.* ◆ selective seratonin uptake inhibitor (antidepressant drug)

SSS *abbrev.* ◆ Secretary of State for Scotland ◆ sick sinus syndrome ◆ Simplified Spelling Society ◆ standard scratch score

SSSA *abbrev.* ◆ Scottish Salmon Smokers' Association ◆ Scottish Schools Swimming Association

SSSI *abbrev.* ◆ site of special scientific interest

SSSR *abbrev.* ◆ Soyuz Sovietskikh Sotsialisticheskikh Respublik (Russian, = Union of Soviet Socialist Republics)

SSSU *abbrev.* ◆ Scottish Speed Skating Union

SST *abbrev.* ◆ Scottish Scenic Trust ◆ supersonic transport

SSTA *abbrev.* ◆ Scottish Secondary Teachers' Association

SSTC *abbrev.* ◆ sold subject to contract

SSU *abbrev.* ◆ Sunday School Union

s/susp. *shortening* ◆ sports suspension

SSW *abbrev.* ◆ south-south-west

ST *abbrev.* ◆ Belize Airways ◆ Inverness (British vehicle registration mark) ◆ sanitary towel ◆ septic tank ◆ Standard Time ◆ Stoke-on-Trent (UK postcode) ◆ Summer Time

St *contraction* ◆ Saint ◆ Strait ◆ Street

st *abbrev.* ◆ short ton

st *contraction* ◆ seat

st. *shortening* ◆ stanza ◆ stone (weight) ◆ street ◆ strophe ◆ stumped (cricket)

STA *abbrev.* ◆ Sail Training Association

Sta *contraction* ◆ Santa (Italian, Portuguese, Spanish, = saint) (of a woman) ◆ Señorita (Spanish, = Miss)

sta. *shortening* ◆ station ◆ stationary

StAAA *abbrev.* ◆ St Andrew's Ambulance Association

stab. *shortening* ◆ stabilizer

stacc. *shortening* ◆ staccato (Italian, = detached) (music)

Staffs. *shortening* ◆ Staffordshire

Stags *acronym* ◆ sterling accruable government securities

stand. *shortening* ◆ standard

Start *acronym* ◆ Strategic Arms Reduction Talks ◆ Strategic Arms Reduction Treaty

stat. *shortening* ◆ statim (Latin, = immediately) ◆ statistic ◆ statute

Stat. Hall *contraction* ◆ Stationers' Hall

STAUK *abbrev.* ◆ Seed Trade Association of the United Kingdom

STB *abbrev.* ◆ Sacrae Theologiae Baccalaureus (Latin, = Bachelor of Sacred Theology) ◆ Scottish Tourist Board

stbd *contraction* ◆ starboard

STC *abbrev.* ◆ short-title catalogue ◆ Standard Telephones and Cables Ltd ◆ subject to contract

STD *abbrev.* ◆ Sacrae Theologiae Doctor ◆ sexually transmitted disease ◆ subscriber trunk dialling

std *contraction* ◆ standard

STE *abbrev.* ◆ Society of Telecom Executives

Ste *contraction* ◆ Sainte (French, = Saint) (of a woman)

Sté *contraction* ◆ Société (French, = Company)

Stem *acronym* ◆ scanning transmission electron microscopy

sten. *shortening* ◆ stenographer ◆ stenography

steno. *shortening* ◆ stenographic

stenog. *shortening* ◆ stenographer ◆ stenography

Step *acronym* ◆ Special Temporary Employment Programme

ster. *shortening* ◆ sterling

St. Ex. *shortening* ◆ Stock Exchange

stg *contraction* ◆ seating ◆ sterling

stge *contraction* ◆ storage

STGWU *abbrev.* ◆ Scottish Transport and General Workers' Union

STH *abbrev.* ◆ somatotrophic hormone

sth *contraction* ◆ south

sthn *contraction* ◆ southern

STIM *abbrev.* ◆ scanning transmission ion microscope

stip. *shortening* ◆ stipend ◆ stipendiary ◆ stipulation

STIR *abbrev.* ◆ surplus to immediate requirements

Stir. *shortening* ◆ Stirlingshire (former Scottish county)

stk *contraction* ◆ stock

STLO *abbrev.* ◆ scientific and technical liaison officer

STM *abbrev.* ◆ Sacrae Theologiae Magister ◆ scanning tunnelling microscope ◆ scientific, technical and medical ◆ short-term memory

stn *contraction* ◆ station

stnry *contraction* ◆ stationery

STO *abbrev.* ◆ senior technical officer ◆ Stockholm (British vehicle registration mark)

stockrm *contraction* ◆ stockroom

STOL *abbrev.* ◆ short take-off and landing

STOLVCD *abbrev.* ◆ short take-off and landing, vertical climb and descent

Stop *acronym* ◆ suction termination of pregnancy

Stopp *acronym* ◆ Society of Teachers Opposed to Physical Punishment

STP *abbrev.* ◆ Sacrae Theologiae Professor (Latin, = Professor of Sacred Theology) ◆ scientifically treated petroleum (colloquial name for a hallucinogenic drug)

stp *abbrev.* ◆ standard temperature and pressure

STR *abbrev.* ◆ Stuttgart (airport baggage label)

str *abbrev.* ◆ surplus to requirements

str *contraction* ◆ steamer

Str. *shortening* ◆ Strasse (German, = Street)

str. *shortening* ◆ straight ◆ strait ◆ strength ◆ strings ◆ stroke (rowing) ◆ strong ◆ structure

stratig. *shortening* ◆ stratigraphy

strep. *shortening* ◆ streptococcal ◆ streptococcus

STATES OF THE USA

For each state the official abbreviation (where one exists) is followed by that used in the US postcode system.

Ala, AL *Alabama*	**La, LA** *Louisiana*	**NY** *New York*
Alas., AK *Alaska*	**Me, ME** *Maine*	**OH** *Ohio*
Ariz., AZ *Arizona*	**Md, MD** *Maryland*	**Okla, OK** *Oklahoma*
Ark., AR *Arkansas*	**Mass., MA** *Massachusetts*	**Oreg., OR** *Oregon*
Calif., CA *California*	**Mich., MI** *Michigan*	**Pa, PA** *Pennsylvania*
Col., CO *Colorado*	**Minn., MN** *Minnesota*	**RI** *Rhode Island*
Conn., CT *Connecticut*	**Miss., MS** *Mississippi*	**SC** *South Carolina*
Del., DE *Delaware*	**Mo., MO** *Missouri*	**SDak, SD** *South Dakota*
Fla, FL *Florida*	**Mont., MT** *Montana*	**Tenn., TN** *Tennessee*
Ga, GA *Georgia*	**Nebr., NB** *Nebraska*	**Tex., TX** *Texas*
HI *Hawaii*	**Nev., NV** *Nevada*	**UT** *Utah*
ID *Idaho*	**NC** *North Carolina*	**Va, VA** *Virginia*
Ill., IL *Illinois*	**NDak, ND** *North Dakota*	**Vt, VT** *Vermont*
Ind., IN *Indiana*	**NH** *New Hampshire*	**Wash., WA** *Washington*
Ia, IA *Iowa*		**Wis., WI** *Wisconsin*
Kan., KS *Kansas*	**NJ** *New Jersey*	**WVa, WV** *West Virginia*
Ky, KY *Kentucky*	**NMex, NM** *New Mexico*	**Wyo., WY** *Wyoming*

STRG *abbrev.* ◆ Scottish Tory Reform Group

string. *shortening* ◆ stringendo (Italian, = tightening)

Strive *acronym* ◆ Society for the Preservation of Rural Industries and Village Enterprises

STS *abbrev.* ◆ Scottish Tartans Society ◆ Scottish Text Society

STSF *abbrev.* ◆ Scottish Target Shooting Federation

STSO *abbrev.* ◆ senior technical staff officer

STTA *abbrev.* ◆ Scottish Table Tennis Association

STUC *abbrev.* ◆ Scottish Trades Union Congress

stud. *shortening* ◆ student

STV *abbrev.* ◆ Scottish Television ◆ single transferable vote

stvdr *contraction* ◆ stevedore

stwy *contraction* ◆ stairway

SU *abbrev.* ◆ Aeroflot (airline baggage code) ◆ Glasgow (British vehicle registration mark) ◆ Scripture Union ◆ Soviet Union

Su. *shortening* ◆ Sunday

sub. *shortening* ◆ subaltern ◆ subeditor ◆ subito (Italian, = suddenly) (music) ◆ subject ◆ subjunctive ◆ submarine ◆ subordinate ◆ subscription ◆ subsidiary ◆ substitute

SUBAW *abbrev.* ◆ Scottish Union of Bakers and Allied Workers

subd. *shortening* ◆ subdivide ◆ subdivision

subed. *shortening* ◆ subeditor

subj. *shortening* ◆ subject ◆ subjective ◆ subjunctive

Sub-Lieut. *shortening* ◆ Sub-Lieutenant

Sub-Lt *contraction* ◆ Sub-Lieutenant

subs. *shortening* ◆ subsistence

subseq. *shortening* ◆ subsequent

subsp. *shortening* ◆ subspecies

subst. *shortening* ◆ substantive ◆ substitute

substand. *shortening* ◆ substandard

succ. *shortening* ◆ success ◆ successive ◆ successor

SUD *abbrev.* ◆ Sudan (international vehicle registration)

Suds *acronym* ◆ sudden unexplained death syndrome

Suff. *shortening* ◆ Suffolk

suff. *shortening* ◆ sufficient ◆ suffix

suffr. *shortening* ◆ suffragan

suffoc. *shortening* ◆ suffocation

sug. *shortening* ◆ suggestion

Sult. *shortening* ◆ Sultan

SUM *abbrev.* ◆ surface-to-underwater missile

sum. *shortening* ◆ sume (Latin, = take) ◆ summary ◆ summer

sums *contraction* ◆ summons

Sun. *shortening* ◆ Sunday

Suns *acronym* ◆ sonic underwater navigation system

SUNY *abbrev.* ◆ State University of New York

sup. *shortening* ◆ superfine ◆ superior ◆ superlative ◆ supine ◆ supplement ◆ supra (Latin, = above) ◆ supreme

Sup. Ct. *shortening* ◆ Superior Court ◆ Supreme Court

super. *shortening* ◆ supernumerary

superhet. *shortening* ◆ superheterodyne

superl. *shortening* ◆ superlative

supp. *shortening* ◆ supplement ◆ supplementary

suppl. *shortening* ◆ supplement ◆ supplementary

supr. *shortening* ◆ superior ◆ supreme

Supt *contraction* ◆ Superintendent

Sur. *shortening* ◆ Surrey

surf *acronym* ◆ spent unreprocessed fuel

surg. *shortening* ◆ surgeon ◆ surgery ◆ surgical

Surg. Cdr *contraction* ◆ Surgeon Commander

Surg. Gen. *shortening* ◆ Surgeon General

Surg. Lt-Cdr *contraction* ◆ Surgeon Lieutenant-Commander

Surg.-Maj. *shortening* ◆ Surgeon-Major

surr. *shortening* ◆ surrender ◆ surrogate

surv *acronym* ◆ standard underwater research vessel

surv. *shortening* ◆ survey ◆ surviving

Surv.-Gen. *shortening* ◆ Surveyor-General

SUS *abbrev.* ◆ Scottish Union of Students

Sus. *shortening* ◆ Susanna (book of Bible)

susp. *shortening* ◆ suspend ◆ suspension

Suss. *shortening* ◆ Sussex

SUT *abbrev.* ◆ Society for Underwater Technology

Suth. *shortening* ◆ Sutherland (former Scottish county)

SV *abbrev.* ◆ Sancta Virgo (Latin, = Holy Virgin) ◆ Sanctitas Vestra (Latin, = your Holiness) ◆ Saudi Arabian Airlines ◆ simian virus

Sv *shortening* ◆ sievert

sv *abbrev.* ◆ sub verbo (Latin, = under the word) ◆ sub voce (Latin, = under the heading)

s/v *abbrev.* ◆ surrender value

SVA *abbrev.* ◆ Scottish Volleyball Association

SVC *abbrev.* ◆ superior vena cava

svce *contraction* ◆ service

SVD *abbrev.* ◆ swine vesicular disease

svg *contraction* ◆ saving

S-VHS *abbrev.* ◆ Super Video Home System

SVO *abbrev.* ◆ subject, verb, object

SVP *abbrev.* ◆ s'il vous plaît (French, = please)

svr *abbrev.* ◆ spiritus vini rectificatus (Latin, = rectified spirit of wine)

SVQ *abbrev.* ◆ Seville (airport baggage label)

SVS *abbrev.* ◆ still-camera video system

SW *abbrev.* ◆ Glasgow (British vehicle registration mark) ◆ short wave ◆ small women's (clothing size) ◆ south-west ◆ south-western ◆ south-west London (UK postcode)

S/W *abbrev.* ◆ software

Sw. *shortening* ◆ Sweden ◆ Swedish ◆ Swiss

SWA *abbrev.* ◆ Scotch Whisky Association ◆ Society of Women Artists ◆ Namibia (international vehicle registration; orig. South-West Africa)

SWACS *abbrev.* ◆ Space Warning and Control System

swalk *acronym* ◆ sealed with a loving kiss

Swap *acronym* ◆ Scottish Women Against Pornography

Swapo *acronym* ◆ South-West Africa People's Organization

swb *abbrev.* ◆ short wheelbase

swbd *contraction* ◆ switchboard

Swed. *shortening* ◆ Sweden ◆ Swedish

Swet *abbrev.* ◆ Society of West End Theatres

SWF *abbrev.* ◆ single white female

SWFA *abbrev.* ◆ Scottish Women's Football Association

SwFr *abbrev.* ◆ Swiss franc (monetary unit)

SWG *abbrev.* ◆ Song Writers' Guild of Great Britain

swg *abbrev.* ◆ standard wire gauge

SWHA *abbrev.* ◆ Scottish Womens' Hockey Association

Swift *acronym* ◆ Society for Worldwide Interbank Financial Transmission

swing *acronym* ◆ sterling warrant into gilt-edged stock

Switz. *shortening* ◆ Switzerland

swl *abbrev.* ◆ safe working load

SWLA *abbrev.* ◆ Society of Wildlife Artists

SWM *abbrev.* ◆ single white male

SWMF *abbrev.* ◆ South Wales Miners' Federation

swot *acronym* ◆ strengths, weaknesses, opportunities and threats (product marketing analysis)

SWP *abbrev.* ◆ Socialist Workers' Party

swp *abbrev.* ◆ safe working pressure

SWPF *abbrev.* ◆ single white professional female

SWR *abbrev.* ◆ standing-wave ratio

SWRI *abbrev.* ◆ Scottish Women's Rural Institute

SWS *abbrev.* ◆ static water supply ◆ Swansea (airport baggage label)

SWT *abbrev.* ◆ Scottish Wildlife Trust

SX *abbrev.* ◆ Edinburgh (British vehicle registration mark) ◆ Sundays excepted

SXB *abbrev.* ◆ Strasbourg (airport baggage label)

SY *abbrev.* ◆ Seychelles (international vehicle registration) ◆ Shrewsbury (UK postcode) ◆ steam yacht

SYD *abbrev.* ◆ Sydney (airport baggage label)

SYHA *abbrev.* ◆ Scottish Youth Hostels Association

syll. *shortening* ◆ syllable ◆ syllabus

sym. *shortening* ◆ symbol ◆ symmetrical ◆ symphony ◆ symptom

symp. *shortening* ◆ symposium

syn. *shortening* ◆ synod ◆ synonym ◆ syonymous ◆ synthetic

sync. *shortening* ◆ synchronized ◆ synchronous

synd. *shortening* ◆ syndicate

synon. *shortening* ◆ synonymous

synop. *shortening* ◆ synopsis

synth. *shortening* ◆ synthesizer ◆ synthetic

SYR *abbrev.* ◆ Syria (international vehicle registration)

Syr. *shortening* ◆ Syria ◆ Syriac ◆ Syrian

syr. *shortening* ◆ syrup

sys. *shortening* ◆ system

syst. *shortening* ◆ system ◆ systematic

SYY *abbrev.* ◆ Stornoway (airport baggage label)

SZ *abbrev.* ◆ Down (British vehicle registration mark)

SZG *abbrev.* ◆ Salzburg (airport baggage label)

T

T *abbrev.* ◆ tablespoon ◆ tenor (music)
◆ tesla ◆ Thailand (international vehicle
registration) ◆ thousand (car mileage)
◆ Thursday ◆ Tuesday

t *abbrev.* ◆ tare ◆ temperature ◆ tense
◆ tera- ◆ tome (French, = volume) ◆ ton
◆ tonne ◆ transitive ◆ troy

TA *abbrev.* ◆ Exeter (British vehicle
registration mark) ◆ Taunton (UK
postcode) ◆ Territorial Army
◆ Transactional Analysis ◆ Tricycle
Association

Ta *symbol* ◆ tantalum (chemical element)

ta *abbrev.* ◆ target area ◆ time and
attendance

TAA *abbrev.* ◆ Territorial Army
Association

TA & VRA *abbrev.* ◆ Territorial, Auxiliary
and Volunteer Reserve Association

TAB *abbrev.* ◆ Tobago (airport baggage
label) ◆ typhoid-paratyphoid A and B
(vaccine)

TAB *shortening* ◆ tabulator (name of
typewriter etc key)

tab. *shortening* ◆ table (displayed list etc
in book) ◆ tabulation ◆ tabulator

Tabmac *acronym* ◆ The All British
Martial Arts Council

TAC *abbrev.* ◆ Theatres Advisory
Council ◆ Tobacco Advisory Council

tacan *acronym* ◆ tactical air navigation

Tafe *pronounced* tay-fee *acronym*
◆ Technical and Further Education

tafubar *acronym* ◆ things are fucked up
beyond all recognition

Tag *acronym* ◆ Towpaths Action Group

Tag. *shortening* ◆ Tagalog

TAH *abbrev.* ◆ total abdominal
hysterectomy

Tai. *shortening* ◆ Taiwan

tal *abbrev.* ◆ traffic and accident loss

Talisman *acronym* ◆ Transfer
Accounting Lodgement for Investors
and Stock Management

TAM *abbrev.* ◆ tactical air missile

Tam *acronym* ◆ Television Audience
Measurement

Tam. *shortening* ◆ Tamil

Tamba *acronym* ◆ Twins and Multiple
Births Association

tan *shortening* ◆ tangent

Tanca *acronym* ◆ Technical Assistance to
Non-Commonwealth Countries

T & A *abbrev.* ◆ tonsils and adenoids

T & AVR *abbrev.* ◆ Territorial and Army
Volunteer Reserve

t & b *abbrev.* ◆ top and bottom

t & e *abbrev.* ◆ test and evaluation ◆ tired
and emotional (drunk) ◆ travel and
entertainment ◆ trial and error

T & G *abbrev.* ◆ Transport and General
Workers' Union

t & g *abbrev.* ◆ tongued and grooved
(woodwork)

t & o *abbrev.* ◆ taken and offered

t & p *abbrev.* ◆ theft and pilferage

TandRA *acronym* ◆ Tennis and Rackets
Association

t & s *abbrev.* ◆ toilet and shower

T & SG *abbrev.* ◆ Television and
Screenwriters' Guild

T & T *abbrev.* ◆ taxed and tested (of
second-hand cars) ◆ Trinidad and
Tobago

TAP *abbrev.* ◆ Trasportes Aéreos
Portugueses (airline baggage code)

tar. *shortening* ◆ tariff

TARO *abbrev.* ◆ Territorial Army Reserve of Officers

Tars *acronym* ◆ The Arthur Ransome Society

TAS *abbrev.* ◆ Tashkent (airport baggage label) ◆ true air speed

Tas. *shortening* ◆ Tasmania ◆ Tasmanian

TASM *abbrev.* ◆ tactical air-to-surface missile

TASS *acronym* ◆ Technical, Administrative and Supervisory Section (AEUW) ◆ Telegrafnoye Agentsvo Sovietskovo Soyuza (Russian, = Telegraph Agency of the Soviet Union)

TAT *abbrev.* ◆ thematic apperception test ◆ tired all the time ◆ transatlantic telephone cable

TAUN *abbrev.* ◆ Technical Assistance of the United Nations

Taurus *acronym* ◆ Transfer and Automated Registration of Uncertified Stock

taut. *shortening* ◆ tautology

tav. *shortening* ◆ tavern

TAVR *abbrev.* ◆ Territorial and Army Volunteer Reserve

TAVRA *abbrev.* ◆ Territorial, Auxiliary and Volunteer Reserve Association

taw *abbrev.* ◆ twice a week

tax. *shortening* ◆ taxation

TB *abbrev.* ◆ Liverpool (British vehicle registration mark) ◆ torpedo boat ◆ tubercle bacillus ◆ tuberculosis

Tb *symbol* ◆ terbium (chemical element)

tb *abbrev.* ◆ trial balance

TBA *abbrev.* ◆ The Buying Agency (Department of Environment procurement agency)

tba *abbrev.* ◆ to be advised ◆ to be agreed ◆ to be announced ◆ tyres, batteries, accessories

tb & s *abbrev.* ◆ top, bottom and sides

tbcf *abbrev.* ◆ to be called for

TBD *abbrev.* ◆ torpedo-boat destroyer

tbd *abbrev.* ◆ to be determined

TBF *abbrev.* ◆ Teachers' Benevolent Fund

TBI *abbrev.* ◆ throttle-body injection ◆ total body irradiation

tbl *abbrev.* ◆ through bill of lading

TBM *abbrev.* ◆ tactical ballistic missile ◆ tuberculous meningitis

TBO *abbrev.* ◆ time between overhauls

TBS *abbrev.* ◆ Tbilisi (airport baggage label)

tbs. *shortening* ◆ tablespoonful

tbsp. *shortening* ◆ tablespoonful

TBT *abbrev.* ◆ tributyl tin

TC *abbrev.* ◆ Air Tanzania (airline baggage code) ◆ Bristol (British vehicle registration mark) ◆ travellers' cheque ◆ tre corde (Italian, = three strings) (direction to pianist to release left-hand pedal) ◆ Trusteeship Council (UN) ◆ Turkey (international civil aircraft marking)

Tc *symbol* ◆ technetium (chemical element)

tc *abbrev.* ◆ time check ◆ true course

TCA *abbrev.* ◆ tricyclic antidepressant

TCB *abbrev.* ◆ Thames Conservancy Board ◆ tumour cell burden

TCBM *abbrev.* ◆ trans-continental ballistic missile

TCCB *abbrev.* ◆ Test and County Cricket Board

TCD *abbrev.* ◆ Chad (international vehicle registration; French name Tchad) ◆ Trinity College, Dublin

TCDD *abbrev.* ◆ tetrachlorobenzodioxin (environmental pollutant)

TCE *abbrev.* ◆ trichloroethylene (solvent)

TCF *abbrev.* ◆ Touring Club de France

tcf *abbrev.* ◆ trillion cubic feet

TCGF *abbrev.* ◆ T-cell growth factor

tchg *contraction* ◆ teaching

tchr *contraction* ◆ teacher

TCI *abbrev.* ◆ Touring Club Italiano

TCJCC *abbrev.* ◆ Trades Councils Joint Consultative Committee

TCL *abbrev.* ◆ Trinity College of Music, London

T-CLL *abbrev.* ◆ T-cell chronic lymphatic leukaemia

TCM *abbrev.* ◆ Trinity College of Music, London

TCP *abbrev.* ◆ transmission control protocol ◆ trichlorophenylmethyliodisalicyl (antiseptic)

TCPA *abbrev.* ◆ Town and Country Planning Association

TD *abbrev.* ◆ Galashiels (UK postcode) ◆ Manchester (British vehicle registration mark) ◆ tardative dyskinesia ◆ Teachda Dála (Gaelic, = Member of the Dáil) ◆ Teaching Diploma ◆ technical drawing ◆ Territorial Decoration ◆ Tunisian Dinar (monetary unit)

td *abbrev.* ◆ technical data ◆ test data ◆ time delay

TDA *abbrev.* ◆ Timber Development Association ◆ Timber Drying Association

TDD *abbrev.* ◆ telecommunications device for the deaf

TDE *abbrev.* ◆ total digestible energy

TDDL *abbrev.* ◆ time-division data link

TDG *abbrev.* ◆ Timeshare Developers Group

TDL *abbrev.* ◆ tunable diode laser

TDM *abbrev.* ◆ time-division multiplexing

TDMA *abbrev.* ◆ time-division multiple access

TDN *abbrev.* ◆ total digestible nutrients

TDP *abbrev.* ◆ technical development plan

tdr *abbrev.* ◆ tous droits réservés (French, = all rights reserved)

TDRSS *abbrev.* ◆ tracking and data-relay satellite system

tds *abbrev.* ◆ ter die sumendus (Latin, = to be taken thrice daily)

TE *abbrev.* ◆ Air New Zealand (airline baggage code) ◆ Manchester (British vehicle registration mark)

Te *symbol* ◆ tellurium (chemical element)

te *abbrev.* ◆ thermal efficiency

t/e *abbrev.* ◆ time-expired ◆ twin-engined

TEAC *abbrev.* ◆ Technical Education Advisory Council

Teach *abbrev.* ◆ Teacher Education Admissions Clearing House

Tear *acronym* ◆ The Evangelical Alliance Relief Fund

Tec *acronym* ◆ Training and Enterprise Council

tech. *shortening* ◆ technical ◆ technician ◆ technique ◆ technology

techn *contraction* ◆ technician

techn. *shortening* ◆ technique

Tech(CEI) *abbrev.* ◆ Technician (Council of Engineering Institutions)

technol. *shortening* ◆ technological ◆ technology

Tedco *acronym* ◆ Thames Estuary Development Company

Tedis *acronym* ◆ Trade Electronic Data Interchange System (EC)

TEE *abbrev.* ◆ Telecommunications Engineering Establishment ◆ total energy expenditure ◆ Trans-Europe Express

TEF *abbrev.* ◆ Textile Employers' Federation

Tefl *acronym* ◆ Teaching English as a Foreign Language

teg *abbrev.* ◆ top edges gilt

TEL *abbrev.* ◆ tetraethyl lead (petrol additive)

tel. *shortening* ◆ telegraph ◆ telegram ◆ telephone

telecom. *shortening* ◆ telecommunications

teleg. *shortening* ◆ telegraphy

teleph. *shortening* ◆ telephony

TELO *abbrev.* ◆ Tamil Eelam Liberation Organization

TEM *abbrev.* ◆ transmission electron microscopy

temp. *shortening* ◆ temperature ◆ temporal ◆ temporary ◆ tempore (Latin, = in the time of)

Templar *acronym* ◆ Tactical Expert Mission Planner (a military computer)

temp. prim. *shortening* ◆ tempo primo (Italian, = original speed) (music)

ten. *shortening* ◆ tenant ◆ tenement
◆ tenor (voice) ◆ tenuto (Italian, = held)
(music)

tency *contraction* ◆ tenancy

Tenn. *shortening* ◆ Tennessee

TENS *abbrev.* ◆ transcutaneous electrical
nerve stimulation

Tepid *acronym* ◆ tastes expensive,
pension inadequate, dammit

TEPP *abbrev.* ◆ tetraethyl pyrophosphate
(pesticide)

ter. *shortening* ◆ terrace ◆ territorial
◆ territory

terat. *shortening* ◆ teratology

Tercom *acronym* ◆ terrain contour
matching

term. *shortening* ◆ terminal ◆ terminate
◆ termination ◆ terminology

TermNet *acronym* ◆ International
Network for Terminology

terr. *shortening* ◆ terrace ◆ territory

terrd *contraction* ◆ terraced

tert. *shortening* ◆ tertiary

TES *abbrev.* ◆ Times Educational
Supplement

Tesco *acronym* ◆ T E Stockwell and J
Cohen

Tesl *acronym* ◆ Teaching of English as a
Second Language

Tesol *acronym* ◆ Teaching of English to
Speakers of Other Languages

Tessa *acronym* ◆ Tax-Exempt Special
Savings Account

test. *shortening* ◆ testament ◆ testimonial
◆ testimony

Teut. *shortening* ◆ Teutonic

TeV *abbrev.* ◆ tera-electron volt

tewt *acronym* ◆ tactical exercise without
troops

Tex. *shortening* ◆ Texas

text. *shortening* ◆ textile ◆ textual

text. rec. *shortening* ◆ textus receptus
(Latin, = the received text)

TF *abbrev.* ◆ Iceland (international civil
aircraft marking) ◆ Reading (British
vehicle registration mark) ◆ Telford
(UK postcode)

tf *abbrev.* ◆ tax-free

TFA *abbrev.* ◆ Tenant Farmers'
Association ◆ total fatty acids

tfc *contraction* ◆ traffic

TFOF *abbrev.* ◆ Taxi Fleet Operators'
Federation

tfr *abbrev.* ◆ transfer

TFS *abbrev.* ◆ testicular feminization
syndrome

TFSC *abbrev.* ◆ Turkish Federated State
of Cyprus

TFSK *abbrev.* ◆ Turkish Federated State
of Kibris (Cyprus)

TFSR *abbrev.* ◆ Tools for Self Reliance

TFTA *abbrev.* ◆ Traditional Farm-Fresh
Turkey Association

TFU *abbrev.* ◆ telecommunications flying
unit

TFX *abbrev.* ◆ tactical fighter,
experimental

TG *abbrev.* ◆ Cardiff (British vehicle
registration mark) ◆ Guatemala
(international civil aircraft marking)
◆ Tate Gallery ◆ Thai Airways (airline
baggage code, international flights)
◆ Togo (international vehicle
registration) ◆ Townswomen's Guild
◆ transformational grammar

TGAT *pronounced tee-gat acronym* ◆ Task
Group on Assessment and Testing

T-gate *contraction* ◆ ternary selector gate

tgb *abbrev.* ◆ tongued, grooved and
beaded

TGD *abbrev.* ◆ Titograd (airport baggage
label)

TGE *abbrev.* ◆ transmissible
gastroenteritis

TGF *abbrev.* ◆ transforming growth
factor

TGI *abbrev.* ◆ Target Group Index

TGIA *abbrev.* ◆ Toy and Giftware
Importers' Association

TGIF *abbrev.* ◆ thank God it's Friday

tgt *contraction* ◆ target

TGUK *abbrev.* ◆ Timber Growers United
Kingdom Ltd

TGV *abbrev.* ◆ Train à Grande Vitesse
(French, = High Speed Train)

TGWU *abbrev.* ◆ Transport and General Workers' Union

TH *abbrev.* ◆ Swansea (British vehicle registration mark) ◆ Thai Airways (airline baggage code, domestic flights)

Th *symbol* ◆ thorium (chemical element)

Th. *shortening* ◆ Thursday

Thai. *shortening* ◆ Thailand

ThB *abbrev.* ◆ Theologiae Baccalaureus (Latin, = Bachelor of Theology)

THC *abbrev.* ◆ tetrahydrocannabinol (component of cannabis)

THD *abbrev.* ◆ total harmonic distortion

ThD *abbrev.* ◆ Theologiae Doctor (Latin, = Doctor of Theology)

THE *abbrev.* ◆ Technical Help to Exporters

theat. *shortening* ◆ theatre ◆ theatrical

theol. *shortening* ◆ theologian ◆ theological ◆ theology

theor. *shortening* ◆ theorem ◆ theoretical ◆ theory

theoret. *shortening* ◆ theoretical

theos. *shortening* ◆ theosophical ◆ theosophist ◆ theosophy

therap. *shortening* ◆ therapeutic

therm. *shortening* ◆ thermometer ◆ thermostatic

thermochem. *shortening* ◆ thermochemical ◆ thermochemistry

thermodyn. *shortening* ◆ thermodynamics

thermom. *shortening* ◆ thermometer

THES *abbrev.* ◆ Times Higher Education Supplement

thes. *shortening* ◆ thesis

thesp. *shortening* ◆ thespian

Thess. *shortening* ◆ Thessalonians (books of Bible)

THF *abbrev.* ◆ Trust House Forte

THI *abbrev.* ◆ temperature-humidity index

thk *contraction* ◆ thick

ThM *abbrev.* ◆ Theologiae Magister (Latin, = Master of Theology)

thor. ◆ thorax ◆ thoracic

thoro. *shortening* ◆ thoroughfare

thou. *shortening* ◆ thousand

thp *abbrev.* ◆ thrust horsepower

THR *abbrev.* ◆ Teheran (airport baggage label) ◆ total hip replacement

thr. *shortening* ◆ through

THT *abbrev.* ◆ Terence Higgins Trust

Thu. *shortening* ◆ Thursday

Thur. *shortening* ◆ Thursday

Thurs. *shortening* ◆ Thursday

TI *abbrev.* ◆ Costa Rica (international civil aircraft marking) ◆ Texas International Airlines (airline baggage code) ◆ thermal imaging

Ti *symbol* ◆ titanium (chemical element)

TIA *abbrev.* ◆ Telecommunications Industry Association ◆ Tirana (airport baggage label)

TIB *abbrev.* ◆ Tourist Information Bureau

Tib. *shortening* ◆ Tibet ◆ Tibetan

Tibor *acronym* ◆ Tokyo Inter-Bank Offered Rate

TIC *abbrev.* ◆ Timber Industries Confederation

TICCIH *abbrev.* ◆ The International Committee for the Conservation of the Industrial Heritage

tid *abbrev.* ◆ ter in die (Latin, = three times a day)

TIF *abbrev.* ◆ Theatre Investment Fund

tif *abbrev.* ◆ telephone interference factor

Tiff *acronym* ◆ tagged-image file format

TIG *abbrev.* ◆ tungsten inert gas

TIH *abbrev.* ◆ Their Imperial Highnesses

TIIAL *abbrev.* ◆ The International Institute of Applied Linguistics

TILS *abbrev.* ◆ Technical Information and Library Service

TIM *abbrev.* ◆ time is money

Tim. *shortening* ◆ Timothy (books of Bible)

timp. *shortening* ◆ timpani

TIMS *abbrev.* ◆ The Institute of Management Sciences

Tina *acronym* ◆ there is no alternative

tinct. *shortening* ◆ tincture

TIP *abbrev.* ◆ terminal interface processor ◆ Tripoli (airport baggage label)

Tipp. *shortening* ◆ County Tipperary

TIR *abbrev.* ◆ Transports Internationaux Routiers (French, = International Road Transport)

TIRC *abbrev.* ◆ Tobacco Industry Research Committee

TIS *abbrev.* ◆ Technical Information Service

tis. *shortening* ◆ tissue

Tit. *shortening* ◆ Titus (book of Bible)

tit. *shortening* ◆ title ◆ titular

TIU *abbrev.* ◆ Telecommunications International Union

TJ *abbrev.* ◆ Liverpool (British vehicle registration mark) ◆ triple jump (athletics)

TJA *abbrev.* ◆ Table Jellies Association

TK *abbrev.* ◆ Exeter (British vehicle registration mark) ◆ Turk Hava Yollari (airline baggage code)

tkg *contraction* ◆ taking

tkgs *contraction* ◆ takings

TKO *abbrev.* ◆ technical knockout (boxing)

tkr *contraction* ◆ tanker

tks *contraction* ◆ thanks

tkt *contraction* ◆ ticket

TKU *abbrev.* ◆ Turku (airport baggage label)

TL *abbrev.* ◆ Lincoln (British vehicle registration mark) ◆ thermoluminescent ◆ Turk lirasi (Turkish, = Turkish lira) (monetary unit)

Tl *symbol* ◆ thallium (chemical element)

tl *abbrev.* ◆ total loss

TLA *abbrev.* ◆ Toy Libraries Association

TLC *abbrev.* ◆ tender loving care ◆ thin-layer chromatography ◆ total lung capacity

tld *contraction* ◆ tooled

TLEH *abbrev.* ◆ true love and everlasting happiness

TLG *abbrev.* ◆ Theatrical Ladies' Guild

TLL *abbrev.* ◆ Tallinn (airport baggage label)

TLMI *abbrev.* ◆ The Leprosy Mission International

TLO *abbrev.* ◆ Technical Liaison Officer

tlo *abbrev.* ◆ total loss only

TLR *abbrev.* ◆ twin-lens reflex (camera)

TLRS *abbrev.* ◆ Tramway and Light Railway Society

TLS *abbrev.* ◆ Times Literary Supplement ◆ Toulouse (airport baggage label)

TLU *abbrev.* ◆ table look-up

TLV *abbrev.* ◆ Tel Aviv (airport baggage label)

TM *abbrev.* ◆ Luton (British vehicle registration mark) ◆ tactical missile ◆ technical manual ◆ test manual ◆ Their Majesties ◆ trade mark ◆ training manual ◆ transcendental meditation ◆ trench mortar

Tm *symbol* ◆ thulium (chemical element)

tm *abbrev.* ◆ true mean

TMA *abbrev.* ◆ Trans-Mediterranean Airways (Lebanese national airline)

TMBA *abbrev.* ◆ Twins and Multiple Births Association

tmbr *contraction* ◆ timber

TMD *abbrev.* ◆ theatre missile defence

tmkpr *contraction* ◆ timekeeper

TML *abbrev.* ◆ three-mile limit

TMO *abbrev.* ◆ telegraphic money order

TMPDF *abbrev.* ◆ Trade Marks, Patterns and Designs Federation

tmpry *contraction* ◆ temporary

TMS *abbrev.* ◆ Tramway Museum Society

tmv *abbrev.* ◆ true mean value

TN *abbrev.* ◆ Newcastle upon Tyne (British vehicle registration mark) ◆ Tennessee (US postcode) ◆ Tonbridge (UK postcode) ◆ tradename ◆ true north ◆ Tunisia (international vehicle registration)

tn *abbrev.* ◆ telephone number

tn *contraction* ◆ ton ◆ train

tn. *shortening* ◆ tonne

TNA *abbrev.* ◆ Tamil National Army

TNC *abbrev.* ◆ transnational corporation

TNF *abbrev.* ◆ tumour necrosis factor

TNG *abbrev.* ◆ Tangier (airport baggage label)

tng *contraction* ◆ turning

TNM *abbrev.* ◆ tactical nuclear missile

TNN *abbrev.* ◆ Taiwan (airport baggage label)

TNP *abbrev.* ◆ Théâtre National Populaire (French, = National Popular Theatre)

TNPG *abbrev.* ◆ The Nuclear Power Group

TNT *abbrev.* ◆ trinitrotoluene (explosive)

TNTC *abbrev.* ◆ too numerous to count

TNW *abbrev.* ◆ theatre nuclear weapon ◆ tactical nuclear warfare

TO *abbrev.* ◆ Nottingham (British vehicle registration mark) ◆ Tax Officer ◆ telegraph office ◆ Transport Officer ◆ turn over

t/o *abbrev.* ◆ take-off ◆ turnover

Tob. *shortening* ◆ Tobit (book of Bible)

tob. *shortening* ◆ tobacco ◆ tobacconist

ToB *abbrev.* ◆ Tour of Britain (cycling)

Toc H *abbrev.* ◆ Talbot House (orig. telegraphic code for TH; Talbot House was the charity's London headquarters)

tod *abbrev.* ◆ time of delivery

TOE *abbrev.* ◆ Theory of Everything

Toefl *pronounced* ter-ful *acronym* ◆ Test of English as a Foreign Language

tog. *shortening* ◆ together

ToL *abbrev.* ◆ Tower of London

tom. *shortening* ◆ tomato ◆ tomus (Latin, = volume)

tomat. *shortening* ◆ tomato

tonn. *shortening* ◆ tonnage

TOO *abbrev.* ◆ time of origin ◆ to order only

TOP *abbrev.* ◆ temporarily out of print ◆ termination of pregnancy

top. *shortening* ◆ topographical ◆ topography

Topic *acronym* ◆ Teletext Output Price Information Computer

topog. *shortening* ◆ topographer ◆ topographical ◆ topography

topol. *shortening* ◆ topological ◆ topology

Tops *abbrev.* ◆ Theatre Organ Preservation Society ◆ Training Opportunities Scheme

tor *abbrev.* ◆ time of receipt

torn. *shortening* ◆ tornado

torp. *shortening* ◆ torpedo

tos *abbrev.* ◆ temporarily out of stock ◆ terms of service

Toshiba *acronym* ◆ Tokyo Shibaura Denki KK (Japanese, = Tokyo Shibaura Electrical Corporation)

tot *abbrev.* ◆ time over target

tot. *shortening* ◆ total ◆ totally

tour. *shortening* ◆ tourism ◆ tourist

tourn. *shortening* ◆ tournament

TOW *abbrev.* ◆ tug of war

TOWA *abbrev.* ◆ Tug of War Association

tox. *shortening* ◆ toxicological ◆ toxicology

toxicol. *shortening* ◆ toxicological ◆ toxicologist ◆ toxicology

TP *abbrev.* ◆ Portsmouth (British vehicle registration mark) ◆ to pay ◆ third party

T/P *abbrev.* ◆ title page

tp *abbrev.* ◆ target practice ◆ teaching practice

tp *contraction* ◆ township ◆ troop

tPA *abbrev.* ◆ tissue plasminogen activator

TPC *abbrev.* ◆ Tall Persons Club of Great Britain

tpd *abbrev.* ◆ tons per day

TPE *abbrev.* ◆ Taipei (airport baggage label)

tph *abbrev.* ◆ tons per hour

TPI *abbrev.* ◆ tax and prices index ◆ Town Planning Institute

tpi *abbrev.* ◆ teeth per inch ◆ tracks per inch ◆ turns per inch ◆ threads per inch

TPLF *abbrev.* ◆ Tige People's Liberation Front

tpm *abbrev.* ◆ tons per minute

TPN *abbrev.* ◆ total parenteral nutrition

TPO *abbrev.* ◆ Tree Preservation Order

TPR *abbrev.* ◆ temperature, pulse, respiration ◆ Trust for the Protection of Reptiles

Tpr *contraction* ◆ Trooper

tpr *contraction* ◆ teleprinter

TPS *abbrev.* ◆ Tax Payers' Society ◆ Thomas Paine Society

tpt *contraction* ◆ transport ◆ trumpet

TQ *abbrev.* ◆ Las Vegas Airlines (airline baggage code) ◆ Torquay (UK postcode)

TQM *abbrev.* ◆ total quality management

TQV *abbrev.* ◆ St Moritz (airport baggage label)

TR *abbrev.* ◆ Portsmouth (British vehicle registration mark) ◆ Territorial Reserve ◆ transmit–receive ◆ Truro (UK postcode) ◆ Turkey (international vehicle registration)

T/R *abbrev.* ◆ transmitter-receiver

tr. *shortening* ◆ tinctura (Latin, = tincture) ◆ transactions ◆ transfer ◆ transitive ◆ translated ◆ translator ◆ transpose ◆ treble (singer's voice) ◆ trill ◆ trustee

trac. *shortening* ◆ tractor

Trace *acronym* ◆ test equipment for rapid automatic check-out evaluation (before aircraft take-off)

trad. *shortening* ◆ traditional

trag. *shortening* ◆ tragedy ◆ tragic

trans. *shortening* ◆ transaction ◆ transfer ◆ transit ◆ transitive ◆ translated ◆ translation ◆ transpose ◆ transverse

transcr. *shortening* ◆ transcription

transf. *shortening* ◆ transfer ◆ transferred ◆ transference

transl. *shortening* ◆ translation ◆ translator

translit. *shortening* ◆ transliteration

transp. *shortening* ◆ transparent ◆ transpose

trav. *shortening* ◆ travel ◆ traveller

TRC *abbrev.* ◆ Thames Rowing Club

Trd *contraction* ◆ Trinidad

TRDA *abbrev.* ◆ Timber Research and Development Association

treas. *shortening* ◆ treasurer ◆ treasury

trem *acronym* ◆ transport emergency

trem. *shortening* ◆ tremolando (Italian, = shaking)

trf *abbrev.* ◆ tuned radio frequency

trf *contraction* ◆ tariff

trf. *shortening* ◆ transfer

TRG *abbrev.* ◆ Tory Reform Group

trg *contraction* ◆ training

TRH *abbrev.* ◆ Their Royal Highnesses ◆ thyrotrophin-releasing hormone

TRI *abbrev.* ◆ Thrombosis Research Institute

trib. *shortening* ◆ tribal ◆ tributary

trid. *shortening* ◆ triduum (Latin, = three days)

trig. *shortening* ◆ trigonometric ◆ trigonometry

trigon. *shortening* ◆ trigonometric ◆ trigonometry

Trin. *shortening* ◆ Trinidad ◆ Trinidadian ◆ Trinity

Trip. *contraction* ◆ Tripos

tripl. *shortening* ◆ triplicate

TRM *abbrev.* ◆ trademark

trml *contraction* ◆ terminal

TRN *abbrev.* ◆ Turin (airport baggage label)

tRNA *abbrev.* ◆ transfer ribonucleic acid

TRNC *abbrev.* ◆ Turkish Republic of Northern Cyprus

trng *contraction* ◆ training

TRO *abbrev.* ◆ Temporary Restraining Order

TROBI *abbrev.* ◆ Tree Register of the British Isles

trom. *shortening* ◆ trombone

trombst *contraction* ◆ trombonist

trop. *shortening* ◆ tropic ◆ tropical

trp *contraction* ◆ troop

TRRL *abbrev.* ◆ Transport and Road Research Laboratory

TRS *abbrev.* ◆ Trieste (airport baggage label)

trs. *shortening* ◆ transfer ◆ transpose

trsp. *shortening* ◆ transport

TRSR *abbrev.* ◆ taxi and runway surveillance radar

TRSSGM *abbrev.* ◆ tactical range surface-to-surface guided missile

Truron. *shortening* ◆ Truronensis (Latin, = of Truro)

TS *abbrev.* ◆ Cleveland (UK postcode) ◆ Dundee (British vehicle registration mark) ◆ Samoa Airlines (airline baggage code) ◆ Television Society ◆ Theosophical Society ◆ Tolkien Society ◆ Training Ship ◆ transsexual ◆ typescript

ts *abbrev.* ◆ tensile strength

t/s *abbrev.* ◆ transshipment

TSA *abbrev.* ◆ Training Services Agency ◆ tumour-specific antigen

TSB *abbrev.* ◆ Trustee Savings Bank

TSBA *abbrev.* ◆ Trustee Savings Banks Association

TSE *abbrev.* ◆ transmissible spongiform encephalopathy

TSFA *abbrev.* ◆ The Securities and Futures Authority

TSG *abbrev.* ◆ Tibet Support Group

TSgt *abbrev.* ◆ Technical Sergeant

TSH *abbrev.* ◆ Their Serene Highnesses ◆ thyroid-stimulating hormone

TSh *abbrev.* ◆ Tanzanian shilling (monetary unit)

TSH-RF *abbrev.* ◆ thyroid-stimulating-hormone-releasing factor

tsi *abbrev.* ◆ tons per square inch

TSO *abbrev.* ◆ town sub-office ◆ Trading Standards Officer

TSP *abbrev.* ◆ textured soya protein

tsp. *shortening* ◆ teaspoon

TSR *abbrev.* ◆ tactical strike reconnaissance ◆ terminate and stay resident ◆ Trans-Siberian Railway

TSRB *abbrev.* ◆ Top Salaries Review Body

TSS *abbrev.* ◆ time-sharing system ◆ toxic shock syndrome

TSSA *abbrev.* ◆ Transport Salaried Staffs Association

TSU *abbrev.* ◆ this side up

tsvp *abbrev.* ◆ tournez, s'il vous plaît (French, = please turn over)

TSW *abbrev.* ◆ Television South West

TT *abbrev.* ◆ Exeter (British vehicle registration mark) ◆ teetotal ◆ telegraphic transfer ◆ time trial (cycling) ◆ Tourist Trophy (motor cycling) ◆ Trinidad and Tobago (international vehicle registration) ◆ tuberculin tested

TTAW *abbrev.* ◆ Table Tennis Association of Wales

TTBT *abbrev.* ◆ Threshold Test Ban Treaty

TTF *abbrev.* ◆ Timber Trade Federation

TTFN *abbrev.* ◆ ta-ta for now

TTL *abbrev.* ◆ through the lens

TTNS *abbrev.* ◆ The Times Network Systems (database system for schools)

TTRA *abbrev.* ◆ Tourist Trophy Riders' Association

TTS *abbrev.* ◆ teletypesetting

TTT *abbrev.* ◆ team time trial (cycling) ◆ Tyne Tees Television

TTTA *abbrev.* ◆ Timber Trade Training Association

TU *abbrev.* ◆ Chester (British vehicle registration mark) ◆ trade union ◆ transmission unit ◆ Tunis Air (airline baggage code) ◆ Tupolev (Soviet aircraft manufacturer)

Tu. *shortening* ◆ Tuesday

TUA *abbrev.* ◆ Telecommunications Users' Association

TUBCS *abbrev.* ◆ Trade Union Badge Collectors' Society

Tube *acronym* ◆ The Union of Bookmakers' Employees

tuberc. *shortening* ◆ tubercular ◆ tuberculosis

TUC *abbrev.* ◆ Trades Union Congress

TUCC *abbrev.* ◆ Transport Users' Consultative Council

TUCGC *abbrev.* ◆ Trades Union Congress General Council

Tue. *shortening* ◆ Tuesday

Tues. *shortening* ◆ Tuesday

TUG *abbrev.* ◆ Telephone Users' Group

TUI *abbrev.* ◆ Trade Unions International of Public and Allied Employees

TUIAFPW *abbrev.* ◆ Trade Unions International of Agricultural, Forestry and Plantation Workers

TUIREG *abbrev.* ◆ Trade Unions International Research and Education Group

TUIWC *abbrev.* ◆ Trade Unions International of Workers in Commerce

TUIWE *abbrev.* ◆ Trade Unions International of Workers in Energy

TULF *abbrev.* ◆ Tamil United Liberation Front

TUN *abbrev.* ◆ Tunis (airport baggage label)

turb. *shortening* ◆ turbine

Turk. *shortening* ◆ Turkey ◆ Turkish

turp *acronym* ◆ trans-urethral resection of the prostate

TV *abbrev.* ◆ Haiti Trans Air (airline baggage code) ◆ Nottingham (British vehicle registration mark) ◆ television ◆ transvestism ◆ transvestite

TVA *abbrev.* ◆ taxe sur la valeur ajoutée (French, = value-added tax)

TVE *abbrev.* ◆ Television Trust for the Environment

TVEI *abbrev.* ◆ Technical and Vocational Education Initiative

TVP *abbrev.* ◆ textured vegetable protein

TVRO *abbrev.* ◆ television, receive only (sort of aerial)

TW *abbrev.* ◆ Chelmsford ◆ Trans World Airlines ◆ Twickenham (UK postcode)

TWA *abbrev.* ◆ Trans-World Airlines

TWh *abbrev.* ◆ terawatt hour

TWIF *abbrev.* ◆ Tug of War International Federation

TWIMC *abbrev.* ◆ to whom it may concern

TWOC *acronym* ◆ taking without owner's consent

TWR *abbrev.* ◆ Trans World Radio

TWU *abbrev.* ◆ Tobacco Workers' Union

TX *abbrev.* ◆ Cardiff (British vehicle registration mark) ◆ Texas (US postcode)

TY *abbrev.* ◆ Newcastle upon Tyne (British vehicle registration mark)

TYC *abbrev.* ◆ Thames Yacht Club

TYO *abbrev.* ◆ Tokyo (airport baggage label)

typ. *shortening* ◆ typical ◆ typist ◆ typographical ◆ typography

typh. *shortening* ◆ typhoon

typog. *shortening* ◆ typographical ◆ typography

Tyrol. *shortening* ◆ Tyrolean ◆ Tyrolese

TZ *abbrev.* ◆ Belfast (British vehicle registration mark)

U

U *abbrev.* ◆ union ◆ unionist ◆ united ◆ Universal (film censorship classification) ◆ university ◆ upper-class

U *symbol* ◆ uranium (chemical element)

u *abbrev.* ◆ unified atomic mass unit ◆ unit ◆ upper

UA *abbrev.* ◆ Leeds (British vehicle registration mark) ◆ United Airlines (airline baggage code) ◆ United Artists (film company)

ua *abbrev.* ◆ unauthorized absence ◆ under age ◆ unter anderen (German, = among other things)

UAE *abbrev.* ◆ United Arab Emirates

UAM *abbrev.* ◆ underwater-to-air missile

u & lc *abbrev.* ◆ upper and lower case (capital and ordinary letters)

u & o *abbrev.* ◆ use and occupancy

UAR *abbrev.* ◆ United Arab Republic

uas *abbrev.* ◆ upper air space

UAU *abbrev.* ◆ Universities Athletic Union

uAwg *abbrev.* ◆ um Antwort wird gebeten (German, = reply requested)

UB *abbrev.* ◆ Burma Airways (airline baggage code) ◆ Leeds (British vehicle registration mark)

UBF *abbrev.* ◆ Union of British Fascists

UB40 *abbrev.* ◆ Unemployment Benefit Form 40 (card held by unemployed person and entitling him to state benefits etc)

U-boat *contraction* ◆ Unterseeboot (German, = submarine) (English term for German submarines in both world wars)

UBR *abbrev.* ◆ Uniform Business Rate

UBS *abbrev.* ◆ United Bible Societies

UC *abbrev.* ◆ central London (British vehicle registration mark) ◆ University College

Uc *abbrev.* ◆ Universal, particularly suitable for children (film censorship classification)

uc *abbrev.* ◆ una corda (Italian, = one string) (direction to pianist to depress left-hand pedal) ◆ upper-case (capital letter)

u/c *abbrev.* ◆ undercharge

UCAR *abbrev.* ◆ Union of Central African Republics

Ucatt *acronym* ◆ Union of Construction, Allied Trades and Technicians

UCC *abbrev.* ◆ Union Carbide Corporation ◆ Universal Copyright Convention

Ucca *acronym* ◆ Universities' Central Council on Admissions

UCI *abbrev.* ◆ Union Cycliste Internationale (French, = International Cycling Union)

UCL *abbrev.* ◆ University College, London

UCLA *abbrev.* ◆ University of California at Los Angeles

UCM *abbrev.* ◆ University Christian Movement

UCR *abbrev.* ◆ unconditioned reflex

UCS *abbrev.* ◆ unconditioned stimulus

UCW *abbrev.* ◆ Union of Communication Workers

UCWRE *abbrev.* ◆ Underwater Countermeasures and Weapons Research Establishment

UD *abbrev.* ◆ Oxford (British vehicle registration mark) ◆ United Dairies

ud *abbrev.* ♦ unfair dismissal ♦ ut dictum
(Latin, = as said)

UDA *abbrev.* ♦ Ulster Defence
Association

UDC *abbrev.* ♦ Universal Decimal
Classification ♦ Urban Development
Corporation ♦ Urban District Council

UDF *abbrev.* ♦ Ulster Defence Force
♦ United Democratic Front (South
Africa)

UDHR *abbrev.* ♦ Universal Declaration of
Human Rights

UDI *abbrev.* ♦ Unilateral Declaration of
Independence

UDM *abbrev.* ♦ Union of Democratic
Mineworkers

UDR *abbrev.* ♦ Ulster Defence Regiment

UDT *abbrev.* ♦ United Dominions Trust

UDUP *abbrev.* ♦ Ulster Democratic
Unionist Party

UE *abbrev.* ♦ Dudley (British vehicle
registration mark)

UEA *abbrev.* ♦ Universal Esperanto
Association ♦ University of East Anglia

Uefa *pronounced* oo-ee-fa *acronym*
♦ Union of European Football
Associations

UEL *abbrev.* ♦ United Empire Loyalists

UER *abbrev.* ♦ university entrance
requirements

UF *abbrev.* ♦ Brighton (British vehicle
registration mark) ♦ United Free
Church

u/f *abbrev.* ♦ unfurnished

Ufaw *acronym* ♦ Universities Federation
for Animal Welfare

UFC *abbrev.* ♦ United Free Church
(Scotland) ♦ Universities Funding
Council

UFF *abbrev.* ♦ Ulster Freedom Fighters

Ufo *pronounced* oo-foe *acronym*
♦ unidentified flying object

UG *abbrev.* ♦ Leeds (British vehicle
registration mark)

Ug. *shortening* ♦ Uganda ♦ Ugandan

u/g *abbrev.* ♦ underground

UGC *abbrev.* ♦ University Grants
Committee

UH *abbrev.* ♦ Cardiff (British vehicle
registration mark)

UHF *abbrev.* ♦ ultra-high frequency

UHT *abbrev.* ♦ ultra-heat-treated ♦ ultra
high temperature

UHV *abbrev.* ♦ ultra high vacuum

UI *abbrev.* ♦ Londonderry (British vehicle
registration mark)

ui *abbrev.* ♦ ut infra (Latin, = as below)

UJ *abbrev.* ♦ Shrewsbury (British vehicle
registration mark)

UJD *abbrev.* ♦ Utriusque Juris Doctor
(Latin, = Doctor of Both Laws) (canon
and civil)

UK *abbrev.* ♦ Air UK (airline baggage
code) ♦ Birmingham (British vehicle
registration mark) ♦ United Kingdom

UKA *abbrev.* ♦ Ulster King of Arms

UKADGE *abbrev.* ♦ United Kingdom Air
Defence Ground Environment

UKAEA *abbrev.* ♦ United Kingdom
Atomic Energy Authority

UKCC *abbrev.* ♦ United Kingdom
Central Council for Nursing,
Midwifery and Health Visiting

UKgal *abbrev.* ♦ United Kingdom gallon

Ukias *acronym* ♦ United Kingdom
Immigrants' Advisory Service

UKPA *abbrev.* ♦ United Kingdom Pilots'
Association

UKPIA *abbrev.* ♦ United Kingdom
Petroleum Industry Association Ltd

Ukr. *shortening* ♦ Ukraine ♦ Ukrainian

UL *abbrev.* ♦ central London (British
vehicle registration mark) ♦ university
library

ul *abbrev.* ♦ upper limit

ULA *abbrev.* ♦ uncommitted logic array

ULCC *abbrev.* ♦ ultra-large crude carrier
(oil-tanker)

ULF *abbrev.* ♦ ultra-low frequency

ULM *abbrev.* ♦ universal logic module

ULMS *abbrev.* ♦ underwater long-range
missile system

ULN *abbrev.* ♦ Ulan Bator (airport
baggage label)

ULS *abbrev.* ♦ unsecured loan stock

ult. *shortening* ◆ ultimate ◆ ultimately ◆ ultimo (Latin, = in the last) (month)

Ultra *acronym* ◆ Unrelated Live Transplant Regulatory Authority

ulto *contraction* ◆ ultimo (Latin, = in the last) (month)

ULV *abbrev.* ◆ ultra low volume

UM *abbrev.* ◆ Air Zimbabwe (airline baggage code) ◆ Leeds (British vehicle registration mark)

umbl. *shortening* ◆ umbilical

UMDS *abbrev.* ◆ United Medical and Dental Schools

UMFC *abbrev.* ◆ United Methodist Free Churches

Umist *acronym* ◆ University of Manchester Institute of Science and Technology

ump. *shortening* ◆ umpire

UN *abbrev.* ◆ Exeter (British vehicle registration mark) ◆ United Nations

UNA *abbrev.* ◆ United Nations Association

unab. *shortening* ◆ unabridged

unacc. *shortening* ◆ unaccompanied

unaccomp. *shortening* ◆ unaccompanied

unan. *shortening* ◆ unanimous

unasgd *contraction* ◆ unassigned

unatt. *shortening* ◆ unattached

unattrib. *shortening* ◆ unattributed

unauth. *shortening* ◆ unauthorized

unb. *shortening* ◆ unbound

Unbro *acronym* ◆ United Nations Border Relief Operation

unc. *shortening* ◆ uncertain

Uncast *acronym* ◆ United Nations Conference on the Applications of Science and Technology

Unced *acronym* ◆ United Nations Conference on Environment and Development

Uncitral *acronym* ◆ United Nations Commission on International Trade law

unclass. *shortening* ◆ unclassified

Unclos *acronym* ◆ United Nations Conference on the Law of the Sea

uncond. *shortening* ◆ unconditional

UNCSTD *abbrev.* ◆ United Nations Conference on Science and Technology for Development

Uncro *abbrev.* ◆ United Nations Confidence-Restoring Operation (in Croatia)

Unctad *acronym* ◆ United Nations Conference on Trade and Development

Undof *acronym* ◆ United Nations Disengagement Observer Force

UNDP *abbrev.* ◆ United Nations Development Programme

Undro *acronym* ◆ United Nations Disaster Relief Organization

Unef *pronounced* yoo-nef *acronym* ◆ United Nations Emergency Force

Unep *pronounced* yoo-nep *acronym* ◆ United Nations Environment Programme

Unesco *pronounced* yoo-nes-co *acronym* ◆ United Nations Educational, Scientific and Cultural Organization

unexpl. *shortening* ◆ unexplained ◆ unexploded ◆ unexplored

UNFAO *abbrev.* ◆ United Nations Food and Agriculture Organization

Unficyp *pronounced* un-fi-sipe *acronym* ◆ United Nations Force in Cyprus

UNFPA *abbrev.* ◆ United Nations Fund for Population Activities

ung. *shortening* ◆ unguentum (Latin, = ointment)

UNGA *abbrev.* ◆ United Nations General Assembly

UNHCR *abbrev.* ◆ United Nations High Commission for Refugees ◆ United Nations High Commissioner for Refugees

UNHQ *abbrev.* ◆ United Nations Headquarters

Unicef *pronounced* yoo-ni-sef *acronym* ◆ United Nations Children's Fund (orig. United Nations International Children's Emergency Fund)

Unido *pronounced* yoo-nee-do *acronym* ◆ United Nations Industrial Development Organization

Unidroit *acronym* ◆ Institut International pour l'Unification du Droit Privé (French, = International Institute for the Unification of Private Law)

unif. *shortening* ◆ uniform

Unifil *pronounced* yoo-ni-fil *acronym* ◆ United Nations Interim Force in Lebanon

Unikom *acronym* ◆ United Nations Iraq-Kuwait Observation Mission

unis. *shortening* ◆ unisoni (Italian, = in unison) (music)

Unit. *shortening* ◆ Unitarian ◆ Unitarianism

Unita *acronym* ◆ União Nacional por Independência Total de Angola (Portuguese, = National Union for the Total Independence of Angola)

univ. *shortening* ◆ universal ◆ university

unkn. *shortening* ◆ unknown

unm. *shortening* ◆ unmarried

unmod. *shortening* ◆ unmodernized

Unmogip *acronym* ◆ United Nations Military Observer Group in India and Pakistan

UNO *abbrev.* ◆ United Nations Organization

unop. *shortening* ◆ unopposed

Unosom *acronym* ◆ United Nations Operation in Somalia

unp. *shortening* ◆ unpaged ◆ unpaid

unpd *contraction* ◆ unpaid

Unprofor *acronym* ◆ United Nations Protection Force (in Croatia, Bosnia etc)

unpub. *shortening* ◆ unpublished

Unref *acronym* ◆ United Nations Refugee Emergency Fund

Unrra *acronym* ◆ United Nations Relief and Rehabilitation Administration

Unrwa *pronounced* un-ruh *acronym* ◆ United Nations Relief and Works Agency (for Palestinian refugees)

unsat. *shortening* ◆ unsatisfactory ◆ unsaturated

UNSC *abbrev.* ◆ United Nations Security Council

UNSG *abbrev.* ◆ United Nations Secretary General

unst. *shortening* ◆ unstable

UNTC *abbrev.* ◆ United Nations Trusteeship Council

UNTT *abbrev.* ◆ United Nations Trust Territory

UNWCC *abbrev.* ◆ United Nations War Crimes Commission

UNSC *abbrev.* ◆ United Nations Security Council

UNTSO *abbrev.* ◆ United Nations Truce Supervision Organization

UO *abbrev.* ◆ Exeter (British vehicle registration mark)

UOM *abbrev.* ◆ Union of Myanmar

UP *abbrev.* ◆ Bahamas Air (airline baggage code) ◆ Newcastle upon Tyne

---

COUNTIES OF THE UNITED KINGDOM

Generally accepted abbreviations exist for less than half of the UK counties, and those are listed here and in their alphabetical place in the dictionary. The dictionary also contains some other county abbreviations which are not generally regarded as established.

Beds.	*Bedfordshire*	**Ferm.**	*Fermanagh*	**Northants**	*Northamptonshire*
Berks.	*Berkshire*	**Glos.**	*Gloucestershire*	**Northumb.**	*Northumberland*
Bucks.	*Buckinghamshire*	**Hants**	*Hampshire*	**Notts.**	*Nottinghamshire*
Cambs.	*Cambridgeshire*	**Herts.**	*Hertfordshire*	**Oxon.**	*Oxfordshire*
Ches.	*Cheshire*	**IOW**	*Isle of Wight*	**Som.**	*Somerset*
Corn.	*Cornwall*	**Lancs.**	*Lancashire*	**Staffs.**	*Staffordshire*
Derby.	*Derbyshire*	**Leics.**	*Leicestershire*	**War.**	*Warwickshire*
Dur.	*County Durham*	**Lincs.**	*Lincolnshire*	**Wilts.**	*Wiltshire*

(British vehicle registration mark)
♦ United Presbyterian ♦ United Press
♦ University Press

up *abbrev.* ♦ under proof (alcohol)

up. *shortening* ♦ upper

UPC *abbrev.* ♦ United Presbyterian
Church ♦ Universal Postal Convention
♦ Universal Product Code

uphol. *shortening* ♦ upholstery

UPI *abbrev.* ♦ United Press International

UPNI *abbrev.* ♦ Unionist Party of
Northern Ireland

UPOW *abbrev.* ♦ Union of Post Office
Workers

UPS *abbrev.* ♦ uninterruptible power
supply

UPU *abbrev.* ♦ Universal Postal Union

UPUP *abbrev.* ♦ Ulster Popular Unionist
Party

uPVC *abbrev.* ♦ unplasticized polyvinyl
chloride

UPW *abbrev.* ♦ Union of Post Office
Workers

UR *abbrev.* ♦ Luton (British vehicle
registration mark) ♦ Ukraine
(international vehicle registration)
♦ unconditioned reflex

Ur. *shortening* ♦ Urdu ♦ Uruguay
♦ Uruguayan

ur. *shortening* ♦ urine

URA *abbrev.* ♦ Urban Regeneration
Agency

urb. *shortening* ♦ urban

URBM *abbrev.* ♦ ultimate-range ballistic
missile

URC *abbrev.* ♦ United Reformed Church

Urd. *shortening* ♦ Urdu

URF *abbrev.* ♦ uterine relaxing factor

urg. *shortening* ♦ urgent ♦ urgently

URI *abbrev.* ♦ upper respiratory infection

urol. *shortening* ♦ urology

URT *abbrev.* ♦ upper respiratory tract

URTI *abbrev.* ♦ upper respiratory tract
infection

Urtu *acronym* ♦ United Road Transport
Union

Uru. *shortening* ♦ Uruguay ♦ Uruguayan

US *abbrev.* ♦ Glasgow (British vehicle
registration mark) ♦ unconditioned
stimulus ♦ Under-Secretary ♦ United
Service ♦ United States

us *abbrev.* ♦ ut supra (Latin, = as above)

u/s *abbrev.* ♦ unserviceable ♦ useless

USA *abbrev.* ♦ United States of America
♦ United States of America
(international vehicle registration)
♦ United States Army

USAF *abbrev.* ♦ United States Air Force

USC *abbrev.* ♦ Ulster Special
Constabulary

USCL *abbrev.* ♦ United Society for
Christian Literature

Usdaw *acronym* ♦ Union of Shop,
Distributive and Allied Workers

USec *abbrev.* ♦ Under-Secretary

usf *abbrev.* ♦ und so fort (German, = and
so on)

USG *abbrev.* ♦ United States Government

USGA *abbrev.* ♦ United States Golfing
Association

USgal *abbrev.* ♦ United States gallon

USh *abbrev.* ♦ Uganda shilling (monetary
unit)

USI *abbrev.* ♦ United Service Institution

USIA *abbrev.* ♦ United States Information
Agency

USM *abbrev.* ♦ underwater-to-surface
missile ♦ unlisted securities market

USN *abbrev.* ♦ United States Navy

USNG *abbrev.* ♦ United States National
Guard

USPG *abbrev.* ♦ United Society for the
Propagation of the Gospel

USS *abbrev.* ♦ ultra-sound scanning
♦ Under-Secretary of State ♦ United
States Ship ♦ Universities
Superannuation Scheme

USSC *abbrev.* ♦ United States Supreme
Court

USSR *abbrev.* ♦ Union of Soviet Socialist
Republics

usu. *shortening* ♦ usual ♦ usually

USW *abbrev.* ♦ ultrashort waves
♦ ultrasonic waves

usw *abbrev.* ◆ und so weiter (German, = and so forth)

UT *abbrev.* ◆ Leicester (British vehicle registration mark) ◆ unit trust ◆ urinary tract ◆ Utah (US postcode)

Ut. *shortening* ◆ Utah

ut. *shortening* ◆ utility

UTC *abbrev.* ◆ Universal Time Co-ordinates ◆ University Training Corps

utd *contraction* ◆ united

ut dict. *shortening* ◆ ut dictum (Latin, = as directed)

UTI *abbrev.* ◆ urinary tract infection

util. *shortening* ◆ utility room

ut inf. *shortening* ◆ ut infra (Latin, = as below)

UTS *abbrev.* ◆ ultimate tensile strength

ut sup. *shortening* ◆ ut supra (Latin, = as above)

UU *abbrev.* ◆ central London (British vehicle registration mark) ◆ Ulster Unionist

UUM *abbrev.* ◆ underwater to underwater missile

UUP *abbrev.* ◆ Ulster Unionist Party

UUUC *abbrev.* ◆ United Ulster Unionist Council

UUUP *abbrev.* ◆ United Ulster Unionist Party

uuV *abbrev.* ◆ unter üblichem Vorbehalt (German, = errors and omissions excepted)

UV *abbrev.* ◆ central London (British vehicle registration mark) ◆ ultraviolet

UVA *abbrev.* ◆ ultraviolet radiation A (in the wavelength range 320–80 nanometres)

UVB *abbrev.* ◆ ultraviolet radiation B (in the wavelength range 280–320 nanometres)

UVC *abbrev.* ◆ ultraviolet radiation C (below 320 nanometres in wavelength)

UVF *abbrev.* ◆ Ulster Volunteer Force

UVL *abbrev.* ◆ ultraviolet light

UVR *abbrev.* ◆ ultraviolet radiation

UW *abbrev.* ◆ central London (British vehicle registration mark)

U/w *abbrev.* ◆ underwriter

u/w *abbrev.* ◆ underwater ◆ unladen weight

UWCE *abbrev.* ◆ Underwater Weapons and Countermeasures Establishment

Uwist *acronym* ◆ University of Wales Institute of Science and Technology

UX *abbrev.* ◆ Shrewsbury (British vehicle registration mark)

ux. *shortening* ◆ uxor (Latin, = wife)

UXB *abbrev.* ◆ unexploded bomb

UY *abbrev.* ◆ Worcester (British vehicle registration mark)

UZ *abbrev.* ◆ Belfast (British vehicle registration mark)

Uz. *shortening* ◆ Uzbek ◆ Uzbekistan

V

V *abbrev.* ◆ Vergeltungswaffe (German, = reprisal weapon) (of the second-world-war German flying bombs V1 and V2) ◆ victory ◆ Vatican City (international vehicle registration) ◆ vatu (Vanuatu monetary unit) ◆ volt

V *symbol* ◆ vanadium (chemical element)

v *abbrev.* ◆ vacuum ◆ vel (Latin, = or) ◆ velocity ◆ verb ◆ verse ◆ verso ◆ versus ◆ vertical ◆ very ◆ vide (Latin, = see) ◆ violin ◆ voce (Italian, = voice) ◆ volume ◆ von (German, = of) ◆ vowel

VA *abbrev.* ◆ Peterborough (British vehicle registration mark) ◆ Vicar Apostolic ◆ Vice-Admiral ◆ Virginia (US postcode)

Va *contraction* ◆ Virginia

va *abbrev.* ◆ verb active ◆ verbal adjective

va *contraction* ◆ viola

v/a *abbrev.* ◆ voucher attached

va & i *abbrev.* ◆ verb active and intransitive

vac. *shortening* ◆ vacancy ◆ vacant ◆ vacation ◆ vacuum

vacc. *shortening* ◆ vaccination ◆ vaccine

VAD *abbrev.* ◆ Voluntary Aid Detachment

VAdm *abbrev.* ◆ Vice Admiral

vag. *shortening* ◆ vagabond ◆ vagina ◆ vaginal ◆ vagrant

val. *shortening* ◆ valley ◆ valuation ◆ value

valid. *shortening* ◆ validate ◆ validation

van. *shortening* ◆ vanilla

Van *acronym* ◆ value-added network

V & A *abbrev.* ◆ Victoria and Albert Museum

v & l *abbrev.* ◆ vodka and lime

v & t *abbrev.* ◆ vodka and tonic

V & V *abbrev.* ◆ verification and validation

VANS *abbrev.* ◆ value-added network service

var. *shortening* ◆ variant ◆ variation ◆ variety ◆ various

var. lect. *shortening* ◆ varia lectio (Latin, = variant reading)

varn. *shortening* ◆ varnish

vas. *shortening* ◆ vasectomy

vasc. *shortening* ◆ vascular

Vascar *acronym* ◆ visual average speed computer and recorder (speed-trap device)

VAT *acronym* ◆ Value Added Tax

Vat. *shortening* ◆ Vatican

Vat. Lib. *shortening* ◆ Vatican Library

VB *abbrev.* ◆ Maidstone (British vehicle registration mark)

vb *contraction* ◆ verb

vbl *contraction* ◆ verbal

V-bomber *contraction* ◆ a bomber of the Victor, Vulcan or Valiant types

VC *abbrev.* ◆ Coventry (British vehicle registration mark) ◆ Vatican City ◆ vice-chairman ◆ vice-chancellor ◆ vice-consul ◆ Vickers Commercial (used in names of aircraft manufactured by them, eg VC10) ◆ Victoria Cross ◆ Viet Cong

vc. *shortening* ◆ violoncello

VCC *abbrev.* ◆ Veteran Car Club of Great Britain

VCE *abbrev.* ◆ Venice (airport baggage label)

VCH *abbrev.* ◆ Victoria County History

vcl. *shortening* ◆ violoncello

VCR *abbrev.* ◆ video cassette recorder

215

VD *abbrev.* ◆ venereal disease
◆ Volunteer Decoration
VDH *abbrev.* ◆ valvular disease of the heart
VDI *abbrev.* ◆ virtual device interface
VDJ *abbrev.* ◆ video disk jockey
VDQS *abbrev.* ◆ vin délimité de qualité supérieure (French, = quality wine from a specified region)
VDR *abbrev.* ◆ video-disk recording
VDRL *abbrev.* ◆ Venereal Disease Reference Laboratory Test
VDT *abbrev.* ◆ video display terminal
VDU *abbrev.* ◆ visual display unit
VE *abbrev.* ◆ Peterborough (British vehicle registration mark) ◆ vaginal examination ◆ Victory in Europe (at the close of World War II)
veg. *shortening* ◆ vegetable ◆ vegetarian
veh. *shortening* ◆ vehicle ◆ vehicular
Ven. *shortening* ◆ Venerable
Venet. *shortening* ◆ Venetian
Venez. *shortening* ◆ Venezuela ◆ Venezuelan
vent. *shortening* ◆ ventilate ◆ ventilation
ver. *shortening* ◆ verification ◆ verify ◆ verse
Ver. *shortening* ◆ Verein (German, = Company)
verb. sap. *shortening* ◆ verbum sapienti sat est (Latin, = a word is sufficient to the wise)

vers *acronym* ◆ versed sine
vers. *shortening* ◆ version
vert. *shortening* ◆ vertebra ◆ vertical
VES *abbrev.* ◆ Voluntary Euthanasia Society
ves. *shortening* ◆ vespere (Latin, = at evening)
vesp. *shortening* ◆ vespere (Latin, = at evening)
vet. *shortening* ◆ veterinary
VF *abbrev.* ◆ Norwich (British vehicle registration mark) ◆ ventricular fibrillation ◆ video frequency ◆ voice frequency
VFA *abbrev.* ◆ Victoria Falls (airport baggage label)
VFM *abbrev.* ◆ value for money
VG *abbrev.* ◆ Norwich (British vehicle registration mark) ◆ Vicar-General
vg *abbrev.* ◆ very good
VGA *abbrev.* ◆ video graphics array
vgc *abbrev.* ◆ very good condition
VGH *abbrev.* ◆ very good health
vgl. *shortening* ◆ vergleiche (German, = compare)
VGO *abbrev.* ◆ Vigo (airport baggage label)
VGSOH *abbrev.* ◆ very good sense of humour
VH *abbrev.* ◆ Australia (international civil aircraft marking) ◆ Huddersfield (British vehicle registration mark)

INTERNATIONAL VEHICLE REGISTRATION MARKS

There are about 170 marks in current use, and all of them are listed in this dictionary at their alphabetical place. This panel lists those most likely to be seen in the United Kingdom.

A	*Austria*	**FL**	*Liechtenstein*	**IL**	*Israel*
B	*Belgium*	**GB**	*United Kingdom*	**IRL**	*Ireland*
CH	*Switzerland*	**GBA**	*Alderney*	**L**	*Luxembourg*
D	*Germany*	**GBG**	*Guernsey*	**MC**	*Monaco*
DK	*Denmark and Greenland*	**GBJ**	*Jersey*	**N**	*Norway*
		GBM	*Isle of Man*	**NL**	*Netherlands*
E	*Spain*	**GBZ**	*Gibraltar*	**P**	*Portugal*
F	*France*	**GR**	*Greece*	**S**	*Sweden*
FI	*Finland*	**I**	*Italy*	**SF**	*Finland*

vhc *abbrev.* ◆ very highly commended
VHD *abbrev.* ◆ video high density
VHE *abbrev.* ◆ very high energy
VHF *abbrev.* ◆ very high frequency
VHS *abbrev.* ◆ video home system
VHT *abbrev.* ◆ very high temperature
VHY *abbrev.* ◆ Vichy (airport baggage label)
VI *abbrev.* ◆ virgo intacta (Latin, = a virgin)
vi *abbrev.* ◆ verb intransitive ◆ vide infra (Latin, = see below)
VIA *abbrev.* ◆ Visually Impaired Association
vib. *shortening* ◆ vibraphone ◆ vibration
VIC *abbrev.* ◆ Vicenza (airport baggage label)
Vic. *shortening* ◆ Victorian
vic. *shortening* ◆ vicar ◆ vicarage ◆ vicinity
Vict. *shortening* ◆ Victorian
vid. *shortening* ◆ vide (Latin, = see)
VID *abbrev.* ◆ virtual image display
VIE *abbrev.* ◆ Vienna (airport baggage label)
vill. *shortening* ◆ village
VIP *abbrev.* ◆ very important person
VIR *abbrev.* ◆ Victoria Imperatrix Regina (Latin, = Victoria, Empress and Queen)
vis. *shortening* ◆ viscount
visc. *shortening* ◆ viscosity ◆ viscount
vit. *shortening* ◆ vitreous
vix. *shortening* ◆ vixit (Latin, = lived)
viz. *shortening* ◆ videlicet (Latin, = namely)
VJ *abbrev.* ◆ Gloucester (British vehicle registration mark) ◆ Victory over Japan (at the close of World War II) ◆ video jockey
VK *abbrev.* ◆ Newcastle upon Tyne (British vehicle registration mark)
VL *abbrev.* ◆ Lincoln (British vehicle registration mark)
vl *abbrev.* ◆ varia lectio (Latin, = variant reading)
vl. *shortening* ◆ violin
vla *contraction* ◆ viola
VLBC *abbrev.* ◆ very large bulk carrier (ship)

VLBW *abbrev.* ◆ very low birth weight
VLC *abbrev.* ◆ Valencia (British vehicle registration mark)
VLCC *abbrev.* ◆ very large crude carrier (oil tanker)
VLCD *abbrev.* ◆ very low calorie diet
VLDB *abbrev.* ◆ very large database
VLDL *abbrev.* ◆ very low density lipoprotein
vle *contraction* ◆ violone
VLF *abbrev.* ◆ very low frequency
VLLW *abbrev.* ◆ very low level waste (nuclear)
vln *contraction* ◆ violin
VLSI *abbrev.* ◆ very large scale integration
vltg. *shortening* ◆ voltage
vlv. *shortening* ◆ valve ◆ valvular
VM *abbrev.* ◆ Manchester (British vehicle registration mark) ◆ Virgin Mary ◆ virtual machine
vM *abbrev.* ◆ vorigen Monats (German, = last month)
VM/CMS *abbrev.* ◆ Virtual Machine, Conversational Monitor System
VMD *abbrev.* ◆ Veterinariae Medicinae Doctor (Latin, = Doctor of Veterinary Medicine)
VMH *abbrev.* ◆ Victoria Medal of Honour
VMS *abbrev.* ◆ Virtual Machine System
vmt *abbrev.* ◆ very many thanks
VN *abbrev.* ◆ Middlesborough (British vehicle registration mark) ◆ Vietnam (international vehicle registration)
VNO *abbrev.* ◆ Vilnius (airport baggage label)
VO *abbrev.* ◆ Nottingham (British vehicle registration mark) ◆ Veterinary Officer ◆ voice over
vo *contraction* ◆ verso
VOA *abbrev.* ◆ Voice of America (radio station of US Information Agency)
voc. *shortening* ◆ vocal ◆ vocalist ◆ vocational ◆ vocative
vocab. *shortening* ◆ vocabulary
vocat. *shortening* ◆ vocative
VOG *abbrev.* ◆ Volgograd (airport baggage label)

VOL *abbrev.* ◆ Volos (airport baggage label)

vol. *shortening* ◆ volatile ◆ volume ◆ voluntary ◆ volunteer

volc. *shortening* ◆ volcanic ◆ volcano

volum. *shortening* ◆ volumetric

VOP *abbrev.* ◆ very oldest procurable (on brandy etc bottle)

VP *abbrev.* ◆ Birmingham (British vehicle registration mark) ◆ verb phrase ◆ Vice-President

vp *abbrev.* ◆ vanishing point ◆ verb passive

VPC *abbrev.* ◆ vente par correspondance (French, = mail order)

vpd *abbrev.* ◆ vehicles per day

vph *abbrev.* ◆ vehicles per hour

VPO *abbrev.* ◆ Vienna Philharmonic Orchestra

vps *abbrev.* ◆ vibrations per second

VR *abbrev.* ◆ Manchester (British vehicle registration mark) ◆ Victoria Regina (Latin, = Queen Victoria) ◆ virtual reality ◆ Volunteer Reserve ◆ vulcanized rubber

vr *abbrev.* ◆ variant reading ◆ verb reflexive

VRAM *abbrev.* ◆ video random-access memory

VRI *abbrev.* ◆ Victoria Regina et Imperatrix (Latin, = Victoria, Queen and Empress) ◆ viral respiratory infection

VRN *abbrev.* ◆ Verona (airport baggage label)

VRO *abbrev.* ◆ vehicle registration office

VRZ *abbrev.* ◆ Veronezh (airport baggage label)

VS *abbrev.* ◆ Luton (British vehicle registration mark) ◆ Veterinary Surgeon ◆ Virgin Atlantic Airways (airline baggage code)

vs *abbrev.* ◆ vide supra (Latin, = see above) ◆ volti subito (Italian, = turn over quickly) (music)

vs *contraction* ◆ versus

VSAM *abbrev.* ◆ virtual storage access method

VSCC *abbrev.* ◆ Vintage Sports Car Club

VSD *abbrev.* ◆ ventricular septal defect

VSL *abbrev.* ◆ Venture Scout Leader

VSO *abbrev.* ◆ very superior old (on brandy etc bottle) ◆ Vienna State Opera ◆ Voluntary Service Overseas

VSOP *abbrev.* ◆ very superior old pale (on brandy etc bottle)

VSR *abbrev.* ◆ very special reserve (on wine etc bottle)

VSS *abbrev.* ◆ vital signs stable

VSTOL *abbrev.* ◆ vertical and short take-off and landing

VSUK *abbrev.* ◆ Vegetarian Society of the United Kingdom Ltd

VT *abbrev.* ◆ India (international civil aircraft marking) ◆ Stoke-on-Trent (British vehicle registration mark) ◆ vatu (Vanuatu currency unit) ◆ ventricular tachycardia ◆ Vermont (US postcode)

Vt *contraction* ◆ Vermont

vt *abbrev.* ◆ verb transitive

VTE *abbrev.* ◆ Vientiane (airport baggage label)

vtg *abbrev.* ◆ voting

VTO *abbrev.* ◆ vertical take-off

VTOHL *abbrev.* ◆ vertical take-off, horizontal landing

VTOL *abbrev.* ◆ vertical take-off and landing

VTOVL *abbrev.* ◆ vertical take-off, vertical landing

VTR *abbrev.* ◆ videotape recorder

VU *abbrev.* ◆ Manchester (British vehicle registration mark) ◆ varicose ulcer ◆ volume unit

Vulg. *shortening* ◆ Vulgate

vulg. *shortening* ◆ vulgar

VV *abbrev.* ◆ Northampton (British vehicle registration mark)

vv *abbrev.* ◆ vice versa

VVO *abbrev.* ◆ very very old (on brandy etc bottle) ◆ Vladivostok (airport baggage label)

VW *abbrev.* ◆ Very Worshipful ◆ Volkswagen (German, = People's Car) (motor manufacturer)

Vw *contraction* ◆ View

VX *abbrev.* ◆ Chelmsford (British vehicle registration mark)

VY *abbrev.* ◆ Leeds (British vehicle registration mark)

vy *abbrev.* ◆ various years

VZ *abbrev.* ◆ Tyrone (British vehicle registration mark)

W

W *abbrev.* ✦ Wales ✦ watt ✦ Wednesday ✦ Welsh ✦ west ✦ western ✦ white ✦ winter ✦ women ✦ women's (clothing size) ✦ won (Korean monetary unit)

w *abbrev.* ✦ week ✦ weight ✦ wicket (cricket) ✦ wide ✦ widow ✦ width ✦ wife ✦ with ✦ won ✦ word

WA *abbrev.* ✦ Sheffield (British vehicle registration mark) ✦ Washington (US postcode) ✦ West Africa ✦ Western Australia

WAA *abbrev.* ✦ Women's Auxiliary Association

WAAA *abbrev.* ✦ Women's Amateur Athletic Association

WAAF *abbrev.* ✦ Women's Auxiliary Air Force

WACCC *abbrev.* ✦ Worldwide Air Cargo Commodity Classification

waf *abbrev.* ✦ with all faults

WAfr *abbrev.* ✦ West Africa

WAG *abbrev.* ✦ Gambia (international vehicle registration) ✦ Writers' and Artists' Guild

Wagbi *acronym* ✦ Wildfowl Association of Great Britain and Ireland

WAGGGS *abbrev.* ✦ World Association of Girl Guides and Girl Scouts

Waif *acronym* ✦ World Adoption International Fund

WAL *abbrev.* ✦ Sierra Leone (international vehicle registration)

Wal. *shortening* ✦ Walloon

WAN *abbrev.* ✦ Nigeria (international vehicle registration)

wan *acronym* ✦ wide-area network

W & M *abbrev.* ✦ William and Mary

w & s *abbrev.* ✦ whisky and soda

w & t *abbrev.* ✦ wear and tear

War. *shortening* ✦ Warwickshire

war. *shortening* ✦ warrant

WARC *abbrev.* ✦ World Administrative Radio Conference ✦ World Alliance of Reformed Churches

WAS *abbrev.* ✦ Washington (airport baggage label)

warr. *shortening* ✦ warranty

Wash. *shortening* ✦ Washington

Wasp *acronym* ✦ white Anglo-Saxon Protestant

WATA *abbrev.* ✦ World Association of Travel Agents

Wat. *shortening* ✦ County Waterford

WAW *abbrev.* ✦ Warsaw (airport baggage label)

WAYC *abbrev.* ✦ Welsh Association of Youth Clubs

WB *abbrev.* ✦ Sheffield (British vehicle registration mark) ✦ Warner Brothers ✦ World Bank

Wb *shortening* ✦ weber

WBA *abbrev.* ✦ West Bromwich Albion ✦ whole body activity ✦ World Boxing Association

WBC *abbrev.* ✦ white blood cell ✦ World Boxing Council

WBF *abbrev.* ✦ World Bridge Federation

wbi *abbrev.* ✦ will be issued

WBR *abbrev.* ✦ whole body radiation

WBS *abbrev.* ✦ whole body scan

WC *abbrev.* ✦ Chelmsford (British vehicle registration mark) ✦ water closet ✦ West Central

wc *abbrev.* ✦ without charge

W/C *abbrev.* ✦ Wing Commander

wca *abbrev.* ✦ worst-case analysis

WCC *abbrev.* ✦ War Crimes Commission ✦ World Council of Churches

W/Cdr *contraction* ◆ Wing-Commander
WCRA *abbrev.* ◆ Women's Cycle Racing Association
WCT *abbrev.* ◆ World Championship Tennis
WD *abbrev.* ◆ Dominica (international vehicle registration) ◆ Dudley (British vehicle registration mark) ◆ War Department ◆ Works Department
wd *contraction* ◆ would
2-w/d *abbrev.* ◆ two-wheel drive
4-w/d *abbrev.* ◆ four-wheel drive
WDA *abbrev.* ◆ Welsh Development Agency
WDC *abbrev.* ◆ Woman Detective Constable
WDH *abbrev.* ◆ Windhoek (airport baggage label)
WDR *abbrev.* ◆ West-Deutscher Rundfunk (German, = West German Radio)
WDS *abbrev.* ◆ Woman Detective Sergeant
wdth *contraction* ◆ width
WE *abbrev.* ◆ Sheffield (British vehicle registration mark)
w/e *abbrev.* ◆ weekend ◆ week ending
WEA *abbrev.* ◆ Workers' Educational Association
Wed. *shortening* ◆ Wednesday
Weds. *shortening* ◆ Wednesday
wef *abbrev.* ◆ with effect from
Wen *acronym* ◆ Women's Environmental Network
w/end *contraction* ◆ weekend
Wes. *shortening* ◆ Wesleyan
Westm. *shortening* ◆ Westminster ◆ Westmorland
Westmeath *abbrev.* ◆ County Westmeath
WET *abbrev.* ◆ Western European Time
WEU *abbrev.* ◆ Western European Union
Wex. *shortening* ◆ County Wexford
WF *abbrev.* ◆ Sheffield (British vehicle registration mark)
wf *abbrev.* ◆ wing forward ◆ wrong fount
WFA *abbrev.* ◆ Women's Football Association

WFB *abbrev.* ◆ World Fellowship of Buddhists
WFC *abbrev.* ◆ World Food Council (UN)
WFD *abbrev.* ◆ World Federation of the Deaf
WFEO *abbrev.* ◆ World Federation of Engineering Organizations
WFP *abbrev.* ◆ World Food Programme (UN)
WFTU *abbrev.* ◆ World Federation of Trade Unions
WG *abbrev.* ◆ Grenada (international vehicle registration) ◆ Sheffield (British vehicle registration mark) ◆ Welsh Guards
wg *abbrev.* ◆ water gauge ◆ wire gauge
Wg/Cdr *contraction* ◆ Wing Commander
WGer *abbrev.* ◆ West Germany
WGlam *abbrev.* ◆ West Glamorgan
WGmc *abbrev.* ◆ West Germanic
WGU *abbrev.* ◆ Welsh Golfing Union
WH *abbrev.* ◆ Manchester (British vehicle registration mark)
Wh *abbrev.* ◆ watt-hour
wh *abbrev.* ◆ wing half
wh. *shortening* ◆ which
WHA *abbrev.* ◆ World Hockey Association
whb *abbrev.* ◆ wash-hand basin
whf *contraction* ◆ wharf
whfg. *shortening* ◆ wharfage
WHML *abbrev.* ◆ Wellcome Historical Medical Library
WHO *abbrev.* ◆ World Health Organization
WI *abbrev.* ◆ West Indies ◆ Wisconsin (US postcode) ◆ Women's Institute
WIA *abbrev.* ◆ wounded in action
WIC *abbrev.* ◆ Wick (airport baggage label)
Wick. *shortening* ◆ County Wicklow
wid. *shortening* ◆ widow ◆ widower
Wigorn. *shortening* ◆ Wigorniensis (Latin, = of Worcester)
Wilts. *shortening* ◆ Wiltshire
wimp *acronym* ◆ windows, icons, menus, pointer
wint. *shortening* ◆ winter

Winton. *shortening* ◆ Wintoniensis (Latin, = of Winchester)

WIP *abbrev.* ◆ work in progress

wip. *shortening* ◆ wiper

Wipo *acronym* ◆ World Intellectual Property Organization

Wis. *shortening* ◆ Wisconsin

Wisd. *shortening* ◆ Wisdom of Solomon (book of Bible)

wit. *shortening* ◆ witness

WITA *abbrev.* ◆ Women's International Tennis Association

WJ *abbrev.* ◆ Sheffield (British vehicle registration mark)

WJC *abbrev.* ◆ World Jewish Congress

WK *abbrev.* ◆ Coventry (British vehicle registration mark)

wk *contraction* ◆ weak ◆ week ◆ work

wkg *contraction* ◆ working

wkly *contraction* ◆ weekly

wkt *contraction* ◆ wicket (cricket)

wky *contraction* ◆ weekly

WL *abbrev.* ◆ Oxford (British vehicle registration mark) ◆ St Lucia (international vehicle registration) ◆ waiting list ◆ wavelength

WLA *abbrev.* ◆ Women's Land Army

WLF *abbrev.* ◆ Women's Liberal Federation

WLG *abbrev.* ◆ Wellington (airport baggage label)

WLM *abbrev.* ◆ Women's Liberation Movement

WLR *abbrev.* ◆ Weekly Law Reports

WLTM *abbrev.* ◆ would like to meet

WM *abbrev.* ◆ Liverpool (British vehicle registration mark) ◆ well maintained ◆ white male

WMA *abbrev.* ◆ Working Mothers' Association

WMC *abbrev.* ◆ Working Men's Club ◆ World Methodist Council

WMCIU *abbrev.* ◆ Working Men's Club and Institute Union Ltd

wmk *contraction* ◆ watermark

WMM *abbrev.* ◆ World Movement of Mothers

WMO *abbrev.* ◆ World Meteorological Organization

wmp *abbrev.* ◆ with much pleasure

WNB *abbrev.* ◆ weekly news bill

WNCCC *abbrev.* ◆ Women's Nationwide Cancer Control Campaign Ltd

wndp *abbrev.* ◆ with no down payment

wndw *contraction* ◆ window

WNE *abbrev.* ◆ Welsh National Eisteddfod

wnl *abbrev.* ◆ within normal limits

WNO *abbrev.* ◆ Welsh National Opera

WNP *abbrev.* ◆ Welsh National Party

WNW *abbrev.* ◆ west-north-west

WO *abbrev.* ◆ Cardiff (British vehicle registration mark) ◆ War Office ◆ warrant officer ◆ wireless operator

wo *abbrev.* ◆ walkover ◆ wie oben (German, = as above) ◆ written order

w/o *abbrev.* ◆ without ◆ written off

Woar *acronym* ◆ Women Organized Against Rape

woc *abbrev.* ◆ without compensation

wocs *abbrev.* ◆ waiting on cement setting

WoO *abbrev.* ◆ Werke ohne Opuszahl (German, = works without an opus number) (enumeration of Beethoven's unpublished works)

Worcester. *shortening* ◆ Worcesteriensis (Latin, = of Worcester)

Worcs. *shortening* ◆ Worcestershire (former English county)

Worm *acronym* ◆ write once, read many times

Wosac *pronounced* woe-sack *acronym* ◆ worldwide synchronization of atomic clocks

WOSB *pronounced* wos-bee *acronym* ◆ War Office Selection Board

WOW *abbrev.* ◆ waiting on weather ◆ War on Want ◆ Women Against the Ordination of Women

WP *abbrev.* ◆ Worcester (British vehicle registration mark) ◆ word-processing ◆ word-processor ◆ Warsaw Pact

wp *abbrev.* ◆ weather permitting

Wp. *shortening* ◆ Worship ◆ Worshipful

WPA *abbrev.* ♦ World Presbyterian Alliance

wpb *abbrev.* ♦ wastepaper basket

WPBSA *abbrev.* ♦ World Professional Billiards and Snooker Association

WPC *abbrev.* ♦ Woman Police Constable

Wpfl *contraction* ♦ Worshipful

WPGA *abbrev.* ♦ Women's Professional Golfers' Association

WPI *abbrev.* ♦ wholesale price index

wpm *abbrev.* ♦ words per minute

WPMSF *abbrev.* ♦ World Professional Marathon Swimming Federation

WR *abbrev.* ♦ Leeds (British vehicle registration mark) ♦ Western Region ♦ West Riding (former division of Yorkshire) ♦ Wilhelmus Rex (Latin, = King William)

WRAAC *abbrev.* ♦ Women's Royal Australian Army Corps

WRAAF *abbrev.* ♦ Women's Royal Australian Air Force

WRAC *abbrev.* ♦ Women's Royal Army Corps

WRAF *abbrev.* ♦ Women's Royal Air Force

WRC *abbrev.* ♦ Water Research Centre

WRI *abbrev.* ♦ war risks insurance ♦ Women's Rural Institute

WRNR *abbrev.* ♦ Women's Royal Naval Reserve

WRNS *abbrev.* ♦ Women's Royal Naval Service

WRO *abbrev.* ♦ war risks only ♦ Wroclaw (airport baggage label)

WRP *abbrev.* ♦ Workers' Revolutionary Party

WRRA *abbrev.* ♦ Women's Road Records Association (cycling)

wrt *abbrev.* ♦ with respect to

WRU *abbrev.* ♦ Welsh Rugby Union

WRVS *abbrev.* ♦ Women's Royal Voluntary Service

WS *abbrev.* ♦ Bristol (British vehicle registration mark) ♦ Western Samoa (international vehicle registration) ♦ Writer to the Signet

WSC *abbrev.* ♦ World Series Cricket

w/shop *shortening* ♦ workshop

WSJ *abbrev.* ♦ Wall Street Journal

WSW *abbrev.* ♦ west-south-west

WT *abbrev.* ♦ Leeds (British vehicle registration mark) ♦ Nigeria Airways (airline baggage code) ♦ weekly takings

wt *contraction* ♦ weight

w/t *abbrev.* ♦ wireless telegraphy

WTA *abbrev.* ♦ Women's Tennis Association

WTB *abbrev.* ♦ Welsh Tourist Board

WTO *abbrev.* ♦ Warsaw Treaty Organization

WTT *abbrev.* ♦ World Team Tennis

WTUC *abbrev.* ♦ World Trade Union Conference

WU *abbrev.* ♦ Leeds (British vehicle registration mark)

PRINCIPAL WORLD AIRLINES

The list below shows the baggage-label codes of 20 of the main carriers. Many more will be found in the dictionary.

AF	Air France	**LH**	Lufthansa	**SA**	South African Airways
AI	Air India	**LO**	Polish Airlines	**SK**	Scandinavian Airlines
AZ	Alitalia	**LV**	El Al	**SN**	Sabena
BA	British Airways	**OA**	Olympic Airways	**SU**	Aeroflot
CI	China Airlines	**OS**	Austrian Airlines	**TW**	Trans World Airlines
EI	Aer Lingus	**PA**	Pan American		
JL	Japan Air Lines	**QF**	Qantas		
KL	KLM				

WV *abbrev.* ◆ Brighton (British vehicle registration mark) ◆ St Vincent (international vehicle registration) ◆ West Virginia (US postcode)

w/v *abbrev.* ◆ weight in volume

WVa *abbrev.* ◆ West Virginia

WVS *abbrev.* ◆ Women's Voluntary Service

WW *abbrev.* ◆ Leeds (British vehicle registration mark) ◆ walnut wood trim ◆ world war

w/w *abbrev.* ◆ wall to wall ◆ weight for weight

WWF *abbrev.* ◆ Worldwide Fund for Nature (orig. World Wildlife Fund) ◆ World Wrestling Federation

WWO *abbrev.* ◆ Wing Warrant Officer

WWSU *abbrev.* ◆ World Water Ski Union

WWW *abbrev.* ◆ World Weather Watch

WX *abbrev.* ◆ Leeds (British vehicle registration mark) ◆ women's extra (clothing size)

WY *abbrev.* ◆ Leeds (British vehicle registration mark) ◆ Wyoming (US postcode)

Wy *contraction* ◆ Way

Wyo. *shortening* ◆ Wyoming

WYSIWYG *abbrev.* ◆ what you see is what you get

WZ *abbrev.* ◆ Belfast (British vehicle registration mark)

WZO *abbrev.* ◆ World Zionist Organization

PRINCIPAL AIRPORTS OF THE WORLD

These label codes will enable you to check where your own (and other people's!) luggage is bound for. Many more can be found in the dictionary.

AMS	*Amsterdam*	**CAI**	*Cairo*	**NDH**	*Delhi*
ANK	*Ankara*	**DAM**	*Damascus*	**PAR**	*Paris*
ARN	*Stockholm*	**DCA**	*Washington*	**PEK**	*Beijing*
ATH	*Athens*	**GVA**	*Geneva*	**ROM**	*Rome*
BEG	*Belgrade*	**HAG**	*The Hague*	**SIN**	*Singapore*
BER	*Berlin*	**HEL**	*Helsinki*	**STO**	*Stockholm*
BGW	*Baghdad*	**HKG**	*Hong Kong*	**VIE**	*Vienna*
BKM	*Moscow*	**JNB**	*Johannesburg*	**WAS**	*Washington*
BRN	*Bern*	**LON**	*London*	**WAW**	*Warsaw*
BUD	*Budapest*	**MAD**	*Madrid*	**WLG**	*Wellington*
BUE	*Buenos Aires*	**MOW**	*Moscow*	**ZRH**	*Zurich*

X

X *abbrev.* ◆ Christ (from the shape of the Greek capital letter chi, the initial of *Christos*) ◆ former film-censorship classification, limiting exhibition to those over 16 years of age

XA *abbrev.* ◆ Mexico (international civil aircraft marking)

XB *abbrev.* ◆ Mexico (international civil aircraft marking)

XC *abbrev.* ◆ Mexico (international civil aircraft marking)

x-c *abbrev.* ◆ cross-country (skiing)

xd *abbrev.* ◆ ex dividend (excluding dividend)

XDR *abbrev.* ◆ extended dynamic range (cassettes)

Xe *symbol* ◆ xenon (chemical element)

XH *abbrev.* ◆ Honduras (international civil aircraft marking)

XI *abbrev.* ◆ Belfast (British vehicle registration mark)

xi *abbrev.* ◆ ex interest (without interest)

xlwb *abbrev.* ◆ extra-long wheelbase

Xm. *shortening* ◆ Christmas (the X reproduces the shape of the Greek capital letter chi, the initial of *Christos*)

Xmas *pronounced* ex-mass *acronym* ◆ Christmas (the X reproduces the shape of the Greek capital letter chi, the initial of *Christos*)

Xn *contraction* ◆ Christian (the X reproduces the shape of the Greek capital letter chi, the initial of *Christos*)

xn *abbrev.* ◆ ex new (without the right to new shares)

Xnty *contraction* ◆ Christianity (the X reproduces the shape of the Greek capital letter chi, the initial of *Christos*)

XR *abbrev.* ◆ X-ray

xr *abbrev.* ◆ ex rights

X-ref. *shortening* ◆ cross-reference

XRT *abbrev.* ◆ X-ray therapy

XRY *abbrev.* ◆ Jerez de la Frontera (airport baggage label)

XS *abbrev.* ◆ cross-section

xs *abbrev.* ◆ expenses

Xt *contraction* ◆ Christ (the X reproduces the shape of the Greek capital letter chi, the initial of *Christos*)

Xtian *shortening* ◆ Christian (the X reproduces the shape of the Greek capital letter chi, the initial of *Christos*)

xw *abbrev.* ◆ ex warrants (excluding warrants)

XY *abbrev.* ◆ Burma (international civil aircraft marking)

xyl. *shortening* ◆ xylophone

XZ *abbrev.* ◆ Armagh (British vehicle registration mark) ◆ Burma (international civil aircraft marking)

Y

Y *abbrev.* ◆ yen (Japanese monetary unit) ◆ yuan (Chinese monetary unit)

Y *symbol* ◆ yttrium (chemical element)

y *abbrev.* ◆ yard ◆ year

YA *abbrev.* ◆ Afghanistan (international civil aircraft marking) ◆ Taunton (British vehicle registration mark)

YAR *abbrev.* ◆ Yemen Arab Republic (international vehicle registration)

YB *abbrev.* ◆ Taunton (British vehicle registration mark) ◆ Year Book

Yb *symbol* ◆ ytterbium (chemical element)

YC *abbrev.* ◆ Taunton (British vehicle registration mark) ◆ yacht club ◆ Young Conservative ◆ youth club

YC & UO *abbrev.* ◆ Young Conservative and Unionist Organization

YD *abbrev.* ◆ Taunton (British vehicle registration mark)

yd *contraction* ◆ yard

YE *abbrev.* ◆ central London (British vehicle registration mark) ◆ Yemen (international civil aircraft marking) ◆ Your Excellency

Yem. *shortening* ◆ Yemen ◆ Yemeni

Yeo. *shortening* ◆ Yeomanry

YES *abbrev.* ◆ Youth Employment Service ◆ Youth Enterprise Scheme

YF *abbrev.* ◆ central London (British vehicle registration mark)

YFC *abbrev.* ◆ Young Farmers' Club

YFCU *abbrev.* ◆ Young Farmers' Clubs of Ulster

YG *abbrev.* ◆ Leeds (British vehicle registration mark)

YH *abbrev.* ◆ central London (British vehicle registration mark) ◆ youth hostel

YHA *abbrev.* ◆ Youth Hostels Association

YHANI *abbrev.* ◆ Youth Hostels Association of Northern Ireland

YHZ *abbrev.* ◆ Halifax, Nova Scotia (airport baggage label)

YI *abbrev.* ◆ Iraq (international civil aircraft marking)

Yid. *shortening* ◆ Yiddish

YJ *abbrev.* ◆ Brighton (British vehicle registration mark)

YK *abbrev.* ◆ central London (British vehicle registration mark) ◆ Cyprus Turkish Airlines ◆ Syria (international civil aircraft marking)

YL *abbrev.* ◆ central London (British vehicle registration mark)

YM *abbrev.* ◆ central London (British vehicle registration mark)

YMCA *abbrev.* ◆ Young Mens' Christian Association

YMCU *abbrev.* ◆ Young Men's Christian Union

YMFS *abbrev.* ◆ Young Men's Friendly Society

YMHA *abbrev.* ◆ Young Men's Hebrew Association

YN *abbrev.* ◆ central London (British vehicle registration mark)

Yn *contraction* ◆ yen (Japanese currency unit)

YO *abbrev.* ◆ central London (British vehicle registration mark)

yo *abbrev.* ◆ year old

yob *abbrev.* ◆ year of birth

yod *abbrev.* ◆ year of death

yom *abbrev.* ◆ year of marriage

Yop *acronym* ◆ Youth Opportunities Programme

Yorks. *shortening* ◆ Yorkshire

YOW *abbrev.* ◆ Ottowa (airport baggage label)

YP *abbrev.* ◆ central London (British vehicle registration mark)

YQB *abbrev.* ◆ Quebec City (airport baggage label)

YR *abbrev.* ◆ central London (British vehicle registration mark) ◆ Romania (international civil aircraft marking)

yr *contraction* ◆ year ◆ younger ◆ your

yrbk *contraction* ◆ yearbook

YRl *abbrev.* ◆ Yemeni riyal

yrly *contraction* ◆ yearly

yrs *contraction* ◆ yours

YS *abbrev.* ◆ El Salvador (international civil aircraft marking) ◆ Glasgow (British vehicle registration mark)

YT *abbrev.* ◆ central London (British vehicle registration mark) ◆ Yukon Territory

ytd *abbrev.* ◆ year to date

YTS *abbrev.* ◆ Youth Training Scheme

YTV *abbrev.* ◆ Yorkshire Television

YU *abbrev.* ◆ central London (British vehicle registration mark) ◆ Yale University ◆ Yugoslavia (international civil aircraft marking) ◆ Yugoslavia (international vehicle registration)

Yugo. *shortening* ◆ Yugoslavia ◆ Yugoslavian

Yuk. *shortening* ◆ Yukon Territory

YUL *abbrev.* ◆ Montreal (airport baggage label)

yuppy *acronym* ◆ young urban professional

YV *abbrev.* ◆ central London (British vehicle registration mark) ◆ Venezuela (international civil aircraft marking) ◆ Venezuela (international vehicle registration)

YVR *abbrev.* ◆ Vancouver (airport baggage label)

YW *abbrev.* ◆ central London (British vehicle registration mark)

YWCA *abbrev.* ◆ Young Women's Christian Association

YWG *abbrev.* ◆ Winnipeg (airport baggage label)

YWHA *abbrev.* ◆ Young Women's Hebrew Association

YX *abbrev.* ◆ central London (British vehicle registration mark)

YY *abbrev.* ◆ central London (British vehicle registration mark)

YZ *abbrev.* ◆ Londonderry (British vehicle registration mark)

Z

Z *abbrev.* ◆ zaire (Zairean monetary unit) ◆ Zambia (international vehicle registration)

z *abbrev.* ◆ zenith ◆ zero ◆ zone

ZA *abbrev.* ◆ Albania (international civil aircraft marking) ◆ South Africa (international vehicle registration; in Afrikaans, Zuid Afrika)

ZAG *abbrev.* ◆ Zagreb (airport baggage label)

Zam. *shortening* ◆ Zambia

Zanu *acronym* ◆ Zimbabwe African National Union

Zapu *acronym* ◆ Zimbabwe African People's Union

ZB *abbrev.* ◆ Zen Buddhism

zB *abbrev.* ◆ zum Beispiel (German, = for example)

ZCCT *abbrev.* ◆ Zoo Check Charitable Trust

Zech. *shortening* ◆ Zechariah (book of Bible)

zeg *abbrev.* ◆ zero economic growth

zen. *shortening* ◆ zenith

Zeph. *shortening* ◆ Zephaniah (book of Bible)

zH *abbrev.* ◆ zu Händen (German, = by the hands of) (care of) ◆ zu Händen (German, = to the hands of) (for the attention of)

Zift *acronym* ◆ zygote intrafallopian transfer

Zip *acronym* ◆ Zone Improvement Plan (US postcode system)

ZK *abbrev.* ◆ New Zealand (international civil aircraft marking)

ZL *abbrev.* ◆ New Zealand (international civil aircraft marking)

Zl. *shortening* ◆ zloty (Polish monetary unit)

ZM *abbrev.* ◆ New Zealand (international civil aircraft marking)

Zn *symbol* ◆ zinc (chemical element)

ZO *abbrev.* ◆ Zionist Organization

zool. *shortening* ◆ zoological ◆ zoologist ◆ zoology

ZP *abbrev.* ◆ Paraguay (international civil aircraft marking) ◆ Virgin Air (airline baggage code)

zpg *abbrev.* ◆ zero population growth

Zr *symbol* ◆ zirconium (chemical element)

ZRE *abbrev.* ◆ Zaire (international vehicle registration)

ZRH *abbrev.* ◆ Zurich (airport baggage label)

ZS *abbrev.* ◆ Union of South Africa (international civil aircraft marking) ◆ Zoological Society

Zs. *shortening* ◆ Zeitschrift (German, = periodical)

ZSI *abbrev.* ◆ Zoological Society of Ireland

ZSL *abbrev.* ◆ Zoological Society of London

ZST *abbrev.* ◆ Zone Standard Time

ZT *abbrev.* ◆ Union of South Africa (international civil aircraft marking)

ZUM *abbrev.* ◆ Zimbabwe Unity Movement

ZW *abbrev.* ◆ Zimbabwe (international vehicle registration)

ZZ *abbrev.* ◆ vehicle temporarily imported to UK (British vehicle registration mark)